# THE ECONOMICS OF RELIGION: ANTHROPOLOGICAL APPROACHES

# RESEARCH IN ECONOMIC ANTHROPOLOGY

## Series Editor: Donald C. Wood

Recent Volumes:

Volume 20: Research in Economic Anthropology – Edited by B. L. Isaac

Volume 21: Social Dimensions in the Economic Process – Edited by N. Dannhaeuser & C. Werner

Volume 22: Anthropological Perspectives on Economic Development and Integration – Edited by N. Dannhaeuser & C. Werner

Volume 23: Socioeconomic Aspects of Human Behavioral Ecology – Edited by M. Alvard

Volume 24: Markets and Market Liberalization: Ethnographic Reflections – Edited by N. Dannhaeuser & C. Werner

Volume 25: Choice in Economic Contexts: Ethnographic and Theoretical Enquiries – Edited by D. Wood

Volume 26: The Economics of Health and Wellness: Anthropological Perspectives – Edited by D. Wood

Volume 27: Dimension of Ritual Economy – Edited by E. C. Wells & P. McAnany

Volume 28: Hidden Hands in the Market: Ethnographies of Fair Trade, Ethical Consumption and Corporate Social Responsibility – Edited by Geert De Neve, Peter Luetchford, Jeffrey Pratt & Donald C. Wood

Volume 29: Economic Development, Integration, and Morality in Asia and the Americas – Edited by Donald C. Wood

Volume 30: Economic Action in Theory and Practice: Anthropological Investigations – Edited by Donald C. Wood

RESEARCH IN ECONOMIC ANTHROPOLOGY VOLUME 31

# THE ECONOMICS OF RELIGION: ANTHROPOLOGICAL APPROACHES


EDITED BY

**LIONEL OBADIA**

*Department of Anthropology, Université Lyon 2 – Lumière, Lyon, France*

**DONALD C. WOOD**

*Department of Medical Information Science, Akita University Graduate School of Medicine, Akita, Japan*



Emerald

United Kingdom – North America – Japan
India – Malaysia – China

Emerald Group Publishing Limited
Howard House, Wagon Lane, Bingley BD16 1WA, UK

First edition 2011



**British Library Cataloguing in Publication Data**
A catalogue record for this book is available from the British Library

ISBN: 978-1-78052-228-9
ISSN: 0190-1281 (Series)

Printed and bound by CPI Group (UK) Ltd, Croydon, CR0 4YY

# CONTENTS

## PART III: EXPERIMENTAL STUDIES – BEHAVIOR UNDER CONTROLLED CONDITIONS

# LIST OF CONTRIBUTORS


| | |
|---|---|
| *Billy Baum* | Department of Environmental Science and Policy, University of California, Davis, CA, USA |
| *Simon Coleman* | Centre for the Study of Religion, University of Toronto, Toronto, ON, Canada |
| *Andrés Dapuez* | Department of Anthropology, Johns Hopkins University, Baltimore, MD, USA |
| *Andrés Dzib May* | Mexican Commission for the Development of Indigenous People, Valladolid, Yucatan, Mexico |
| *Ed Edsten* | Graduate Group in Animal Behavior, University of California, Davis, CA, USA |
| *Charles Efferson* | Santa Fe Institute, Santa Fe, New Mexico, USA |
| *Sabrina Gavigan* | Independent Researcher, Ellicott City, MD, USA |
| *Natsuko Higa* | Graduate School of Human and Environmental Studies, Kyoto University, Kyoto, Japan |
| *Benjamin Jewell* | School of Human Evolution and Social Change, Arizona State University, Tempe, AZ, USA |
| *Isabelle Jonveaux* | Institut für Religionswissenschaft, Universität von Graz (Austria), Centre d'Etudes Interdisciplinaires des Faits Religieux (CEIFR), Paris, France |

| | |
|---|---|
| *Mark Lubell* | Department of Environmental Science and Policy, University of California, Davis, CA, USA |
| *Nathalie Luca* | Centre d'Etudes Interdisciplinaires des Faits Religieux (CEIFR), Centre National de la Recherche Scientifique (CNRS), Paris, France |
| *Richard McElreath* | Department of Anthropology, University of California, Davis, CA, USA |
| *Riccardo Nanini* | Institute for Advanced Study, New Europe College, Bucharest, Romania |
| *Lionel Obadia* | Department of Anthropology, Université Lyon 2 – Lumière, Lyon, France |
| *Brian Paciotti* | Department of Environmental Science and Policy, University of California, Davis, CA, USA |
| *Peter Richerson* | Department of Environmental Science and Policy, University of California, Davis, CA, USA |
| *Raquel Romberg* | Department of Sociology and Anthropology, Tel Aviv University, Tel Aviv, Israel |
| *Peter Seele* | Faculty of Communication Sciences, University of Lugano, Lugano, Switzerland |
| *Asonzeh Ukah* | Department for the History of Religions, University of Bayreuth, Bayreuth, Germany |
| *Tim Waring* | School of Economics, University of Maine, USA |

*Donald C. Wood* Department of Social Medicine, Akita University School of Medicine, Akita, Japan

*Amber Wutich* School of Human Evolution and Social Change, Arizona State University, Tempe, AZ, USA

# ECONOMICS *AND* RELIGION, ECONOMICS *IN* RELIGION, ECONOMICS *OF* RELIGION: REOPENING THE GROUNDS FOR ANTHROPOLOGY?

## ABSTRACT

*The "economics of religion" has grown into a new and groundbreaking approach to the study of religious beliefs, preferences, attitudes, belongings, organizations, and dynamics. This chapter circumscribes its epistemological area, outlines some of the major developments in the field, allows place for the presentation of both important theoretical models (market theory, rational choice, supply-and-demand) and crucial criticisms that have been directed toward them. If the "economics of religion" partakes of an attempt to explain religion in ancient or recent history, in the conceptual prism of economics, the general movement known as globalization has accelerated the convergence of economics and cultural/social analysis in religious studies. Anthropology, however, has gone its own way regarding economic issues. It has been somewhat reluctant to espouse the principles of "economics of religion," even while being convinced of its relevance. Some recent anthropological works on globalization and religion are presented here as examples of this ambivalent contribution of anthropology to the economics of religion in global settings.*

Bodhisattva
I'm gonna sell my house in town…
– Steely Dan, *Bodhisattva* from Countdown to Ecstasy (1973)

In the late 1980s and early 1990s a new economic approach to the study of religion emerged within the social sciences. Concepts like "religious markets," "consuming religion," "supply-and-demand" strategies, or "religious entrepreneurship" have colonized the lexicon of the sciences of religion. More than the lexical extension of the economic terminology, by the end of the first decade of this century these concepts had come to belong to a paradigm, whose relevance and outcomes have been widely discussed. This introductory chapter does not aim at cataloguing all the publications concerned, more or less directly, with economics of religion – this would be far too ambitious, given the sheer number of works involved. Many vivid accounts have indeed been written on the "economics of religion" and more precisely, on the *sociological* developments within this broad perspective. The purpose of this Introduction – and this volume – is to open up and explore a not-yet-fully-inaugurated discussion with *anthropology* and religion.

Scholars in the social and historical sciences of religion have, on many occasions, and with different intentions, examined the wide-ranging and complex relationships between religion and economy. The major part of the scholarly research on this topic has been devoted to the study of the impact of economic activity or values on religion, and reciprocally, following Weber's research on economic ethics in different religions. "Religion and economy" has been recast by the context of *globalism* – as contemporary conditions of societies and religions, and as a new perspective on the sociology of religion, beyond classical "national" studies (Clarke, 2006). Two different stances on the relationship between religion and economic globalization stem from this new perspective: on the one hand, globalization is seen as a *threat* to religion, and on another hand it is seen as a *chance* for religion to become revitalized and spread, which is actually more accurate – and interesting (Obadia, 2010). Globalization is far from being a consensual concept in the social sciences and humanities; quite the reverse, it is permeated with ambiguity (Van Der Bly, 2005). However, "economic globalization," though only *one among* the different approaches to globalization (Sklair 1999), is often considered to represent globalization as a whole. Even the Indian-born American anthropologist Arjun Appadurai, more inclined to focus on *cultural* dimensions of globalization, maintains that "Globalization is inextricably linked to the current workings of capital on a global basis. Its most striking feature is the runaway quality of global finance" (Appadurai, 2001, p. 4).

Sociologist Malcom Waters (2001) traces a distinction between *symbolic* and *material* globalized items (religion partaking on the first category) in the same all-embracing context of globalization. French sociologist Jean-Paul Willaime, in a reverse approach, distinguishes a symbolic (in his own words, "spiritual") and an economic one, insisting upon their coexistence as different globalizations (Willaime, 2004, p. 59). Sudhir H. Kale, professor in marketing in the United States, declares that "spirituality and the process of globalization have, for the most part, gone hand in hand, each shaping the course of each other" since "throughout millennia religious evangelism has contributed as much to foreign exportation and travel as the hunt for gold or spices" (2004, p. 96). These three examples reveal that global economy and global religions can be considered empirically and theoretically separated, yet intimately associated. We will retain, for convenience, three conceptual slogans to illustrate these relationships: economy *and* religion, economy *in* religion (or religious economy), and economy *as* religion (see *infra*). Not in the slightest sense, they should be considered here as "types" or "categories" in which one could distribute empirical facts and analyze them accordingly: yet, the voluminous body of evidence on the impact of religious ideas on economic growth, the existence of religious commodities (sacred or cultic furniture) in identifiable markets, the rise of a "Muslim" or a "Buddhist" economy (selling goods in conformity with religious precepts), the repletion of contemporary economies – especially the most secular ones – with metaphors of the sacred, and even the social and religious sciences terminology already account for analogical terms ("economies of ritual," "moral/cultural economy," etc.).

## ECONOMICS *OF* RELIGION: THE EMERGENCE OF THE FIELD

The economics of religion is something more than the previous approaches. According to contemporary researchers, its genealogy traces back to the Scottish philosopher Adam Smith (1723–1790) and his *Theory of Moral Sentiments* (1759) and later to German sociologist Max Weber (1864–1920) and his works on economy and religion – especially his opus *The Protestant Ethic and the Spirit of Capitalism* (1903–1904). But as an academic movement the economics of religion coalesced as something new beginning with the early works of American sociologists Peter Berger (1970s/1980s), Rodney Stark, Robert Finke, and many others (1980s/1990s) and economist Laurence Iannaccone (late 1980s).

In 1993, Warner was among the first sociologists to predict the employment of supply–demand and rational choice theories (as developed by Stark & Bainbridge, 1985) – and consequently, to a certain extent, economics – in the study of religion. Warner carefully identified new perspectives, more relevant for the description and analysis of the shape of North American religion, that were, in the early 1990s, yet a "work-in-progress" paradigm. A few years later, Iannaccone (1998), attempted to circumscribe the field of economics of religion, which was by this time diverse and complex, and a growing body of literature that was already challenging the attempts to inventory it exhaustively. He viewed the field as an interdisciplinary combination between studies in religion and economics, explaining:

> Studies of religion promise to enhance economics at several levels: generating information about a neglected area of "nonmarket" behaviour; showing how economic models can be modified to address questions about belief, norms, and values; and exploring how religion (and, by extension, morals and culture) affect economic attitudes and activities of individuals, groups, and societies. (1998, p. 1465)

Iannaccone distinguishes *economics of religion* from *religious economics* (or religious economies, i.e., economy and economic theory and practice as they are promoted by confessional actors) and his contribution to the former field can logically be considered as both pioneering and influential. He has striven for outlining and assembling theoretical issues in a single framework, but he also provided empirically based analysis, using quantitative methods and qualitative inquiries. Iannaccone is still a prominent author, aiming at mixing economists' and sociologists' perspectives on religious individuals and organizations' behavior. The application to the study of tools and models first coined in the "classical" frames of economics nevertheless raises epistemological issues, and has nurtured critical debates. Methodologically speaking, Iannaccone's "economic theory" is based upon quantitative approaches to case studies (Church loyalty, religious preferences, religious-driven economic behaviors…) but more qualitative and experimental foci are illustrated by "game theory," and "rational choice" theory, both linked, though not always directly, to the rise and development of the economics of religion. "Game theory" and "rational choice" theory work from rather different origins in religious studies, but the influence of the French philosopher Blaise Pascal (1623–1662) – yet, scarcely mentioned – is of primary importance. Pascal introduced the concept of a "wager" on the existence of God, and then, in a certain way, paved the way to game theory: since Man cannot be definitely assured of the existence of a supernatural being named "God," the only solution is to *wager* that God exists. The "wager theory" relies upon the axiom (or presupposition) of the actor's rationality in the context of religion, generally considered as "irrational." The economics of religion or the economic modelization of religious behaviors presuppose another epistemological foundation of the theory of the social actor. Stark, Iannaccone, and Finke claim that the economics of religion celebrate the end of an out-dated tradition in which religious behavior was associated with "primitive," "prescientific," and "non-rational," and above all, "irrational" (the model of *homo religiosus*), whereas, on the contrary, religion comes under a rational choice (1996, p. 434). The shift from irrationality to rationality, however, embarks on a discussion of the very nature of "rationality": is it an ideological rationality (rationalism) or an economic (calculated and more instrumental) one? Since the "economies" of "religions" can be framed as interfaces between "supply" and "demand" (Stark & Finke, 2000), rational choice theory has developed, within the economics of religion, alongside two distinct but interrelated theoretical approaches: the "supply-side" (the production of religious goods) and the "demand-side" (the individual's choice of these "goods") (Sherkat & Ellison, 1999). Focusing on rational choice in religion nevertheless gave rise to controversies (Bruce, 1999; Chaves, 1995; Iannaccone, 1991; Mellor, 2000), for after all, supply-and-demand theories depend at least in some ways on assumptions of individual choice, free from social determinants, and inspired by neoliberal economic models. In reality, rational choice is deeply embedded in cultural and social contexts (Ellison, 1995), and the study of the economics of religion does not erase the power of religious ideas to shape collective identities (Iannaccone, 1992, 1998). But the model of rationality underlying social behavior is also applied in inquiries on specific segments of social feelings or of behavior, not always directly linked to religion, as is the case of altruism, for instance (Simon, 1993).

It might sound odd, however, to "treat" religious facts as if they were economic in nature and form. It is common wisdom that most of the great religions of the world have developed a sense of suspicion or disgust toward economic matters and finance (though they all have had to cope with business affairs). From the ancient rise of a monetary economy to the recent extension of global capitalism, "materialistic" aspects of human production have been considered ambivalent by contrast with "symbolic" or "metaphysical" aspects: the former essential but polluting. According to Michel de Certeau, in the late 1980s, religious beliefs were "drying up" as such, "in holidays" and shifting toward nonreligious forms, including "economic" ones (1990). The French philosopher and sociologist was among the very first to suggest intuitively that religious behaviors, in the late 1970s, were soon to be replaced by economic motivations and meanings. On the other hand, Vincent Miller's theological rejoinder of consumerism in religion heralded a chance for "genuine" religious feelings to regenerate after the failures of a purely instrumental and economic attitude to religion, to provide *meaning* (Miller, 2003).

Utilizing concepts from economics in the study of religion is nevertheless far from new. Sociologists, like Pierre Bourdieu, began engaging issues of "ritual economy" or "symbolic economy" (*of* religion and *in* religion) decades ago. Following Max Weber, Bourdieu developed a complex model of religious entrepreneurship and consumption, in which (individual and institutional) actors are accumulating "symbolic capital," but this economic metaphor does not lead all the way to a focus on the *economics of religion* – and a "market" theory, even if Bourdieu refers to this – but rather to a political sociology of religious "fields" (Bourdieu, 1971).

## CONCEPTUAL SHIFTS: FROM "FIELD" TO "MARKET" AND THE EMERGENCE OF "RELIGIOUS CONSUMERISM"

Modernity and globalization are supposed to have dramatically changed the religious landscape of societies: migrations, missions, schisms in major religious organizations, and the diversification of beliefs, have reshaped – to varying degrees – the demographics, geography, and social morphology of religion in societies that are considered to be more "modern," with the deepest international connections and broadest transnational (human and symbolic) fluxes. Spiritual "seekers" or "converts," "consumers," or "shoppers," have become new models of religious behavior. "Seekers," "converts," or "pilgrims" can be said to exemplify the new mobility paradigm in religion studies, but in the framework of community-based theories of Durkheim (Hervieu-Léger, 2000; Warburg, 2001), while "shoppers" or "consumers" seem to illustrate a radical transformation, not empirically speaking (for they are the same people), but theoretically speaking: the latter mold their attitude in the framework of economic-like relationships to religion, as if "choosing" and "picking" religious "goods" in a "marketplace" (Mathews, 2000).

The shift from (Bourdieu's) "religious field" to (contemporary, and especially, American sociology) "spiritual supermarket" is a major conceptual shift. Here lies one of the most salient differences with Bourdieu's almost economic sociological theory of religion: in Bourdieu's terms, people are passive agents, determined by processes of religious "capitalization," while these new actor-figures rest upon another conception of social agency, in which the individual is a much more "free" and "active" actor in his/her relationship with religion (Verter, 2003), in a context where religious worldviews that used to be "canopies" (all-embracing systems of meaning shaping individuals and societies' lives) have turned into "markets" (stocks of religious "goods," produced by competing organizations, in which individuals "pick and choose") (Jelen, 2002). These two shifts (field to market, agent to actor) accompany a change in the course of the social science study of religion, from a focus on "economy and religion" to the newer one on the "economics of religion," and which presupposes the adoption of certain predicates:

(1) Economic theories are not contradictory with, but relevant to, the study of religion.
(2) The (individual or collective) actors' relationship to religion is motivated by understandable and rational intentions – *homo religiosus* can be considered, in this theoretical context, as a kind of *homo economicus*.
(3) Religious elements – ideas, symbols, beliefs, practices, etc. – can be labelled as "goods" (even "commodities") in the context and in the site of their production, promotion, circulation, and appropriation.
(4) The logics of organizational arrangements and institutional dynamics of religious traditions and landscapes can be understood and explained with reference to concepts of economics and political economy.

Additionally, some scholars maintain that the "market" logics concern more directly expanding or missionizing religions, and especially new religious movements, rather than world religions or mainstream churches (on the situation in France, see Hervieu-Léger, 2000; Schlegel, 1995). Others feel that, on the other hand, churches have also engaged in the same dynamics of exchange of material and symbolic "goods" (Iannaccone, 1991). Bryan Turner has also argued that contemporary fundamentalist religions, although ethically and politically in contradiction with the way they represent themselves (especially for Islam – Turner, 1994, pp. 90–91), nevertheless align themselves with the logics of consumer culture and the dynamics of expanding capitalism (Turner, 2004).

Peter Berger was perhaps the first sociologist to coin the expression "spiritual supermarket" (1969, p. 137), with the purpose of recounting innovative dynamics in religions. Since then, the application of economic models to the understanding of religious pluralism has been launched on the premise of a shift from Weberian and Bourdieusian "monopoly" to "market" pluralism (Finke & Stark, 1989, and more recently York, 1999), and on the evidence that contemporary religious contexts exemplify a shift from "regulation" (closed economy – monopolistic) to "deregulation" (open economy – pluralistic) (Wortham, 2004). More than sociology, this model is also framed in a *political economy of the sacred*, since religious organizations nowadays act like "firms" (Stark, 2004) or "entrepreneurs" (Greeley, 1989) in a "religious market." Among many others, Thomas Luckmann (2003) believes that historical transformations of religion, in modern Europe, have led to a "market" shaped religious landscape: "An essential characteristic of the 'modern' privatised social form of religion is de-monopolization of the production and distribution of world-views. (Religious) collective representations are produced and distributed in a relatively open market" including "a variety of sources [that] supplies the market of world-views" distributed by "relatively new suppliers" (Luckmann, 2003, p. 281). Moreover, in the context of globalization, and in the "global perspective" recently adopted by sociologists of religion, "religious marketplaces" have become a dominant feature of "religious life in the global village" (Kurtz, 2007, pp. 15–16).

Market theory, rational choices, and models in the economics of religion have nevertheless been accused of reductionism, extracting from religious activity its own essence (Bryant, 2000) or more specifically by targeting their theoretical foundations. Thomas Csordas has addressed critical rejoinders to the recurrent use of the market metaphor in religious sciences: "Particularly misleading [...] is the kind of metaphorical reduction that goes beyond causal priority to assert that processes of religious change can be adequately described as if they were economic, in terms of a 'spiritual marketplace' where people 'buy in' to a system of beliefs or 'shop on' a religious identity" (2009, p. 2). On this, he adds:

> The market metaphor has been taken up relatively uncritically in the popular media as well as in emerging scholarly literature on religion and globalization." [It] might be especially seductive in the case of postsocialist Europe, where capitalism has flooded into an economic vacuum to create an emerging global market simultaneously with the florescence of religious freedom and a multitude of religious possibilities ranging from orthodox to New Age. However, there is more than a semantic difference in describing the religious situation in this part of the world as a 'cultic milieu' [Kürti, 2001] rather than a 'spiritual marketplace' insofar as these terms carry different connotations about motivation, agency, identity and experience." (*Ibid.*, pp. 2–3)

These criticisms of the market theory are twofold. What Csordas points at here, is the fact that the market theory should apply in very specific contexts marked by the cultural and sociological influence of capitalism, and, in a rather different vein, that the model of "religious marketplace," standing as an alternative to more classical sociological terminology, refers explicitly to a neoliberal context *and* ideology. From an epistemological point of view, it is indeed interesting to note that the "marketplace" metaphor was coined in the context of North America, both in terms of the empirical data it relies on and the theoretical grounds upon which it has been framed. Bryan Turner, then, correctly recalls that the "new paradigm" of the economics of religion exists in contrast to the situation with religion in the "Old" continent (Europe) and the theoretical models of secularization, and in the "New" society (America) and the economic-inspired approach to religion: from

Alexis de Tocqueville to Laurence Iannaccone and other supporters of the economics of religion, one can wonder to what extent the latter is not firmly embedded in an "American exceptionalism" regarding religious matters (Turner, 2010, p. 9). Anthropologically speaking, hence, the main question concerns the opportunity to *transpose* economic models of religion beyond the American context, and their relevance there. The marketplace theory is now a conventional reference for highlighting the dynamics of religion in the context of multicultural societies – in South America, for instance.

The issue of pluralism, more broadly, has been a crucial hallmark in the integration of market theories – or the like – in the vocabulary of the social sciences of religion, but yet, it is a much-disputed point (crucial for demonstrating the theoretical relevance of the economics of religion): does the de-monopolization of great and powerful world belief systems and the rise of pluralistic spiritual landscapes lead to a situation of competition between religions, and therefore, take the shape of "markets"? "Economics of religion" enthusiasts are convinced, having conducted much quantitative and historical research in support of such a theory (see, e.g., Stark, Finke, & Iannaccone, 1995). According to Finke and Stark (1989) religious diversity increases pluralism and competition, and, from the economic point of view, contemporary forms of religious participation (on the individuals' side) and of regulation (on the institutions' side) should then be subjected to market effects. Many sociologists have, in contrast, argued that a powerful link between pluralism and a religious open economy is far from assured (Chaves & Gorski, 2001; Voas, Olson, & Crockett, 2002), and some scholars have been eager to stress the *methodological* limits of the "market theory" (Ahdar, 2006). Moreover, one may ask, does the relevance of the economics of religion need to be corroborated by *facts* (even offering no positive and definite evidence) or to be ascertained with the theoretical *posture* of scholars?

Warner (1993) was instrumental in asserting that the newer (American) economics of religion contrasts sharply with the "old" (European) model of secularization and triumphs over it. Yet again, the American case proves that divergent logics, pluralism (open economy), and monopolistic exclusivism (closed economy) can coexist in the same national context (Wortham, 2004), and consequently that "market" effects are not necessarily as widespread as the new paradigm suggests. McCleary and Barro have further demonstrated that the secularization hypothesis, upon which the "old" European theory was founded, was *also* relevant in the case of North America, where the per capita GDP has a negative effect on religiosity (2006, p. 62). Are the two paradigms definitely incompatible (substitutive one to another) or do they touch on *different* segments of the *same* religious landscape, perhaps subsequently adding to our comprehension of contemporary religious complexity? This question raises the issues of the respective nature, compatibility, and relevance of the paradigms. First, the oppositional identity of the "new" paradigm (versus the "old" one) is, in this century, hardly acceptable, at least when the former is supposed to *replace* the latter: an increasing body of research today cannot relinquish one or the other, but rather combines them (Barro, 2004). Second, the distinctive features of the two perspectives may have been overstressed, as with their theoretical unity as "paradigms." Terry Rey's revision of Pierre Bourdieu's sociology of religion contains theoretical evidence proving that, epistemologically speaking, "field" theory and "market" theory were not opposite paradigms for the French sociologist but different terminological ways to describe and analyze similar phenomena, since, in Bourdieu's theory: "Market (*le marché*) is interchangeable with the term 'field' (*le champ*), and other terms crucial to this theory of practice, such as 'profit' (*le bénéfice*), 'interest' (*l'intérêt*), 'capital' (*le capital*) and 'investment' (*l'investissement*) are also usually associated with economics' (2004, p. 332) and "Bourdieu is asserting that all fields conform to a certain economic logic that is 'capable of treating all practices, including those purporting to be disinterested or gratuitous, and hence non economic, as economic practices directed towards maximalizing of material or symbolic profit'" (Rey, 2004, p. 333, quoting Bourdieu, 1977, p. 183). Third, Gary Bouma has maintained that a market situation even recreates or reinforces a "field" configuration, since: "Competitors recognize each other as being legitimate operators in a religious market while in conflict one or more groups seek the exclusion or annihilation of the other" (2007, p. 200). French political scientist Olivier Roy (recently) turned his attention to the topic of new conditions facing religions in global settings – after having studied the globalization of Islam (Roy, 2004) and its encounters with Western modernity in detail – and came to question the ontological status of the "religious marketplace" (asking whether it is metaphor or reality). Roy does recognize that religions are "shaped" by market effects, especially in the case of conversions (2008, p. 41), and that among these effects, religions notably adopt "languages of marketing" in order to adjust to new conditions (p. 206). But more interesting to our discussion here is the recalling by Roy of the inner tension generated by ideological debates in economic theory, which is crucial for the extension and the limitation of the application of economic models in the study of religion: do economic metaphors in religious studies relate to Marxism, making them synonymous for "alienation," or do they aid in the promotion of the neoliberal ideal of "rational" and "free" actor (2008, p. 208)?

To sum up, in simple terms, what can be seen as the main problem of the market theory approach – and more generally, the economics of religion – can be summarized as follows: reference to "marketplace" and the derivative terminology (such as "open economy") can be used in a *metaphoric* sense. "Market" is hence the illustration or the *analogical* model of logics and dynamics underlying the activities and representations of religious actors and institutions (in the case of religious pluralism). A large part of sociological research alludes to such metaphorical abstractions. But reference to "marketplace" or other concepts borrowed from economics are relevant when the forms and processes observed are in a tangible manner related (in a way or another) to economic dimensions of human life, and have an effective impact on the religious sphere. To borrow from the American anthropologist Clifford Geertz (1976), who stated that anthropological terminology should be "experience-near concepts" (in contrast with "experience-distant concepts"), we could distinguish between "economy-near concepts" and "economy-distant concepts" in the economics of religion. Concepts of the first category are to be used when religious behavior is *effectively* impacted by economic factors, whereas concepts of the second category are to be used when religious behavior is *metaphorically comparable* with economic logics or processes.

## GLOBAL CAPITALISM AND THE CULTURAL LOGICS OF ECONOMY

The extension of the capitalistic system to the global scale also led religious organizations to convert themselves into "enterprises" governed by the logic of "branding" religion in a competitive space (the "marketplace") (Einstein, 2008; Moore, 1994). If Weber was the first to stress these economic contours and the logics of religious landscapes, he did not, however, consider that economic influences on religions had been different at different times in history. The legacy of Weber has been much acknowledged but sidestepped by accounts of the contextual features of so-called "late modernity" and "globalization," that is, the rise of a global culture and neoliberal *ethos*. In the context of the fast development of this "consumer culture," as a by-product of the extension of the globalization of capitalism, consumerist attitudes in religion have been widely recorded and came to be studied in depth, in particular in the context of North American Christianity (Twitchell, 2007).

In France, sociologist Jean-Louis Schlegel (1995) has coined the locution *religions à la carte*, depicting religious traditions as a "menu" of "meals" that "clients" can select and "consume." Schlegel has never envisioned a truly economic religion, and neither did scholars in economics of religion. Laurence Iannaccone, despite his status as a leading figure in the field, is sensitive to the distinction between what he calls "secular commodities" and "religious commodities," with only the latter being concerned with existential and ultimate meanings (supernatural forces, explanations of life, and life after death, etc.), but this does not change the *process* of production, distribution, and consumption in a context of rational calculation of costs and benefits (Iannaccone, 1992), and the same goes for the spiritual marketplace, in contrast with material markets (Mathews, 2000).

Economy can however be more than a context or a metaphor; it can be *sacred*. Philosopher Walter Benjamin (in 1921) opened the debate on "economy *as* religion," still pursued today, and certain scholars still maintain that, analogically or not, the contemporary capitalist system resembles (a) religion and creates religious attitudes. Benjamin, however, described capitalism as a cult without dogma nor theology, but presenting similar features (scarcity of resources) and generating religious feelings (faith, guilt, debt, and more). Hans G. Ulrich, after Benjamin, considers – in opposition to Weber – that the Christian religion (in its protestant form) did not *create* or *favor* capitalism, but has *converted to* capitalism itself (Palaver, 2007). David Chidester has labelled "monetary religion" the new cults founded around the world for which "money" has become sacred (2005, p. 111ff). If Max Weber did underline the "abstract" character of money, and also the incompatibility between the ethics of "great" religions and monetary economy, Chidester inversely points out the similar nature of money and religion since they both are "symbolic systems" (2005, p. 112). He even emphasizes that, contrary to the idea that the development of a monetary economy (especially in the cultural sphere) was a threat to religious ideas and beliefs, money is now afforded a religious meaning and it stands "at the centre of a moral economy, a material spirituality, an almost religious mystery" (*ibid.*). Aiming at highlighting the very similar functions of religion and economy as the media of exchange, Chidester connects money with blood (in the case of gang violence turning "religious" in South Africa and the United States), and just as blood is sacred in religious thought, "money is sacred" and plays a key role in the political economy of the sacred (p. 113). Thus, whereas Weber was convinced that religion and economy were by nature two different realms of psychological and social life, Chidester underscores the parallels between them, alluding to Bataille. Money, like religion, is a "scarce resource" that creates "symbolic surplus" (Chidester, 2005, p. 116) and it partakes of an "economy of expenditure" based upon "the sacred truths of symbols" (p. 117). Chidester demonstrates that under certain conditions, and to a certain extent, the economic approach allows scholars and students in religion to reexamine religious thought, attitudes, places, logics, and organizations that are subjected to more or less radical transformations. In the same vein but with different conclusions, Spickard (2008) is convinced that, in his study of the transnational missionary activism of the Japanese sect Sekai Kyusei Kyo, the similarities between the global dynamics of enterprises and the global dissemination and reorganization of religions allows scholars to merge them into a single analytical model. He is otherwise attentive to the fact that economic models pertain, in such an intellectual context, to analogical thinking. Referring to *economics* is nevertheless threatened by a caricature reduction of what and how sociologists study religion (for economists) and what and how economists analyze markets and rationality (for sociologists), and therefore:

> [E]conomic metaphors help us understand religious life but not transparently. As an economic "product," religions are a lot more like Disneyland than they are like rolled steel. Sociologists of religion who blather on about religious markets and rational actors would do well to actually read the works of those trying to understand the business world. They would see what one does not find in their current work: that markets are complex, that there is no one right way to produce goods for them, and that culture matters. (p. 124)

Among others, Peter Wagner's (2001) critique of the identification of modernity in general, and modern economy more precisely, with capitalism, contributes to such conceptual revisions.

## ANTHROPOLOGICAL PERSPECTIVES?

The relative absence of anthropologists from the larger field of *economics of religion* is noteworthy. Or, at least, their contributions yet remain fairly discreet, but this has always been the case for trendy or topical concepts – anthropologists were also reluctant to jump into the "modernity" dispute (Hefner, 1998), and are slowly but prudently engaging in "globalization studies" (Guillén, 2002) despite the invitation of scholars from other disciplines. Succinctly, what is the relevance of the views and concepts of economics for anthropologists studying religion? The *anthropology of religion* is a distinct field of knowledge, separate from economic anthropology, and to a certain extent, these sectors of anthropology have only had occasional exchanges. Combined models of religion and economics belong to a singular intellectual genealogy, rather different from the one claimed by sociologists. But surprisingly, much of anthropology's theoretical inheritance comes from sociologists or scholars of the French *Collège de Sociologie*: George Bataille and his theory of "expenditure" (*dépense*) coined in 1933 but published in his *La part maudite* in 1949, Robert Hertz' theory of ritual and the obligation to "expend" (offerings) in his *Sociologie religieuse et folklore* (1907–1917), Marcel Mauss' conceptualization of the Gift (*le don*) as exchange and counter-exchange in his *Essai sur le don* (published 1923–1924, in *L'Année Sociologique*) and, of course, Emile Durkheim's pioneering views of ritual as symbolic economies (as accumulation and distribution processes of symbolic capital) in his *Les formes élémentaires de la vie religieuse* (published 1912) (recently recapitulated by Neubert, 2008).

In parallel, anthropological perspectives on marketplaces consider them as "social and cultural institutions" in which religion can play a role (for instance, Geertz, 1968), but are not religious per se, or unlikely to be considered as such. More timely are the globalizing expressions of religion, which are concomitant with, and to a certain extent linked to, economic globalization, as studied by contemporary anthropologists like Mathews (2000), Chidester (2005), or Csordas (2009), among others. To what extent, then, do the concepts and methods of the economics of religion take part in a widespread change of attitude among individuals and collective actors (people and organizations) toward religion? Thomas Csordas (2009) has recently drawn attention to the limits of the highly seductive but fairly criticized conceptual apparatus of the economics of religion, spotlighting the changing epistemological nature of religious features, and the hazards of overstressing the influence of economic contextual factors on religion:

> [O]ne can talk about the economics of religion without treating religion literally or metaphorically as a commodity, and one can recognize that religious activities are subject to economic constraints, including market forces, without suggesting that religion operates according to the laws of the market. [But] global religious activity is neither determined by economic globalization nor describable on the model of economy decision making. It is more productive to understand globalization from the outset as a multidimensional process, with religion, popular culture, politics and economics as necessarily coeval and intimately intertwined… (Csordas, 2009, p. 3)

Critics, however, target a possible bias: the "economization" of theories of religion, in which (almost) *all* in religion (beliefs, behaviors, organization, or dynamics) can be interpreted in religious terms. Some scholars prudently address this issue, and even see in Adam Smith the precursor of this "economic imperialism" (Anderson, 1988), that is, the preeminence of the economic factor over all other ones, resulting in an economic overemphasis in the study of religion (see Mellor, 2000), whereas the "economy and religion" approach had cautiously examined the respective impact of one on the other, and reciprocally. Roland Robertson (1992), before Olivier Roy (2008), but in a more detailed reflection, also questioned the underlying ideological determinants and epistemological outcomes of this economic turn in the sociology of religion. All things considered, the two ideal-types of *homo religiosus* and *homo economicus* still hardly merge into a single model. Rationality, a controversial concept, though vital in the economics of religion and in the model of *homo economicus*, is tributary to utilitarian views of social behavior, unlike the functional and emotional aspects of religion, so crucial in the classical theory of Emile Durkheim – and his followers – constructing a nonutilitarian model of *homo religiosus*. Philip Mellor (2000, p. 276) summarizes the difficulty in reconciling the two perspectives:

> Parsons (…) detected an anti-religious impulse in utilitarian economics, not simply in the sense of a rational scepticism, bit in its tendency to see religion simply as commodity rather than something fundamental to social order. Contemporary applications of rational choice to religion both repudiate and reinforce Parsons' criticisms. One the one hand, they are not only free of any rationalist hostility to religion, but have been eager to emphasize the contemporary importance and vitality of religion (…). On the other hand, however, religion is simply a market commodity much like everything else (…). In short, this approach does not endow religion with the elementary sociological significance it had for Durkheim.

Even if the question of whether the *economics of religion* only contributes to a new conceptual and methodological approach of religion, in addition to previously existing ones, or epitomizes a theoretical revolution, it remains that the field of knowledge opened by the economics of religion is both promising and fruitful. After all, even though in recent decades economists have been criticized for discussing various dimensions of social and cultural life (crime, sex, war, etc.) in economic terms – as if *everything* could be explained in the lens of economic theories – it would be senseless and inappropriate to disqualify *economics of religion* as the new "economic-inspired" fashion. But as an empirically based, contextualized, and comparative study of human behavior, anthropology has been mainly interested in the issues of economy *and* religion, rather than *of* religion. If most contemporary anthropologists refer to Weber when they have to tackle the issue of "religion and economy," one must not forget that anthropological theory also includes its own models. Weber, who was not only a remarkable sociologist and a skilled historian of religion, however put a focal emphasis upon world religions and especially monotheistic ones (Judaism, Christianity, Islam), but paid little attention to "primitive" (nontheistic) ones. In the same vein, but in rather different way, Paul Radin's study of "primitive religion" (1937) was interested in the role of "economic factors" in the evolution of religion. According to Radin, "primitive theologies" as symbolic systems, and "primitive theologians" as social status (shamans, priests, sorcerers) appeared early in the history of mankind and religion, as responses to unstable economic conditions of gatherers-hunters and ancient societies. He directly lays emphasis upon the double contribution of economy in ancient religious change: first, as productive processes, and second, as the driving force for the emergence of a nonproductive social stratum, the "primitive theologians."

Most of the work done on the *economics of religion* paradigmatic theoretical body have been conducted in the Western landscape of (mono)theistic religious traditions. Moreover, the North American national context circumscribes the field of inquiries, as Warner indeed recalls: "The newer paradigm [economics of religion] stems not from the old one [secularization], which was developed to account for the European experience, but from an entirely independent vision inspired by American history" (1993, p. 1045). To what extent, and under which epistemological conditions, is the "newer paradigm" relevant for conventional empirical objects and the theoretical subject matter of anthropology? In other words, how does it shed a new light on ancient themes and fieldwork, or, in a sensibly different way, does it improve our anthropological knowledge of new empirical objects, such as globalizing religions or local religions impacted by the outcomes of political and economic modernization processes? A famous example is the Comaroffs' reference to "occult economies" in changing South Africa: the economic and political fluctuations and the antagonistic encounter between "millennial capitalism" and the "culture of neoliberalism" create conditions for the rise of "occult economies" (secret economies of the occult) in which magic and witchcraft are supposed to inflect the material course of economic production and accumulation (Comaroff & Comaroff, 1999). Moreover, political issues surrounding the tension between religious or magical forces, and those of the economy in the same South African context drives anthropologists to investigate the "political economy of religious violence" and highlight the processes underlying the "demonic economies of violence" (Feldman, 2002). As a final point on this, Dawid Venter (1999) has also pointed to the close relationship between the extension of (exported) global capitalism in Africa and the rise of new (local) churches, and illuminated the crucial role of economic (international) forces in the reshaping of indigenous religious landscapes. Further, China's changing religious landscape and the reshaping of political modes of religious regulation between traditions has also encouraged scholars to apply the economic approach in the Confucian-communist but spiritually mosaic country (Yang, 2010) but to adjust it to the specific sociological and anthropological profile (Vermander, 2009). In this small sample of case studies, "economy" is both an environment for changing religious expressions and the metaphorical modelization of the process of change itself. And this might be the core problem of *economics of religion*: economy has two distinct ontological statuses, the (empirical) "reality" and the (abstract) "model of reality." In his study of the globalization of popular culture (and religion), South African anthropologist David Chidester judiciously overturns the idea (for instance, maintained by Spickard) that the model of economic enterprises has become a yardstick to which religious organizations rearrange themselves, and unveils the strategies of transnational corporations to align themselves with the model of world religions (2005, chap. 7). Secularism is definitely what it used to be (seen) and just as Robertson (1989, p.13) asserts that global conditions favor the "religionization of politics and the politicization of religion," there is evidence that they also encourage *the economization of religion and the religionization of economy*.

## RELIGIOUS ECONOMICS, BEYOND DISCIPLINARY BOUNDARIES

To what extent, nevertheless, does this *economic turn* in religious studies epitomize a theoretical revolution? This volume neither seeks to validate such a revolution, nor to undermine it. Do we have to follow Ted Jelen when, for instance, he emphasizes the "unfinished business" in *economics of religion*? The ambitions of the editors and authors of this volume of *Research in Economic Anthropology* are more humble – to provide original theoretical reflections and empirical case studies in order to foster and prolong the debates. This Introduction was written mainly in order to trace a (yet blurry) frontier between four distinct aspects of the *problématique*: economy *and* religion, economy *in* religion, economy *as* religion, and the economics *of* religion. This latter area offers stimulating and challenging perspectives on religion, despite (or more precisely *because of*) the theoretical and epistemological issues it raises. All in all, the new paradigm of "religious economics" no longer relates to a specific disciplinary framework (economics, political economy, sociology, etc.) but rather stands for a transdisciplinary approach to religious behaviors. Under the encompassing banner of "economics of religion" exists a wide range of theoretical approaches, empirical objects, and methodological tools. The goal of this volume of *REA* is to present a significant (yet not exhaustive) sample of research that can be done, using a panel of diverse apparatuses from ethnography to experimental measures, in Western "developed" countries, in their former colonies, and in other parts of the world as well.

As is the case with most recent *REA* volumes, this volume is divided into several sections, defined primarily here by the approaches of the authors. Part I is a collection of five essays that are mainly concerned with theoretical issues surrounding the intersections of economic behavior and religious belief, and exploring the *economics of religion*. Although generally informed to varying degrees by the ethnographic experiences of the authors, these concentrate on concepts and themes more than on specific places and events. In the first chapter, Peter Seele explores the relationship between trust and religious faith. Here, he moves from institutional economics to a more nuanced discussion of individual religious behavior, but a behavior that is guided by faith in "higher powers" that can provide social capital which, in turn, leads to greater security and also to group cohesion when the members are bound by shared feelings and sets of values. Next, Simon Coleman explores what he sees as two phases of research on the global phenomenon of Prosperity Christianity, a movement that teaches believers that it is fully acceptable for them to amass and enjoy material wealth bestowed on them by Christ – an earlier phase centering on the question of why Prosperity Christianity caught on as quickly as it did in the United States over the last 60 years or so, and then spread rapidly outward to Latin America, Africa, and Asia, and a later phase seeking to answer the question of how it spread and adapted. Coleman identifies sacrifice as the theme running through both phases of research and examines this point in his essay leading to a consideration of "not only the economics of religion, but also religion as religious practice" (to borrow the author's words). In the third chapter, Riccardo Nanini considers the general theme of how religious behavior can be economic, and vice-versa, when the latter is at first assumed to not necessarily be "proper." Here, an association mediates between the Roman Catholic Church, with which it is closely associated, and the "economy" (seen as nonreligious) in-line with Catholic Social Teaching and (explicit or implicit) papal approval. Nanini shows a quest here for a "third way" between the cold calculations of ("pure") capitalism and the moral doctrines emanating from Vatican City. However, there are many confounders, such as the global diversity of Catholicism. In the fourth chapter of Part I, Isabelle Jonveaux continues with the theme of mediation between economic (profane?) versus religious (sacred?) activities – but this time it is a symbolic, mental mediation, as the economic production of communion bread ("the host") in monastic communities in France for a market (although a rather closed one) is upheld as a nonbusiness enterprise. The haunting question here is that of how a price can be placed on the body of Christ. Yet, as an item it must be produced somewhere and somehow. Jonveaux shows here how *the host* becomes even more meaningful when produced in a nonbusiness and sacred environment, and how economics as religious practice might be justified in this sense. This chapter rests more heavily than the preceding three on the author's personal fieldwork experience, but because it places the overarching concept of a "noneconomic economy" before the explication of activities on-site (because of the emphasis on analysis over taking the reader to a place, so to speak) it has been included in Part I of this volume. Finally, to wrap up this section, Lionel Obadia explores the place and role of economy in the contemporary globalization of Buddhism, and questions three conceptual models: Buddhism and economy, Buddhist economics, and economics of Buddhism. Albeit explicitly and ethically opposed to any kind of economic activity, Buddhism's asceticism has nevertheless perpetually consented to arrangements with surrounding economic conditions, and even participated in the accumulation of wealth – hence the conundrum hinted at in the epigraph to this Introduction. Contemporary Buddhist criticisms of damaging social outcomes of a global capitalistic market and of global culture assume a similar ambivalent posture, given the fact that, without it, the worldwide spread of Buddhism could not have been possible. Ultimately, in theory and in practice, Buddhism turns out to be paradoxically *against* and *in support of* a global financial economy, as well as to contain a symbolic economy of merit accumulation. Buddhism therefore appears to be an ideal example of religious confrontation with different models of *economics of religion*.

Part II of this volume offers an array of ethnographic case studies that serve to take the reader to a place, or that rely more heavily on particular ethnographic data to argue a point, than the essays in the preceding section. In the first chapter here, Raquel Romberg investigates the accumulation of *spiritual capital* among Puerto Rican faith healers – exploring the subtle "differences between materiality as the conduit for the sacred" on the one hand, and "as the manifestation of the sacred" on the other (in the author's words). In doing so, she directly addresses the important issue of resolving the disconnection between the material world and the spiritual world – a problem that lies at the heart of many debates on religion and even at the core of most major religious belief systems, as witnessed again in the song lyrics at the top of this Introduction. Also, in its approach, Romberg's chapter ties into the themes explored by Coleman, Jonveaux, and Obadia in Part I, backing them in this case with ethnographic evidence from Puerto Rico. The next chapter also deals with the relationship between the material and the spiritual, in this case as it is played out in the form of participation in cargo cults in Yucatan, Mexico, which are marked by a mix of native Mayan and imported Catholic beliefs. Here, for example, Andrés Dapuez and colleagues show how gift items become more meaningful when the giver is more spiritually and socially involved in the gift exchange network than otherwise. Furthermore, as would be expected in cargoes, material wealth is both sanctioned by God and ultimately bestowed on believers by their ancestors, reverence for whom helps to perpetuate the entire system. Protestant admonitions against materialism are not welcome. In the middle chapter of this section, and echoing the theme of Coleman's chapter in Part I, Asonzeh Ukah investigates an increase in religious involvement with the economy – and the economic – in Nigeria, a country which has experienced much social change in recent decades, including tremendous population growth that shows no sign of abating. The focus here is the Redeemed Christian Church of God, a Pentecostal organization that has been remarkably successful not only in attracting converts but also in channeling their economic behavior in certain directions. Not only this, but as Ukah shows, the Church actually shifted from an initial aversion to materiality to a political position that fully embraces and justifies it, allowing the organization to flourish and to make new inroads into banking and national politics. Ukah's chapter adds much weight to the argument that religious faith is today a powerful element in human economic behavior – one that economists overlook at their own peril when constructing theoretical models. Prosperity Christianity again takes center stage in the fourth chapter of this section of the volume, which resonates off Ukah's West Africa case study. Here, Nathalie Luca applies the comparative method in studying the adaptations of multilevel marketing (MLM) – an early postwar American invention – to different cultural contexts (South Korea, Haiti, and France). Permeated with Christian ideological overtones (consider Amway, for example) bearing a striking resemblance to Prosperity Christianity (which merges here with compassionate capitalism, according to the author), these direct-selling networks have taken on elements of different religious systems in the three different parts of the world represented here, to varying degrees of success. In South Korea, economic success became linked with Christianity (and pro-American sentiment) in the country's early competition with its communist neighbor on the north side of the 38th parallel, and MLM tapped into this rather well. In Haiti, however, MLM failed to integrate itself well with preexisting Protestantism and overcome a general acceptance of suffering as devotional testament, despite an apparent initial acceptance, and instead it fell into competition with churches. In France, though, MLM seems to have experienced better success than in Haiti, partly by "selling" a different sort of "Americanism" – the idea that each person is responsible for his or her own destiny and that nothing is preordained. But this has also come with a price: a dilution of MLM's Christian overtones. In the last chapter of Part II, Natsuko Higa examines generosity in the form of donations to the Church among Wesleyan Methodists in the Kingdom of Tonga. She relies on both qualitative and quantitative ethnographic data to argue that what might at first appear to be a purely competitive practice is actually a more complex system of competition and cooperation tied to individual and group status within small village communities. Gifts flow into the country from the outside in the form of remittances – the object of much attention in economic anthropology of late – and then cash and other forms of wealth flow to the churches and then back out again. Economy *in* religion: the Church is here a conduit for economic exchange that links local residents and distant Tongans as well.

Finally, Part III consists of two chapters which seek to better understand human economic behavior vis-à-vis religious sentiment by observing actions under controlled conditions. In the first, Brian Paciotti and colleagues report on the outcomes of a study drawing on the work of experimental economics they conducted on a university campus using students as subjects. Noting that there has been considerable disagreement among scholars regarding feelings of trust and the unifying power of religion, Paciotti and colleagues evaluated student performance in several different games in both religious and secular settings, which led them to conclude that feelings of generosity, trust, and cooperation are not necessarily stronger between people of similar religious beliefs (in all settings). On the other hand, in the next and final chapter of this volume, Benjamin Jewell and Amber Wutich argue that religious sentiment ("Christian norms" in this case) was a strong factor in water-sharing arrangements in a water-scarce environment in Bolivia. Based on "in-field" controlled experiments and backed by ethnographic observations, the authors found that community members sharing the same religious views were more generous with one another, which would seem to suggest opportunities for greater economic cooperation in a variety of forms between such persons in such a setting. To be sure, the points being measured and the conditions and study designs were quite different in the two chapters of this section, but taken together they seem to indicate a need for more comparative research on these issues across a wider range of geographic, environmental, and cultural settings. In addition, they also call attention to the importance of integrating theoretical, ethnographic, and experimental evidence in our quest for a more thorough understanding of economy *and, in,* and *as* religion – of the *economics of religion.* This is, ultimately, the goal of this 31st volume of *REA*.

## REFERENCES


Ahdar, R. (2006). The idea of "religious markets". *International Journal of Law in Context, 2*(1), 49–65.

Anderson, G. M. (1988). Mr. Smith and the preachers: The economics of religion in the Wealth of Nations. *The Journal of Political Economy, 96*(5), 1066–1088.

Appadurai, A. (2001). Grassroots globalization and the research imagination. In: A. Appadurai (Ed.), *Globalization* (pp. 1–21). Durham, NC: Duke University Press.

Barro, R. (2004). Religious faith and economic growth: What matters most – Belief or belonging? *The Heritage Foundation.* Retrieved from http://heritage.org/Research/Religion/h1841.cfm. Accessed on March 28, 2008.

Berger, P. (1969). *A rumor of angels: Modern society and the rediscovery of the supernatural.* New York, NY: Anchor Books.

Bouma, G. (2007). Religious resurgence, conflict, and the transformation of boundaries. In: P. Beyer & L. G. Beaman (Eds.), *Religion, globalization and culture* (pp. 187–202). Leiden: Brill.

Bourdieu, P. (1971). Genèse et structure du champ religieux. *Revue française de sociologie, 12*(3), 295–334.

Bourdieu, P. (1977). *Outline of a theory of practice.* Cambridge, MA: Cambridge University Press.

Bruce, S. (1999). *Choice and religion: A critique of rational choice theory.* Oxford: Oxford University Press.

Bryant, J. M. (2000). Cost–benefit accounting and the piety business: Is *homo religiosus* at bottom a *homo economicus*? *Method and Theory in the Study of Religion, 12*, 520–548.

Certeau, M. de (1990). *L'invention du quotidien. (1) Arts de faire.* Paris: Gallimard.

Chaves, M. (1995). On the rational choice approach to religion. *Journal for the Scientific Study of Religion, 34*, 98–104.

Chaves, M., & Gorski, P. S. (2001). Religious pluralism and religious participation. *Annual Review of Sociology, 27*, 261–281.

Chidester, D. (2005). *Authentic fakes: Religion and American popular culture.* Berkeley, CA: University of California Press.

Clarke, P. B. (2006). *New religions in global perspective: A study of religious change in the modern world.* London: Routledge.

Comaroff, J., & Comaroff, J. L. (1999). Occult economies and the violence of abstraction: Notes from the South African postcolony. *American Ethnologist, 26*(2), 279–303.

Csordas, T. (2009). Modalities of transnational transcendence. In: T. Csordas (Ed.), *Transnational transcendence: Essays on religion and globalization* (pp. 1–29). Berkeley, CA: University of California Press.

Einstein, M. (2008). *Brands of faith: Marketing religion in a commercial age*. London: Routledge.

Ellison, C. G. (1995). Rational choice explanations of individual religious behavior: Notes on the problem of social embeddedness. *Journal for the Scientific Study of Religion, 34*, 89–97.

Feldman, A. (2002). Strange fruit: The South African truth commission and the demonic economies of violence. In: B. Kapferer (Ed.), *Beyond rationalism: Rethinking magic, witchcraft and sorcery* (pp. 234–365). New York, NY: Berghahn Books.

Finke, R., & Stark, R. (1989). Evaluating the evidence: Religious economies and sacred canopies. *American Sociological Review*, *54*(6), 1054–1056.

Geertz, C. (1968). *Islam observed: Religious development in Morocco and Indonesia*. New Haven, CT: Yale University Press.

Geertz, C. (1976). From the native's point of view. In: K. H. Basso & H. A. Selby (Eds.), *Meaning in anthropology* (pp. 221–237). Albuquerque: University of New Mexico Press.

Greeley, A. (1989). *Religious change in America*. Cambridge, MA: Harvard University Press.

Guillén, M. F. (2002). Is globalization civilizing, destructive or feeble? A critique of five key debates in the social science literature. *Annual Review of Sociology*, *27*, 235–260.

Hefner, R. W. (1998). Multiple modernities: Christianity, Islam and Hinduism in a globalizing age. *Annual Review of Anthropology*, *27*, 83–104.

Hervieu-Léger, D. (2000). *Religion as a chain of memory*. New Brunswick, NJ: Rutgers University Press.

Iannaccone, L. (1991). The consequences of religious market structure: Adam Smith and the economics of religion. *Rationality and Society*, *3*(2), 156–177.

Iannaccone, L. (1998). Introduction to the economics of religion. *Journal of Economic Literature*, *36*(3), 1465–1495.

Iannaccone, L. R. (1992). Religious markets and the economics of religion. *Social Compass*, *39*(1), 123–131.

Jelen, T. G. (Ed.) (2002). *Sacred markets, sacred canopies: Essays on religious pluralism*. Lanham, MD: Rowman and Littlefield.

Kale, S. H. (2004). Spirituality, religion, and globalization. *Journal of Macromarketing*, *24*(2), 92–107.

Kurtz, L. R. (2007). *Gods in the global village: The world's religions in sociological perspective* (2nd ed.). Thousand Oaks, CA: Pine Forge Press.

Luckmann, T. (2003). Transformations of religion and morality in modern Europe. *Social Compass*, *50*(3), 275–285.

Mathews, G. (2000). *Global culture/individual identity: Searching for home in the cultural supermarket*. New York, NY: Routledge.

McCleary, R. M., & Barro, R. J. (2006). Religion and economy. *Journal of Economic Perspectives*, *20*(2), 49–72.

Mellor, P. A. (2000). Rational choice or sacred contagion? "Rationality," "non-rationality," and religion. *Social Compass*, *47*(2), 273–292.

Miller, V. (2003). *Consuming religion: Christian faith and practice in a consumer culture*. New York, NY: Continuum.

Moore, R. L. (1994). *Selling God: American religion in the marketplace of culture*. New York, NY: Oxford University Press.

Neubert, F. (2008). Indicating commitment: The notion of dépense in the study of religion and ritual. *Journal of Classical Sociology*, *8*(2), 306–320.

Obadia, L. (2010). Religion and globalization. In: B. Turner (Ed.), *The new companion for the sociology of religion* (pp. 477–497). Oxford: Blackwell.

Palaver, W. (2007). Challenging capitalism as religion: Hans G. Ulrich's theological and ethical reflections on the economy. *Studies in Christian Ethics*, *20*(2), 215–230.

Radin, P. (1937). *Primitive religion: Its nature and origin*. New York, NY: Viking Press.

Rey, T. (2004). Marketing the goods of salvation: Bourdieu on religion. *Religion*, *34*(4), 331–343.

Robertson, R. (1989). Globalization, politics and religion. In: J. Beckford & T. Luckmann (Eds.), *The changing face of religion* (pp. 10–23). London: Sage.

Robertson, R. (1992). The economization of religion? Reflections on the promises and limitations of the economic approach. *Social Compass*, *39*(1), 147–157.

Roy, O. (2004). *Globalised Islam: The search for a new Ummah*. London: Hurst.

Roy, O. (2008). *La Sainte ignorance: Le temps de la religion sans culture*. Paris: Le Seuil.

Schlegel, J.-L. (1995). *Religions à la carte*. Paris: Hachette.

Sherkat, D. E., & Ellison, C. G. (1999). Recent developments and current controversies in the sociology of religion. *Annual Review of Sociology*, *25*, 363–394.

Simon, H. A. (1993). Altruism and economics. *The American Economic Review*, *83*(2). (Papers and Proceedings of the 105th Annual Meeting of the American Economic Association, pp. 156–161).

Sklair, L. (1999). Competing conceptions of globalization. *Journal of World-Systems Research*, *2*, 143–162.

Spickard, J. V. (2008). Organizational transformations in global religions: Rethinking the relationships between organization, culture and market. In: A. W. Geertz & M. Warburg (Eds.), *New religions and globalization* (pp. 109–127). Aarhus, Denmark: Aarhus University Press.

Stark, R. (2004). *Sociology* (9th ed). Belmont, CA: Wadsworth.

Stark, R., & Bainbridge, W. S. (1985). *The future of religion, secularisation, revival and cult formation*. Berkeley, CA: University of California Press.

Stark, R., & Finke, R. (2000). *Acts of faith: Explaining the human side of religion*. Berkeley, CA: University of California Press.

Stark, R., Finke, R., & Iannaccone, L. R. (1995). Pluralism and piety: England and Wales, 1851. *Journal for the Scientific Study of Religion*, *34*(4), 431–444.

Stark, R., Iannaccone, L. R., & Finke, R. (1996). Religion, science, and rationality. *American Economic Review* (Papers and Proceedings, pp. 433–437).

Turner, B. S. (1994). *Orientalism, postmodernism and globalism*. London: Routledge.

Turner, B. S. (2004). Fundamentalism, spiritual markets and modernity. *Sociology*, *38*(1), 195–202.

Turner, B. S. (2010). Mapping the sociology of religion. In: B. S. Turner (Ed.), *The new Blackwell companion to the sociology of religion* (pp. 1–29). Oxford: Wiley-Blackwell.

Twitchell, J. B. (2007). *Shopping for God: How Christianity went from in your heart to in your face*. New York, NY: Simon & Schuster.

Van Der Bly, M. (2005). Globalization: A triumph of ambiguity. *Current Sociology*, *53*(6), 875–893.

Venter, D. (1999). Globalization and the cultural effects of the world – Economy in a semiperiphery: The emergence of African indigenous churches in South Africa. *Journal of World-Systems Research*, *5*, 104–126.

Vermander, B. (2009). Réveil religieux et sortie de la religion en Chine contemporaine. *Perspectives Chinoises/China Perspectives, 4*, 4–17.
Verter, B. (2003). Spiritual capital: Theorizing religion with Bourdieu against Bourdieu. *Sociological Theory, 21*(2), 50–174.
Voas, D., Olson, D. V. A., & Crockett, A. (2002). Religious pluralism and participation: Why previous research is wrong. *American Sociological Review, 67*(2), 212–230.
Wagner, P. (2001). Modernity, capitalism and critique. *Thesis Eleven, 66*(1), 1–31.
Warburg, M. (2001). Seeking the seekers in the sociology of religion. *Social Compass, 48*(1), 91–101.
Warner, R. S. (1993). Work in progress toward a new paradigm for the sociological study of religion in the United States. *The American Journal of Sociology, 98*(5), 1044–1093.
Waters, M. (2001). *Globalization* (2nd ed.). New York, NY: Routledge.
Willaime, J-P. (2004). *Europe et religions: Enjeux du XXIe siècle*. Paris: Fayard.
Wortham, R. A. (2004). Religious choices and preferences: North Carolina's Baskin Robbins effect? *Sociation Today, 2*(1). Retrieved from http://www.ncsociology.org/sociationtoday/v21/religion.htm. Accessed on March 21, 2008.
Yang, F. (2010). Religious awakening in China under communist rule: A political economy approach. In: B. Turner (Ed.), *The new companion for the sociology of religion* (pp. 429–455). Oxford: Blackwell.
York, M. (1999). Le supermarché religieux: ancrages locaux du Nouvel Age au sein du réseau mondial. *Social Compass, 46*(2), 173–179.

Lionel Obadia
Donald C. Wood

# PART I
# THEORETICAL ISSUES – CONCEPTS AND PROBLEMS

# TRUST, FAITH AND CALCULATIVENESS: A THEORETICAL EXTENSION OF O. WILLIAMSON'S 'INSTITUTIONAL TRUST'

Peter Seele

## ABSTRACT

*This chapter aims to develop an institutionalist concept of faith based on Williamson's concept of 'institutional trust' and Coleman's contribution to 'placement of trust'. As a starting point, it considers the social capital literature on trust from the perspective of institutional economics and economic anthropology. 'Institutional faith' posits as a normative state the inevitability of trust with regard to certain questions human beings cannot answer. This has a behaviour-channelling effect which makes, e.g. for institutional stability. The proposed concept is evaluated critically by contrasting it with T. Kuran's concept of 'preference falsification' in the Hindu caste system. Finally, the concept is challenged by today's Hindu fundamentalism and makes a differentiation between fundamentalism and institutional faith.*

**The Economics of Religion: Anthropological Approaches**
**Research in Economic Anthropology, Volume 31, 3–21**

**ISSN: 0190-1281/doi:10.1108/S0190-1281(2011)0000031004**

## INTRODUCTION: SOCIAL CAPITAL AS STARTING POINT

It is a common observation from everyday life, and from everyday world politics, that decisions – be they economic, personal, political or military in kind – are motivated by, and legitimated through, backgrounds in belief that presuppose the existence of the religious convictions of the individual. Economic theory has, with very few exceptions, not considered this adequately. In the literature on Economics of Religion (e.g. Iannaccone, 1998; Mc Cleary & Barro, 2006), we predominantly find rational choice approaches that do not entirely capture the influence of religion on decisions. Promising approaches come from Institutional Economics, also taking path-dependent processes, premmference falsifications (Kuran, 1995a, 1995b) or customs (Schlicht, 1998) into account. Also, J. Ensminger's (1994, 1997) work relating anthropology to institutional economics has contributed to the discussion in the economics of religion field in a positive way. Another major contribution is the work from economic anthropologists (Gramajo, 2007; Landa, 1994; Wood, 2007). But 'mainstream' economic theories such as classical or neo-classical ones, with their primarily quantitative methodologies (sometimes disparaged as 'autistic' by their critics), provide only a very limited theoretical framework for describing the fuzziness and complexity implied by religious convictions and their impact on decision-making.

As a starting point, this chapter brings in findings on social capital to explain motivations also influenced by trust-based relations, by beliefs and religious faith. A valuable source in the field is literature from anthropology that partly criticizes the social science approach to social capital[1] (Durrenberger, 2002) or introduces a more dense description of social capital in anthropological terms grounding the concept in ethnography (Schneider, 2006). However, trust as underlying concept is a key to understanding social capital. The aim here is to transfer Williamson and Coleman's concepts of (institutional) trust to religion, in particular to the concept of faith. Institutional faith, as introduced here, emphasizes the behaviour-channelling existence of the individual's religious orientation, which, through people's material actions, increases the stability of the entire institutional structure and thus its persistence potential.

## TRUST AND FAITH

The parameters of *trust* and *social capital*, rarely used and accepted only by a small number of economic theorists, do not suffice to represent and describe religion adequately. Institutional economic analysis has demonstrated that religious matters can be expressed through existing concepts and terms of institutional economics, e.g. by reference to form-less rules, 'spiritual enforcement' (Hull & Bold, 1994) or expanded concepts of rationality, but a practical application seems impossible. This is not the place, however, to discuss the various charges made against the expansion of institutional economics as 'theory imperialism' or 'economic imperialism'. Rather, we will try to redraw the borders through an expansion of vocabulary.

If religion matters, then, it does so in the sense that religious conviction of – or faith in – something transcendent counts for the perception of the transcendent. Statements about 'the metaphysical' would not be admissible. Yet, the existence of conviction in the form of mental models is enough to attest that religion matters. By reference to Coleman (1990) and to Luhmann (1987, 1989), it can be shown that trust is an act of faith without any material basis when the trusting player acts as though he had certain knowledge of the future (Luhmann, 1989, p. 8). This state of being certain about something uncertain requires a faith. In this context, the institutional frame determines the ideologies by which the players' mental models will make transcendence matter.

In general, the claim that religion matters points to the conclusion that metaphysical orientation will not lead to the secular world's being surrendered to its own developmental laws, but rather to this world's endowment, through the attempt of transcending it, with a new, peculiar dynamics (Eisenstadt, 1984, p. 356). This is where trust in routine becomes important and is produced, e.g. by rituals. In religion, ritual achieves the application and enforcement of this development, in that it creates an 'instantaneous transcendence reference': Stietencron (2001, p. 110) asserts that ritual itself demands routine, precise action and the knowledge and the correct use of powerful formulae. On the basis of the assertion that religion matters in analogy to Williamson's term 'institutional trust', the term 'institutional faith' will be introduced. This calls for an explanation of what is meant by *faith*, and how this semantic field relates to religion.

Following Eisenstadt, it can be shown that in religion, the physically not-present world of the metaphysical, which is perceived as 'other', also facilitates the shaping of the material world. Evidence of this is persistent criterion of a religion's sustained developmental path. As a characteristic of the institutional form, Eisenstadt identifies the existence of an encompassing culture and the central importance of the religious sphere (1984, p. 337). This means that the rules of religion, implicit and explicit alike must be seen as connected. While this may be obvious for implicit rules, the claim is harder to verify with regard to explicit rules. Therefore, the concept of institutions as rules in connection with trust will be presented.

## CONCEPTS OF TRUST AND WILLIAMSON'S 'INSTITUTIONAL TRUST'

Luhmann's sociological study of trust is helpful in conceptualizing trust in religious terms, as it deals with the function of transcending time through the mechanism of trust: For Luhmann (1989), the main function of trust is to reduce the complexity of action contexts and to facilitate decision-making and actions for all players. The trust mechanism works in situations when the risk exceeds certain well-defined limits. Thus, Luhmann takes the view that trust only becomes effective in situations in which uncertainty – whether through complexity or through irresolution – overcomes the will to make a decision. Trust, as a unificatory bond between parties beyond rationally perceived vulnerability, will bring about action. In *Social Systems*, Luhmann terms the basis for this bond, and for trust, a 'risky advance' (1987, p. 23) which must be made for trust to come about. Trust, he argues, does not simply follow from the past; it exceeds the information it possesses from the past, and it risks a prediction of the future. The action of trusting reduces the future's complexity (*ibid.*, p. 20). The aspect of bridging the gap between present and future, Luhmann addresses in a way useful to the present study in his work on trust (1989): He provides a tentative theoretical connection between trust and religious faith when he points out that those who trust anticipate the future, acting as though it was certain. One might think, he says, that those who trust surmount time, or at least time differences (*ibid.*, p. 8) (the problem that time is not practically certain beyond the immediate present need not be addressed here). Much more central is that through trust, the present establishes a relationship that reaches into the future, transforming a certain choice from something possible into something probable and turning it further (through action according to the decision made on the basis of trust) into something potentially, and then actually, real in the present. The basis of this mechanism is beyond empiricism in terms of perception, although it can be made plausible through the principle of path dependency. We are thus dealing with a paradoxical relationship, since trust as explained by Luhmann only comes to bear when risk is exceeded. Thus, trust exists and evolves as a negative action coordinate. In that sense, trust constitutes a kind of 'inner reserve', but with the difference to financial inner reserves that its replacement is near impossible. Between the actors concerned, and in terms of the process of trust development, trust is non-renewable. That does not mean, however, that a new basis for trust could not be established within a certain frame of rules, albeit one that would likewise have to be created anew.

As we now have dealt with trust and the function of transcending time by trust-based relationships, we will now turn to O. Williamson and his concept of institutional trust. In the following text, it will be attempted to develop from the term 'institutional trust' the term 'institutional faith'. Williamson (1996, 1993) differentiates between *calculative*, *personal* and *institutional* trust. The latter constitutes a synthesis of the two complementary variants of trust in that it integrates elements of both, assuming a mediating and stabilizing function:

(1) *Calculative trust* is a terminological sleight of hand by which Williamson captures the intentional utilization of behaviour which is only constituted through the non-utilization of trust. Calculative trust constitutes an oxymoron, or a contradiction in terms, insofar as through the intentional utilization of trust, trust itself (which is 'fragile')[2] is being negated. Thus, Williamson's term is effectively a critique of the use of the term 'trust'. He also points out that 'trust' and 'risk' are often mistakenly used synonymously (Williamson, 1996, p. 275). Williamson concludes his discussion of trust with a critique of calculative trust: 'The irony is that the limits of calculativeness are realized by examining user-friendly terms – of which "trust" is one – in a thoroughly calculative way' (*ibid.*). In his general definition of trust – one that does not refer to one of the three categories only – it becomes clear again that for Williamson, as well as for Noorderhaven (1996), calculative trust is not actually trust at all: 'Trust is warranted when the expected gain from placing oneself at risk to another is positive, but not otherwise' (Williamson, 1996, p. 257).

(2) *Personal trust*, on the other hand, is characterized by non-calculability according to Williamson. He names three criteria of personal trust: '(1) the absence of monitoring, (2) favourable or forgiving predilections, and (3) discreteness' (Williamson, 1996, p. 273). These three criteria make it clear that personal trust is not a resource to be utilized, but rather one that relies on relationships that span longer periods of time. Thus, they constitute an atmosphere of governance without form-bound instruments of governance, which would be applicable in a purpose-bound

manner. Williamson calls this peculiar nature 'almost non-calculable', which from the point of view of propositional logic appears at first glance to be another contradiction in terms, but it transports the relationship structure and the fuzziness that are the very central characteristics of trust. Williamson further emphasizes the intimacy of personal trust, which finds particular expression in the third criterion of discretion (1996, p. 275).

(3) *Institutional trust*, according to Williamson, constitutes a category of trust that is at the same time personal and intentional. It may be seen as the dialectical principle of the other two categories. From personal trust, it is distinguished by accounting for the 'social and organizational context'. This endows institutional trust with a utilitarian dimension, which is not, however, as Williamson insists, calculative in an obvious sense: Institutional trust refers to the social and organizational context within which features are exogenous, institutional trust has the appearance of being non-calculative. In fact, however, transactions are always organized (governed) with reference to the institutional context (environment) of which they are a part. Calculativeness thus always reappears (*ibid.*, also Williamson, 1993).

In the following text we will concentrate on institutional trust because institutional trust is our transfer point for institutional faith: Since social action and transactions are context-bound, a calculative element finds entrance into institutional trust. In this context, Williamson refers to institutional trust also as 'hyphenated trust' (*ibid.*, p. 268). To him, there are six interconnected contexts for institutional trust, which he sketches briefly as follows (*ibid.*, p. 268f): (1) *Societal culture*: The main importance of culture, for purposes of economic organization, is that it serves as a check on opportunism; (2) *Politics*: Legislative and judicial autonomy serve credibility purposes; (3) *Regulation*: It can serve to infuse trading confidence into otherwise problematic trading relations; (4) *Professionalization*: The obligation to fulfil the definition of a role is especially important for professionals; (5) *Networks*: Credibility turns on whether these reputation effects work well or poorly; (6) *Corporate culture*: It displays both spontaneous and intentional features and works mainly within particular organizations.

Following Williamson, one may then view trust as a mechanism of governance which reduces transaction costs. Karpe cautions, however, that the term 'transaction costs' needs to be broadened if trust is to be accounted for. According to him, the term would then need to include a field quite alien to economic terminology, taking in a transaction atmosphere influenced by socio-cultural conditions (Karpe, 1997, p. 76). The development of the term 'institutional trust' thus builds on Williamson's work. As Karpe showed with regard to Williamson's term, such a step necessarily entails, in addition, the broadening of the term 'transaction costs'. From the six domains of institutional trust, the point that appears most promising for the present study is professionalization. For this reason, and for reasons of brevity, the other five domains will not be discussed here in detail.

In the context of institutional trust, Williamson comments on professionalization: 'the obligation to fulfil the definition of a role is especially important for professionals' (1996, p. 268). This view clearly shows that Williamson's explanation of trust is very much tied to the secular. The 'obligation' Williamson mentions for professionals is additionally legitimated. Irrespective of whether this metaphysical legitimation is real or not, it stabilizes the worldly order as a controlling effect.

In the case of religion, this means that secular and sacred matters form a unit which – as history shows – is characterized by remarkable stability. The aspect of dialectical mutuality is the very precondition for the existence of institutions in general, as Aoki points out. This is what he means when he calls institutions 'symbolic systems of belief' (Aoki, 2001, p. 18) and claims that an institution will only continue to exist 'if the agents mutually believe in it' (p. 10). Here, too, mutuality forms the basis for an institution's validity as long as its factors of influence are accepted as binding and players believe in them. For the concept of institutional trust and institutional faith, it is significant to note that for an institution to be relevant, the belief in it is sufficient to keep up the institution. Generally speaking, this refers to an institution's credibility, resulting from the frame of rules in accordance with players' expectations, which reduces the players' decision-making costs. Belief is then the opposite of doubt, constituting a self-sufficient habit of mind. Therefore, it can be stated that the basis of persistence is dependent on the features of the institutional members' belief – or faith.

Among these features, one may point to the absence of doubt; doubt would cause high transaction costs in the form of opportunity and decision-making costs if trust or faith is involved. Belief, on the one hand, reduces transaction costs. On the other hand, belief causes high set-up costs, which – in the form of social capital – turns into an obstacle to change because of the high amount of sunk costs resulting from them. It becomes more difficult to reach the critical mass necessary for institutional change if players believe strongly in a shared set of institutions.

## THE TERM 'FAITH' AND ITS INHERENT DIFFICULTIES

In the following text, the term *faith* will be introduced to facilitate its use as a terminological supplement to institutional theory in the form of 'institutional faith'. 'Faith' connotes both trust and religious belief, both of which are crucial constituents of religion. To develop 'institutional faith' from Williamson's 'institutional trust' is thus to draw attention to the deeper nature of the trust entailed by religious belief.

This affinity between 'trust' and 'faith' is also emphasized by Kasper and Streit in their discussion of the connection between long-term views and prosperity: 'In many communities, people who interact take a long-term view and do not play opportunistic end games. They understand that their prosperity depends on mutual, ongoing and rule-bound interaction as well as on trust and good faith' (1999, p. 262). 'Faith' is not used in a religious sense here. Yet, the term does refer to sustained, persisting and also prosperity-conserving rule systems, which already hints at the behaviour-channelling direction of the term 'institutional faith'. Growth based on competitive advantage is the opportunistic counter-strategy. This does not cater to the long-term time frame made possible by 'institutional trust' and 'institutional faith', but it yields much higher returns and can increase prosperity significantly in a short time. It ought to be pointed out again that the argument and terminology developed here does not pursue ethical aims, but rather attempts to provide an analytical description of the parameters affecting institutional change.

'Institutional faith' will also take in the trust-deepening function of religious belief in order for the description of economic processes to be able to account for the existence of metaphysically motivated behaviour. Thus, it must be differentiated between belief in general and religious belief in particular. An example, Stenmark (1994, p. 290) neatly sums up this distinction, facilitating the inclusion of religious belief in the concept of 'institutional faith'. Institutional theory is increasingly concerned with behaviour, the acquisition of knowledge and the mental models of players. Accordingly, it is crucial for a complete understanding of players to take into account the component of their religious convictions and beliefs. The next step is then to ask how *faith* manifests itself in religion, if 'institutional faith' in general is to be explained. Badrinath offers a terminological differentiation that aims at clarifying the difference between 'belief' and 'faith': 'And it is faith upon which every human relationship, personal or collective, is everywhere visibly founded. Whereas belief relates primarily to the mind and its instruments; faith involves participation of feelings' (2000, p. 176). Both authors seem to agree that 'faith' encompasses existential matters of non-material needs and has found little employment as an economic category for that reason. When economics increasingly turns towards informal, non-material historical matters, the component of 'faith' becomes relevant and useful. To sum up, 'institutional faith' emphasizes the behaviour-channelling existence of players' metaphysical orientation, which through their material actions increase the stability of the entire institutional structure, and thus its persistence potential. And, when an existing terminology is supplemented, it must be examined regarding how far the proposed supplement is original, or which existing approaches may be built on or connected to.

## PLACEMENT OF TRUST VERSUS PLACEMENT OF FAITH

At this point, the term 'institutional faith' can now be characterized by reference to Coleman's (1990) four points from his 'Placement of Trust'.

1. *Trust* and *faith* must be distinguished in one further respect in order to clarify the expanded scope of the latter: The difference between *trust* and *faith* lies in the involved parties. In the case of *trust*, this means worldly entities (both natural persons and legal entities) and/or institutions (implicit and explicit). In the case of *faith* on the other hand, the relationship exists between a worldly entity (which can here only be the natural person with their needs) and a metaphysical entity, the existence of which need only be assumed by the player in order to establish this relationship. Therefore, the relevant question to ask is the question of placement: '[T]he placement of trust allows an action on the part of the trustee that would not have been possible otherwise' (p. 97). Regarding *faith*, this is equally true, with the differences between the two terms remaining in place. The consequences of this point can differ significantly: '[I]f the trustee is trustworthy, the person who places trust is better off than if trust were not placed, whereas if the trustee is not trustworthy, the trustor is worse off than if trust were not placed' (p. 98). In this context, the differentiation between the basis of the concerned parties is important. The player 'placing' his faith is the natural person,

while the object of faith is the metaphysical entity, whose trustworthiness or religious legitimation cannot be established. Conversely, this means that it is only the player's faith that establishes the relationship. If the differentiation between trust and faith described above is accepted, Coleman's second point also applies to faith.

2. '[T]he action of placing trust involves the trustor's voluntarily placing resources at the disposal of another party (the trustee), without any real commitment from that other party' (p. 98). Again, transference must be made by reference to the differentiation of terms. The commitment of the 'other party', which in the case of faith is again the metaphysical entity, depends on the firmness of belief on the part of the believer. This can be massively disturbed through worldly events. If one disregards non-confirmable claims of miracles and acts of revelation, there is no communication of commitment by the metaphysical entity towards the worldly player. In any case, commitment consists of the self-perceived relationship to the metaphysical entity.
3. A more difficult point is the question of voluntariness. It emerged that freedom is very limited through the mere existence of an order of hereditary station exacting great influence on individual players with regard to the roles they have to fulfil.
4. '[T]ime lag: Each has to do with future actions on the part of the trustee' (*ibid.*). The problem of time can be in the context of the term 'trust'. Luhmann's (1989, p. 8) assertion that the player in the trust relationship behaves as though he could surmount time, as though he were certain of the future, comes very close to the expectation connected with religious *faith*, but the returns of the actions based on trust and faith are only reaped in the afterlife. It is useful to point out here that Coleman uses the term 'trustee', making use of its commercial connotations. The players invest a non-material value into their relationship with the metaphysical entity, expecting, after the time lag mentioned above, the otherworldly pay-off in the same non-material 'currency'. By accounting for 'institutional faith', the existence of this 'currency' explains the behaviour-channelling of religiously motivated players.

Thus, Coleman's four points can demonstrate how *trust* and *faith* are related. On the other hand, the difference in the qualities of the concerned entities is grave. If this difference is taken to be implicitly understood, *faith* and *trust* can be used synonymously with regard to the four points.

## THE QUESTION OF ENFORCEMENT IN 'INSTITUTIONAL FAITH'

One important question remains to be answered: What motivates a worldly player to enter into a relationship with a metaphysical entity, for the existence of which there is no testimony outside the player's perception? One economic reason is the reduction of transaction costs repeatedly mentioned above: reducing complexity entails cheaper decision-making and lower opportunity costs. The enforcement guarantee of contracts between worldly players of the same faith in a metaphysical entity and its enforcement authority is a cheaper alternative to elaborate 'third party enforcement institutions'. North explains this, probably without thinking of metaphysical entities, when he states that if formal enforcement guarantee through a third party matters, it is important to define exactly what this means: In principle, he points out, enforcement guarantee would require a neutral instance with the ability to measure a contract's attributes and to enforce contract compliance, both without any cost (1992, p. 70). Modern societies do not require this cost reduction any longer, since they have developed a mode of exchange through the high transaction costs of enforcement guarantee that can do without metaphysical entities. North points out the negative aspect of this when he says that the enforcement of contract fulfilment through a third party is a great problem in economies aiming to practice impersonal exchange (*ibid.*). This differentiation is an ideal one in the academic sense. In reality, such a bipolar division of positions will not be encountered. Neither does every player who believes in a metaphysical entity adhere to worldly contracts, nor would impersonal exchange be possible without a basic trust in fulfilment, for which there would be no certainty.

Apart from the argument of transaction cost reduction through stability induced by 'institutional faith', Coleman also posits a kind of existential basic need for entering relationships of trust and faith: '[a]ctors sometimes have a strong need to place trust' (1990, p. 107). He points to situations in which trust becomes inevitable because of the lack of other ways out: 'The most extreme case of a need to place trust is that of a person in a desperate situation from which he cannot extricate himself without help' (*ibid.*). In the sense of the above differentiation between *trust* and *faith*, *faith* can also address a way out of existential despair arising from the limitations of the human mind and the unanswerability of the so-called 'ultimate questions' of human existence. Through a relationship with something transcendent, which must not be doubted by the player, this possibility of despair can be mitigated. 'Institutional faith' thus posits as a normative state the inevitability of trust with regard to certain questions human beings cannot answer. This has a behaviour-channelling effect which makes for stability.

## CONFRONTING 'INSTITUTIONAL FAITH' WITH KURAN'S CONCEPT OF 'PREFERENCE FALSIFICATION' IN THE HINDU CASTE SYSTEM

The above constitutes an attempt to assess the functional effect of religious preferences on actions in general and economic actions in particular. In the following text, the theses' inevitable vulnerability to attack will be critically examined by reference to a model that would have to reject institutional faith as a preference falsification. This model comes from Timur Kuran's work (especially 1994, 1995a) on preference falsification, which is particularly well-suited to a critical examination of the theses presented here because it contains an application of the preference falsification thesis. Kuran argues that individuals have authentic, genuine needs that are not satisfied because they interpret them wrongly or are manipulated from the outside. He defines preference falsifications as 'the act of misrepresenting one's genuine wants under perceived social pressures' (1995a, p. 3). He elaborates, '[p]reference falsification aims specially at manipulating the perceptions others hold about one's motivations or disposition' (p. 4). He exemplifies with regard to the South Asian caste system: 'It has been asserted that no one subscribes in earnest to the doctrine of karma – nor, for that matter, to the other props of Hindu ideology. In this view, Indians simply pretend to accept Hindu ideology' (p. 197). If that were so, the Hindu world would have persisted for *c.* 2,500 years through its members' powers of simulation, although in reality, these members want something entirely different from their 'Hindu ideology'. It is argued here that institutional faith provides the conditions how the institutional framework persisted.

The historical fact alone that Hindus have repeatedly fought bloody wars for the sake of the Hindu world would seem to leave little room for assertions like Kuran's. He focuses on the caste system especially, and he claims that it could, and can, exist through the preference falsification of its members: 'I shall propose that members of all castes have contributed to the system's perpetuation, often through preference falsification' (Kuran, 1995a, p. 128). Kuran rightly states that all caste members did and do contribute to perpetuating the caste system. If the faith in the caste order's righteousness and obligatory nature were anything but authentic, this set of form-less rules would hardly have persisted for so long. Kuran seems trapped by his own premises, at least with regard to the extreme case of the caste system. Thus, he concludes his discussion of the caste system with a rhetorical question:

> Granted that during the first phase [the first 1,000 years] of the caste system India prospered, it is not self-evident why the lower castes would have considered this a reason for upholding the status quo. Why would untouchables have supported an institution that condemned them to poverty, subjugation, and humiliation? (Kuran, 1995a, p. 131)

It is plain that in Kuran's system, at least, the thesis advanced in this study of institutional faith has no room. Thus, it must be asked whether the terms introduced here can legitimately claim to make a contribution to theory. This question cannot be answered here; it requires external discussion. But by accepting the notion that transcendence matters and that there is such a thing as institutional faith, on the basis of the above institutional economic discussion, a tentative answer can be proposed. This incapability of doubting that which exists is based on the existence of institutional faith. In Kuran's example, the acceptance of the Hindu doctrine can then explain why the untouchables should support an institution 'that condemned them to poverty, subjugation, and humiliation'. The form-less rules that can be identified as religious rules are the behaviour-channelling influence of institutional faith. Especially, the time lag argument of institutional faith, presented above in analogy to Coleman's fourth point, can be referred to in order to answer Kuran's question. The time lag inherent in institutional faith that stretches beyond the extent of earthly life can explain, even in Kuran's example of the untouchables, why players should accept their lives and not act according to the 'actual' preferences Kuran alleges. Only by accounting for the fact that transcendence matters, the scope of the preference order can be broadened so as to explain that which Kuran declares unexplainable. Depending on one's point of view, this is comparable to Timur Kuran's hypothesis of *self-reproducing social pressure*.[3]

This discussion may illustrate how 'institutional faith' can be of use for terminology on trust and social capital by rendering explainable players' behaviour that would have to be seen as encoded in terms of existing terminology, if it were to be discussed at all. In order to introduce the term of institutional faith, it is useful to locate it with regard to existing terminology, i.e. to point out possible points of interconnection at which institutional faith can be applied and employed.

The first point, also with regard to the genesis of the term, is trust in general and Williamson's institutional trust in particular. The proximity stems from the development of the term institutional faith. A further 'neighbour' in terms of terminology is the category of 'custom' introduced by Schlicht, which he defines as follows: 'A custom consists of a set of habitual, emotional, and cognitive regularities. These regularities may be described by rules which assign certain behavioural, emotional, and cognitive responses to emerging conditions' (Schlicht, 1998, p. 87). According to North's dichotomy of implicit and explicit rules, custom constitutes the most extreme case in the spectrum of implicit rules. In that regard, it must be asserted that institutional faith expands the spectrum in terms of the form of rule and thus transcends it, as it were. In terms of their mental models, unlike in terms of religious institutionalization, matters of faith are implicit rules for religious actors, although they also make for strong commitment. The informality of rules is even greater in institutional faith than in the case of custom, since the partner in the regulatory relationship is perceived to have a metaphysical source. With regard to the four components of custom named by Schlicht,[4] institutional faith can be mapped in terms of the terminological matrix of 'custom'. However, the term 'institutional faith' facilitates a differentiation that explicitly accounts for the significance of religious rules, while 'custom' provides a fuzzy frame for religious rules alongside other fuzzy regulatory structures of a cultural kind.

## FAITH AND/OR FUNDAMENTALISM? THE EXAMPLE OF 'HINDU FUNDAMENTALISM'

If individuals' behaviour is influenced by religious rules and a strongly binding, freedom-restricting commitment to these rules the question is: In how far must one then expect this faith-based commitment to constitute that which is often referred to as 'religious fundamentalism?' Or, to put the question differently: What is the difference between 'institutional faith' and religious fundamentalism? It must be pointed out at this early point that the term 'fundamentalism' is used in a highly rhetorical way in the literature.[5]

In order to safeguard the term 'institutional faith' against the charge of being mere rhetoric or the 'arrogation of knowledge', and to develop it as a functionally descriptive term, the following text will explain by reference to the Hindu world how 'institutional faith' differs from 'fundamentalism'. The first question must be, is there religious fundamentalism in the Hindu world?

Frykenberg argues that owing to neo-Hinduist policy, religious fundamentalism has emerged and is still an issue (MacGovan, 2008).

> The presence of Hindu fundamentalism in India, as epitomized by the BJP-VHP-RSS [*Bharatiya Janata Party, Vishwa Hindu Parishad, Rashtriya Swayamsevak Sangh*] 'family', entails a contradiction between reality and rhetoric. The insistence of these fundamentalists that the concepts 'Hindu' and 'Indian' are synonymous and interchangeable, and that 'Hindutva' alone encompasses all matters – religious or political, social or cultural – lies at the heart of this contradiction. To insist on holding to the original meaning of 'Hindu' as 'native of India' or 'Hindustani', and to advance the view that all religious associations, beliefs, or customs in India which do not adopt the norms of Hindutva (i.e. Brahmanic, Puranic, Sanskritic, or Vedic norms) are 'alien' and 'not native to India', is to insist upon something which, on the very face, is not possible. (Frykenberg, 1993, p. 251)

Frykenberg actually deems it possible that this fundamentalism might lead to the destruction of India: To many in India, the BJP–RSS–VHP position and influence has been disruptive of everything which has provided balance and security to the political system. By its appeal to 'Hindutva' [*Hinduness*], to 'one nation', to 'religion' over 'secularity' and to 'majority community' dominance, Hindu fundamentalism is more than a militantly defensive reaction in the name of 'fundamentals'. It is a raw bid for power which, by breaking the delicate balance of contractual support for the political system, risks the destruction of India itself (*ibid.*, p. 252f).

Lal, on the other hand, argues that the Hindu world's very nature does not permit the development of fundamentalism in the conventional sense, thus contradicting Frykenberg's basic assumption:

> Being a Hindu has always meant adherence to a way of life (that is, a particular social system) rather than to any specific religious philosophy. With no central church or central dogma, Hinduism has no religious fundamentals which can be used to identify or organize a Hindu fundamentalist movement. As many current leaders of the Hindu nationalist party (the BJP) have emphasized, Hindu fundamentalism is a contradiction in terms. (Lal, 1993, p. 410)

The contradiction ought not to deter us at this point. It seems more probable that the very organization which Frykenberg charges with promulgating Hindu fundamentalism should make a claim for such a contradiction. The rhetorical nature of the term and its use thus becomes apparent. Lal, on the other hand, proposes the term of a historically grown 'Hindu nationalism' and thus endows the subject with a secular connotation: 'The current wave of support for the BJP is better described, therefore, as representing Hindu nationalism' (Lal, 1993, p. 411).

The basic problem seems to stem from the mingling of religious and secular matters. Neither Frykenberg nor Lal can solve this problem. Nevertheless, the position of Lal referring to the BJP rhetoric that intrinsically there is no such thing as Hindu fundamentalism seems to be odd, to say the least when looking at the Hindutva and its civil war-like encounters with members of other religions, especially Moslems and Christians.

Kuran, on the other hand, offers a criterion of differentiation against the highly tendentious term of fundamentalism in view of the economic consequences: 'What I am suggesting is that fundamentalist economics is shaped heavily by the secular forces from which its proponents claim immunity' (1993, p. 298). This makes it clear that the 'metaphysical orientation and legitimation' has been re-transcended into a secular force which does not meet the requirements of 'institutional faith' – as proposed here – any more, since transcendence no longer matters as the prime leading maxim of players.

Kuran (p. 289) further elaborates how fundamentalism might be differentiated from faith by referring to the economic agenda: 'Many fundamentalist movements have an economic agenda. This means not that their participants want to enrich themselves – which they might and often do – but that they wish to restructure economic systems to conform with the stipulations of their respective religions'. Therefore, as long as the agenda mainly serves to satisfy transcendent matters, the term 'institutional faith' will be employed. When this preference allocation and the relationship between decisions switches over, the term 'fundamentalism' will be used.

It must be pointed out, however, that there are players in the name of faith who belong to the category of religious fundamentalists. If one takes into account the political turn towards neo-Hinduism, as Frykenberg (1993) does, the potential for religious fundamentalism appears even greater.

## CONCLUSIONS

The idea of social capital and trust as described here with theoretical anchoring in institutional economics, economic anthropology and sociology can be seen as an attempt to approach the complexity of how religious convictions influence practical decisions on the side of the individual as well as on the side of a group with shared beliefs. Oliver Williamson's concept of trust and here his idea of 'institutional trust' allows us to build a bridge from institutional economic theory to religious motivated behaviour. The step from trust to faith as proposed in the term 'institutional faith' then allows us to think of institutional settings where non-empirical entities such as perceived gods and goddesses become counterparts of social contracts and producers of social capital. The outcome of faith-based and religiously channelled behaviour can be seen in institutional and structural stability of the members of a specific group. At the same time freedom of choice is reduced when individuals act in the name of a specific faith. This reduction might hinder innovation and adaptation but produces cohesion and predictability of behaviour within the group. This, on the other hand, opens the doors for uncritical following of religious fundamentalists and their inner worldly intentions and ambitions.

## NOTES

1. Some economists consider social capital to be a commodity (Dasgupta, 1988; Dasgupta & Serageldin, 1999) which is rightly criticised.
2. Writes Williamson (1985, 64f): 'One of the implications of opportunism is that "ideal" cooperative modes of economic organization, by which I mean those where trust and good intentions are generously imputed to the membership, are very fragile. Such organizations are easily invaded and exploited by agents who do not possess those qualities'.
3. Thus, Kuran answers his own question at another point: 'I myself have addressed the issue of why the "untouchables" who lie at the foot of India's caste hierarchy commonly accept doctrines, like karma and dharma, that sanctify their lowly social status. In a nutshell, my explanation hinges on self-reproducing social pressures that, over the ages, have regulated Indian public discourse on matters of vice and virtue, rights and responsibilities, and life and death. With the costs of independent reflection making Indians of all ranks derive their worldviews largely from public discourse, the central tenets of Hinduism eventually came to be accepted by many as self-evident truths' (Kuran, 1994, p. 772).
4. Writes Schlicht (1998, p. 5): 'A web of reinforcements, Entitlements and obligations, Smooth and lumpy changes, Fuzziness'.
5. Among others, Frykenberg asserts this in his essay on 'Hindu Fundamentalism and the Structural Stability of India' (1993, p. 251).

## REFERENCES

Aoki, M. (2001). *Toward a comparative institutional analysis*. Cambridge, MA: MIT Press.
Badrinath, C. (2000). *Finding Jesus in Dharma*. Delhi: ISPCK.
Coleman, J. S. (1990). *Foundations of social theory*. Cambridge, MA: Belknap Press.

Dasgupta, P. (1988). Trust as a commodity. In: D. Gambetta (Ed.), *Trust: Making and breaking cooperative relations* (pp. 49–72). Cambridge, MA: Oxford.

Dasgupta, P., & Serageldin, I. (1999). *Social capital: A multifaceted perspective*. Washington, DC: World Bank.

Durrenberger, P. (2002). Why the idea of social capital is a bad idea. *Anthropology News, 43*(9), 5.

Eisenstadt, S. N. (1984). Die Paradoxie von Zivilisationen mit außerweltlichen Orientierungen. In: W. Schluchter (Ed.), *Max Webers Studie über Hinduismus und Buddhismus* (pp. 333–363). Frankfurt a. M.: Suhrkamp.

Ensminger, J. (1994). The political economy of religion: An economic anthropologist's perspective. *Journal of Institutional and Theoretical Economics, 150*(4), 745–754.

Ensminger, J. (1997). Transaction costs and Islam: Explaining conversion in Africa. *Journal of Institutional and Theoretical Economics, 153*(1), 4–29.

Frykenberg, R. E. (1993). Hindu fundamentalism and the structural stability of India. In: M. E. Marty & R. S. Appleby (Eds.), *Fundamentalism and the state* (pp. 233–256). Chicago, IL: University of Chicago Press.

Gramajo, A. M. (2007). Choice in economic contexts: Ethnographic and theoretical enquiries. *Research in Economic Anthropology, 25*, 217–238.

Hull, B. B., & Bold, F. (1994). Hell, religion, and cultural change. *Journal of Institutional and Theoretical Economics, 150*(3), 447–464.

Iannaccone, L. (1998). Introduction into the economics of religion. *Journal of Economic Literature, XXVI*, 1465–1496.

Karpe, J. (1997). *Institutionen und Freiheit. Grundlegende Elemente moderner Ökonomik*. Münster: LIT Verlag.

Kasper, W., & Streit, M. E. (1999). *Institutional economics: Social order and public policy*. Cheltenham, UK: Edward Elgar.

Kuran, T. (1993). Fundamentalism and the economy. In: M. E. Marty & R. S. Appleby (Eds.), *Fundamentalism and the state* (pp. 289–302). Chicago, IL: University of Chicago Press.

Kuran, T. (1994). Religious economics and the economics of religion. *Journal of Institutional and Theoretical Economics, 4*, 769–775.

Kuran, T. (1995a). *Private truths, public lies: The social consequences of preference falsification*. Cambridge, MA: Harvard University Press.

Kuran, T. (1995b). *Legacies of conformism*. Cambridge, MA: Harvard University Press.

Lal, D. (1993). The economic impact of Hindu revivalism. In: M. E. Marty & R. S. Appleby (Eds.), *Fundamentalism and the state* (pp. 410–429). Chicago, IL: University of Chicago Press.

Landa, J. T. (1994). *Trust, ethnicity, and identity: Beyond the new institutional economics of ethnic trading networks, contract law, and gift-exchange*. Ann Arbor, MI: University of Michigan Press.

Luhmann, N. (1987). *Soziale Systeme-Grundriss einer allgemeinen Theorie*. Frankfurt a. M.: Surkamp.

Luhmann, N. (1989). *Vertrauen: Ein Mechanismus der Reduktion sozialer Komplexität*. Stuttgart: Enke.

MacGovan, J. (2008). Pious carnage: The rise of Hindu fundamentalism in India. In Commonweal Foundation (Ed.), *Commonweal: A review of public affairs, literature and the arts* (Vol. 152, Issue 2, p. 2). New York, NY: Commonweal Pub.

Mc Cleary, R., & Barro, R. (2006). Religion and economy. *Journal of Economic Perspectives, 20*(2), 49–72.

Noorderhaven, N. G. (1996). Opportunism and trust in transaction cost economics. In: J. Groenewegen (Ed.), *Transaction cost economics and beyond* (pp. 105–128). Boston, MA: Academic Publishers.

North, D. C. (1992). *Institutionen, institutioneller Wandel und Wirtschaftsleistung*. Tübingen: Mohr.

Schlicht, E. (1998). *On custom in the economy*. Oxford, MA: Clarendon Press.

Schneider, J. A. (2006). Anthropological relevance and social capital. *Anthropology News*, p. 4.

Stenmark, M. (1994). *Rationality in science, religion, and everyday life: A critical evaluation of four models of rationality*. Notre Dame, IN: University of Notre Dame Press.

Stietencron, H. von (2001). *Der Hinduismus*. München: Beck.

Williamson, O. E. (1985). *The economic institutions of capitalism. Firms, markets, relational contracting*. New York, NY: Free Press.

Williamson, O. E. (1993). Calculativeness, trust, and economic organization. *Journal of Law & Economics*, *XXXVI*, 453–486.

Williamson, O. E. (1996). *The mechanisms of governance*. Oxford: Oxford University Press.

Wood, D. C. (2007). Introduction. *Research in Economic Anthropology*, *25*, 1–23.

# PROSPERITY UNBOUND? DEBATING THE "SACRIFICIAL ECONOMY"

Simon Coleman

## ABSTRACT

*I present here a review and critique of social scientific analyses of the global spread of Prosperity Christianity. My argument is that at least two phases of research can be discerned: an initial phase where economic factors are given strong causal explanatory force in accounting for the upsurge in Health and Wealth congregations; and a more recent phase that complicates our understandings of the relationships between religious and economic action. My review of the literature reveals that sacrifice is a theoretical trope common to both phases of writing, and in the latter half of the chapter I explore the ways in which notions of the sacrificial economy can point to nuanced understandings of the forms of materiality deployed in many Prosperity contexts. The wider implications of this chapter refer in part to how we might understand notions of rational and irrational action in relation to economic behavior; and also to an appreciation of the ways in which ritual action can be productive of, and not merely a response to, perceived ambiguity and risk.*

**The Economics of Religion: Anthropological Approaches**
**Research in Economic Anthropology, Volume 31, 23–45**

**ISSN: 0190-1281/doi:10.1108/S0190-1281(2011)0000031005**

# INTRODUCTION

In December 2009, a headline article of the American magazine *The Atlantic Monthly* asked a provocative question: "Did Christianity Cause the Crash?" Any reader piqued enough to read the article would quickly have discovered that, rather than blaming the whole of Christianity for the economic meltdown that affected many parts of the world from 2008, the author was actually focusing on one particular branch of the faith. The opening lines of the piece state:[1]

> America's mainstream religious denominations used to teach the faithful that they would be rewarded in the afterlife. But over the past generation, a different strain of Christian faith has proliferated – one that promises to make believers rich in the here and now. Known as the prosperity gospel, and claiming tens of millions of adherents, it fosters risk-taking and intense material optimism. It pumped air into the housing bubble. And one year into the worst downturn since the Depression, it's still going strong.

So it might seem that a certain group of Christians, and not just bankers, created an air of economic optimism too fragile for the world to sustain. But even from just this short paragraph, we surely see much to debate. Note for instance the vagueness of that phrase "over the last generation." It suggests an effective rhetorical contrast with the supposed asceticism of earlier times, and yet it comes at a cost – later acknowledged by the author – of passing too quickly over the long history of Prosperity-oriented theologies in the United States, the religiously motivated responses to America's Gilded Age that the historian Jackson Lears chronicles so vividly in such books as *Rebirth of a Nation* (2009) and *Something for Nothing* (2003).[2] Take note also of the swift movement from the "risk-taking" of this "different strain" of Christianity toward the undoubted catastrophe of the present period, as if causality could be asserted through textual juxtaposition. Finally, there is the intriguing sting in the tail, the counter-intuitive observation that is meant to sustain our interest throughout the rest of the article: the claim that the Depression has come, the bubble has indeed burst, and yet Prosperity churches still float on an air of optimism. Indeed, later in the piece we are invited to explore the idea that the state of economic disaster might actually provide a propitious growing-ground for such a gospel. As the author puts it, she is attempting to find out "whether 'prosperity' could possibly still seem enticing, or even plausible, in this distinctly unprosperous moment." The answer? "Very much so, as it turns out."[3]

In the following text, I do not intend to focus on questions of causality and blame, though I suspect that even journalists searching for a headline might find it hard to pin all the responsibility for global financial meltdown on to a single strain of Christianity. Rather, I think that the piece raises interesting issues for anthropologists about Prosperity practices and their relationship to what we conventionally define as economic behavior. In one respect, the article is right to point out the popularity of such churches among Latino and African American populations in the United States, and to present their expansion as a diffuse ideological wave rather than a single, well-defined denomination or movement. And yet the article's perspective is also deeply parochial in its focus on just one side of "the Atlantic." It talks of "a shift in the [North] American conception of divine Providence and its relationship to wealth"[4] but we need to remember that manifestations of the Prosperity Gospel have found fertile ground in Latin America as well as among Latinos in America, in Africa as well as among African Americans, and even in certain parts of "secular" Europe. What interests me in this review, then, is how scholars have attempted to analyze the Prosperity Gospel in different parts of the world, to locate its relationship to "the economy," and in the process to reveal some of the reasons behind its apparent popularity. Much of the article is taken up by an attempt to juxtapose, but also to compare and critique, a sample of such writings. More generally, I argue that these debates have laid out in useful relief significantly different approaches to the analysis of religion and its relationship to economics.

There are many reasons why "Prosperity Christianity" attracts both attention and divided opinion among numerous constituencies – academic and otherwise. If we go back briefly to the *Atlantic* article, for instance, we might consider how the piece explores the power of religion to actually make a difference, to go beyond the exercise of private piety in affecting economic behavior at varying scales of action. We learn of the lives of impoverished and aspirant believers who hope for cars, jobs, houses, and how such desire taps into a modified form of the American Dream that has impacts on national levels of speculation and debt. And there is the inevitable questioning of whether this is *really* religion that we are dealing with, or at least religion of an "authentic" variety. Thus, the author describes how a pastor joins some men of his church as they weep, jump, and raise their Bibles before an altar that contains both anointing oils and the keys to a Mercedes Benz. Religion in this image is presented as both powerful and yet implicitly morally weakened by the focus of its aspirations and assumptions about how to achieve the "Dream." Religion of the older generation, of the asceticism that Max Weber would have recognized, presents a story of what American denominations "used to teach." But such a model of the

Protestant Ethic is undermined as religion no longer acts to constrain, but rather encourages, consumption without responsibility.

Among anthropologists and other social scientists, we see more complex understandings of the relationship between religious and economic aspiration, and yet again the question is raised as to whether such analysis creates certain hierarchizations of value: we are unlikely to present Christians as the sole instigators of global economic collapse, but do we nonetheless have a tendency to assume that we can channel the primary significance of "religious" action into an "economic" frame? More generally still, what are we to make of the connections between religious action and materiality that we see in prosperity practices?

These are broad questions, and my answer here is inevitably restricted in focus and scope. After initially considering some of the work done by social scientists on the economic aspects of Prosperity Christianity, I go on to argue that a common theoretical trope in the literature is that of "sacrifice." While the use of this term intriguingly echoes the language of theological discourse, it also raises questions concerning the operation of agency that reveal some significant distinctions in analytical approach. By reflecting on these distinctions, we are led to consider not only the economics *of* religion, but also economics *as* religious practice.

## SPREADING THE MESSAGE

Stephen Hunt's important survey of the worldwide spread of "Faith" or "Prosperity" Christians (2000, p. 332) describes it as an immensely successful expression of "evangelical fundamentalism," albeit less a movement than an aggregation of roughly similar ministries, with the United States constituting a center of diffusion through the mobility of its pastors, the popularity of American ministries' training courses, and other mission and media activity. While sharing with other Pentecostals an emphasis on Baptism in the Spirit and revivalism, the Prosperity Gospel is said to be distinguished by a more materialist orientation and positive conception of the spiritual self. In these terms, "health and wealth" form part of a wider package of salvation, since the Atonement of Christ is regarded as having the power to remove not just sin but also sickness and poverty from the life of the believer.

While it is true that some regions of the world – such as the Indian subcontinent and the Middle-East – have proved more resistant to Faith ideas, Hunt observes that the teachings have found fertile soil in many places. In the nations of the Pacific Rim it resonates with what he sees as an emergent capitalist culture of growing urban conurbations and crowded inner cities. A good example of this phenomenon is provided by the Yoido Full Gospel Church, based in Seoul – with over a million members probably the largest Protestant congregation in the world.[5] In Latin America, homegrown ministries have spread rapidly in recent decades, partly inspired by exported US models, and in 1977 Brazil hosted the foundation of what is now a globally diffused denomination, The Universal Church of the Kingdom of God (UCKG). Faith congregations and ministries have also flourished in many parts of Africa, in particular those already marked by nineteenth century missionary endeavors, and often act "as a form of motivation for rising out of the dire conditions experienced by some of the poorest people on earth" (*ibid.*, p. 342). In Western Europe, Prosperity ideas have frequently proved controversial not only because of their departures from orthodox Christian theology, but also because of their seemingly vulgar, "North American" attributes. Yet, here, as elsewhere, we see Prosperity ideas influencing even established congregations that would not necessarily present themselves as part of any like-minded movement. Hunt observes that many of the more receptive congregations have been in inner cities, marked by working-class contexts but also by ethnic enclaves, such as the socially and economically aspirant Redeemed Christian Church of God, which over the past two decades or so has formed a dynamic part of the neo-Pentecostal scene in London while remaining predominantly Nigerian in its appeal. Turning to other parts of Europe, Hunt argues for parallels between post-Soviet contexts and the emergent economies in Latin America and the Pacific Rim: "Poland, the Czech and Slovak Republics, and Hungary, in particular, have been receptive to the new gospel," in "one package of spiritual and economic liberty" (*ibid.*, p. 339).

The preceding paragraph can do little more than illustrate the spread of variants of the Faith Gospel, but we can at least note the increasing prominence of Prosperity ideas in recent decades, both in defined denominations and in more diffuse forms, alongside the more general reemergence of Pentecostal, neo-Pentecostal, and charismatic varieties of Christianity. So how might we explain the popularity of this gospel in so many different parts of the world? We shall come back to Hunt's view below but first I want to turn to a book that provided one of the first attempts by social scientists to explain the global "Faith" phenomenon.

In *Exporting the American Gospel*, Steve Brouwer, Paul Gifford, and Susan Rose (1996) trace the emergence of a religious ideology that in their interpretation is inherently linked with the expansion of global capital. For them (*ibid.*, p. 1) this "transnational religious culture" flourishes in the megacities of the developing world. At the same time, it is a "quintessentially American faith, which promises material 'blessings' and spiritual 'power encounters' to all" (*ibid.*, pp. 5–6), building upon an American Gospel of Wealth that was originally preached to middle-class congregations in the nineteenth century. The book contains three assumptions that are pertinent here. First, the sense of a religious faith existing parallel to, indeed maintaining an elective affinity with, a globalizing economic tendency: "For Christian fundamentalism in particular, the universalizing of the faith is intertwined with the homogenizing influences of consumerism, mass communication, and production in ways that are compatible with the creation of an international market culture by global capitalist institutions" (*ibid.*, p. 3). Second, the linking of the efflorescence of such religion with the answering of what are assumed to be basic human requirements. For instance, Prosperity Theology is said to have spread rapidly from the United States to other middle-class groups of Christians, who are seen as having an unlimited number of "needs" to be met in such widely divergent places as Sweden, South Africa, and South Korea. Finally, there is the assertion that the faith can in fact appeal across different economic situations, since it has spread to the "lower classes" (*ibid.*, p. 9) and is often "embraced by poorer people" (*ibid.*, p. 198).

What are we to make of such assertions? For Hunt (2000, p. 333), they represent an example of what he calls the "hegemonic model" of explanation, with echoes of dependency theory and assumptions that Christianity is acting as a modernizing, Westernizing force – in effect producing a new form of cultural dominance in postcolonial contexts. Nonetheless, he has some sympathy for the view that Faith ideas present a religious justification for a Western, free market economy (*ibid.*, p. 334; see also Roberts, 1995), valorizing both an individualized ethic of consumerism and a spirit of entrepreneurship. Furthermore, the appearance of hegemony is reinforced for him by the very form that Prosperity practices take, with the standardization of core doctrines combining with the deployment of worldwide systems of communication through electronic media. In this view, such religion seems to come close to an evangelical version of "McDonaldization" (*ibid.*, p. 334; Ritzer, 1993).

At the same time, Hunt points to some of the limitations of the hegemonic model. He notes that a "grand narrative" model of religious ideology emanating from a single center clearly fails to appreciate the ways in which cultural influence can flow in reciprocal dimensions, or indeed the different meanings attributable to any cultural package (*ibid.*, p. 335). For him, the extent to which the Faith message is endorsed, whether in standardized, modified, or syncretic modes, also depends upon "the preexisting" religious context. Following David Martin (1990), Prosperity is therefore seen by Hunt as a particular example of a more general tendency of global Pentecostalism to offer solutions to problems and to deal with the needs of distinct socioeconomic groups.

Stepping back ourselves from these earlier social scientific debates over the popularity of Prosperity discourses,[6] we can observe some development in the complexity of the argument. A hegemonic model that reproduces the very homogeneity it detects within Faith Christianity is partially challenged by a perspective that emphasizes the importance of acknowledging diversities in cultural production, flow, and interpretation. Nonetheless, what is retained in both analyses is a sense of such religion as potential response to economic and more broadly human "need." Its appeal is ultimately related to material circumstances, whether providing affinities with the entrepreneurial spirits of wealthy congregations in North America or ideological panaceas for poor churches in parts of Africa.

## MONEY FROM NOTHING

Hunt's survey appeared in 2000. A year earlier another paper was published that was clearly relevant to the Prosperity theme and yet placed the phenomenon within a still wider historical and theoretical frame. Jean and John Comaroff's *Occult Economies and the Violence of Abstraction* had the subtitle "Notes from the South African Postcolony," though the Comaroffs suggested that the economies they were describing were dramatically on the increase in other postrevolutionary societies as well. Such societies, whether in Europe, Africa, or elsewhere, were depicted as ones in which an optimistic faith in free enterprise was likely to encounter the challenges of neoliberal economics, including unpredictable shifts in demands for labor at global scales, an equivocal role for the state, and uncertainties surrounding the nature of civil society (*ibid.*, p. 294). In this analysis, an occult economy emerges from and responds to such circumstances, involving the deployment of magical means for material ends. More generally, "the magical allure of making money from nothing" indicates a "millennial moment" where "capitalism has an effervescent new spirit – a magical, neo-Protestant zeitgeist – welling up close to its core" (*ibid.*, p. 281).

The Comaroffs' version of the neo-Protestant Ethic involves the ability to gain wealth without perceptible production, but it also implies – to those at the bottom of the economic pile – the working of insidious forces and even sorcery as means of accumulation (1999, p. 282). In contexts where vast wealth appears to concentrate in the hands of just a few citizens, the market becomes a container of mysterious mechanisms of accumulation and distribution. We see the paradox of these occult economies, as they point both to the pursuit of new, magical means for otherwise unattainable ends, and at the same time to the effort to eradicate people held to enrich themselves by such illegitimate deployment of the forces of production and reproduction (*ibid.*, p. 284). Interestingly, much of the weight of this analysis is placed less on class per se than on generational distinctions – forms of extraction typically associated with older people of apparent affluence, who may be accused of aborting natural processes of social reproduction by preventing the next generation from securing the bases of its material existence. Distance is also seen as a key factor. The translocal dimension of dealings in the occult economy seems crucial to the way in which its workings are understood in South Africa, as people "ponder the interplay of mobility and compression in the production of new forms of wealth" (*ibid.*, p. 291).

But how might these issues relate even more directly to Prosperity discourses of the kind discussed by Hunt or Brouwer et al.? In fact, the Comaroffs provide an extended example from fieldwork in rural Tswana, where "discourses of the diabolical" often focus on none other than the UCKG (1999, p. 281). The latter is presented as a new Protestant denomination rumored to issue charmed credit cards that register no debt promises to people who embrace Christ and denounce Satan. It is also a place where Pentecostalism meets neoliberal enterprise, located in a shopping precinct and holding services during business hours, while "appealing frankly to mercenary motives, mostly among the young" (1999, p. 281). This time the altar does not contain the keys to a Mercedes, as in the *Atlantic* example, but is instead decorated with color advertisements for BMWs.

While on the one hand the concreteness of such religious practice resonates with a pragmatism that the Comaroffs see as evident in black Christianity in South Africa, they also note its ambiguous moral valency. Thus, they report an argument among history graduate students at the University of the Northwest as to whether the Universal Church should be seen as the work of the Antichrist or – presumably less threateningly – a vindication of Max Weber (*ibid.*, p. 292). Meanwhile, the Church itself creates its own moral hierarchies, constructing a globalizing picture of Satan "deceiving people all over the world" (*ibid.*, p. 292).

The argument is partly repeated but also extended a year later in the Comaroffs' reflections on how the occult economy is a significant dimension of "millennial capitalism," in other words both "capitalism at the millennium and capitalism in its messianic, salvific, even magical manifestations" (2000, p. 293). Again, the focus is on ways of generating value that appear to be intangible, and are associated with concomitant increases in economic speculation (*ibid.*, p. 295). While the Comaroffs do not claim to be able to measure the precise amount of occult activity compared to the past, they do assert that it has become more evident as a theme within the public sphere not only in Africa but also in such diverse contexts as Asia and the United States (*ibid.*, p. 311). And while new religious movements are taking on "a wide variety of guises" the "fee-for-service, consumer-cult, prosperity-gospel denominations" appear to be especially close to the new neoliberal spirit of the age (*ibid.*, p. 314).

As with the occult economies piece, a central question impelling the Comaroffs' analysis is that of: "Why?" In other words, "how are we to account for the current spread of occult economies and prosperity cults?" (2000, p. 315). In certain respects, their answers seem familiar to scholars accustomed to debates over relative deprivation, albeit adapted to the demands of contemporary globalization. Thus, millennial capitalism is said to contain a confusing and contradictory blend of hope and hopelessness, alongside a privatized sense of religious participation in relation to a market whose benefits remain ever more unattainable, constituted through rapid flows of value across space and time. However, in comparison with *Exporting the American Gospel*, the notion of the occult economy clearly presents a bottom-up rather than top-down analysis: we are urged to look at interpretations of the arcane actions of the market by those excluded from its workings, rather than at the centralized production of religious and economic ideologies.

In common with Hunt, the Comaroffs accept the significance of such denominations as the Universal Church in contributing to the diffusion of cultural influences that can go in numerous directions rather than constituting a one-way "hegemonic" flow. Notably, both the Comaroffs and Hunt also deploy the imagery of magic in describing Prosperity practices. Hunt (1998) talks elsewhere of the "magical moments" created by Faith ministries, focusing on the metaphysical assumptions held by believers as to the power of "confessing" the right words in order to effect reality. For the Comaroffs, magic has other, additional dimensions, emerging in the gap between economic status and the actual ability to raise that status, explaining as well as mitigating one's lack of agency. We might also note how it links with classic anthropological notions of witchcraft and the occult, forming part of an economy of blame as well as explanation. Such magic becomes less a means to self-improvement and more an explanation of the prosperity of immoral others.

Despite these differences, all three sets of authors set as a fundamental task the explanation of why Prosperity practices have become so prominent in recent years. In each case, we are encouraged to think of religious action predominantly as *response* to other events, in particular to a current conjoining of the global and the neoliberal. This kind of explanation is sometimes intellectualist in tone, involving the assumption that believers seek explanations for their status – or lack of status – in relation to others and to "a world gone awry" (Comaroff & Comaroff, 2000, p. 316). It also focuses on structural positioning – in terms of class, generation, and sometimes ethnicity – of believers and to aspiration for economic improvement. Thus, the search for wealth and the search for knowledge become complementary, even as both appear – in these millennial times – to represent the opposite of the rational. In this sense, we might see the Comaroff's imagery of occultation as referring not merely to religious ideas of concealed and illicit practices, but also to analytical assumptions concerning the hidden inequalities of material practices. So the occult economy is about the arcane and malignant forces of personalized, powerful others, but is also a symptom of – even as it misrecognizes – the wider workings of the global economy.

## THE PERFORMANCE OF PROSPERITY

Magic as mystification, occultation as misrecognition: they form powerful images and arguments. But are they enough? For instance, even in their own terms, can they explain the popularity of Prosperity practices among such different constituencies as mobile middle classes and more clearly disempowered populations? This kind of explanatory problem points to a tension evident across the accounts of Faith practices given so far, between religion as site of agency or as de facto site of resignation to one's lot in life. It may be that one answer is provided by the very ambiguity of the economies the Comaroffs describe, since their notion of the occult comprehends both the manipulation of supernatural agency for personal gain and the invocation of it to explain one's own lack of prosperity. Yet, we may wish to question the assumption that religion itself can be accounted for through such a "response" mode, or that what appears to the secular observer as the irrational must be explained through an analytical rationale based on societal or emotional need. In doing so, I suggest, we can profitably move beyond "why" questions (which often assume that a secular orientation is the default mode of being, not in itself requiring further explanation) toward a more multidimensional understanding of how Faith practices articulate the connections between "religious" and "economic" spheres of activity. In doing so, I argue, we move into what I see as an implicit second phase of studies of Prosperity Christianity, where analysis of the connections between these spheres moves away from analytical hierarchies into a more complex model of co-constitution.

One of the more powerful articulations of such a view has been provided by Ruth Marshall (2009), in reflections prompted by work on Nigerian neo-Pentecostalism. Marshall notes the tendency in anthropology to see in such new forms of religiosity the elaboration of a "vernacular language" that functions "to translate into a form of popular knowledge destabilizing processes, such as globalization, relations of domination, and socio-economic crises – in short, to see them principally as forms of the domestication of modernity" (*ibid.*, p. 22; see also Cannell, 2006).[7] The work of the Comaroffs clearly corresponds with this characterization, in the sense that they regard practices relating to prosperity and the occult as mobilized in relation to new forms of desire, allied with intense frustration at being positioned on the margins of sites of wealth. An important question Marshall asks, however, is how "new" these current circumstances are in a continent whose history has long contained fluid boundaries and the continual integration of strangers (*ibid.*, p. 27), and where the challenges of neoliberalism are emergent in contexts still marked by colonial legacies. Rather, for her, an analytical focus on the violent abstractions of capitalism runs the risk of referring less to the specific historical circumstances of believers and more to concerns raised by secular, Western narratives of political critique (*ibid.*, pp. 29–31). Instead of searching for relations of causality that are likely to confirm such a story (the "why" questions, in my terms), Marshall prefers to see such "forces" as globalization, the crisis of the nation-state, new forms of wealth and inequality less as the specific *object* of religious activities, and more as contributing to their "context of plausibility" (*ibid.*, p. 33). Thus, one can "proceed by supposing that religious change is not merely the sign or the effect of change in other domains of human practice, but constitutes rather, in and of itself, a mode of historical and political transformation" (*ibid.*, p. 34). And so born-again Christianity becomes a specific regime of practice, in and through which particular moral and political subjects are produced.

If Marshall writes as a scholar of Christianity, Bill Maurer (2010) tells a broadly similar story from the perspective of an anthropologist of money and finance. In a recent piece discussing the religion "in" and "of" the current financial crisis – what he calls "credit crisis religion" – Maurer produces his own reconsideration of the Comaroffs' (2000) essay. He confesses that he begins his analysis with "Malinowski ... firmly in my back pocket!" (*ibid.*, p. 148), in other words harboring assumptions concerning the frailty of human rationality in the face of uncertainty. Such intellectualist tendencies apart, however, he is concerned to examine what I am characterizing as more structural explanations for millennial capitalist manifestations of religion, and here he does not find modern and Marxist meta-narratives to be satisfactory. Thus, "If the occult economies of millennial capitalism were seen as efforts to grasp the violence of capitalist abstraction, it is because the social scientific attempt to describe those occult economies also partakes of the same hierarchism in the construction of the object of that analytical effort" (*ibid.*, p. 149). Here, I think he agrees with Marshall in not only critiquing the implicit privileging of the economic as primary source and site of explanation, but also suggesting that such analyses too easily tell a story whose conclusions are already known at the very start of the telling. Furthermore, Maurer points – albeit more briefly – to religion as a site of practice, where articulations of faith are also articulations in a more performative sense, pointing to and constituting their contexts, and with "an ontology demand[ing] a stance athwart theories of religion that would pose them as 'reflections' of a second-order logic" (*ibid.*, p. 149).

A double sense of religion as a form of practice, and one where the hierarchical relationship between economic rationality and religious mystification is problematized, is also evident in Daromir Rudnyckyj's (2010) recent conceptualization of what he calls the "spiritual economy." Rudnyckyj's ethnography is based on examining the relationship between Islam and the organization of steel production in Indonesia, and yet his approach responds to some of the same issues surrounding religious responses to neoliberalism as are evident in the Comaroffs' work. His focus on "spiritual economies" is meant to elucidate how economic reforms may be conceived of and enacted as matters of religious piety, not least as spirituality becomes objectified as a site of management, individual accountability, and rationalization through productive labor (*ibid.*, pp. 131–132). An emphasis on transparency as an organizing ethic for such action contrasts directly with the imagery of the occult economy,[8] as does the stress on creating, rather than feeling excluded from, productivity – and indeed on rationalizat*ion* rather than irrationali*ty*. Thus, for Rudnyckyj, the notion of the occult economy is not especially useful in understanding instances where religious practices are combined with corporate norms and sites of industrial production.

It is important to note that many of the people enmeshed in the particular spiritual economy Rudnyckyj describes are supervisory-level employees rather than those at the bottom of the corporate hierarchy (*ibid.*, p. 134). There is a more general theoretical point to be made out of the juxtaposition between his and the Comaroffs' approach, however. In Rudnyckyj's analysis, religious adherence is not regarded as a retreat into magic and mystery but rather as involving the deployment of a set of ascetic practices designed to make humans into specific types of beings (*ibid.*, p. 134; see also Asad, 1993). Whereas occult economies assume that those subjected to the culture of neoliberalism do not fully comprehend the changes in which they are enmeshed, subjects in a spiritual economy do grasp the challenges they face, even though they may not be in complete control of the means to remedy them. And, unlike occult economies, spiritual economies do not assume that the ethnographer possesses a more privileged insight into the predicaments faced than that of informants. So it seems that there is more than a structural difference underlying these two theoretical and spiritual orientations: whereas the occult approach assumes a certain model of agency whereby capitalism can be separated from modern subjects and acts on those subjects from the outside through deception, mystification, and fetishization, in the spiritual economy approach capitalism does not act so much *on* the subject as *through* him or her by effecting certain practices and ethical dispositions (*ibid.*, p. 134). We might see this as producing selves as much as steel.

Rudnyckyj's claim that he is not seeking a privileged insight into the economic predicaments faced by informants can be debated, not least since he is attempting to deploy an anthropological framework to understand their lives and spiritualities. In addition, his assumption that subjects can fully comprehend the changes that surround them may ask too much of any subject, anthropological or otherwise. However, he is clearly pulling in the same analytical direction as Marshall and Maurer. The refusal to see religion as *mere* response to more fundamental structural shifts leads to a reconceptualization of religious activity, whereby the cultures and activities of neoliberalism are both historically specific and made by specific, historical subjects.

This kind of approach also requires us to look more closely at religious activity itself, to see how it is conceptualized and deployed by actors beyond their "misrecognition" of the abstract forces of capitalism that may underlie their situation. Remember therefore that Maurer refers to the ways in which articulations of faith can work in a performative sense; and that Marshall sees born-again Christianity as a specific regime of practice, through which "subjects" are produced. What I want to look at in the following section is to see whether we can see sacrifice as just one site of practice. I do not wish to present it in a totalizing analytical and interpretative fashion as *the* central act of adherence for Prosperity Christians, with identical meanings evident across denominations; not do I explain (away) acts of sacrifice in functionalist terms, as if their existence were accounted for by the ways in which they might help to constitute selves or social contexts. I do wish, however, to point to sacrifice as a trope that appears across different manifestations – and analyses – of Faith Christianity, and moreover one that readdresses problematic issues relating to the ambiguous role of agency in the believer, as well as intersections between so-called religious and so-called economic spheres of action. And, as we shall see, it will also take us back to the theme with which this chapter began: that of the role of hope, risk-taking, and the production of buoyancy even in the face of economic crisis.

## BETWEEN PROSPERITY AND SACRIFICE

James Bielo's (2007) study of Faith Christianity in the United States belongs to what I am characterizing broadly as the second phase of work on such believers – in other words analyses that are less concerned with "why" questions, and more with "how" practices relating to Prosperity interact with wider aspects of believers' lives and self-understandings. Bielo sees himself as arguing that born-again Christian imaginings of financial success are embedded within a particular "cultural logic," and moreover one that does not correspond easily with popular perceptions of such Christians peddling a uniform theology that places faith and success in a causal relationship. Much of Bielo's piece focuses not on abstractions but on the beliefs and actions of a single person, Rick Betcher, who is both a Sunday school teacher and a Christian businessmen. The "logic" that Bielo focuses on relates to the nature of personhood. Believers such as Rick cannot be seen as cynical seekers after wealth for its own sake, but do understand financial success as emergent from one's status as a born-again Christian. Financial accumulation is organized around but also contributes to an understanding of the self as a hardworking as well as prayerful economic agent, and such an orientation helps to explain Rick's decision to leave his job in retail in order to start his own business.

For my purposes what is most significant about Bielo's analysis is the presentation of a positive, Prosperity-based model of practice whose logic is not secular and yet clearly has its own rationality. In this sense, Bielo's model comes close to the "sacrificial economics" model presented by Susan Harding (2000) in her study of a rather more famous preacher and businessman, Jerry Falwell. Harding's study focuses on the language surrounding a Baptist pastor whose theological positions are often at variance with those of neo-Pentecostalists regarding such issues as speaking in tongues and the workings of the Holy Spirit, but who does at times come very close to Health and Wealth orientations in relation to finance.[9] Harding's analysis looks to the ambiguities, even the moral uncertainties, surrounding practices associated with religious commitment, and shows how ritual can be productive of uncertainty alongside certainty in a particular dialectic. She notes (*ibid.*, p. 85) that the miracles – economic and otherwise – claimed by Falwell have in common a "semantic risk or ambiguity, some sort of excess of gap that demands interpretive attention and engagement, choices which place one inside or outside the faith at hand." The claiming of a miracle assumes that the disbelief of secular others will be a precondition of miraculous action (*ibid.*, p. 86). Preachers learn to provoke these kinds of narrative instabilities, since religious commitment precisely "rests on a poetics of faith, not a hermeneutics of suspicion" (*ibid.*, p. 88).

Such poetics of faith are inherently demanding of both pastor and believer. From the 1970s, one of the reasons that Falwell succeeded is that he managed to transform himself and his ministry into objects *worthy* of sacrificial giving from his followers, with the act of asking for money not merely reflecting, but also enacting, spiritual authority and commitment. What seems like fundraising to the unbeliever is translated into a form of religious commitment by the faithful, and "in an important way, the whole point of giving to a God-led ministry is to vacate the commercial economy and to enter another realm, a Christ-centered gospel, or sacrificial, economy in which material expectations are transformed" (Coleman, 2004; Harding, 2000, p. 109). Giving to "Jerry" can be seen as akin to giving to Jesus, but is also a means of positive action in relation to the self:

> If a contributor is financially strapped, the gift is even more meaningful. It is more of a literal sacrifice, and the sense of escape from irksome budgetary constraints is heightened. Fundamental Baptists, the middling and wealthy as well as the poor, try to be careful financial managers, routinely treating themselves to seminars and tapes and manuals that pique their consciousness about the finite flow of money in and out of their hands. Giving sacrificially breaks them out of those cycles. (*ibid.*, p. 123)

Note how in this statement "sacrifice" applies to people in different economic situations. Such action may involve the using up of money, but it is very far from secular models of consumption aimed at immediate personal gratification. Moreover, sacrificial gifts are both distinguished from careful financial management (it is important to give at a time of personal financial pressure, to break out of routinized cycles of prudence) *and* part of it (giving systematically indexes commitment and the believing subject). Such a schema does not see the distribution of wealth as inherently arcane or as the product of magical forces beyond the power of the believer; rather, the very ambiguity surrounding the sources and possibility of the miraculous calls for conscious action on the part of the believer.

We might still of course see followers of Falwell as mere dupes, or the preacher himself as fooled by his own ideology into a misrecognition of his role as an exploiter of the faithful. As we have seen, however, such a view tends to force us into a one-dimensional view of religious action as ultimately explicable through discrete, economic motives; and nor does it capture a sense of how "sacrifice" in these terms is both a mode of submission and a means of engaging in goal-directed, spiritually charged action. Without conflating the very different ethnographic contexts described by the Comaroffs and by Harding, and while acknowledging that American believers may simply see themselves as possessing more agency, what strikes me as significant is the ways in which their analyses present complementary methodological and theoretical approaches to Faith discourse and practice. While the Comaroffs ultimately reach, as we have seen, for a narrative of the almost ineluctable diffusion of neoliberal inequalities in their explanation of religious adherence, Harding's book seems notably lacking in consideration of wider economic or even sociostructural frameworks to understand the actions of a man such as Falwell.[10] On the other hand, while – at least in the essays examined here – the Comaroffs say little about the specifics of ritual practice, Harding's strength is in demonstrating how religious adherence provides narrative means to draw believers into a world of self-construction through the fertile ambiguities of sacrifice. Admittedly, the Comaroffs do mention sacrifice in their account of the South African Universal Church that they have encountered: the local pastor of the church is quoted as stating that "believers have also to 'make their faith practical' by publicly 'sacrificing' as much cash as they can to the movement" (1999, p. 291). This intriguing comment is not followed up, however, as we move swiftly on to a consideration of how the church presents an encounter between Pentecostalism and neoliberal enterprise, and one where it can appeal to merely mercenary motives.

Other more detailed ethnography on the Universal Church shows how a focus on sacrifice can feed into a nuanced model of religio-economic practice, as well as providing possible clues as to how to mediate between Harding's and the Comaroffs' clearly different approaches. For instance, Eric Kramer's (2002) account of research conducted in urban São Paulo and Rio de Janeiro during the 1990s shows how the popular yet controversial UCKG in Brazil appears to be in a very different position to its counterpart in South Africa – for instance it has devised strategies to elect federal congressmen to office in Brasilia – and yet one common feature across universal congregations worldwide appears to be the presence of faith-based "sacrifice." Kramer sees his ethnography among predominantly working-class believers as indicating how "millennial capitalism" has become a defining condition of our age. At the same time, he provides closely described accounts of fundraising practices and the idea that believers visibly test and constitute their religious faith through economic sacrifices. Kramer describes such action as a kind of audacious spiritual wagering, where the interiorized nature of faith itself leads to a kind of productive activity, affirming personal control over money and exchange while drawing on the mediating, material forms used in sacrificial practices. It is perhaps difficult to glean from Kramer's account whether he sees such psychological and emotional "benefits" of sacrifice as helping to explain its popularity among UCKG congregations. However, we can say that his concluding comments suggest a carefully poised analytical position: for Kramer, just as a narrow cultural phenomenology overlooks the universal determinants of a process spanning different societies in space, so a global history of capital can too easily become a teleological form of explanation.[11]

Devaka Premawardhana (in press) has also recently focused on a Universal Church, this time patronized by relatively poor Cape Verdean immigrants in the Dorchester neighborhood of Boston in the United States, and once again he finds sacrifice to be a powerful theme through which to explore controversies around seemingly irrational economic actions. His paper is itself something of a conversion narrative, detailing the transformation of Premawardhana's thinking not toward born-again belief, but away from the assumption that it would be possible to explain believers' participation in abstract terms of alienation and ideological domination. Some of the ethnographic details may by now seem familiar: the urging of members to go beyond regular tithing in their contributions to the church, and even to give money that might have been set aside for such large purchases as a car; certainly also the sense of frustration among immigrants at their proximity to but continued marginality from more prosperous lifestyles. However, Premawardhana reveals certain ethnographic surprises, such as the ways in which believers may reinterpret the financial demands of the church. One man, for instance, talks of how he lacks money to give to the church, but instead contributes with his time and effort; similarly, his wife notes "I don't have money to give, but I have my spirit." As Premawardhana remarks, Evans-Pritchard's (1940) Nuer also found it perfectly acceptable to engage in ritual substitution, sacrificing a wild cucumber in the place of an ox when the latter was not readily available; such action suggests that gifts of time, effort, and devotion offered by the man and woman bring them, no less than money would, into relationships of reciprocity with their church and their God. This kind of action is productive in another sense (and one that has resonances with Kramer's analysis), as while such ritual action may or may not alter "objective" circumstances, it can have an effect on how such circumstances are experienced. The giver comes to understand him – or herself as someone who is *able* to give to their church, and is not merely a recipient of its benefits.

Such ethnography brings us back to reflections on causality and material practice. Premawardhana sees himself as concerned with observing the *effects*, rather than speculating about the *causes*, of symbolic action in a specific context, and so "attempting to take seriously transformative religious experiences without explaining them away through secular modes of rationality and intelligibility." His emphasis is on the need to go beyond seeing the church as "compensatory" in relation to the frustrations of the "real" world. In this view, a narrative of exploitation and alienation can tell us little about experiences of sacrifice that in fact come closer to those described by Godfrey Lienhardt (1961) for Dinka sacrificial rituals, where the significance of ritual action lies less in its technical efficacy and more in the act itself. So for Premawardhana the change is in the subjective experience of the ritual actor, giving him or her the sense of a move from "underlying passivity" in relation to events toward "active construction" in shaping them. This is not so far, I contend from the poetics of Prosperity as described by Harding and others.[12]

## CONCLUDING REMARKS AND WIDER REFLECTIONS

While this chapter has been discussing the potential links between neoliberalism and neo-Pentecostalism, much of the theoretical imagery that has been invoked – of witches, gifts, sacrifice, millennialism, rationality, and alienation – has been of a distinctly more traditional variety.[13] The deployment of such terms, if not exactly constituting a "neo"-stone-age economics, perhaps reflects the tendency of any discipline to interpret the new in terms of established frameworks. At the same time, some of this theoretical vocabulary does important work in our understanding of Prosperity practices. In particular, the shift away from metaphors of consumption toward those of sacrifice emphasizes the complex "economy" in which many believers operate: not merely that of occultation or consumption, but also a combining of ritual and material practice in ways that may help to index as well as constitute personal religious commitment, and which can signal attachment to wider church structures and not merely self-interest. We might say that these are practices imbued with materiality, but not necessarily with materialism, as conventionally understood. Such action does not conform to secular assumptions of economic prudence but nonetheless is likely to contain a rationality of its own, even if we cannot impose a single meaning on to it. Sacrifice, as Hubert and Mauss (1964) originally recognized, is a productive and not merely a destructive act, bringing materiality and reciprocity together in creative ways.

Two other long-standing theoretical frameworks have surely been relevant to the analyses discussed above. One relates to economic practice as "performance" – linked with both ritual and the performative creation of social situations. To the extent that they see themselves as agents and not merely victims of circumstance, many of the Faith adherents we have encountered in this chapter arguably work on the dividing line between imagination and aspiration, positive thinking and positive action. Often, this is precisely the kind of action which makes them appear deluded to secular observers, and it is certainly one of the factors contributing to what Harding might call the "hermeneutic suspicion" evident in the *Atlantic* article quoted at the beginning of this chapter. As Tsing points out in yet another piece published in 2000, however, on "the economy of appearances," the actions of secular corporations seeking investment are frequently themselves precisely performances aimed at becoming self-fulfilling prophecies, as the self-conscious making of a spectacle becomes a necessary aid to gathering investment funds. These kinds of behaviors form their own enchantment, "creating a magic show of peculiar meanings, symbols, and practices" (*ibid.*, p. 119). And as Maurer (2010, pp. 149–150) notes in relation to those critical of financial grandstanding, the moral elevation of investment over speculation itself harks back to a Protestant Ethic. So, one irony may be that Prosperity Christians are closer to secular economic actors than the latter might always admit, even if the power and influence of the latter is vastly greater on a global scale.

A further framework, more implicit in this piece, has related to spheres of exchange. Although his analysis refers to a Californian Vineyard congregation that professes to distance itself from Health and Wealth Christianity, Jon Bialecki (2008) intriguingly talks of the potential coexistence of different modes of economic practice within the church. While "stewardship" draws on a common Christian trope relating to money that is "not their own," in effect erasing the importance of the subject as an agentive force (*ibid.*, pp. 378–379), sacrifice presents a rather different model of agency and origination, where moderation is devalued and lack of hesitation encouraged (*ibid.*, p. 382). We might think of this as a kind of "disciplined extravagance," and in my analysis it indicates the power of sacrifice not merely to respond (as the intellectualist stance would have it) to uncertainty, but actually to *create* a kind of uncertainty – indeed a leap of faith through material means – in ways that can be socially and personally productive, even if such productivity does not in itself provide a single "meaning" of, or suggest a single "function" for, such acts.

While much of this chapter has used an emphasis on practice and performance to challenge models of analysis that privilege economic "explanations" for religious acts, it is important not simple to throw out the materialist baby along with the hegemonic bathwater. For instance, the power and sophistication of the Comaroffs' approach indeed point to wider structures of inequality that must not be discarded by microscale phenomenological analyses that look no further than the walls of a particular church. To change the metaphor somewhat, the devil is rather in the *hierarchical* detail, in the presentation of economic positioning as (over-)powerful explanatory force. So in answering the question "Did Christianity Cause the Crash?" we might respond, typically for anthropologists, with worries about the question itself, indeed even with a kind of reversal of its causality: What is it about a global financial crash that makes us want to blame a certain branch of Christianity? For we can be sure that so-called "irrationalities" are concealed in many parts of our lives, and not merely those we choose to label religious.

## NOTES

1. Retrieved from http://www.theatlantic.com/magazine/archive/2009/12/did-christianity-cause-the-crash/7764/

2. Robert Wauzzinski's (1993) *Between God and Gold* traces the interface between Protestant Evangelicalism and the Industrial Revolution in the nineteenth and early twentieth centuries, arguing for a continuity in discourses of personalism and implicit or explicit materialism that has run through at least some strands of American evangelicalism from the 1800s to the present-day. Kramer (2002) notes that the post-World War II Pentecostal healing and charismatic revivals in the United States, from the late 1940s through America's postwar economic boom, brought forth shifts in the emphasis of certain Pentecostal themes, such as healing and material well-being. According to Bielo (2007), "prosperity theology" itself reemerged on a national scale in the 1950s with the genesis of the Full Gospel Men's Business Fellowship, and the populist writings of Norman Vincent Peale. It expanded from the 1970s through such preachers as Oral Roberts, Kenneth Copeland, and Kenneth Hagin; currently prominent preachers in the United States include Joel Osteen, T. D. Jakes, and Creflo Dollar.

3. Retrieved from http://www.theatlantic.com/magazine/archive/2009/12/did-christianity-cause-the-crash/7764/

4. Retrieved from http://www.theatlantic.com/magazine/archive/2009/12/did-christianity-cause-the-crash/7764/

5. Though Hunt also points out that the church also displays many differences from its American counterparts, including teachings on demonology, shamanism, and animism that emerge from the Korean context.

6. For a fuller review of earlier relevant writings, see Coleman (2000).

7. Marshall (2009, pp. 22–23) also directs her argument toward what she sees as Meyer and Geschiere's (1999) argument that globalization reinforces the production of cultural difference, implying a causal relationship between the intensification of global flows and a new and pressing "need" for forms of cultural and political closure. Compare also Robbins (2007), who sees the Comaroffs' work on South Africa more generally as providing an account of the formation of a culture engaged with capitalism, in the process sidelining the study of Christianity per se.

8. See also Geschiere's (2003, p. 163) comparison of the occult and the transparent.

9. Thus, Harding (2000, p. 114) refers to the text of a 1976 promotion, describing the sacrificial giving of people from all walks of life that had built Falwell's ministry thus far, and reminding readers of Luke 6:38: "Give, and it shall be given unto you."

10. Bialecki (2008, p. 377) also notes that, because Harding's project is consciously orientated toward analyzing the rhetoric of Falwell and other church elites, we are often unable to see how this dynamic fully plays out in everyday Christian life.

11. In this context, it may be significant that Kramer talks of an "affinity" rather than a relationship of causality between the "accentuated magicality" present in Brazilian UCKG notions of entrepreneurial success and believers' consciousness of neoliberal capitalism.

12. Indeed, this attitude echoes Harding's (1987) depiction of the wider process of becoming a believer through the manipulation of rhetoric, involving the shift from being a "listener" to being a "speaker."

13. Maurer (2010, p. 148) too sees such work on the apocalyptic religious visions attending the apparent global triumph of neoliberal capitalism as contributing to a

much longer anthropological tradition of considering "those moments when the domains of the economy and religion, mysticism, and magic are barely separable and seem to merge into one: to the devils in commodity fetishism (Taussig, 1980)" as well as the spirits of capitalist work discipline.

# REFERENCES


Asad, T. (1993). *Genealogies of religion: Discipline and reasons of power in Christianity and Islam*. Baltimore, MD: The Johns Hopkins University Press.

Bialecki, J. (2008). Between stewardship and sacrifice: Agency and economy in a Southern California charismatic church. *Journal of the Royal Anthropological Institute*, *14*(2), 372–390.

Bielo, J. (2007). "The mind of Christ": Financial success, born-again personhood, and the anthropology of Christianity. *Ethnos*, *72*(3), 315–338.

Brouwer, S., Gifford, P., & Rose, S. (1996). *Exporting the American Gospel: Global Christian fundamentalism*. London: Routledge.

Cannell, F. (2006). Introduction: The anthropology of Christianity. In: F. Cannell (Ed.), *The anthropology of Christianity* (pp. 1–50). Durham, NC: Duke University Press.

Coleman, S. (2000). *The globalisation of charismatic Christianity: Spreading the Gospel of Prosperity*. Cambridge, MA: Cambridge University Press.

Coleman, S. (2004). The charismatic gift. *Journal of the Royal Anthropological Institute*, *10*(2), 421–442.

Comaroff, J., & Comaroff, J. (1999). Occult economies and the violence of abstraction: Notes from the South African postcolony. *American Ethnologist*, *26*(2), 279–303.

Comaroff, J., & Comaroff, J. (2000). Millennial capitalism: First thoughts on a Second Coming. *Public Culture*, *12*(2), 291–343.

Evans-Pritchard, E. (1940). *The Nuer: A description of the modes of livelihood and political systems of a Nilotic people*. Oxford, MA: Clarendon.

Geschiere, P. (2003). On witch doctors and spin doctors: The role of "experts" in African and American politics. In: B. Meyer & P. Pels (Eds.), *Magic and modernity: Interfaces of revelation and concealment* (pp. 159–182). Stanford, CA: Stanford University Press.

Harding, S. (1987). Convicted by the Holy Spirit: The rhetoric of fundamental Baptist conversion. *American Ethnologist*, *14*(1), 167–181.

Harding, S. (2000). *The book of Jerry Falwell: Fundamentalist language and politics*. Princeton, NJ: Princeton University Press.

Hubert, H., & Mauss, M. (1964). *Sacrifice: Its nature and function*. Chicago, IL: University of Chicago Press.

Hunt, S. (1998). Magical moments: An intellectualist approach to the neo-Pentecostal Faith Ministries. *Religion*, *28*, 271–280.

Hunt, S. (2000). "Winning ways": Globalisation and the impact of the Health and Wealth Gospel. *Journal of Contemporary Religion*, *15*(3), 331–347.

Kramer, E. (2002). Making global faith universal: Media and a Brazilian prosperity movement. *Culture and Religion*, *3*(1), 21–47.

Lears, J. (2003). *Something for nothing: Luck in America*. New York, NY: Viking Penguin.

Lears, J. (2009). *Rebirth of a nation: The making of modern America, 1877–1920*. New York, NY: Harper Collins.

Lienhardt, G. (1961). *Divinity and experience: The religion of the Dinka*. Oxford, MA: Clarendon Press.

Marshall, R. (2009). *Political spiritualities: The Pentecostal revolution in Nigeria*. Chicago, IL: University of Chicago Press.

Martin, D. (1990). *Tongues of fire: The explosion of Protestantism in Latin America*. Oxford, MA: Basil Blackwell.

Maurer, W. (2010). Credit crisis religion. *Religion and Society*, *1*, 146–155.

Meyer, B., & Geschiere, P. (Eds.). (1999). *Globalization and identity: Dialectics of flow and closure*. Oxford, MA: Blackwell.

Premawardhana, D. (in press). Transformational tithing: Sacrifice and reciprocity in a neo-Pentecostal church. *Nova Religio*, *15*(4), May 2012.

Robbins, J. (2007). Continuity thinking and the problem of Christian culture: Belief, time and the anthropology of Christianity. *Current Anthropology*, *48*(1), 5–38.

Roberts, R. (Ed.) (1995). *Religion and the tradition of capitalism in contemporary America*. London: Routledge.

Rosin, H. (2009, December). Did Christianity cause the crash? *Atlantic Magazine*. Retrieved from http://www.theatlantic.com/magazine/archive/2009/12/did-christianity-cause-the-crash/7764/

Ritzer, G. (1993). *The McDonaldization of society: An investigation into the changing character of contemporary social life*. Thousand Oaks, CA: Pine Forge Press.

Rudnyckyj, D. (2010). *Spiritual economies: Islam, globalization, and the afterlife of development*. Ithaca, NY: Cornell University Press.

Taussig, M. (1980). *The devil and commodity fetishism in South America*. Chapel Hill, NC: The University of North Carolina Press.

Tsing, A. (2000). Inside the economy of appearances. *Public Culture*, *12*(1), 115–144.

Wauzzinski, R. (1993). *Between God and gold: Protestant evangelicalism and the industrial revolution, 1820–1914*. Toronto, ON: Associated University Presses.

# A CATHOLIC ALTERNATIVE TO GLOBALIZATION? THE *COMPAGNIA DELLE OPERE* AS A MEDIATOR BETWEEN SMALL AND MEDIUM ENTERPRISES AND CATHOLIC SOCIAL TEACHING

Riccardo Nanini

## ABSTRACT

*As testified by its secular history, Catholic Social Teaching is closely bound to the various attempts that have been made at putting it into practice. Today, one of the most interesting ones is that of the enterprises' association* Compagnia delle Opere. *Particularly in Italy, the* Compagnia *wants to become an important point of reference for Small and Medium Enterprises, the heart of Italian production system, through a new socioeconomic concept, based on the Subsidiarity Principle and the growth of the nonprofit sector. In many ways, it aims to create an alternative to classical capitalism, also supported by Benedict's XVI recent social encyclical; nevertheless, numerous ambiguities persist.*

**The Economics of Religion: Anthropological Approaches**
**Research in Economic Anthropology, Volume 31, 47–76**

**ISSN: 0190-1281/doi:10.1108/S0190-1281(2011)0000031006**

# INTRODUCTION

Capitalism is one of the basic elements of modernity, as it developed within Western societies. However, even within these there are movements, traditions, (sub)cultures, and religions that tend to see themselves – often antagonistically – as sharply antithetical to what the Western world has "become," in recent decades or even in the last few centuries. Their antithetical character is particularly evident by the way that they confront the capitalistic system. This chapter considers the relationship between economy and religion by observing the tension between them, played out in a specific case of trying to resolve this tension.

One of the "movements, traditions, (sub)cultures, and religions" referred to here is the Roman Catholic Church (RCC – see Table 1). The way in which the RCC views the economy and capitalism is indissolubly bound, at least for almost 120 years, to its view of society and politics, namely of all that is situated, so to speak, outside of it: modernity. Indeed, economy is considered within the global context of the so-called Catholic Social Teaching (CST), which was formed in 1891 with Leo XIII's encyclical *Rerum novarum*. From the beginning, it was characterized by its opposition both to liberal individualism and to different forms of collectivism. At the center of the CST lies the Subsidiarity Principle (SP), connected with the growth of intermediate communities – families as well as free associations – which intended to break the (historically determined) bipolarity between the individual and the state. This principle is based on the Christian idea of a human being, seen as a dynamic interlacement of both transcendent and immanent attributes.

The development of this social doctrine kept up with the increase in the intensity of laity activity. In particular, this commitment was realized within the so-called Catholic Movement, which arose in the 19th century under the

***Table 1.*** Abbreviations Commonly Used in this Chapter.

| | |
|---|---|
| CdO, *Compagnia* | *Compagnia delle Opere* |
| CL | *Comunione e Liberazione* |
| CST | Catholic Social Teaching |
| IC | Industry Clusters |
| RCC | Roman Catholic Church |
| SME | Small and Medium Enterprises |
| SP | Subsidiarity Principle |

shield of Catholic Action, the mother association of worldwide Catholic laypeople, and evolved differently in different countries and in different political and social contexts. In Italy, "Social Catholicism" has been especially fruitful; you have only to bear in mind the "Work of the Congress" (*Opera dei Congressi*, 1874–1907), a sort of national coordination organization for social and charitable activities scattered across the territory; or the "Italian People's Party" (*Partito Popolare Italiano*, 1921–1926), a Christian (but not clerical) party founded by Don Luigi Sturzo as soon as the Catholic laypeople were allowed to participate in political life and which was shortly blighted by the Fascist regime; or remember "Christian Democracy," Don Sturzo's party's heir, which unceasingly governed Italy until the early 1990s. The CST represents for these movements a sort of lodestar: a source of inspiration, a series of theoretical assumptions to put into practice, but also a guideline whose limits cannot be exceeded, and thus a system. This is, at least, its self-conception: often, the inspiration was ignored, the implementation allowed to languish, and the limits unobserved.

In this chapter, I present one of these laity phenomena, which only appeared in 1986 and continue to be very active across Italy: the *Compagnia delle Opere* ("Companionship of Works", CdO), a peculiar enterprise association. What makes it interesting is not only its close relationship to the RCC – also and especially with Pope John Paul II as well as Cardinal Joseph Ratzinger, who later became Pope Benedict XVI – but also its claim to apply CST's principles to the economic and entrepreneurial sphere of life in particular. Loyal to the RCC's thinking, the CdO puts at the center of its reflections the SP, which it claims is applied both social-politically as well as institutionally and strictly economically, by underlining Small and Medium Enterprises (SMEs) and Industry Clusters (*distretti industriali*, ICs), always at the heart of the Italian production system, to relaunch at new bases.

On the one hand, the CdO represents a very significant example of the CST's application, mainly because of the choice to be able to bypass a political party's commitment and to directly refer to the place where social life is molded and regulated. This "place" is the economy in a broad sense, as it is comprehended by the CST and by the CdO; it includes not only production, taxation, and distribution, but also how resources are employed, and human relations. On the other hand, I believe that the interaction between the CdO and the CST is far more interesting than it might first appear: what at the beginning – that is, during John Paul's II papacy, which in my opinion represented the "dogmatization" of the CST – emerges as an enthusiastic but slavish implementation attempt turns into a creative CST elaboration. It is an elaboration that culminates in the more or less implicit reception within Benedict XVI's social encyclical *Caritas in veritate* (2009), in which many elements are recognizable as typical of the CdO, or at least of the "atmosphere" that the CdO has created over 20 years within Italian politics and society. A current and authoritative papal document affirms that topics that only a few years ago very little specialists knew of, today belong to the CST, and that the CdO, through its clever use of the mass media and during a relatively short time, made the following familiar, although not alone, for a large audience: the "third sector"/"civil economy," "welfare society," subsidiarity, etc.

The papal support gives to the CdO a great impetus. Nevertheless, it is not enough for us to understand if the pattern that this association offers really constitutes an alternative to the globalized capitalistic system. Rather, my impression is that many obscure points and obstacles remain. These relate in particular to the cultural and social background that this pattern, deep-rooted in Italy, necessarily presupposes: a certain type of cultural Catholicism. Without this Catholicism, the SP's application, and therefore a proper "alternative," becomes questionable.

## CATHOLIC SOCIAL TEACHING AND SUBSIDIARITY PRINCIPLE

For Catholicism, the end of the State of the Church, performed in 1870 by the very young Kingdom of Italy, represents a huge turning point. From the RCC's point of view, this symbolizes and summarizes all that, during a long span of time, was at first external and extraneous and then became openly adverse to it, a threat to its existence: the ideology of enlightenment, liberalism, nationalism, and a socialist movement; in short, modernity. Above all, the RCC was forced to admit that it did not lie anymore, so to say, at the center of the world, although – to make use of Émile Poulat's expression – it continues to pretend to be "un monde," a closed universe that does not admit anything outside of itself (cf. Poulat, 1986, pp. 9–10).

The "sacrilege" of the Italian troops, the rationalist atheism as "venom," the modern State ideology, and the ideas that permeated workers' claims required appropriate response. Especially under Pius IX's long and vigorous papacy (1846–1878), these responses appeared in disapproval documents like the encyclical *Quanta cura* or *Syllabus errorum* (1864)[1], as well as in the First Vatican Council's convocation (1869–1870), with the unexpected dogmatization of papal infallibility. But what marks an "evolution" within the RCC is the creation of a Catholic "social doctrine": in fact, a purely defensive attitude turns into a first attempt to open the institution to the outside. The "new things" to which the title of the first social encyclical refers (Leo's XIII *Rerum novarum*, 1891)[2] could no longer be ignored – or worse, even played down. Indeed, the CST is not based on empty foundations: already several decades before, different laity activities existed.

For more than a century, the CST survived social developments, historical phases, political events, and the evolution of economy. Its history is marked by the papal documents, which at regular intervals celebrate and update Leo XIII's *Magna Charta* by adapting the CST to the times and to the personalities of the different Popes. The CST is strictly bound to the Catholic Movement (*Movimento Cattolico*), both socially and politically.

For the first time, the SP is explicitly mentioned and expounded in *Quadragesimo anno*, a Pius XI encyclical letter (1931; cf. Pius IX, 1931);[3] however, it represents an attribute of Catholic thinking ever since the beginning of modernity and is a CST cornerstone. It frames a "stepped" society pattern, where between the state and the individual as two extremes, the so-called "intermediate bodies" play a key role: first of all for families, but also free citizen associations, whose task is to reach where individuals cannot reach, the more complex are the needs to satisfy; the state only intervenes where (differently sized) intermediate bodies are overextended. According to this pattern, it is not the state that lies at the center of the society, but the person, both as an individual – indeed not as a "monad" – and as a member of a "natural" community (a family) or of a chosen one (an intermediate body): individual as a person, as a dynamic interlacement that reflects both the Trinitarian love between the Father, the Son, and the Holy Spirit and God's love for human beings (cf. Nanini, 2004).

Thus, at the center of its own concerns the CST poses at all times a twofold rejection: on the one hand, it rejects the individualistic (liberal) pattern; on the other hand, it wants to have nothing to do with the collectivistic systems claimed by the different forms of statism and Marxism. Instead it underlines a "middle way," the way of persons, of families, of intermediate communities, of free citizens' associations, of a moderate but resolute communitarian antistatism.

Over many decades, this basic attitude has not changed. The SP is characterized as the heart, the fundament, and the synthesis of the CST. What changes, is the way in which the Catholic social doctrine is implemented within the different historical contexts; the space that it wins, its theological and pastoral position, or the accentuations of some aspects of it to others' detriment. In this sense, the expression "Third Way" plays an important role, as well as the disputes that have sprung up around it, given the wide use of this concept outside of a Christian understanding of economy and politics. Can it be said, in relation to the CST, that there is a "Third Way," alternative to capitalism as well as collectivism or statism? To what extent is this way a "third" way? These are important questions. However, we must also ask: is it really a "way," that is, a journey with a certain goal? Or, is it rather a sort of road sign, with the only aim to show a general direction – one of the various ways to reach the destination? And: what is the SP's role?

The Second Vatican Council (1962–1965) constitutes another conclusive turning point within Church history. Its *aggiornamento* attempt has not only to do with a structure renewal, but also with the relations to modernity – one that *Rerum novarum* began to see objectively, although with condemnation. The core issue is the autonomy that the RCC as a "monde" is ready to grant to what has developed as an independent "monde," namely the modern world. Pope John XXIII, the Second Vatican Council's initiator, wanted to read the "sign of the times" (cf. *Humanae salutis*, No. 4; quotation from Mt 16:3)[4] and to see in the contemporary world "immense possibilities in the field of the apostolate" (cf. John XXIII, 1961, No. 260). The optimism that he conveys to the Council assembly seems to produce a new self-conception of Catholicism, summarized in the Pastoral Constitution *Gaudium et spes*, that is, the Council's final document.[5] As aphoristically explained by an Italian sociologist, Salvatore Abbruzzese, before the Second Vatican Council "it was a question of bringing back the world to Christ," whereas, after the Council "it is a question of recognizing Christ in the world" (cf. Abbruzzese, 1991, p. 80).

All of this affects the CST. In the encyclicals *Mater et magistra* (1961; cf. John XXIII, 1961) and above all in *Pacem in terris* (1963)[6], there is a significant emphasis on the autonomy of the laity, the will to act more independently – more "anonymously" – through simple laypeople with their own choices. It cannot be said that the SP disappears; however, it is a fact that the SP is practically not mentioned in John's XXIII encyclicals, and neither in the Council's documents. Also Pope Paul VI, successor to John XXIII, did not seem to particularly love the SP; in general, it seems that he even wanted to diminish the CST's importance which it obtained from the preconciliar Popes. In fact, Paul VI's apostolic letter *Octogesima adveniens* (1971) shows a sort of reduction; the CST becomes a "social instruction," whose task is at most to offer very general norms that Catholics have to adapt to different contexts (cf. Menozzi, 2000, pp. 89–90; Prandi, 1981, p. 194). An authoritative Church historian speaks here even of an "invitation to relativising" what – namely the CST – previously was presented as "definitive and inherent to the human nature itself" (cf. Acerbi, 1987, p. 126).

The "Third Way" problem does not exist for the counciliar Popes. Both John XXIII and Paul VI limit themselves to a generic condemnation of liberalism and collectivism because of their godlessness as well as their ideological character (cf. John XXIII, 1961, No. 198; Paul VI, 1971, No. 34–35). Or rather, it is not the "thirdness" that is questioned, but the fact that the CST is seen as a "way" and so implicitly put on the same level of these ideologies.

It is a risk that John Paul II, Paul VI's successor after John Paul I's short interlude, on the contrary, willingly accepts to take. With Karol Wojtyla (John Paul II), an unprecedented systematization and "canonisation" takes place within the CST. It not only becomes a doctrine again, but in my opinion undergoes a thorough "dogmatization" process: it is almost raised to an article of faith. It is not an accident that a CST digest, edited by the Pontifical Council for Justice and Peace, appeared in 2004 (cf. Pont. Counc. for Justice a. Peace, 2005), drawn up according to the pattern of the Catechism of the Catholic Church (1992).[7] The *Compendium of the Social Doctrine of the Church* intends even to catechetically set what, until this moment, was an object of separate papal documents and open to several interpretation nuances.

The manifesto of John Paul II's social doctrine is *Centesimus annus*, an encyclical written one hundred years after *Rerum novarum* (1991; cf. John Paul II, 1991). Referring to the first social encyclical, the Pope underlines the "permanent value" of its teaching and the need of a doctrinal continuity with it: *Rerum novarum* "created a lasting paradigm for the Church" (cf. John Paul II, 1991, No. 2–3, 5). On the one hand, these unequivocal words are related to what some commentators regard as a "restoration," based on the Council's reduction and normalization (cf., e.g., Zizola, 2003); and on the other hand, they testify to the force and determination with which John Paul II intends to guide the Church (catchword: "New Evangelisation").

The failure of real Socialism (1989–1991), to which John Paul II himself was not extraneous, represents in his social doctrine the end of a political and economical era. The mirror of communist ideology reflects in negative the Christian concept. This concept presents itself as overcoming the false alternative between collectivism and capitalism, that is, between two equal and contrary modalities to reduce human beings to "a series of social relationships" (cf. John Paul II, 1991, No. 13). The Catholic "Third Way" – nevertheless, an expression that neither John Paul II nor his successor Benedict XVI (Joseph A. Ratzinger), accept (cf., e.g., Benedict XVI, 2005, No. 29; John Paul II, 1987, No. 41; ) – is a "third" one, so to say, in the sense of an *Aufhebung*; but its characteristic as a "way" is emphasized as in the *Rerum novarum*'s time. Its task is to create a new situation and to actively introduce in the public domain a multipolarity, breaking the state-market duopoly: the intermediate communities claimed by the SP have to concretely become the protagonists of such a perspective change, of such a tension to an "integral and solidary humanism" (cf. John Paul II, 1991, No. 49).

Benedict XVI has a difficult task: to continue to predicate this "integral and solidary humanism" by using, at the same time, the slight clearance bequeathed by Wojtyla's dogmatization. What is left to add to this doctrinal corpus? Ratzinger seeks to trace such a system back to its theological basics, first of all the theological virtue of *caritas*, indissolubly bound to *veritas*. His first encyclical, *Deus caritas est* (2005; cf. Benedict XVI, 2005), and above all his recent social one, *Caritas in veritate* (2009; cf. Benedict XVI, 2009), put the CST in its own doctrinal context and implicitly warn against the risk of closing it in a system: first, it is "the proclamation of the truth of Christ's love in society" (cf. Benedict XVI, 2009, No. 12, 5). However, it seems also that *Caritas in veritate* wants to further specify the ways in which the CST can be put into practice. Whereas John Paul II limits himself to wishing for the state-market duopoly's breaking as well as the intermediate communities' success, Benedict XVI de facto goes on to support concrete applications of these new perspectives and of the SP as their keystone.[8]

In any case, the CST's developments in the past 30 years are closely connected with application attempts made by the laity: on the one hand, the CST is a direct inspiration source, and on the other hand it significantly takes account of the laity activities. The impression is that the impetus given to the CST by John Paul's II great charisma gave rise to and directed many laity actors, and that these conferred on it specific contents and enriched it with "experience." Despite Ratzinger's fears, the CST became a system, and not just theoretically: it became a sort of "current" or "sensibility," if not yet a proper "party," hegemonic within Catholicism. The CdO, I believe, shows all this very clearly.

## "AN IDEAL CRITERION," AN "OPERATIVE FRIENDSHIP"

The CdO is an enterprise association founded on the 11th of July, 1986, in Milan, officially recognized by the Italian Department of Finance as a Trade Union association of Italian companies (1993) and by the Italian

Department of Interiors as a charitable institution (1988) and as a nonprofit body (1998; cf. Associazione *Compagnia delle Opere*, 2003). The CdO currently includes approximately 35,000 enterprises.[9] This growth occurred mainly during the past 10–15 years (cf. Associazione *Compagnia delle Opere*, 2008, p. 5). The current CdO president, following Giorgio Vittadini's long leadership (1989–2003) and Raffaello Vignali's shorter one (2003–2008), is M. Bernard Scholz, a German management-consultant and publicist.[10]

Within the CdO, about 1,000 nonprofit organizations coexist among an overwhelming majority of profitable enterprises (about 97%). Small and tiny enterprises with at most five employees are prevalent (45%); only very few firms employ more than 100 employees (2%). Thus, the turnover generally remains quite low: two-thirds of the CdO members have annual proceeds of 1,500,000 euros or below, and only about 2% bring in over 25,000,000. It is an association of small – often tiny – and medium enterprises that work in particular within the service sector (42%) and subordinate industries (27%), as well as commerce (19%). The territorial arrangement is also interesting: the most CdO members (about 60%) are situated in Lombardy, the richest and most dynamic Italian region; its national house branches number 40.[11] Only a negligible minority is located outside Italy; it looks like a sort of "colonization" pursued by the head office, with 15 foreign branches, above all in Latin America and in Europe.[12] Added to this are 25 liaison offices for profit and nonprofit organizations (cf. Associazione *Compagnia delle Opere*, 2008, p. 8). Together, the CdO members form a wide network, employing in total about 500,000 people. Already in 2003 the total annual turnover amounted to about 74,000,000 euros, meaning that the CdO gains nearly 14,000,000 euros annually (cf. Marinetti, 2003, p. 15; Pinotti & Viafora, 2010, pp. 85–86).

The *Compagnia* is sectored in four main areas: *CdO-Imprese*, addressed to profitable enterprises, *CdO-Opere sociali*, directed to nonprofit organizations, *CdO-Persona*, involved with individuals and their problems, and finally *CdO-Estero*, dedicated to relations with foreign markets as well as to the implementation of the CdO outside Italy. Every sector refers to specific operative fields, like "Human Capital," "Enterprise Training," "Innovation," "Internationalization," "Work and Schooling," or "Banks and Finance." There are also more tightly circumscribed activity spheres, like *CdO-Sport*, *CdO-Agroalimentare*, or *CdO-Informatica*, as well as an important trade fair occurring yearly in Milan, named *Matching*. Finally, there is the *Fondazione per la Sussidiarietà* ("Subsidiarity Foundation") that promotes the SP culturally and educationally as well as within enterprises and many other bodies.[13]

The *Compagnia* slogan, "An Ideal Criterion, an Operative Friendship," efficaciously summarizes its self-conception and its way of operation. On the one hand, it is important to bring out people's creativity and put them in concrete forms within the firms and organizations that they lead or to which they belong, as well as to create effective instruments by a relations' network: one of the most successful instruments undoubtedly being that of tariff agreements given to CdO members and stipulating many concerns of every kind (motor vehicles industries, insurances companies, financial groups, telecommunication firms, and so on).[14] On the other hand, it is fundamental to conform to an ideal that guides individuals and enterprise action (cf. Associazione *Compagnia delle Opere*, 2003). In other words, from an "Ideal Criterion" arises an "Operative Friendship."

"Ideal Criterion" is the key to understanding what the CdO is. The first article of its statute explains this clearly:

> The Association, *in the path of the Catholic presence in Italian society and according to the Social Doctrine of the Catholic Church*, promotes and defends both in Italy and in the world human dignity and work, as well as the presence of works and enterprises in the social context, encouraging thus a concept of a market whose rules understand and respect the individual in each aspect, dimension, and moment of his life. (Associazione *Compagnia delle Opere*, 1986, paragraph 1 – italics added)

Therefore, the *Compagnia* is a Catholic enterprise association. On the one hand, it refers to the "Catholic presence in society" and on the other hand to the CST, in order to promote work, free enterprise, and "works" in the perspective of a specific market concept.

What the CdO does is not merely paying a formal and vague tribute to the RCC as an institution – it is a very staunch one. The CdO is deep-rooted in social Catholicism and takes place within the great flourishing of charisma-based ecclesial movements occurring in the post-war period, especially after the Second Vatican Council. It is a sort of "emanation" of an Italian ecclesial movement that arose in 1954 in Milan under the priest Don Luigi Giussani (1922–2005): *Comunione e Liberazione* (CL). A brief description of CL seems appropriate here.

CL is a Catholic movement; its aim being an "education to the faith." In its conception, the faith means to acknowledge Jesus Christ's incarnation, death, and resurrection, as well as the redeeming role of the Church founded by him as an historical event that, as such, can only be accepted or rejected. At the same time, this event is characterized as a total and absolute answer to man's peculiar thirst for the infinite, that Don Giussani calls the "religious sense." Thus, to accept Christianity's historical truth means to understand that it is the height of a reality – of a "universe"

– whose structure is deeply Christian, that is, entirely fashioned on God's love for human beings; a love that is realized by the Son's mission. This means that nothing is unrelated to faith: history, art, thought, politics, society, economy. The basis of all human expressions, according to CL, is the Christian structure of reality.[15]

Thus, CL's history is the history of different attempts made to grasp this structure, according to the three movement's dimensions: culture, charity, and mission. As it sprang out of a school (Don Giussani was a religion teacher in a Milanese secondary school for many years), the movement is closely connected to the youth. It has been so especially since the "revolution" of 1968 in Italy, which ran well into the following decade. At its core, the so-called *Caritativa* was practiced as a weekly aid initiative for needy children and families in rural districts. When the *ciellini* (the CL's members) became students, the *Cattolici Popolari* ("People's Catholics") – a group active in university politics alongside the gauchiste "student movement" – was created. At the same time, CL watched with interest the political activity within the *Democrazia Cristiana*, that is, the Christian Democratic Party that has ruled Italy since the republic's foundation (1946): the *Movimento Popolare* ("People's Movement") arose and quickly became a main constituent of the party, by openly standing in dispute with other more "secular" sectors (cf. Nanini, 2010, pp. 111–153).

All of these attempts represent the implementation of one of Don Giussani's main assumptions, namely "presence." In contrast to a society and a culture that for a long time deviated from the Church and therefore from God – and in contrast, in part, to the RCC itself, too, criticized for surrendering to "protestantizing" tendencies associated with the "dominant mentality" and its "dissolution anthropology" – CL sees itself as a "Church fragment" that seeks to rediscover within the world and to push the world to rediscover the Christian structure of reality with its own testimony. It attempts to plant a "seed" that should grow through the realization of "works," intended as implementations of an act aimed at satisfying needs, whatever they may be. So, "presence" is the conditio sine qua non for the CL's ecclesial dimension, and at the same time its demonstration. "Presence" does not assume a definite and definitive form, but changes depending on situations and necessities (cf. Nanini, 2010, pp. 89–109).

## "MORE SOCIETY, LESS STATE"

The CdO came up in the middle of the 1980s as an association of very few enterprises. The "legend" says that its beginning was due to the difficulties of a small Sicilian wine industry from Alcamo consisting of CL sympathizers. Don Giussani himself challenged his people to make something so that it can sell its own – "excellent" – wine (see, e.g., Farina, 2001).

At this time, the *Movimento Popolare* exerted a great influence on Italian politics through its activities within the *Democrazia Cristiana*, although it is also socially involved with the creation and development of refectories, students' hostels as well as youth employment centers. However, the CL founder was not pleased with its political activity, for the fear that it might become a hostage of power games, and above all of the "totalitarianism" inherent in the state distanced from the people's real needs. Thus, it is necessary to pay attention to the social dimension, and this is what CL increasingly does. Between 1986–1987 and 1993 – the year in which *Movimento Popolare* ended – the CdO played an increasingly important role, in contrast with the pronounced decrease of *Movimento Popolare*'s party political activity. This brought a halt to its function, although external causes also contributed to its end. In particular, the *Tangentopoli* affair was a major cause. From that point on, the CdO has constantly increased its member base as well as its public standing. An efficacious mass media policy, skilfully crafted by its president, Vittadini, plays a key role in this.

Unquestionably, what stands out in the CdO history is its continued adherence to CL politics, similar to the former *Movimento Popolare*. But the *Compagnia* has done this by using other means, by striving to originate a "reformist," (i.e., cross-party) alliance to achieve its own aims, although it takes a liking to Silvio Berlusconi (who first became prime minister in 1994) and his conservative coalition. Here, the *Intergruppo per la sussidiarietà* ("Intergroup for Subsidiarity") is worth mention. This is a cross-party parliamentarian group, consisting of members from nearly all parties, which arose in 2002 and is still active today. Through lobby-like activism, it pursues a subsidiary transformation of the state and its institutions (cf. Nanini, 2010, pp. 254–276).

But the CdO is foremost an enterprise association. Or rather, it is an enterprise network, where the enterprises' "good" agrees with the network's aims, largely identified with an application of the SP as wide and deep as possible, above all within the Italian context. So, enterprises become elements of a very ambitious plan aimed at putting into practice, according to specific lines, CST's most salient points.

The starting point is a little revolution, implemented within the *Compagnia*: the abandoning, primarily on the theoretical level, of the subdivision between profitable enterprises and nonprofit organizations. On the one hand, the task is to "humanize" profit concerns and concretely open them to "charity" and "gratuitousness"; to consider workers "like brothers" and not as counterparts, and to let them actively take part in enterprise life; to invest for the long run, without looking only at quarterly gains; to patrimonialize gains by reinvesting them for enterprise development, paying attention to research and innovation; to assign in part proceeds and free time to charity activities (cf. interview with ex-CdO president Vignali – Nanini, 2010, pp. 360–362).

On the other hand, it is necessary to free the nonprofit sphere – also known as the Third Sector, Social Enterprise, or (as favorite denomination) Civil Economy – of a romantic misunderstanding, according to which it is identified with volunteering as an "Indian reservation," that is, a socially heroic, but economically and politically almost trifling field. So, Vignali explains: "The non-profit logic begins only *after* getting any profit, not before. It concerns the fact that gains are not redistributed, but not that it is forbidden to get profit" (cf. Nanini, p. 362). Civil Economy is not marginal and offers many public utility services in various fields, above all, but not only, health, welfare, education, and culture. In order to gradually become one of the economy's protagonists, it has to assume business features: efficiency, productivity, continuity, more financial capacity, greater concern size, professionalization, and innovation (cf. Vittadini, 2002c).

Most of all, the nonprofit sector must be free to develop in this sense: in this respect, state responsibility is not small. So, we come back to the "political" matter, namely to the CdO attempt to influence in different ways a subsidiarity-based state reform. The theoretical and practical abandoning of the subdivision between profitable firms and nonprofit organizations involves an enormous strengthening of the Civil Economy, till it breaks the state-market duopoly within society: on the one hand the market as a realm of absolute profit, and on the other hand, the state control on all services supplies. Within the welfare state pattern, the state has as its main job the operation of wealth redistribution, by directly stating how resources assigned to services are to be used: it is the "from the cradle to the grave" pattern. According to the *Compagnia*, this pattern is in a critical position: inefficient and expensive, rigid and not sustainable, vulnerable to patronage systems as well as to corruption. Above all, this pattern greatly restricts citizens' freedom, participation, and responsibility; de facto, they are reduced to passive and resigned subjects (cf. Vittadini, 2002a, pp. XV, XVII).

The new pattern to introduce, according to the slogan that CdO has unceasingly repeated since 1986 – "More Society, less State" – is that of the welfare society. Vittadini defines this as "a rainbow world" (Cf. Meeting per l'Amicizia tra i Popoli di Rimini, 2002): a self-organized society, one built "from below" the state with its administrative units, gainful agents, and of course civil economy. It is a society where the citizens' free choice principle is in force: a society that thus promotes "virtuous competition" among these three actors (cf. Vittadini, 2002b). It is a society, at the same time, where the state no longer has a "father of a family" or "watchdog" task, but a "supervisor" function: it has namely to fix rules, to watch over abuses, and to evaluate the quality of supplied services (cf. Vittadini, 1994). Of course, there are also operative instruments to implement this pattern: coupons and vouchers, fiscal subsidiarity, and quality accreditation (cf., e.g., Vittadini, 2001a, p. 305, 2001b).[16]

## "HOW MANY BILL GATES DID WE KILL WITHOUT KNOWING IT?"

Thus, we are dealing here with a concept that intends to "transfigure" enterprises in many respects. By shuffling the cards, it transforms the nonprofit sector, a marginal one in itself, into an economic actor in every respect, while at the same time inverting the welfare state logic with its absolute state preeminence by wealth redistribution, as well as introducing welfare society.

However, according to the CdO this "revolution" does not represent an absolute beginning, but wants to refer to an already existing tradition, namely that of the SMEs. Always, the SMEs are the basics of the Italian production system; they repeatedly "saved" the Italian economy during the past 40 years. For the *Compagnia*, SMEs have both a symbolic and practical value. They are the result of a long historical process that created a "welfare society ahead of its time." Only Italian unification, in 1861, could destroy it by imposing an unnatural and ideologically ruinous statism. The SMEs are the concretization on the economic level of the intermediate bodies claimed by the CST.

For the CdO, it is not possible to understand the SMEs' meaning if they are not viewed within their historical and cultural context, that is, Italy, understood not as a state but as a nation or a people, as a Catholic country, as the place where Catholicism, so to say, became culture in a full and supreme way. Vittadini calls it a "great country," a "masterpiece," because it is based on the "ability to observe," "a typically Catholic feature": "Ability to imagine the latent reality structure" (cf. Da Rold, 2001), namely the close Christian configuration of all existence, which we noted above with reference to CL. It was not because of its raw materials, its military power, or its national consciousness that Italy became one of the most industrialized countries in the world, says the CdO co-founder, but because of the ability of innumerable "Egos" to work together (cf. Vittadini, 1998, p. 57; 2000b, p. 44). Its Catholic matrix, according to Vittadini, allowed the Italian people to create, since the Middle Ages, a very particular society, the incubator of *authentic* capitalism; a capitalism that, unlike usually thought, was invented by Italian monks and merchants. Italian society, he emphasizes, was the culture medium of the first universities, guilds and brotherhoods, hospitals and welfare activities, schools, pawn agencies, and later cooperatives, savings and cooperative banks, trade unions, and training colleges (cf. Vittadini's statements in Falsitta, Turco, Vittadini, Maroni, & Gualaccini, 2001, p. 163).

The SMEs, so to say, are a sort of "spin-off" of the intermediate bodies that from the Middle Ages progressively built the Italian "Welfare Society ahead of its time": they arose from the same mentality, the same culture, the same faith, the same "ability to observe" and "imagine" the close Christian structure of all reality, says Vittadini. That is the reason why, according to him, they represent an "anomaly:" the "Italian anomaly," a "virtuous anomaly" that prevails despite all practical as well as ideological obstacles, first of all capitalism "protestantization" or "Calvinization" (cf. Banca Europa, 2001, p. 89). Rejoining them to the nonprofit organizations, making them ideally and practically protagonists of the civil economy, and thus making them integral parts of a new welfare society means nothing more than giving them what is due them.

Their conformation shows all this. In the opinion of the CdO' masterminds, the SMEs did not develop depending on a planning from the top, but took place from below, on the basis of needs and abilities within specific places, in short: in a subsidiary way. In a nearly natural way, they created industrial zones specialized in manufacturing certain items (e.g., shoes and textiles, furniture, machine-building, taps and fittings, etc.). Nowadays, these industrial zones are named ICs, number over 200, and constitute the industrial evolution of traditional local craft specializations (cf. Quadrio Curzio & Fortis, 2005, pp. 91–93).

ICs are not to be confused with simple assemblages of industries of similar concerns. They are socio-territorial entities where several enterprises not only exist, but also populations that interact within. The ICs are communities where homogeneity both on the economic and the social level exists, and where both the economic and the social level closely interpenetrate. Firms tend to increase, often "per gemmation," that is, through ex-workers that found other jobs; labor is very skilled and the related know-how becomes a peculiarity of the respective cluster; a high cooperation level between enterprises is usual (common plans, promotional activities, pools etc.). On the social and cultural level, "identity spirit" and territory affection become central within the common industry cluster "self-understanding" (cf. Quadrio Curzio & Fortis, 2005, p. 99).

Although in the past praiseworthy, the Italian SMEs and ICs are now facing an unavoidable decline. Beginning in the 1990s they started to show symptoms of yielding, above all because of market globalization and of the "new scientific-technologic-industrial revolution" (cf. Quadrio Curzio & Fortis, pp. 115–121), a revolution that they fundamentally failed to navigate. The Italian production system, as it stands now, is totally inadequate. For the CdO, it is necessary to preserve all that is positive within the SMEs and ICs – indeed, a great benefit – but also to look for new ways. The new ways go through planning, technology (research and development) as well as a "new agreement" between all society and economy actors (cf. Quadrio Curzio & Fortis, 2005, pp. 129–133). It is necessary to put into practice a "de facto horizontal subsidiarity" (cf. Quadrio Curzio & Fortis, 2005, pp. 134–136), able to merge progress and solidarity; an "ecosystem," to borrow Vignali's words (cf. Bogliari, 2006, pp. 46–47).

This "ecosystem" has to be based on innovation, understood not only as a process, but also as an attitude, namely as "a dimension that concerns every enterprise area as well as enterprise nature: creativity, risk, knowledge, confidence, complexity, etc." (cf. Vignali, 2006a, p. 24). Innovating means going beyond "economic Darwinism" and giving a new meaning to the word "competition" (*concorrenza*), or rather, going back to the old one: *concorrenza* comes from the Latin word *concurrere*, "to run together," "to cooperate," "to contribute together" (cf. Bogliari, 2006, pp. 46–47; Nanini, 2010, p. 358). In short, innovating means looking at the past and, at the same time, looking at the future.

The IC concept, a deeply Italian one, was even exported: for instance to Korea, to the Silicon Valley, and to Bangalore. In an interview Vignali said: "The most successful foreign production areas were inspired by the Italian SMEs network" (cf. Nanini, 2010, p. 358). Thus, Vignali wonders, how can it be possible that even where ICs arose and developed, they now are in decline? It is necessary to look at prosperous foreign stories. According to the ex-president of the *Compagnia*, the Italian ICs have to follow Silicon Valley's example and become complex systems or "meta-systems," where not only enterprises with their products and services providers exist, but also a knowledge system (universities and research centers), a finance system (credit institutions), a policy system (the territorial state articulation), as well as the so-called "bridge-subjects," namely the elements able to connect the different actors in the *concurrere* logic, by preserving culture, ideal aspects, sense of belonging, and community ties (cf. Vignali, 2006a, pp. 134–136). The ICs – which already were "local markets" – according to Vignali have to promote the creation of new enterprises, to pay better attention to customer needs, and to be more inclined to embrace risk, on the grounds of the inherent flexibility and adaptability of their own components, as well as of a fundamental "immaterial asset," namely the widespread "confidence" that they produce (cf. Vignali, 2006a, pp. 137–139).

According to the CdO leaders, all this is impossible without a radical change in the roots where SMEs and ICs are to be found – a change in the state machinery, especially in the Italian one, but also in the banking system (reluctant to loan), in the employment and professional training sector (still too inelastic), and in the education system, CL's and CdO's favorite area from the start. "How many Bill Gates did we kill without knowing it?" Vignali rhetorically wonders (cf. Vignali, 2006b). The alternative, he thinks, lies between the risk of becoming a sort of Florida (or worse, Argentina) – an old-people's country or a bankrupt one – and the challenge to consequently and diffusely apply the SP together with all that it implies (cf. Vittadini, 2003a, 2003b).

The role that CdO wants to play here is a crucial one. It intends to become a "bridge subject," doomed to contribute to multi-level network creation: among the different SMEs, between SMEs and financial and credit system agencies, between SMEs and state articulations, between SMEs and the "knowledge system." The potential to create "networks of networks," nationally and internationally, of course, is not excluded (cf. Vignali, 2006a, pp. 171–174). In particular, the CdO aims at becoming one of the main connections between the society and the economy: Vittadini calls it "a virtual and multi-sectorial industry cluster," with an especially educational, sensitization purpose (cf. Vittadini & Sala, 2005, footnote 16 p. 196). It is not a coincidence that another CL's "emanation" through the CdO, the forementioned *Fondazione per la Sussidiarietà* led by Vittadini, whose functions in this sense are of eminently cultural and formative character, has visibly increased in recent years.

## "APPLIED SUBSIDIARITY:" THE LOMBARDY PATTERN

An important element to add here is the role played by Lombardy. As already said, the majority of the CdO members as well as the *Compagnia* have residence in Lombardy, the most industrialized Italian region. But the fact that this region has been led since 1995 by Roberto Formigoni, a man closely bound to CL, and whose fourth mandate will expire in 2015, is especially interesting. He has been for many years *Movimento Popolare*'s president, and from the very beginning a militant supporter of *Forza Italia* – Berlusconi's party.[17]

For the past 17 years, Formigoni has tried to apply CdO's main principles, in the limits of his powers and of the political clearance at his disposal. Institutionally, supported in this regard by one of his allies (the separatist party *Lega Nord*) he attempted to carry out federalism and devolution demands nationwide, by taking to extremes his "governor" powers; on the regional level, he gave space to the SP by exploiting the objective vivacity and social sensibility of the Lombard people. If in Italy there is a "welfare society ahead of its time," it is primarily in Lombardy.

The "Lombardy pattern" is based on what Vittadini calls "applied subsidiarity" (cf. Vittadini, 2000a, p. 193); on its part, this is concretely based on the "accreditation" system, used in several sectors: health politics, family and social politics, education politics, enterprise support, professional training, and employment politics. In each of these sectors, citizens fundamentally have free choice concerning the most qualified structure to satisfy their needs, or the way to realize their goals. The region supplies coupons and vouchers that completely or partly refund expenses or give contributions or loans on favorable conditions. Thus, there exist "school coupons," "socio-medical vouchers," "honour loans" for families in financial straits, and "technological vouchers" to support enterprise innovation, for instance. This implies that there must be a sufficient number of suitable structures, which can be public, classically private or led by nonprofit organizations. All these undergo constant quality controls and are then accredited. However, the concrete role played here by the ICs and their transformation in Silicon Valley-like networks is not very clear. Anyway, it must be said that in this respect a regional government cannot do very much.

Actually, the Lombardy pattern has always been not free from criticism – most notably, the high costs of this system, especially in the health sector, as well as the establishment of patronage relations based on CdO-affiliate firms, which are the overwhelming majority of the accredited ones. There have also been several judicial proceedings against close members of Formigoni's staff (cf. Barbacetto, 2000, 2001; Pinotti & Viafora, 2010, pp. 143–180). However, this "applied subsidiarity" attempt shows very clearly how the welfare society should be according to the *Compagnia*: a "supervisor" state that gives place to civil economy and, therefore, transforms the state-market duopoly in a "tripoly" where the most "suitable" enterprises (those able to transcend the border between profit and nonprofit) – several of which are actually associated with the CdO – become crucial economic actors. Within the Lombardy pattern – the nearest pattern to the ideal – the *Compagnia* becomes the main "bridge subject," if not the only one.

## *COMPAGNIA DELLE OPERE* AND CATHOLIC SOCIAL TEACHING

Thus, it is clear that the CdO's activism acts on two levels: the macro-political one, so to say, and the strictly entrepreneurial one. They are closely bound: without a welfare society-oriented macro-political change, enterprises as conceived by the CdO would not be able to adequately develop; but without a paradigm shift within enterprise-conceiving, a subsidiary state reform would not have a chance of success.

I believe that all of this implies that the name of the game is a very particular economy concept. For the CdO, the economy has not only to do with the market, that is, with sending and acquiring goods and service, but it is also a great place where all social life grows: besides classically thought market and finance, it includes taxation as well as wealth redistribution systems, social, health, welfare, and education policies, and all that serves to get work done in a society – also and primarily politics in a broad sense. Consequently, economy has to do with the *humanum* as a whole. It is not a coincidence that one of the CdO headwords is "human capital:" human beings – with their education, their culture, their work, their needs, and their creativity – are the true capital of concern. The production of free goods and services is enclosed in an "ideological" system that does not reject it – against leftist parties, the *Compagnia* often declares that "before redistributing it is necessary to produce" – but sets this up according to its own criteria.

Within the CdO, economy is thus incessantly "humanized" and "moralized," and this humanization and moralization process occurs by introducing a solid and weighty factor: civil economy seen within the SP's logic. Civil economy represents the attempt to merge both capitalism and solidarity – not to a posteriori add a "humanizing" dimension to an essentially inhumane system (in this respect, the constant CdO polemic against capital yields is quite meaningful), but to create something new on the basis both of the free market thought and of the Christian charity logic. Actually, these new aspects, according to the *Compagnia*, have always existed: *authentic* capitalism, arisen and developed in a Catholic and deeply subsidiary culture, and then blurred by protestant, Calvinistic, and after all atheistic modernity. In this context, it is noteworthy that CdO's masterminds unceasingly polemize against Max Weber and his theory about the "Protestant ethic" and the "spirit of capitalism," or rather, against its *warped* interpretation (according to them). It is also noteworthy that this controversy assumes a well-established position on the scientific level, too: one has only to bear in mind, for instance, Rodney Stark's argument in support of a "rational choice theory" in *The Victory of Reason* (cf. Stark, 2005).[18]

The CdO is a Catholic enterprise association that intends to apply the CST's main principles, first of all the SP. Although these principles have not essentially changed for more than a century, as we saw, the CST has played different roles depending on the time, the ecclesial atmosphere, as well as the personality of the respective pontiffs. It is not a coincidence that the *Compagnia* flourished even under the leadership of John Paul II – a Pope who had the matter particularly at heart. Affinity between Don Giussani with his movement and the CdO, in particular, and the Polish Pope is a common feeling deep-rooted in a very similar view of the faith and the way to live it: in a papal audience to the *ciellini* in 1980, John Paul II went as far as to affirm: "Your way of facing human problems is very near to mine, or rather, I can say that they are the same" (cf. John Paul II, 1980).

At the beginning, CL's reception of John Paul II's CST was indeed enthusiastic, although not very original. But from the CL's social turning point, that is, from the CdO's birth, a continuous widening and explicating attempt developed in the movement. Subsidiarity, "rediscovered" by John Paul II after twenty years of "oblivion" due to the Council Popes, as in a chain reaction, comprised all the other main points of the *Compagnia:* What is the meaning of concretely using the SP? What is the meaning of finding an alternative to collectivism as well as liberal capitalism forms? John Paul II's interpretation of the CST demands to put it in practice; it has to incarnate in a specific proposal. This proposal, however generic it may be, does not allow a very wide margin of manoeuvre; actually, it cannot look very differently as it looks within the CdO: from welfare society to the SMEs assembled in ICs, the Italian economic pattern, however, needs adjustments and improvements, at least ideally conforms with that one thought by John Paul II. This is CdO's firm belief, and by observing the *Compagnia*'s concept by the light of the CST it is difficult to say that it is erroneous.

Even more so, it is difficult to say that it is erroneous by reading the last written social encyclical, Benedict XVI's above-mentioned *Caritas in veritate*. Beyond doctrinal statements (love and its relation to truth) as well as moral and cultural ones (relativism and technocracy criticism, necessity of an authentic and integral human being's development, role played by public welfare, civic function of faith, etc.), it is striking that the Pope wanted not only to reaffirm CST's significance and intrinsic unity, but also to underline the fact that it is not a closed system and that the RCC "does not have a technical solution to offer" (cf. Benedict XVI, 2009, No. 12, 9). Nevertheless, these assertions seem to clash with the de facto dogmatization realized by John Paul II and also with what the current Pope writes even in this encyclical letter.

In fact, *Caritas in veritate* goes so far as to make very specific statements, as it is highlighted by authoritative commentators.[19] It is wrong to think that economy can "solve all social problems through the simple application of *commercial logic*"; in fact, the market is an instrument in the hands of man, which can "be used badly" by "man's darkened reason." Economy "must be structured and governed in an ethical manner," and "in commercial relationships the principle of gratuitousness and the logic of gift as an expression of fraternity can and must *find their place within normal economic activity*" (cf. Benedict XVI, 2009, No. 36). Pope Benedict XVI writes:

> [...] *Every economic decision has a moral consequence* [...] Perhaps at one time it was conceivable that first the creation of wealth could be entrusted to the economy, and then the task of distributing it could be assigned to politics. Today that would be more difficult [...] Hence the canons of justice must be respected from the outset, as the economic process unfolds, and not just afterwards or incidentally. Space also needs to be created within the market for economic activity carried out by subjects who freely choose to act according to principles other than those of pure profit, without sacrificing the production of economic value in the process. The many economic entities that draw their origin from religious and lay initiatives demonstrate that this is concretely possible. (Benedict XVI, 2009, No. 37)

With regard to *Centesimus annus*, Ratzinger mentions "a system with three subjects: the *market*, the *State* and *civil society*," in every one of whose, "to varying degrees and in ways specifically suited to each, the aspect of fraternal reciprocity must be present" (Benedict XVI, 2009, No. 38). About this, he stresses:

> What is needed [...] is a market that permits the free operation, in conditions of equal opportunity, of enterprises in pursuit of different institutional ends. Alongside profit-oriented private enterprise and the various types of public enterprise, there must be room

> for commercial entities based on mutualist principles and pursuing social ends to take root and express themselves. It is from their reciprocal encounter in the marketplace that one may expect hybrid forms of commercial behaviour to emerge, and hence an attentiveness to ways of *civilizing the economy*. Charity in truth, in this case, requires that shape and structure be given to those types of economic initiative which, without rejecting profit, aim at a higher goal than the mere logic of the exchange of equivalents, of profit as an end in itself. (Benedict XVI, 2009, No. 38)

The state-market duopoly had as a result the disappearance of "solidarity in relations between citizens, participation and adherence, actions of gratuitousness," what is more than and different from both the market typical of "*giving in order to acquire*" and the state typical of "*giving through duty*." The state-market duopoly "is corrosive of society," while "economic forms based on solidarity" build up the society and are necessary (cf. Benedict XVI, 2009, No. 39).

The consequence is that also "*business enterprise* involves a *wide range of values,*" beyond both the figure of the "private business leader of a capitalistic bent" and the figure of the "State director"; owing to the needs of workers and society, there are different types of business enterprises, over and above the simple distinction between "private" and "public" (cf. Benedict XVI, 2009, No. 41). The Pope affirms:

> When we consider the issues involved in the *relationship between business and ethics*, as well as the evolution currently taking place in methods of production, it would appear that the traditionally valid distinction between profit-based companies and non-profit organizations can no longer do full justice to reality, or offer practical direction for the future. In recent decades a broad intermediate area has emerged between the two types of enterprise. It is made up of traditional companies which nonetheless subscribe to social aid agreements in support of underdeveloped countries, charitable foundations associated with individual companies, groups of companies oriented towards social welfare, and the diversified world of the so-called "civil economy" and the "economy of communion." This is not merely a matter of a "third sector," but of a broad new composite reality embracing the private and public spheres, one which does not exclude profit, but instead considers it a means for achieving human and social ends. Whether such companies distribute dividends or not, whether their juridical structure corresponds to one or other of the established forms, becomes secondary in relation to their willingness to view profit as a means of achieving the goal of a more humane market and society. It is to be hoped that these new kinds of enterprise will succeed in finding a suitable juridical and fiscal structure in every country. Without prejudice to the importance and the economic and social benefits of the more traditional forms of business, they steer the system towards a clearer and more complete assumption of duties on the part of economic subjects. And not only that: *The very plurality of institutional forms of business gives rise to a market which is not only more civilized but also more competitive*. (Benedict XVI, 2009, No. 46)

About the SP, Benedict XVI says that it is "particularly well-suited to managing globalization and directing it towards authentic human development" and must be "closely linked to the principle of solidarity" (Benedict XVI, 2009, No. 57–58). He even mentions a component of the SP that for the CdO is very important, namely the so-called fiscal subsidiarity, which allows "citizens to decide how to allocate a portion of the taxes they pay to the State" (cf. Benedict XVI, 2009, No. 60). Besides, the state role must be revised: "Once the role of public authorities has been more clearly defined, one could foresee an increase in the new forms of political participation, nationally and internationally, that have come about through the activity of organizations operating in civil society" (Benedict XVI, 2009, No. 24).

As we can see, the issues with whose concretization John Paul II, in his social doctrine, entrusts to the laity in *Caritas in veritate* are dealt with by the light of reflections and experiences of Catholic laypeople within society. The impression is that the drafting of this encyclical letter in many respects also treasured CdO reflections and experiences, or at least the "atmosphere" that the *Compagnia* to a great extent – above all within Italian Catholicism – contributed to diffuse.[20] Undoubtedly, all this strengthens the idea that CdO's interpretation of the CST is among the most authoritative ones, at least in the sense that the *Compagnia* "did the right thing," by understanding John Paul II's dogmatized doctrinal corpus in a way that was fully confirmed by Benedict XVI. To be particularly generous, it can be said that here the CdO plays a crucial role as an outrider, as an explorer of territories of which then the pontiff officially takes possession.[21] In the future, this can even be verified more specifically in relation to the SMEs and ICs. Because of the modality in which the CdO puts this subject in its own understanding of subsidiarity and civil economy, by connecting it to the "glorious past" of the "welfare society ahead of its time," such a subject appears as a consequence that is of course harmonizable with the CST of the past 30 years. Maybe a social encyclical will make a statement also about this one day.

## CONCLUSION

It is difficult to answer the question asked in the title of the present article. Are we experiencing a Catholic alternative to capitalistic system, a system that today is being put to a severe test by a crisis that seems to be a structural one, particularly in a structurally weak country like Italy? What kind of connection exists between this possible alternative – the one proposed by the CdO – and its "ideological" point of reference, namely the RCC's social doctrine?

Within Catholic understanding, it is not capitalism that is the problem, but rather what led it to take the shape it took: modernity blotting out God from its own horizon. Within the understanding of the CST, economy – even less a specific economic system like capitalism – is not and cannot be an independent field of human activity (cf. Il sussidiario, 2009b).[22] Without conversion, sooner or later every economic pattern will reveal itself as a failure. On its part, the CdO proposes a sort of conversion – a return to the past that, according to it, is perfectly able to take on the challenges of the future. In itself, the pattern offered by the *Compagnia* aims at universal application, but such an application is dependent on several significant variables.

De facto, the CdO's pattern presupposes that within society there is a religion or *Weltanschauung*-based institution, an inalienable point of departure to create "intermediate bodies" and, thus, apply the SP. Sure, this institution must not necessarily be the RCC. At any rate, it has to produce, as a precondition, effects that are similar to those produced by Catholicism – in this case, Catholic culture as it was historically realized in Italy. Therefore, such an institution has to be found as a necessary condition. Besides, even Catholicism assumes in reality different forms, depending on place and time; thus, it should not be simplistically identified with the Italian version. In a society, the social and religious pluralism level, the impact of religion on public discourse, the political and economic complexity – and many other factors – play of course an important role, too.

Put quite simply, within CL and the CdO there is a vague attempt to overcome this impasse, by looking at the "religious sense" as a universal a priori and in the United States with Alexis de Tocqueville's eyes, as a sort of Promised Land of subsidiarity (cf. Tocqueville, 1835–1840; Antonini, 2005, p. 64).[23] However, it should not be forgotten that the CdO's development outside Italy has had unequal outcomes: on the one hand, it was successful in Latin America as well as in Spain and Poland, and on the other hand the attempt to establish the *Compagnia* in Germany (a country at least partially Catholic but culturally, politically and economically quite different from Latin or Polish "culture Catholicisms") is still unsuccessful.

The CST, as it developed over the past 30 years, is certainly a great ally of the CdO and its effort to create a "Third Way." Nevertheless, even the RCC's social doctrine runs a risk with its nearly unconditional support, in that it refuses to acknowledge its own character as a "work site" (cf. Pont. Counc. for Justice a. Peace, 2005, No. 86) and put "technical solutions" before the "witness to faith" (cf. Benedict XVI, 2009, No. 9, 15), by revealing itself as a more and more intransigent antagonist of the Western World, so that the tension between the economic and the religious sphere is apparently far from being resolved, at least in this case.

## NOTES

1. For texts of the two documents, see http://www.ewtn.com/library/ENCYC/P9QUANTA.HTM (*Quanta cura*) and http://www.ewtn.com/library/PAPALDOC/P9SYLL.HTM (*Syllabus errorum*).
2. The text of this encyclical can be found at http://www.vatican.va/holy_father/leo_xiii/encyclicals/documents/hf_l-xiii_enc_15051891_rerum-novarum_en.html
3. The SP is treated in particular in No. 79: "Just as it is gravely wrong to take from individuals what they can accomplish by their own initiative and industry and give it to the community, so also it is an injustice and at the same time a grave evil and disturbance of right order to assign to a greater and higher association what lesser and subordinate organizations can do. For every social activity ought of its very nature to furnish help to the members of the body social, and never destroy and absorb them."
4. The Apostolic Constitution with which Pope John XXIII opened the Second Vatican Council (text unavailable in English): http://www.vatican.va/holy_father/john_xxiii/apost_constitutions/1961/index.htm).
5. Text of the Dogmatic Constitution: http://www.vatican.va/archive/hist_councils/ii_vatican_council/documents/vat-ii_cons_19651207_gaudium-et-spes_en.html
6. Text of the encyclical: http://www.vatican.va/holy_father/john_xxiii/encyclicals/documents/hf_j-xxiii_enc_11041963_pacem_en.html
7. Cf. the English edition: *Catechism of the Catholic Church*, Città del Vaticano: Libreria Editrice Vaticana, 2000: http://www.vatican.va/archive/ENG0015/_INDEX.HTM
8. To give an example, *Caritas in veritate* explicitly cites even the so-called "fiscal subsidiarity" (cf. Benedict XVI, 2009, No. 60; see later in this chapter). Thus, George Weigel, John Paul II's biographer and conservative exponent of North American Catholic intelligentsia, is perhaps not completely wrong when he observes that there is a certain dualism within Benedict XVI's last encyclical – due, according to him, to the interference of the Pontifical Council for Justice and Peace – between Ratzinger's typical thought features and a more "sociologistic" and practice-oriented tendency by the Curia (cf. Weigel, 2009); indeed, it would mean an unsolved and perhaps unsolvable situation.
9. For more, see http://www.cdo.it/Home/CDO/tabid/140/Default.aspx
10. For more, see http://www.cdo.it/Home/CDO/IlPresidente/tabid/988/Default.aspx
11. For more, see http://www.cdo.it/Home/CDO/Inostrisoci/tabid/374/Default.aspx; http://www.cdo.it/Home/CDO/Dovesiamo/DovesiamoinItalia/tabid/392/Default.aspx

12. Aside from Italy, CdO is present in Argentina, Brazil, Bulgaria, Chile, France, Israel, Kenya, Paraguay, Peru, Poland, San Marino, Spain, Switzerland, Hungary, and Venezuela (cf. http://www.cdo.it/Home/CDO/DovesiamonelMondo/tabid/397/Default.aspx).

13. Examples are the *Centri di Solidarietà* ("Solidarity Centres"), established to assist the job market; the *Federazione Italiana delle Opere Educative* ("Italian Educational Works Federation"), intended for Catholic schools (250 member schools with about 40,000 students); the *Fondazione Banco Alimentare*, the main Italian Food Bank; *AVSI*, a Non-governmental Organization dedicated to Third World development and present in 32 countries; the *Banco Farmaceutico* ("Pharmaceutical Bank"), occupied with collecting and distributing drugs to people in need; or *Famiglie per l'Accoglienza* ("Reception Families"), that provides hospitality services to minors and adults. Cf. Ass. Compagnia delle Opere, 2008, p. 15.

14. For more, see http://www.cdo.it/Default.aspx?alias=www.cdo.it/serviziecon venzioni

15. See Rondoni (Ed.), 2000, and the texts of Don Giussani's (the *PerCorso* trilogy, Giussani, 2003b (first volume), 2003a (second volume), 2003c (third volume)).

16. Public bodies provide needy citizens with finance resources of various types, disguised as coupons or vouchers, repayments or tax allowances, after establishing a "quality accreditation," that is, evaluation and selection of services that providers scientifically carry out (cf. Vittadini, 2002a, pp. XXIII–XXIV). Fiscal subsidiarity is a SP taxation-based application, according to which tax receipts are partially redistributed on the basis of criteria directly and autonomously chosen by the taxpayers (cf. Antonini, 2005, pp. 19–22; Vittadini, 2002a, p. XXI).

17. In 2009, *Forza Italia* merged with other conservative parties and created the *Popolo delle Libertà* ("Freedoms' People"). On the "Lombardy pattern," see Nanini, 2010, pp. 332–335.

18. Rodney Stark sets capitalism at the end of a Western World evolution, based, according to him, on the "victory of reason," essentially occurring in four stages. He writes: "The rise of the West was based on four primary victories of reason. The first was the development of faith in progress within Christian theology. The second victory was the way that faith in progress translated into technical and organizational innovations, many of them fostered by monastic estates. The third was that, thanks to Christian theology, reason informed both political philosophy and practice to the extent that responsive states, sustaining a substantial degree of personal freedom, appeared in medieval Europe. The final victory involved the application of reason to commerce, resulting in the development of capitalism within the safe havens provided by responsive states. These were the victories by which the West won" (p. xiii).

19. Probably the most authoritative Italian expert on CST, Stefano Zamagni (University of Bologna), said: "[…] This is a very innovative encyclical, because it not only makes a reading of the signs of the times, but takes a step forward: it shows which are the ways to go for solving the problems. The encyclicals *Rerum novarum* and *Centesimus annus* stayed on the defensive: the Church expressed perplexities and doubts and invited men of good will to correct system's errors. But in my opinion

this encyclical has a more propositional character" (Il sussidiario, 2009a). Also see the interview with the new Archbishop of Milan, Card. Angelo Scola, Don Giussani's eminent disciple (Il sussidiario, 2009a).

20. In an interesting article in the Pontifical Institute for Foreign Missions' web page, Gerolamo Fazzini (cf. Fazzini, 2009) points out, among other things, the encyclical's explicit reference (cf. Benedict XVI, 2009, No. 34) to the so-called "economy of communion" of the Focolare Movement, a project of entrepreneurs, workers, managers, consumers and financial operators in Brazil, "with the aim of building and showing a human society where, following the example of the first Christian community in Jerusalem, 'no one among them was in need'" (cf. http://www.edc-online.org/index.php/en.html. Retrieved on August 12, 2009).

21. This is manifested in the press releases of CL and the CdO about *Caritas in veritate*, indeed quite proud: cf. Ass. Compagnia delle Opere, 2009 and Comunione e Liberazione, 2009. Vittadini means regarding this: "In Italy there is already a market very closed to that intended by the encyclical. With SMEs, artisan cooperative firms [...] and CdO, we have here an economy that both accepts market and has an ideal goal" (Vecchi, 2009).

22. Here, Zamagni says that the "true centre" of *Caritas in veritate* as CST's summa are "the criticism as well as the invite to overcome dichotomy between the economical and the social sphere, a dichotomy that characterized the two ideological systems prevailing in 19th century: Anarcho-liberalism and Socialism. For both of them, the economical dimension, either rejected or accepted, was the 'bad' sphere, consisting in profit maximization to the detriment of the rights of the others. On the opposite, there was the social dimension, as the field of those people who tried to offset the sick and perverse happening in the economical dimension".

23. On CL's diffusion in the United States, see Allen, 2005. In the United States, the CL's point of reference is Lorenzo Albacete, priest, journalist, and professor of theology at St. Joseph's Seminary in New York.

## REFERENCES

Abbruzzese, S. (1991). *Comunione e Liberazione. Identità religiosa e disincanto laico.* Roma-Bari: Laterza.

Acerbi, A. (1987). Risposta polemica alla laicizzazione del paese. *Il Regno – Attualità, 32*(565), 43–49.

Allen Jr., J. L. (2005). *Report from Rimini: Italy's biggest public event; What Comunione e Liberazione is; CL in the USA; Spreading the movement; Cardinal Simonis of Holland; A report from Kenya; Women and Islam.* Retrieved from http://www.nationalcatholicreporter.org/word/pfw082605.htm#TopOfPage. Accessed on August 31, 2009.

Antonini, L. (2005). *Sussidiarietà fiscale. La frontiera della democrazia.* Milano: Guerini e Associati.

Associazione *Compagnia delle Opere*. (2003). *An ideal principle, an operative friendship.* Advertising brochure.

Associazione *Compagnia delle Opere*. (2008). *Presentation.* Information brochure.

Associazione *Compagnia delle Opere*. (2009). *Enciclica "Caritas in veritate", bussola preziosa per le sfide dello sviluppo*. Retrieved from http://www.cdo.it/Home/ScholzsuCaritasin Veritate/tabid/2240/Default.aspx. Accessed on July 14, 2009.

Banca Europa. (2001). Oltre il profitto: un nuovo modo di "fare impresa". Interview with G. Vittadini & S. Bicocchi. *Banca Europa*, June 17, 88–93.

Barbacetto, G. (2000). Regione corrotta, nazione infetta. *Diario della settimana*, *5*(45), 36–40.

Barbacetto, G. (2001). Milano da bere, atto secondo. Mircomega, *No. 1*. Retrieved from http://www.societacivile.it/primopiano/articoli_pp/pp_2.html. Accessed on August 11, 2009.

Benedict XVI, Pope. (2005). *Deus caritas est*. Encyclical Letter. Retrieved from http://www.vatican.va/holy_father/benedict_xvi/encyclicals/documents/hf_ben-xvi_enc_20051225_deus-caritas-est_en.html. Accessed on June 29, 2011.

Benedict XVI, Pope. (2009). *Caritas in veritate*. Encyclical Letter. Retrieved from http://www.vatican.va/holy_father/benedict_xvi/encyclicals/documents/hf_ben-xvi_enc_20090629_caritas-in-veritate_en.html. Accessed on June 29, 2011.

Bogliari, F. (2006). Il futuro è il sarto di Cernobbio. Interview with R. Vignali. *Business People*, November, 44–48.

Comunione e Liberazione. (2009). *Il comunicato stampa di Comunione e Liberazione sulla "Caritas in veritate"*. Retrieved from http://www.ilsussidiario.net/articolo.aspx?articolo=30092. Accessed on July 14, 2009.

Da Rold, G. (2001). "Centrosinistra dispotico: noi votiamo per il Polo". I Interview with G. Vittadini. *Il Giornale*, May 11, 5.

Falsitta, V. E., Turco, L., Vittadini, G., Maroni, R., Gualaccini, G. P. (2001). Si scrive non profit, si legge libertà: dal Welfare State alla Welfare Society. Public event occurred at the Meeting per l'Amicizia tra i Popoli di Rimini. In A. Ballarino, N. Celora, F. Bosi, & E. Gaddoni (Eds.), *Sopra il G8: opere alla prova*. Incontri del ciclo: *Compagnia delle Opere*. La prima questione morale è l'educazione. Il Libro del Meeting 2001. Tutta la vita chiede l'eternità (pp. 161–170). Castel Bolognese: Itaca.

Farina, R. (2001). Noi fatturiamo, poi ci pensano gli angeli. Interview with G. Vittadini. *Libero*, August 24.

Fazzini, G. (2009). *"Caritas in veritate", i bersagli nascosti*. Retrieved from http://www.missionline.org/index.php?l=it&art=1432. Accessed on July 17, 2009.

Giussani, L. (2003a). *All'origine della pretesa cristiana. Volume secondo del PerCorso*. Milano: Rizzoli (sixth edition) (First edition Milano: Jaca Book, 1988). [English translation: *At the Origin of the Christian Claim*. Montreal: McGill-Queen's University Press, 1998].

Giussani, L. (2003b). *Il senso religioso. Volume primo del PerCorso*. Milano: Rizzoli (third edition) (First edition Milano: Jaca Book, 1966). [English translation: *The Religious Sense*. Montreal: McGill-Queen's University Press, 1997].

Giussani, L. (2003c). *Perché la Chiesa. Volume terzo del PerCorso*. Milano: Rizzoli (second edition) (First edition Milano: Jaca Book, 1990–1992). [English translation: *Why the Church?* Montreal: McGill-Queen's University Press, 2001].

Il sussidiario. (2009a). *Scola: la testimonianza di Cristo, al cuore dello sviluppo*. Interview with A. Scola. Retrieved from http://www.ilsussidiario.net/articolo.aspx?articolo=30232. Accessed on July 16, 2009.

Il sussidiario. (2009b). *Zamagni: diciotto anni dopo la Chiesa non gioca in difesa ma va all'attacco*. Interview with S. Zamagni. Retrieved from http://www.ilsussidiario.net/articolo.aspx?articolo=30039. Accessed on July 15, 2009.

John XXIII, Pope. (1961). *Mater et magistra*. Encyclical Letter. Retrieved from http://www.vatican.va/holy_father/john_xxiii/encyclicals/documents/hf_j-xxiii_enc_15051961_mater_en.html. Accessed on June 29, 2011.

John Paul II, Pope. (1980). Avviciniamo l'uomo nella cultura. A un gruppo di giovani di Comunione e Liberazione. *La traccia* (1), 65.

John Paul II, Pope. (1987). *Sollicitudo rei socialis*. Encyclical letter. Retrieved from http://www.vatican.va/holy_father/john_paul_ii/encyclicals/documents/hf_jp-ii_enc_30121987_sollicitudo-rei-socialis_en.html. Accessed on June 29, 2011.

John Paul II, Pope. (1991). *Centesimus annus*. Encyclical letter. Retrieved from http://www.vatican.va/holy_father/john_paul_ii/encyclicals/documents/hf_jp-ii_enc_01051991_centesimus-annus_en.html. June 29, 2011.

Marinetti, M. (2003). Il paradiso degli affari. *Panorama – Economy*, (20), 14–22.

Meeting per l'Amicizia fra i Popoli di Rimini. (2002). *Libertà di creare. Workshop sulla Welfare Society*. Public event occurred on 22nd August at the Meeting per l'Amicizia fra i Popoli di Rimini. Retrieved from http://www.meetingrimini.org/detail.asp?c=1&p=6&id=1753&key=3&pfix=. Accessed on August 11, 2009.

Menozzi, D. (2000). *I Papi del '900*. Firenze: Giunti-Casterman.

Nanini, R. (2004). Subsidiaritätsprinzip: der diskrete Charme der katholischen Soziallehre. *Jahrbuch der Stipendiatinnen & Stipendiaten der Friedrich-Naumann-Stiftung*, *5*, 81–88.

Nanini, R. (2010). *An Werke glauben. Theologie, Politik und Wirtschaft bei der Compagnia delle Opere*. "Forum Religion und Sozialkultur – Abteilung A: Religions- und Kirchensoziologische Texte" 21. Berlin-Münster-Wien-Zürich-London: LIT-Verlag.

Paul VI, Pope. (1971). *Octogesima adveniens*. Apostolic letter. Retrieved from http://www.vatican.va/holy_father/paul_vi/apost_letters/documents/hf_p-vi_apl_19710514_octogesima-adveniens_en.html. Accessed on June 29, 2011.

Pinotti, F., & Viafora, G. (2010). *La lobby di Dio*. Fede, affari e politica. La prima inchiesta su Comunione e Liberazione e la Compagnia delle Opere. "Principio attivo – Inchieste e reportage". Milano: Chiarelettere.

Pius IX, Pope. (1931). *Quadragesimo anno*. Encyclical letter. Retrieved from http://www.vatican.va/holy_father/pius_xi/encyclicals/documents/hf_p-xi_enc_19310515_quadragesimo-anno_en.html. Accessed on June 29, 2011.

Pontifical Council for Justice and Peace (Ed.) (2005). *Compendium of the Social Doctrine of the Church*. Città del Vaticano: Libreria Editrice Vaticana. Retrieved from http://www.vatican.va/roman_curia/pontifical_councils/justpeace/documents/rc_pc_justpeace_doc_20060526_compendio-dott-soc_en.html. Accessed on June 29, 2011.

Poulat, É. (1986). *L'Église, c'est un monde. L'Ecclésiosphère*. Paris: Les Éditions du Cerf.

Prandi, A. (1981). Genesi ed evoluzione dell'insegnamento sociale della Chiesa. In: F. Traniello & G. Campanini (Eds.), *Dizionario storico del Movimento Cattolico in Italia 1860–1980. I/1. I fatti e le idee* (pp. 180–195). Torino: Marietti.

Quadrio Curzio, A., & Fortis, M. (2005). L'economia italiana tra sviluppo, declino, innovazione. In: F. per la Sussidiarietà (Ed.), *Un "io" per lo sviluppo* (pp. 73–142). Milano: Rizzoli.

Rondoni, D. (Ed.) (2000). *Communion and liberation. A movement in the church*. Montreal: McGill-Queen's University Press.

Stark, R. (2005). *The victory of reason. How Christianity led to freedom, capitalism, and western success*. New York, NY: Random House.

Tocqueville, A. de. (1835–1840). *De la démocratie en Amérique*. Otley: Paris.

Vecchi, G. G. (2009). *Vittadini: dagli artigiani alle coop, l'Italia vicina all'enciclica*. Interview with G. Vittadini. Originally *Corriere della sera*, July 9. Retrieved from http://www.ilsussidiario.net/articolo.aspx?articolo=30234. Accessed on July 14, 2009.

Vignali, R. (2006a). *Eppur si muove. Innovazione e piccola impresa*. Milano: Guerini e Associati.

Vignali, R. (2006b). Quanti Bill Gates "abbiamo ucciso" senza saperlo? *Il Riformista*, October 2, 6.

Vittadini, G. (1994). Pari dignità al non profit. *Corriere delle opere*, *9*(10), 5. *Originally Il Sole* 24 Ore, November 20.

Vittadini, G. (1998). Sussidiarietà? Sì, grazie. *Tracce – Litterae Communionis*, *25*(6), 56–59.

Vittadini, G. (2000a). Le politiche regionali e la sussidiarietà. *Non Profit*, February, pp. 187–197.

Vittadini, G. (2000b). A ognuno il suo mestiere. *Tracce – Litterae Communionis*, *27*(7), 44–45.

Vittadini, G. (2001a). Sussidiarietà: una tradizione che è modernità. *Non Profit*, March, pp. 297–307.

Vittadini, G. (2001b). *Vallombrosa 2001*. Retrieved from http://www.acli.it/modules/interventi/allegati/154.gabaglio2.doc?POSTNUKESID=iqxguqty. Accessed on August 11, 2009.

Vittadini, G. (2002a). Introduzione. In: Vittadini, G. (Ed.), *Liberi di scegliere. Dal welfare state alla welfare society*. Milano: ETAS, XII-LV.

Vittadini, G. (2002b). Lo statalismo duro a morire. *Il Sole 24 Ore*, April 14, p. 6.

Vittadini, G. (2002c). "Welfare Mix": Stato e privati "concorrono" per erogare servizi di pubblica utilità. *Terzo Settore* (Supplement to *Il Sole 24 Ore*), 1st February, VII.

Vittadini, G. (2003a). Desiderio, opere, politica. Oltre i blocchi. *Tracce – Litterae Communionis*, *30*(6), 35.

Vittadini, G. (2003b). Una guerra da vincere con la fede. *Il Giornale*, November, 18, 5.

Vittadini, G., & Sala, F. (2005). Un nuovo "io" per un nuovo sviluppo. In: F. per la Sussidiarietà (Ed.), *Un "io" per lo sviluppo* (pp. 183–255). Milano: Rizzoli.

Weigel, G. (2009). *Caritas in veritate in Gold and Red*. The revenge of justice and peace (or so they may think). Retrieved from http://article.nationalreview.com/?q=NTdkYjU3MDE2YTdhZTE4NWIyN2FkY2U5YTFkM2ZiMmE=. Accessed on July 12, 2009.

Zizola, G. (2003). *L'altro Wojtyła. Riforma, restaurazione e sfide del Millennio*. Milano: Sperling & Kupfer.

# THE ECONOMY OF THE HOST IN THE MONASTIC WORLD: A NON-ECONOMIC ECONOMY

Isabelle Jonveaux

## ABSTRACT

*Although the host, the future body of Christ in the Catholic Eucharist, seems to lie completely outside of the economic system, it needs to be produced and sold. The majority of host producers are female monasteries for which the production process brings double tension: as an economic activity within a religious utopia (the monastery) and as the economization of something that is considered to be a religious good. This double tension provokes the question, how do the nuns legitimate this economic process in their monastery without desacralizing the symbolic good? Trying to answer this question, nuns typically deny the economic dimension of production and transaction, yet the sheer existence of this economy proves it is accepted. This chapter examines the relationship between economy and religion through an analysis of the ambivalence in the production and marketing process of altar bread.*

'Around 1220, a French monk, Geoffroy de Vendôme, compared the consecrated host to a perfectly minted coin: the round shape of the host, Geoffroy observed, reminds us of the shape of the coin in exactly the same

**The Economics of Religion: Anthropological Approaches**
**Research in Economic Anthropology, Volume 31, 77–97**

**ISSN: 0190-1281/doi:10.1108/S0190-1281(2011)0000031007**

way as the capacity of the host to be the equivalent of salvation reminds us that the coin represents a value' (Todeschini, 2008, p. 15).

The host is the highest symbolic good in the Christian religion, especially for Roman Catholics. The Eucharistic ritual in Catholicism has as its goal the transformation of a piece of unleavened bread into the real body of Christ. But this religious good is also produced, sold and consumed. Though it may seem blasphemous for the religious world to set up an economy around the 'future body of Christ', there is a specific market for it. In many countries, the manufacturers of the host are mainly monastic. In the case of France – the focus of this chapter – there is only one lay producer in the market. Aside from this one, there are about 40 female monastic communities producing and selling ceremonial unleavened bread.

The economy of the host has to be placed in the perspective of the tensions present in the monastery, between religious life and economic activity. Because of its religious significance, the production of hosts can seem to be a compromise between the need for revenue and the desire to maintain a pious life. However, this eminently religious product leaves the cloister to be commercialized and enters a market, governed by religious imperatives. The question arises of how the production and the marketing of this symbolic good should be organized without any form of transaction. Of all the monastic products, the host is the one with the highest religious stakes within the classical economic pattern. The production of hosts brings about double tension: first as an economic activity in the religious utopia, and second as the economization of a religious good. This second tension concerns the majority of monastic products, such as foodstuffs. Studying this market reveals, as if looking through a magnifying glass, the internal mechanisms of the monastic economy. To begin, it must be stressed that this product is made only by female communities. There is an implicit separation of the work between those who make liturgical objects and hosts (women) and those who perform the rituals they are made for (men). This research takes place in a larger sociological research on the monastic economy and is based on field inquiries in a Carmel in France where I conducted interviews with the nuns who are responsible for the host production (2008).

## ECONOMICS AND RELIGION: UNION OR REJECTION

The relationship between economics and religion lies at the background of this chapter. This question, which was at the forefront of the ideas of the founders of sociology, has only rarely been re-examined since then. According to Max Weber, the relationship between salvation religion and rational economics is necessarily antagonistic because economics, through its development, comes into conflict with religious values. On the contrary, he leads us to believe that primitive economy before its rationalization, which dispelled its charm, was not hostile to religion. This means that a certain type of economy could coexist with the religious system, and that it is not the essence of religion and of economy which make them mutually antagonistic. So it is possible to set up an economy which is not antagonistic to religion.

It is possible to investigate the relationship between religion and economics, thanks to the typology of P.J. Welch. For him, economics and religion can interact according to four models: the first is 'economics separate from religion' (Welch & Mueller, 2001, p. 187), when economics is unrelated to religion because of a certain hostility between them. The second one is 'economics in service of religion' – a situation in which 'appeals to religious beliefs or arguments are made to attain economic objectives' (*ibid.*, p. 193). Then, we have 'religion in service of economics', which includes 'situation(s) where appeals to religious beliefs or arguments are made to attain economic objectives' (*ibid.*, p. 193). And finally, there is 'religion and economics in union (...) where religion and economics, rather than being held apart or on in service of the other, work together' (*ibid.*, p. 195). Thanks to this exhaustive typology, we will be able to examine here the kind of relationship which develops between economics and religion in special areas, which is theoretically complete and only religious. So the economy of the host will be a useful example of these relationships, and I will take into account the economic activity in the religious sphere and the economization of a specific religious good.

## *Economics and Monastic Life*

The market of the host occurs in the particular context of monastic life, which is known for its reticence to hold economics. The monastery is above all a religious institution, which in theory should not accept an economy within itself. According to J. Séguy, the monastery is a utopia of the Kingdom of God here already present and yet to come. 'A utopia is a complete ideological system aiming to radically transform the existing global system implicitly or explicitly, by appealing to imaginary (written utopia) or by applying it in practice (practical utopia)' (Séguy, 1971, p. 331).

The monastery is thus a complete system centred on religion and on the preparation for the coming of the Kingdom of God. The architecture of the monastery is an anticipation of this Kingdom.

Work and economy, peculiar to time on Earth, will be absent from Paradise. Nevertheless, the monks, still bound by earthly conditions, must provide for their own needs, and consequently have to work.[1] But these economic activities have to be justified by the monks, so that the coherence of the perfect system of utopia is not challenged. The presence of an economy puts the balance of monastic life at risk because it reintroduces into the monastery what the monks had wanted to abandon by leaving the world. As Weber says, 'in fact, the whole history of monasticism is in a certain sense, the history of a continual struggle with the problem of the secularizing influence of wealth' (2003, p. 174). This antagonism, intrinsic to the nature of utopia, appeared at the very beginning of monastic life and has never been completely allayed. Work has never been taken for granted in monastic life and has always been the object of constant justifications.

## THE HOST: PERFECT INTEGRATION OF ECONOMY IN THE RELIGIOUS UTOPIA?

The justification of work and economy gives rise to various strategies because of the need for reorganization. One of these consists of giving religious signification to the economy, which in this case will no longer be opposed to religion. As Peter Berger observed, 'the fundamental "recipe" of religious legitimation is the transformation of human products into supra or non-human facticities. The humanly made world is explained in terms that deny its human production. The human nomos becomes a divine cosmos' (1969, p. 89). Artistic work, for instance, can be seen as a continuation of divine creation. But the most elevated religious concept a monk can give to work is surely a work which is specifically religious, for instance the production of hosts.

### *Perfect Conditions for Monastic Work*

Making hosts seems, at first, to be the answer to the specific requirements of monastic life. For monks this represents revenues, manual involvement and is useful in the struggle against idleness. This activity could be mechanized, but the nuns choose to keep part of the process manual so as to maintain manual work as a physical balance to prayer. On a website for host-making machines we find some machines that are entirely mechanized and others that need the intervention of the human hand. The latter are specifically intended for the monastic world. At the same time, this work is in itself a religious activity which participates in the principal Christian ritual: it produces nothing less than the body of Christ, which is at the centre of every nun's life.

This production is special because it remains, for the most part, in the strictly religious sphere and so the closed wall of the utopia is not breached. Even the selling of the host is within a religious framework – the nuns making contact with priests or lay parishioners. Only the suppliers of the flour – the raw material – do not belong to this sphere. The commercialization does not require any travelling or any lifting of the rule of enclosure. The enclosure indeed 'protects the utopian society both against external corruption and against the threat of outsiders' (Boudon, 1986, p. 632). To open it for economic reasons would introduce potentially subversive elements in the Kingdom yet to come. The clients come and fetch the bags of hosts at the monastery door where the extern sister[2] meets them. When the monastery does not have an extern sister, a nun or a lay person does the task. The nuns have repositories in the parish and sometimes in individual shops for the customers who do not come to the monastery. And this allows them to avoid having an open commerce. The religious network is then reinvented for commercial transactions and furthermore as the object is standardized, there are no options except for the size and the two sorts of host (white or wholewheat). Customers do not need to see the product before buying it, which further reduces the necessity for communication with the producer.

> It's a work one dreams of because we do not have to leave the monastery. The advantage with hosts is that we can do everything ourselves ... The customers order either by telephone or by fax – not yet by email, but perhaps it will happen one day. As for us, we send parcels out, we have sisters at the reception, we have places where people can buy the hosts – so, there is no need to leave the enclosure. (a bursar sister in a Carmelite monastery)

This economy is therefore truly an enclosed economy which remains completely within the religious sphere. Even the market is closed because everyone is not entitled to buy this product. The monasteries which make the hosts are the ones with the strictest rules of enclosure (see Table 1).

The female communities producing the most hosts are those with the strictest enclosure: Benedictines, Carmelites and Dominicans. Choosing to

***Table 1.*** Female Communities Producing Religious Articles in France. (31.30% of the Benedictine Female Communities Product Religious Articles for the Clergy*).

Percentage of Female Communities Producing Religious Objects (France)

| | Benedictines | Cistercians | Trappists | Carmelites | Dominicans | St. Clare | Visitandines | Chartreuse |
|---|---|---|---|---|---|---|---|---|
| Religious articles for clergy | 31.30 | 18.20 | 10 | 44.70 | 30.80 | 48.90 | 15.80 | 0 |
| Religious articles for lay people | 31.30 | 9.10 | 20 | 31.80 | 46.20 | 31.90 | 15.80 | 50 |
| Total | 62.60 | 27.30 | 30 | 76.50 | 77.00 | 80.80 | 31.60 | 50 |

*In the case of the Chartreuse nuns, the number of cases (only two) is not significant enough to draw a conclusion.

work in this sector is therefore subject to the constraints imposed by the enclosure and by the desire to work in a branch where leaving the monastery is not a necessity. This activity proves that work is accepted, but it also shows the refusal to accept economy and its commercialization and communication – these two aspects being replaced by the monastic values of silence and stability.

## *Work or Religious Mission?*

The production of 'altar bread' is especially adapted to the rule. The various stages of production can be divided into units of activity which can each be done in solitude, as prescribed by the Carmelite rule. But above all, the object produced opens directly onto spiritual meditation, integrating prayer into the act of work. As a bursar nun said, 'it is bound up to a sacrament – this is why it has a meaning'. This kind of work could be linked to what popular theology as 'the highest form of monastic "productivity" was to be found in the increase of the thesaurus ecclesiae [the church's spiritual treasures] through prayer and choir service' (Weber, 2009, p. 143). In this case, it could be seen as a religious work, in the same way as prayer, the offices and the sacraments. Praying during work is even considered to be necessary, given the final purpose of the production: 'It really is a product intended for the celebration of Eucharist. It presupposes a spiritual attitude at the same time', said a nun. This activity is a 'mission', a 'service' and a link in the chain of the Eucharistic ritual. Much more than just work, it can therefore be seen as the archetype of work considered as an ecclesial mission.

As a bursar sister of the Carmel monastery quoted above stated: 'It is not work necessary to sustain life – it is more a mission for the community', and also, 'it is truly work for the Church'. As this particular nun has a degree from an important business school, she understands the economic usefulness of work perfectly well, but gives preference to the religious mission over the question of resources. Nevertheless, she recognizes that it is because the nuns needed an activity in order to subsist that they have taken over this work from another Carmel monastery that closed. In this way, it has been integrated into a perfect system of religious legitimization and has become an ecclesial mission which is not only useful but also essential for the faithful.

This activity seems to reconcile the contradiction between work and monastic life. But for this activity to fit into a perfect monastic life, it would have to be utopian in itself, by announcing, as the rest of the monastic life does, the coming of the Kingdom of God, without the need for any further justification. The production of hosts satisfies this function by contributing to the fulfilment of the Christian ritual. Yet, if the instruments used in the cult, especially the host, help to render God's presence on Earth through the sacrament of the Eucharist, it also implies that the utopian rule has not yet been established. If this were the case, there would be no need to render God's presence, through this material medium. Making Him present emphasized its absence.

Admittedly, taking part in this ritual hastens, in a certain manner, the advent of the Kingdom of God not by bringing us nearer to the end of time, which is something monks can have no influence over, but by bringing into being a tiny parcel of the Kingdom of God during the mass. The production of hosts is an activity which has a perfect religious justification that leads to the elimination of the economic aspect by transforming it into a service. As it remains in the religious sphere, however, it does not further the dissemination of the utopian idea outside the monastery in the way the other products such as foodstuffs and cosmetics do.

## PRODUCTION OF A SYMBOLIC GOOD

### *A Risk of Desacralization?*

By introducing the host into a process of production and commercialization, what should be purely religious is transferred to the economic sphere. Are we not taking away the sacred aura of the 'future body of Christ' by submitting it to purchase and the profane setting of a price (a monetary value)? The sacred value of the host can disappear for the nuns themselves when they become aware of these decisions. A nun in a convent shop in Paris dealing in monastic wares said, 'people think that the sister is thinking about Jesus but in fact she is thinking about the budget'. Thus, whereas the act of consecration of an object is extracted from its ordinary environment, by turning it into a *res sacra*, the economization produces an opposite effect which reintroduces it into everyday life. If what is sacred belongs to the order of the extraordinary, then 'what occurs daily is above all where the economy takes place' (Colliot-Thélène, 1995, p. 75). The nuns try to avoid the risk by weaving a religious envelope around the production in a complete fusion of work and prayer. But what can be done during the production of the host is not as easy to do during commercialization.

### *Process of the Consecration of the Symbolic Good*

The process of the consecration of production begins, in a certain way, from the moment when the raw material enters the monastery. Made by the nuns, the host will not have the same value if it has come from a lay manufacturer. Symbolically and not religiously, 'the operation of production' is the equivalent of a 'symbolic act of transubstantiation, not reducible to a material transformation' (Bourdieu, 1974, p. 21). The term 'transubstantiation' is daring for a product of this sort, but the ultimate transubstantiation for which it is intended begins from the moment of production in the silence and solitude of the cloister. In response to the demand of work in solitude, each valuated unit is divided so as to correspond to a particular workshop. The mixing of the dough, the baking, the moistening and the cutting up into circles, each takes place in a different room. Manufactured in prayer, the host acquires little by little its unique nature, which will culminate in the ritual of the transubstantiation. The sisters insist on the fact they call it 'altar bread' to emphasize that it is not yet the consecrate host. It is still an object and not a person:

> The consecration itself is absent. So it remains just bread or … .Even if it has the shape of the host, we don't make host – we make altar bread. That is why we have to insist that it is altar bread when we are talking about it to people. It is not a host, you see. It is not easy for people because they know what a host is but not altar bread. So it is true that it is important to speak of altar bread so as to avoid merging the two terms indiscriminately. (Sister Louise, in charge of production of altar bread)

And yet the process of sacralization has already begun as it is shown by the fact that the sisters do not use, or only very rarely, unleavened bread for anything except the Eucharistic ritual:

> Sometimes we give a little to families but I don't really like that and we have to explain what it is to them. But when we have requests from bakers or people like that, we are not comfortable with this. That's not what it is for. It's for Christian worship. (Sister Agathe, bursar at the Carmel monastery)

In addition, the person responsible for the production workshop said:

> For example, we have requests from bakers who make nougat for unleavened bread which they use to line the underside of their product. So we said, 'what are we going to do?' Everyone is free to do as they like, but we wanted to think about it together. And we thought, 'we mustn't mix everything up'. What we do really and truly is work for the Church.

This bread, made in prayer, to become the body of Christ, though not yet consecrated according to canonical ritual, cannot be used for any other purpose, or only exceptionally. It is already an object, set apart for implicit consecration. The intention of the nuns to keep the two conceptions separate is underlined by this sort of informal consecration, applied to the altar bread. Although the host has not yet been consecrated by the ritual, the nuns have removed it from the group of normal products which can be found in usual shops. Even though there is no ritual consecration, it amounts to an implicit consecration.

### *Religious Identity of the Producer*

The identity of the producer is not a neutral factor in the process of sacralization. The symbolical dimension of the good is all the more important if the producer himself is consecrated to God. 'It is by creating a scarcity among the producers that the field of symbolic production induces the rarity of the product: the magical power of the "creator", which comes with the position of authority is a capital of authority which can only act if it is set in motion by an authorized person or better, if it is identified with a person or his charisma and guaranteed by a signature' (Bourdieu, 1974, p. 21). The nuns making the hosts are indeed rare in the sense that the scarcity of vocations is diminishing their number and also because their life, cut off as it is from the world, has made them practically invisible in society – the more so, as these orders maintain strict rules of enclosure. As a consequence, the host contains within itself the secret identity of the producer. For the buyer too, the monastic host will have an added value which can be interpreted in different fashions. As a nun said, 'it is important to maintain a bond between the manufacturer of the product and the people concerned'. As Marcel Mauss stated, during the transaction, there remains in the object something of the person who made it. 'The obligation attached to a gift itself is not inert. Even when abandoned by the giver, it still forms a part of him' (Mauss, 1970, p. 9) and this value is even greater when the identity of the producer has links with the function of the object – both being religious in the present case.

The choice of buying from nuns also reveals a desire to help religious communities. Thus, the struggle of the nuns against lay competition is less due to a religious feeling than by a necessity of earning a livelihood. 'It is vital work' – they explain – 'competition must on no account place monasteries in financial difficulties'. But from the religious point of view, is it really necessary that the host should come from a religious environment? If we examine the religious sense of the rite of the Eucharist, this presacralization does not seem in anyway necessary. The rite of the Eucharist is, in effect, an offering, so a gift from the profane world brought by lay people to the divinity. For the ritual offering, 'it always presupposes that the worshiper gives some of his substance or of his goods to his gods' (Durkheim, 1982, p. 344). It is the institutionalization of religious practices and the rationalization of rituals which determine the religious origin of the offerings to ensure the power of the consecrated class and the monopoly of the offerings. The liturgy for the consecration of the Eucharistic speaks about this bread 'which earth has given and human hands have made', assuming a communion between Earth and Heaven by the divine appearance of a divine element. The host made by the nuns is already religious, but this import from within it compensated for by the financial offering of the faithful, which is used indirectly to buy the host.

The path from the producer to the consumer can be summed up thus: the producers through religiously defined work manufacture the symbolic good in a strictly religious sphere. Because it is put on the market, there arise the notions of price and money. The link between the purchaser and the seller is still purely religious since the host is given free during the mass. To be more precise its purchase is financed by the various gifts of the laity to the Church. But the absence of gift does not make it unavailable to the faithful. We can therefore find people who take advantage of the offer without paying. Sandler calls these people 'free riders' (Sandler & Cornes, 1996, p. 30). During the whole process, there is only one step that is truly economic, which is when it is sold. If the nuns want to suppress the economy,

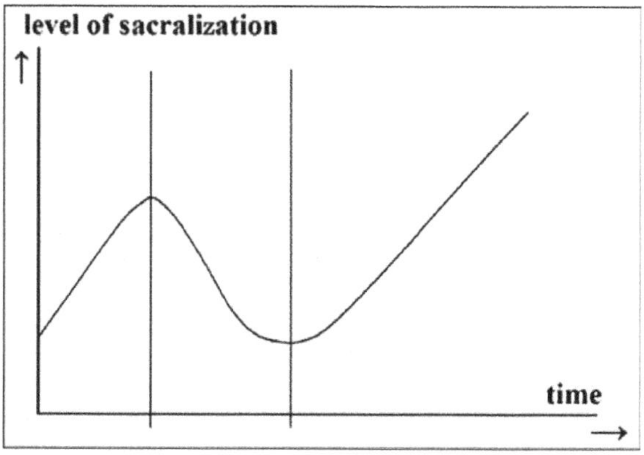


| Production | Commercialization | Transubstantiation |
|---|---|---|
| Prayer | Economy | Ritual |
| Creation | Price | Free access |
| Fraternity | Competition | Communion |
| Nuns | Lay people | Priest |
| RELIGIOUS | ECONOMIC | RELIGIOUS |

*Fig. 1.* Sacralization of the Host from Production to Transubstantiation.

in the whole of the cycle, this step will have to be re-examined. This evolution of the sacralization of this product is shown in Fig. 1.

The central part of the curve in Fig. 1 shows the period of desacralization when the religious object goes through a commercial stage. At this point it loses the symbolical and secret power it had acquired previously. If the nuns wish to attain their ultimate religious goal – but through a religious process only – this is the sector they have to concentrate on, by drawing the curve upwards. The economic transaction would have to be redefined in religious terms on the market itself. But how does the market for the host function?

## THE HOST MARKET: ACCEPTING THE ECONOMY?

Because the host has to be commercialized, a specific market is found round the symbolic good. The nuns, who are the ones offering the product, try to redefine the conditions of this market in order to deny the economic dimension and to guarantee the uniqueness of the symbolic good.

### *Determining Factors of Demand*

The functions that govern the dynamics of supply and demand for this symbolic good are somewhat peculiar compared to the usual concerns of micro-economics. Even if it is subjected to a market, a religious good does not fit all the criteria of the pure and perfect economy.

The demand on the host market is not made up of separate individuals but of a religious organization which purchases the host for larger groups of consumers. None of the latter generally knows anything about the whole economic process preceding the Eucharistic rite. Up to a certain point and in a certain manner, this pattern closely resembles that of free public services which, being financed from taxes, gives the impression of standing outside normal economic circuits. In the case under consideration here, it is a religious service just like confession, for example. In no way does the curve for the demand correspond to the calculations of the consumers who receive the host without paying.

Unlike a normal market, the consumption of the host is in no way influenced by the usual devices of publicity or any other commercial strategy. It strictly depends on religious practices and can only be influenced by religious means. This is why diminishing practice in traditional Christian religion today has a significant effect on the consumption of hosts. The group of host manufacturers in France has seen a fall of 5% in consumption.

### *A Price for the Body of Christ?*

The introduction of variable monetary factors is the element that topples the symbolic good from the religious domain into the economic sphere. It is indeed a contradiction to put a price on the 'future Body of Christ' who, according to Christian liturgy, gives himself freely as a sacrifice during the communion. How can we get around the secularizing force of the price? According to classical theory, demand depends on the price and the revenue of the consumers whereas, in the present case, the absolute necessity of the product for the rite prevents its acquisition depending on the price.

The price is the disturbing element because it reduces what will become the object of divine transubstantiation to something of mere commercial value. The price would be less upsetting if there were no presacralization by the makers as, in this case, it would only set back the beginning of the process of sacralization. In the case of manufacture, which is already religious, it interrupts the sacralization. And yet if we examine this process closely, we notice that the nuns, while making attempts at sacralization, are at the same time applying methods of desacralization to get around the conflict between an object already sacred and the economic market. The distinction they make between altar bread and the host enables them to assert that it is not the body of Christ which is sold under the form of unleavened bread. For how could they possibly sell Christ – to whom they have consecrated their entire lives? The separation, highlighted by the vocabulary, is intended to make a distinction between what still belongs to the commercial order and what is to become purely religious and consequently outside the economic field. The sisters, therefore, tend to set up a barrier between the sacred and the profane, between the terrestrial order and the divine order so as to legitimize what would otherwise be utter profanation. And yet this distinction is not as clean-cut as it seems. From the start, strategies are used for the purpose of sacralization.

How can the price be determined? The demand cannot in fact depend on the price since a low price would not increase the consumption which is held in check by other imperatives. Will the consumer be able to choose the supplier according to the same price? They will not because amongst other things the market price is practically standardized. In fact, a few years ago, the nuns making the hosts did try to decide on a 'fair price':

> It was in the group of producers of altar bread that we tried to work out what the fair selling price should be. It should be fair, we thought, in the sense that we wouldn't lose on it, but that we wouldn't make an excessive profit from it either. Two methods were suggested by two different people. The first was a very classical method of analysis of the cost of production and I was the one who did it here. And then there was a method of added-value which can be interesting. A certain number of monasteries worked it out. The main idea is to examine the production very closely – really closely with great precision … to establish a sort of yardstick by which the production could be measured. The yardstick was worked out by one of the monasteries and then it was used in other monasteries willing to apply the method to the production figures. As for me, I did it one year and I came up with a result close to what I had found with my first result. I used both methods to make sure the price was fair.

This insistence on defining a fair price comes close to wanting to deny there is a price or to overstep the price. To deny the differences in price is almost the same thing as to say that the price itself is not an element in the transaction. Deciding on the fair price by a rational method gives the nuns a clear conscience. Added to which, the price of the raw materials (simply flour and water) unlikely to vary much, will have very little effect on the fixed price on the market. We are here getting close to a situation of oligopoly in which firms agree on the price. In the case of the monasteries, the quasi-uniformity on the market is more the result of the inevitable similarities of the product and of the desire to fix a fair price than a result of any implicit agreement between themselves. The only variations result from different methods of production. Moreover, the insistence of the sisters that this work is a service and a mission means that there is a change in how they perceive the revenues, which are no longer the result of a mercantile act, but are the just reward for a religious service enabling them to live. What is more, it is the Church, through the parishes that buys the hosts and consequently pays the nuns. This payment is not intended to make the nuns rich but to provide for their keep. Money, then, is no longer a means of capitalization. It reassumes its primitive function as an instrument of exchange, which will allow the nuns to buy what is essential. If this is still economics, it is, at any rate, religious economics.

### *From Competition to Mutual Aid*

Competition is one of the basic principles of every market and we shall see how it functions. According to economic theory, pure and perfect competition is made up of an atomicity of economic agents which are represented on the host market by the numerous communities. The homogeneity of the product is perfect as the only possible choice is between white hosts and wholewheat hosts. And this is not a basic difference. Standardization guarantees the conformity of the product since the specifications are fixed by Canon law.[3] Free entry on the market is also guaranteed. In an interview, a sister mentioned the example of a new community in the south of France which had recently entered the market, although another monastic producer was already present in the diocese. It is difficult however to judge the transparency of the market. Though all the producers know each other and are part of the Monastic Association (the group of host manufacturers), there is without a doubt a real lack of information due to the absence of publicity. In spite of this, as we have seen, the price on the market is practically the same everywhere. This market is therefore in a situation of pure but not perfect competition.[4]

But competition is also an important element leading to disenchantment with the economy because it comes into conflict with the values of religion and suppresses the ethic of brotherhood. In this sense competition contributes to the desacralization of the process. The ethic of brotherhood would extend from production to communion, during the mass, if it were not for competition which broaches it (see Fig. 1); hence, the need to redefine competition in religious terms. The religious actors concerned try to transform this competition into mutual aid and more or less explicit collaboration. It is generally accepted implicitly that one of the monasteries has precedence on the market in its diocese. As in the case of oligopoly, a certain sharing of the market can be observed based 'on geographic, territorial or regional differences with each of the producers being, as it were, guaranteed a market' (Abraham-Frois, 1986, p. 254). These agreements are however entirely tacit because contracts of this kind are forbidden by law. According to a nun:

> In fact, we struck a balance quite easily. Each community has a different volume of production. To start with, we work with our region and then when we take on a new client, it is because a producer has closed down. So, in fact, there is not really any competition. Otherwise, we would end up by having monopolies. What is sure is that there is no sharing – we are not allowed to. And production can vary. A community is permanent but it can alter quite quickly. A community which has no vocations will produce less after a certain time. I am talking about quite a sad case of course ... or a community which has lots of vocations could turn out a lot of work. So I give the impression that a sort of balance emerges all by itself.

A sort of 'invisible hand', to borrow Adam Smith's expression, seems to keep the market in balance without the sellers or the purchasers having to agree on anything explicitly. Moreover, this natural equilibrium means that the nuns can transcend the idea of competition which they see as not corresponding to the monastic values of charity and brotherly love. A risk exists that the host might be desacralized by the economic conflict. Thus, a nun said that she 'had no qualms directing a customer to another producer' if she herself does not produce sufficient quantities or if the demand is better satisfied by another producer – for instance, for the size of the host.

In certain ways, the sisters try to surpass the economic imperatives and deny that it is in fact an economy. The following quotation shows this clearly: 'it is for this reason that it is important for us not to do anything else with our bread. We do not sell it to bakeries, because if we did it might be desacralized. That would be business. It really is solely for the Eucharist'. For the sister concerned, the fact that the production is intended for the mass only is enough to avoid the commercial aspect even though the hosts are nevertheless sold. This is at one with the idea, mentioned above, that the income is seen as a reward for service and not as profit from a sale. The integration of the economy necessary for subsistence in the religious utopia is therefore achieved in this case not only by redefining manual work as a religious activity but by disclaiming it is an economy. To surpass the latent conflict between religion and economics, the nuns tend to redefine the seller–buyer relationship. For Max Weber, 'the "silent" trade dramatically represents the contrast between the market community and the fraternal community' (1978, p. 637). And it is thus that economy 'cannot nearly collide with the universal ethics of brotherhood preached by salvation religions' (Tschannen, 1992, p. 131).

The sisters therefore seek to restore the element of universal brotherly love in their transactions, as much with the producers as with the customers to get around the impersonal nature of economics: 'Quite often I leave a note, something to do with liturgy because it is a feast day or else I pass on news of the community. And I think it is important that the people who buy the hosts from us realize there are real people behind the scene'. This sister also thinks it is important that friendly ties be established between the producers of hosts.[5] The reintroduction of the ethics of brotherly love puts a stop to their disenchantment with the economy, which means that even if it does not enable them to deny the existence of the economy, at least they can live a type of economy not in contradiction with religious values. In this way, the transaction assumes a religious dimension once more, and this lessens the desacralization of the product.

### *Negation or Acceptance of the Economy*

The economy of the host is in fact submitted to the double tension of being refused or accepted. Whenever the nuns consent to adapt their offer to the demand, thereby personalizing the object of the transaction, it is to disavow the commercial dimension. In the Carmelite convent I studied, the hosts are generally sold in packs of 10,000 but, as one nun said, 'if a customer asks for 253, they'll get 253' so, therefore, 'it is a service, it is not business'. In much the same way, the sisters are tempted to deny the notion of profitability which is the symbol of outrageous capitalism:

> For a certain number of things, we are helped by a person who used to work for an American firm selling toothpaste. He explained the method used. As for me I quite often disagree with him. I say 'listen, we are not selling cheese!' For instance, there is

> something that really shocked me. The size of the host which is the most profitable to produce is 13 cm. We have to create the need for the customer to buy the 13 cm size. I went to a business school and I know what creating need is. I said to him, 'Listen, I don't agree with you, we are not selling cheese. It is not a product necessary for life, it is more a mission for the community'. If he had said, 'it makes the breaking of the bread easier', I would have accepted that perfectly well. But to say that you must create the need because that way, it is more profitable: No, I would prefer to say that it is more significant for breaking the bread.

This extract taken from an interview demonstrates exactly what Bourdieu had observed concerning the Catholic Church. 'Truth in a religious firm consists in having two truths: the economic truth and the religious truth which denies the first' (Bourdieu, 1994, p. 204). On the one hand, the sister absolutely recognizes the economic dimension and the need to apply rational methods since she herself called on a professional to help her. But on the other hand, she does not admit the validity of his advice based on economic efficiency and not on religious criteria. The only acceptable economy would be the one founded solely on religious criteria. But in another interview she defends the use of the cutting machine capable of punching 50 hosts at a time and minimizing the space lost between circles on the plaque. But the argument she uses for the machine is not its immediate profitability but more that it lessens the labour required from the sisters. As she said, 'making one host at a time would be madness'.

This assertion and negation of the reality of economic life amounts more to a redefinition of the activity than to its total suppression. According to Weber, 'no economic ethic has ever been determined solely by religion' (…) but, 'an economic ethic has, of course, a high measure of autonomy' (1996, p. 332). The economic ethic obviously contains a pure intrinsic logic. It follows that a different sort of economy is applied inside the monastery framework, which is why a nun who attended a business school said, 'we do not have the same attitude in a monastery as in a firm. I can see that quite well when I look at what I studied. I can no longer apply what I learnt at the school because it is out of tune with us'.

Despite the visible attempts to reduce the economy to its simplest expression and to see as religious the various steps in the pre-ritual process, the economy is not really rejected. This is easily shown: if the market exists, it is well and truly because the nuns accept it. Indeed, the long list of attempts to disavow or to redefine it makes us wonder why the market exists at all. It would be perfectly possible to imagine a structure in which the Church would finance the communities for the services they render without having to go through the commercialization of the host. We would not be in a secondary structure then, but in a tertiary structure. In this case, why create a market for something as delicate as the host? What profit is there in it for the nuns? Various hypotheses can be put forward. This choice appears to be an economy of justification allowing the nuns to assert their financial independence from the Church and their very real implication in the only work considered legitimate – that is work that is productive and commercial. By its transition through the market the religious good acquires a 'worldly' dimension, which it has to assimilate to be seen as an offering. It takes on what is common to all humanity and by its secularization it will become all the greater.

At the same time the market is in self-denial because the faithful know so little about it. Apart from the nuns and the lay people concerned in the parishes, who really knows anything about the economic process implied by the host? How many of the faithful who go to communion know that the host has been sold and that a price has been put on it. This market is ignored because it is almost invisible for the consumers. It is only for the direct actors in the process that the desacralization through the economy intervenes. For the consumers, the main recipients, the production in fact seems continuous on account of the total lack of knowledge of what precedes the Eucharist. For the bulk of the faithful, the host appears as if 'ex nihilo' at the moment of consecration and the economic variants are therefore only known to the limited circle of producers and buyers. The existence of procedures of denial and acceptance of the economy can, therefore, be explained either as a theoretical point of view applied to the object or as something intended for the nuns themselves.

In theory, the existence of the market shows that the host is not exclusively intended for the Eucharistic sacrifice. Its journey through the market, which, in theory, puts it in competition with the other non-monastic products shows it could be used for other purposes. For example, hosts, round slices of unleavened bread are sold in Quebec as pastries in bakeries. Though this market creates an illusion of economic freedom, it is misleading since it is, in fact, closed to demand. In France the hosts are sold to religious consumers only and refused to the others. This illusion is, one may say, a commercial process which has been rigged in advance. The food offered, for example, could be used otherwise as a gift. In France, at least, this is not the case: the host is predetermined for communion. Only its journey through the market shows that it comes from the ordinary world. Indeed, the nuns try to make people understand that only monastic hosts are authentic. In an article, a French nun wrote: 'By the way, in your parish, do the hosts come from a monastery? Go and find out'! (Gaulmyn, 2010).

The example of the host market makes us reflect on the links between economy and religion that extend beyond the monastic world. Economic practices in religious institutions have rarely been studied and they are not even listed by L.A. Iannaccone in his *Introduction to the Economics of Religion* (1998). The economy of the host by the support it gives to monastic life corresponds to the configuration of 'economy at the service of religion' described by Welch and Mueller (2001). It is only through economics that religion can preserve itself. No institution can exist without the management of resources. The natural tendency is the one of hostility, 'economics must be kept separate from religion' and it is in order to overcome this theoretical hostility that the nuns manoeuvre to try to find links between economics and religion – this is the fourth step described by Welch.

But this economy of an eminently religious good, set in a consecrated religious context, reveals numerous peculiarities. The actors tend to deny the economy on account of both the object and the context. And so, I come to the same conclusion as L. Bolstanski and E. Chiapello concerning what they called 'natural products' (1999). Though they are in circulation on the market, they can be considered as totally outside the realm of economics. Paradoxically, the very existence of this economy proves it is accepted. This economy, full of contradictions, disavows and asserts itself by the very fact that it exists although it is not even necessary. More interesting are the reasons for its acceptance. Could it be in order to insist on the monastic ideal of physical work to earn a living?

Religion and economics often seem to clash on the question of rationality, but the example of the host market contradicts this. On the contrary religious values can find their place in a redefined economy. As Iannaccone says, 'the economics of religion will eventually bury two myths – that of homo economicus as a cold creature with neither need nor capacity for piety, and that of homo religiosus as a benighted throwback to pre-rational times' (1998, p. 1492). The example I have studied even seems to demonstrate that religious economics require a twofold rationality: the rationality of economic function and the rationality bound up with the demands of religion. The existence of an economy of the host bears witness both to the rationality of the nuns who have voluntarily chosen a market economy over one of services and also to their religious rationality in keeping this economy on the narrow pass of religion.

## NOTES

1. These obligations give rise to numerous reorganizations, which I discussed in my doctoral dissertation defended at the EHESS Paris in December 2009.
2. A sister especially responsible for the relations with outside world.
3. The Code of Canon Law, Canon 924 requires that the hosts be made from wheat flour and water only.
4. Abraham-Frois makes the distinction between pure competition, which requires atomicity, the homogeneity of the product, and free entrance onto the market, and perfect competition, which needs the perfect transparency on the market and the perfect mobility of the factors of production. To achieve this much-vaunted pure and perfect competition, all five conditions must be present. In G. Abraham-Frois, *Micro-économie*. Paris: Economica, 1986, p. 170.
5. There are different commissions according to the sectors of production within the Monastic Association created in 1996. The group of host producers is very active and holds meetings once or twice a year.

## ACKNOWLEDGEMENTS

The author wishes to thank Robert Gryson for help with translation from French to English.

## REFERENCES

Abraham-Frois, G. (1986). *Micro-économie*. Paris: Economica.

Berger, P. (1969). *The sacred canopy: Elements of a sociological theory of religion*. New York, NY: Anchor Books.

Boltanski, L., & Chiapello, E. (1999). *Le nouvel esprit du capitalisme*. Paris: NRF Essais, Gallimard.

Boudon, R. (1986). *Dictionnaire critique de sociologie*. Paris: Puf, article utopie.

Bourdieu, P. (1974). Le couturier et sa griffe: Contribution à une théorie de la magie. *Actes de la Recherche en Sciences Sociales*, *1*(1), 7–37.

Bourdieu, P. (1994). *Raisons pratiques, sur la théorie de l'action*. Paris: Le Seuil.

Colliot-Thélène, C. (1995). Rationalisation et désenchantement du monde: Problèmes d'interprétation de la sociologie de Max Weber. *Archives de Sciences Sociales de Religions*, *89*, 61–81.

Durkheim, E. (1982). *The elementary forms of the religious life*. Boston, MA: Allen & Unwin.

Gaulmyn, I. de. (2010). Les hosties françaises sont soumises à la rude concurrence. *La Croix*. Retrieved from http://www.la-croix.com/Religion/S-informer/Actualite. Accessed on February 28.

Iannaccone, L. R. (1998). Introduction to the economics of religion. *Journal of Economic Literature*, *36*(9), 1465–1496.

Mauss, M. (1970). *The Gift, forms and functions of exchange in archaic societies* (I. Cunnison, Trans.). London: Cohen & West LTD.
Sandler, T., & Cornes, R. (1996). *The theory of externalities, public goods and club goods*. Cambridge, MA: Cambridge University Press.
Séguy, J. (1971). Une sociologie des sociétés imaginées: Monachisme et utopie. *Annales*, *26*(2), 328–354.
Todeschini, G. (2008). *Richesse franciscaine, de la pauvreté volontaire à l'économie de marché*. Paris: Verdier Poche.
Tschannen, O. (1992). *Les théories de la sécularisation*. Genève: Droz.
Weber, M. (1978). *Economy and society*. Berkeley, CA: University of California Press.
Weber, M. (1996). *Sociologie des religions* (J.-P. Grossein, Trans.). Paris: Tel Gallimard.
Weber, M. (2003). *The protestant ethic and the spirit of capitalism* (T. Parsons, Trans.). Mineola, NY: Dover Publications.
Weber, M. (2009). *The protestant ethic and the spirit of capitalism, with other writings on the rise of the West* (S. Kalberg, Trans.). Oxford, MA: Oxford University Press.
Welch, P. J., & Mueller, J. J. (2001). The relationships of religion to economics. *Review of Social Economy*, *59*(2), 185–202.

# IS BUDDHISM LIKE A HAMBURGER? BUDDHISM AND THE MARKET ECONOMY IN A GLOBALIZED WORLD

Lionel Obadia

## ABSTRACT

*Buddhism, a globalizing religion, offers a remarkable opportunity to test different hypotheses and models coined in the field of "economics of religion." Since their foundation over 25 centuries ago, Buddhist ethics have always epitomized extra-worldly and noneconomic philosophies of renunciation. And in the context of globalization, contemporary Buddhist voices praise resistance to the human-engineered damage caused by expansive capitalism. Buddhist traditions have, however, always followed commercial routes and have been involved, although indirectly, in economic affairs. The globalization of Buddhism perpetuates this tendency but also uncovers the rise of "new" relationships between Asian tradition and (capitalistic) economy, in the realm of religious values, behaviors, and organization. This chapter aims at differentiating three models: Buddhism and economy, Buddhist economics, and the economics of Buddhism. It raises questions about the relevance of the "economic"-inspired conceptualization of Buddhist forms and dynamics.*

**The Economics of Religion: Anthropological Approaches**
**Research in Economic Anthropology, Volume 31, 99–120**

**ISSN: 0190-1281/doi:10.1108/S0190-1281(2011)0000031008**

## FOREWORD

In the early 2000s, I resided for several months in northern Mexico, as an invited professor in a local university. It was a good opportunity to make a series of fieldwork observations in the rural, Indian, and almost desert villages of the Pacific Coast. I was (half) surprised to discover, in the local markets (*tianguis*) of small and rather isolated villages, Buddha statues lined up on the stands beside other "ethnic" (Indian) artefacts (like "dream catchers" or *atrapasueños*) and villagers buying them for "good fortune." Among the middle-class strata in bigger towns, I found that the techniques and principles of *Feng Shui* (a Taoist art of controlling spiritual "energies" by means of organizing the material environment) were the latest trends in interior designing, and "Asian" furniture was also bought accordingly from special shops. Back in the center of the country, I found an ad publicizing the upcoming visit, in summer 2001, of a group of Tibetan monks who were invited by Indian priests to perform a ritual on the sacred sites of the desert plains of Zacatecas. I unfortunately did not have the chance to observe this unique performance. This event was supposed to celebrate the unity of "indigenous" religious virtuosi, but it above all unveiled the appeal of Buddhism in a country firmly attached to Christianity, yet open to foreign spiritual influences, especially from a distant and fantasy-laced area – "Buddhist Asia." Buddhist monastic traditions (Southeast Theravada, Japanese Zen, and Tibetan Mahayana) took root in Mexico in the 1990s (Chinese Buddhism having been introduced to them beginning in the 5th century under very different conditions), partly exported from the United States, and then disseminated from Mexico to other countries in South America (Nira, 2009). Followers are nowadays increasing in number and more and more *Latinos* from one side or the other of the American borderland add Buddhist themes and techniques to their own religiosity, without entirely casting aside, however, their cultural-Christian baggage. Buddhism, as with other "Asian traditions," has traveled along transnational routes, in the unexpected context of rural or urban Mexico, and has entered the realm of material or symbolic merchandise far away from "old" Europe, the first Western province where Buddhism took root. It did this first as a religion for a local audience, in the early 20th century (Batchelor, 1994), and from a "new" North American host country (Fields, 1992) but in a rather similar way: by moving through material markets in the form of goods for consumption, by circulating thanks to international economic networks, and by entrenching itself in a plural cultural and religious landscape in which it epitomizes both a "migrant" and a "convert" religion.

In this last case, it is disseminated religiously in a "marketplace." These three (similarly) "economic" (but empirical) faces of Buddhism suffice us to reopen the field of "Buddhism and economy," in the light of the developments of globalization studies and *economics of religion*.

## INTRODUCTION

Buddhism stands nowadays among the fastest-spreading religions in the world. Its traditions have long ago left their original Asian territories and have turned "global." The globalization of Buddhism raises questions about relationships between the ancient Asian tradition and contemporary global conditions. One interesting point regarding the globalization of Buddhism is the paradoxical posture of Buddhist monastic traditions and new movements, both are engaged in diffusion processes owing to economic globalization and are bitter critics of this development (Liogier, 2004; Obadia, 2007). Highly developed societies, especially (but not exclusively) Western ones, have nevertheless been particularly hospitable to the ancient Asian traditions. Buddhism has found appeal there for complex reasons, mostly relating to a Western imagination of the Asian "other" – a certain genre of *orientalism* – but also because it symbolizes a spiritual alternative to the ideologies of "materialism," which was one of the main criticisms of the West coming from Western "Eastern-inspired" counterculture in the 1960s (Pardue, 1968). This, of course, was the "boom" period for Buddhism in the West (Baumann, 1997).

Buddhist iconography or symbols have become stylish items in popular consumer culture: they can be seen on TV (in the United States), in music, in fashion, and aesthetics (Lopez, 1998) and cinematographic productions inspired by Buddhist themes or narratives participate in "orientalist commercializations" (Mullen, 1998). The globalization of Buddhism, within an economic globalization, can therefore be seen through the lens of economics, despite the intellectual resistance such an attempt tends to raise among scholars in Buddhism and the Buddhist religious milieu. Reference to an economic terminology to understand the westward path of Buddhism, as Jan Nattier did in 1998 (Buddhism "transport," "export," and "import"), did not provoke any kind of critical controversy in Buddhist studies or among Buddhists. But when the metaphor turns to a more realistic level, focusing upon merchandising *in* Buddhism (i.e., the existence of material markets in Buddhism) and moreover, the merchandising *of* Buddhism (i.e., the location of Buddhism in spiritual markets), people are sometimes "outraged" (Padgett, 2000, p. 62). Eschewing an extensive survey of contemporary relationships between economy and Buddhism, this chapter aims at highlighting some salient aspects of these relationships, in the context of economic globalization and the globalization of Buddhism. Furthermore, it questions the relevance and limits of the application of theoretical models in the new paradigm of "economics of religion" (see Obadia & Wood's introduction to this volume). Since the late 1980s, especially in the 1990s, I have been doing intensive ethnographic fieldwork research in Buddhist communities (of converts) in France and other countries of Europe (Tibetan oriented, mainly, but as well in Zen, Theravada, and Soka Gakkai settings), and later (late 1990s to mid-2000s) in Buddhist monastic groups in Asia (Tibetans in Nepal). Although mainly theoretical in scope and based upon a review of literature, this essay also relies to a degree on firsthand empirical data.

## BUDDHISM AND ECONOMY

The well-known theory of the famous German scholar Max Weber on religious ethics and capitalism put emphasis upon the idea that a few religious ethics – especially those of Protestantism – displayed "affinities" with economic values and practices, and gave rise to the modern form of capitalism. He, therefore, negated the chances of any other religious system – including Asian religions – favoring or accompanying the progress of an economic system born and developed in Europe. In his *Introduction to the Economic Ethics of World Religion* (German version, 1915) Weber, who is credited to have been a pioneer founder of sociology and one of the leading influences in the economics of religion, placed emphasis upon the "outer-worldly" ethics of Buddhism (a religion of renunciation), and he supported consequently the idea that this "contemplative" (i.e., meditative) belief system preached a soteriology of social inaction, since it centered on the reclusive and ascetic work of monks (*bhikkhu*) and engaged both body and soul in ataraxic and gnostic religiosity. As such, Buddhism considered mundane affairs as a source of corruption (or "poison") and a deviation from the austere "way" (*marga*) of spiritual liberation (*bodhi*). It is true that ancient texts of the Buddhist Canon stipulate that mundane effects, especially those linked with economic activity, like desire (*tanha*), attachment (*upadana*), and avidity (*lobha*), are sources of suffering (*dhukkha*). Weber, however, demonstrated elsewhere that the birth and rapid development of Buddhism were indirectly concerned with the rise of social forms of economic organizations, especially guilds that were, like the newly created Buddhist order in the 6th or 5th century BC, based upon elective relationships rather than on kinship (Weber, 1958). Allowing for capitalism is indeed a distinctive feature of modernity, and that modernity was born in the West (Europe) – they are two premises where the social and historical sciences have largely converged. Henceforth, Buddhism could not be a ferment for the blossoming of modern (economic and cultural) forms in Asia – a controversial point today (Obadia, 2011).

Is Buddhism, as it was portrayed by the 19th century German sociologist, originally (and truly) "reluctant" to engage in any kind of economic activity? The sacred texts – especially the *vinaya*, the code of monastic rules – in certain ways prohibit the use of money, trade, and possessions other than those that are codified and accepted by the socioreligious order (Lamotte, 1976). The Buddhist system singularizes two social bodies: monks (*bhikkhu*), free from economic activity, whose lives are governed by a rigorous ethical code (8 precepts, 10 rules, 4 monastic obligations, 4 basic prohibitions, 227 vows) and a lay substrata (*upasaka*), which is only subject to five basic precepts and is economically productive. In this system, monks provide "symbolic goods" to lay people (services and "merits") and lay people respond by giving (*dana*) "material goods" – a systemic arrangement that allows monks to respect the rules of a "noneconomic" lifestyle while having sources of funding, whereas lay people who are engaged in economic production can access the symbolic resources of (the) religion.

However, important historical and ethnographical data, collected in very different national and cultural contexts, has established that Buddhist monasticism has always been concerned (and associated) with economic activity in the societies hosting and surrounding it. The works of Gregory Schopen, for instance, clearly exhibit the presence of an intense reflection on economic activities within Buddhist monasticism, since these institutions needed to be involved in "business matters," even in the ancient forms of scriptural Buddhism in India (2004). Further, in the *Digha Nikaya* (sacred Buddhist texts) the foundations of happiness lie unambiguously on an economic foundation: Buddhist lay believers might live in economic security (Pali: *atthi-sukha*), enjoy wealth (*bhoga-sukha*), and want to be free from debts (*anana-sukha*).

Contemporary Buddhist studies have accordingly somewhat relativized Weber's perspectives on Buddhism, based upon a limited number of sources and evaluated within the frame of currently outdated theories: the relationships the German sociologist unveils between economy and religion – especially Buddhism – are much more ambivalent than he portrayed them. If ancient Brahmanism was opposed to commerce (a source of symbolic pollution), "primitive" Buddhism on the contrary maintained preferential relationships with it. Not only was the social recruitment of the Buddha targeting merchants and craftsmen (Bailey & Mabbett, 2003, p. 7), since they were based on Buddhist affinities with their "bourgeois" ethics (Gombrich, 1988, p. 78) and on Buddhism's key idea of universalism (an ideological parallel with their own mentality) (Carrithers, 1983), but the geographic extension of Buddhism corresponds to the (both ancient and contemporary) networks of economic exchanges that have been instrumental for the dissemination of monks, pilgrims, ideas, and for the expansion of the belief system. Pande even supports the idea that a monetary economy – coinciding with the emergence of Buddhism – is *complementary* with Buddhist values, since, at the date of birth of Buddhism, the value of each human was economic *in nature* (Pande, 1974). The relationships between Buddhism and economy in the early centuries of the Asian traditions are complex and uneasy to resolve. Was Buddhism eco(nomy)-friendly in its very nature since its birth or was it incidentally driven to moral and praxeologic inflections, in order to adjust to the social and economic changes of its host countries? Answering this question is beyond the scope of this chapter and the expertise of the author. However, between 1999 and 2003, I conducted ethnographic fieldwork in northern Nepal, where Tibetan Buddhists established themselves in the early 1960s, after the Chinese invasion of 1959 and the beginning of the Diaspora. The *Nying-ma-pa* monastery, Thoupten Choeling, was one of the largest hermitages of exiled Tibetan Buddhists in the area. More than 200 monks (*lama*) and nuns (*anila*) lived there at the time of the fieldwork and they devoted part of their time to religious affairs, but most of the monks and nuns (to the notable exclusion of high-rank *lamas*) spent most of their time engaged in productive activities (commerce with villagers, preparing food, repairing the *gompa* sanctuary, etc.) for the whole monastic community. Even if Max Weber insisted upon the "extra-worldly ethics" of Buddhism, Tibetan monasteries are nevertheless organized as economic societies, producing for and exchanging with the rest of society, and they even have created a special status for "bursarship" among monks, who are the treasurers of the monastery, in direct contact with economic affairs and in *direct* contact with *money*. This is not to mention the well-documented historical fact that monasteries, especially in the Tibetan area, were rich and politically powerful places in the history of Buddhism.

According to Buddhist doctrines, money is thus "impure" and everything relating to inner-worldly affairs is antagonistic to the ethics of Buddhist asceticism. Buddhism could therefore be considered as an economy-free religion. Things are, however, not as simple as that. Buddhism – as a religion – was born (it is worth mentioning) in a wealthy milieu; Shakyamuni was a prince living in luxury and comfort before giving up his high status, privileges, and prosperity. Buddhist traditions (monastic orders) have furthermore always had close, if not direct, relationships with the economic development of their host countries, have been shaped by them, and have even participated in the contemporary spread of Buddhism; bypassing political and geographic frontiers, they have additionally had a close relationship with globalization, in the economic (and most common) sense of the term. Buddhist ideas indeed circulate by way of technological circuits (the Internet), Buddhist virtuosi (e.g., *lama*, *roshi*, and *bhikkhu*) use modern modes of transportation, and Buddhist or Buddhist-inspired artefacts are sold all around the world as decorative or liturgical items. In short, to borrow a slogan from a French historian, the contemporary international spread of Buddhism is conveyed by "the carriages of free-trade" (Vallet, 1995, p. 53), and therefore is, time and again, linked with economic affairs.

## "BUDDHIST ECONOMICS"

Buddhism however, in the Western eyes, still epitomizes a noneconomic spirituality (or one opposed to economic affairs). It comes as no surprise, then, that in the 1970s, in the very heart of the worldwide economic crisis when the first major criticisms were on the outcomes of massive industrialization, economist Ernest F. Schumacher published a booklet entitled *Buddhist Economics* (1973). In his words, the "Buddhist economics" was an appropriate response to the dehumanizing effects of mass productivity, market competition, and inequalities in the distribution of wealth. Schumacher's criticisms were not directed toward the economy itself, but rather toward the underlying values of 20th century triumphant capitalism. The modern economy was, in Schumacher's words, driven by materialism and "greed and envy" (1973, p. 30), which are the symbolic "obstacles" (or "poisons of the mind") to enlightenment (*bodhi*) in Buddhist soteriology.

Surprisingly, while the principles of this Buddhist economics are considered to have been framed in the West, they have hardly been applied there, for several reasons. First, the principles of a scriptural Buddhism remain as ideal models for living, but do not correspond with practical expressions of Buddhism (Pryor, 1990, 1991). But as Peter L. Daniels stressed, "the notion of 'Buddhist' economics appears as a profound oxymoron" (2005, p. 246) and the demonstration of an ontological (and antagonistic) distinction between, on the one hand, nonmaterialistic values of a Buddhist, embodied in the ideal of poverty and the discipline of charity, and, on the other hand, values of interest, consumption, or maximization of profit is contrary to the historical acquaintances between the Buddhist orders and the economic life of their host societies. Buddhist key scriptural values indeed reject greed, envy, possession, materialism, and other references associated with modern economics. But beyond this idealistic refusal of economics, Asian societies (like many others around the world) have, however, been flagrantly confronted with the extension of global capitalism, which is seen as a salient feature of modernity. They have had to manage the encounter between their "traditional" systems of values and the "modern" system of production – following Daniel Bell's scheme of an incongruous gap between capitalism as the emblematic embodiment of freedom, the search for happiness, consumption, human and social benefices, and the exemplary epitome of ideological, cultural, and social erosion (Bell, 1976).

Beyond the issue of embeddedness of values in religious scripturalism, the problem with "Buddhist economics" is that it is not exactly Buddhism, or economics, that is interacting, but a certain idea of Buddhism and a certain idea of what mainstream economy is supposed to be (Daniels, 2005). And, similarly, such Weberian conceptions are only intelligible when related to their historical context of enunciation, and the ideas of Schumacher are ideologically significant in a specific social and cultural location. Roli Varma recalled: "the conviction that rapid development of industrial technologies and productivity, between the 1950s and the 1970s, should trigger hazardous consequences, while in the previous decades, the same processes were regarded as the key values of positive 'progress'" (2003). Since then, the critique of the neoliberal modern program – not only the market and industrial systems but also working activities – has relocated moral issues in the agenda of the modern economy, in parallel with the relocation of "culture" in the very heart of productive organizations (Banks, 2006). Furthermore, there exist substantial barriers to combining the logics of capitalistic production and wealth and the ethical principles of Buddhism – even in a Westernized version (which is a more explicit "economic-friendly" version). Asian countries, in contrast, have been much more interested in a conversion of (*certain*) economic sectors by means of Buddhist philosophy. Remarkably, while Buddhist economics has hence been espoused in the context of rich, urban, and highly developed Western societies,

Buddhist-inspired models of local economy have been set up in the context of poor, rural Asian societies (for instance, the Sri-Lankan *Sarvodaya Shramadana* Movement – see Zadek, 1993) supporting the contention of Schumacher (1973) that "Buddhist economics" was more adapted to small-scale societies. A former monarch of the small kingdom of Bhutan, Jigme Singye Wangchuck, indeed introduced in the early 1970s a new tool for the measure of his country's development: "Gross National Happiness" as substitutive of "Gross Domestic Product," with the aim of substituting "well-being" for "consumption" as the main indicator for the population's standard of living. Considering the fast and recent developments of research on "happiness" and economy applied in the context of large-scale societies (for instance, Stanca, 2010), the promises of a Buddhist-inspired and more humanistic economy is perhaps not just a utopia.

## BUDDHISM *AGAINST* GLOBAL ECONOMY AND THE MARKET

The rapid extension of global capitalism at the end of the 20th century has somewhat radicalized Buddhist postures toward the economy: Buddhism has become an official opponent of – or resistant to – global capitalism, and the fact that it is actually a globalized religion has offered it a chance to voice its antiglobalist sentiment. At the 2002 interfaith meeting at Fès (Morocco), Sulak Sivaraksa presented a paper entitled "Buddhism and the Challenge of Modernity in the 21st Century." He asserted:

> The wheels of the global economy are fuelled by insatiable greed. The Buddha, on the other hand, taught that the wheel of righteousness (*dhammacakka* or *buddhacakka*) must control or influence the wheel of power (*anacakka*). In the contemporary world, the quest for greater profit ultimately determines the actions of the rich and powerful, taking precedence over other motives. As such, any top-down attempt to redress class or ecological problems is likely to fail; at best it will only be a palliative. The teachings of the Buddha however state that the rich and powerful, especially the rulers, must have only overriding concern, that of upholding the law of *dhamma*.

Sivaraksa's attitude is not an isolated one. Many other authors – Asian and non-Asian – have condemned the outcomes of the "modern industrial world" and the "modern economy" as a world where the prevailing value is "greed," and the dominant behavior is "consumption." Against this depreciative image of a materialistic modernity, they oppose a "Buddhist" vision, based upon the "dissolution" of these "poisons," a "compassionate" and "altruist" stance toward the world, and the rehabilitation of the "interdependence" between nature and culture (Norberg-Hodge, 1997). The volume edited in 2002 by Allen Badiner, *Mindfullness in the Marketplace*, offers a series of similar and well-documented developments on the topic.

Thai scholar Preecha Changkhwanyuen (2004, p. 247) affirms that "Buddhism is not economic system," quite the reverse: "Buddhist analysis of capitalist economics reveals many unacceptable features of capitalism to Buddhism, *despite the current virtual harmonious coexistence of Buddhism and capitalism*" (italics added). Individualism, separation of morality and economy, consumerism, belief in material happiness, and delusive advertising are among what he calls the "unacceptable features of capitalism to Buddhism" (p. 247). In the same vein, the Vietnamese scholar Hoang Thi Tho declares that "Buddhist thought and market economy are opposite, because Buddhism resists hedonism and never encourages achievement of wealth" (2005, p. 37). In his "Globalization for a Buddhist perspective," Asian Buddhist monk and scholar Pracha Hutanuwatr is more cautious not to criticize globalization *as a whole*, but only effects damaging to local society and culture:

> When we talk about globalization we must remember such aspects as the globalization of the *dominating consumer monoculture and the accompanying devastating environmental effects*. On a more positive note, all around the world we can witness evidence of the rising consciousness of the interconnection of ecological systems and the emergence of global networking among civil society. From a Buddhist perspective, however, *the very core of the globalization process is the globalization of tanah, or craving*. According to Buddhist analysis, *tanah* is the root cause of all suffering. (2000, italics added)

In the context of Western Buddhism, that is, Buddhism as it has been established in the West, the same critical discourses are heard. An example among the many existing nowadays, reverend Alfred Bloom – a Buddhist scholar and practicing Buddhist living in the United States – also calls for a distinction between globalization per se and the *social* effects of *economic* globalization:

> We Buddhists must *recognize the complexity of contemporary* issues and call on our compatriots to resist simplistic and emotional responses to events and situations. It means we must call on our leaders to consider issues in their full context and not seek politically expedient solutions. The Buddhist principle of non-discrimination and equality is related to this understanding. When we recognize the complexity of causation that produces conflicts and suffering, *we must treat each party to the problem equally and fairly*. We must clarify the issues that will lead to reconciliation and the solution to the problem. Buddhists must make clear the superficiality of contemporary notions of globalism and interdependence and work to rectify injustices created by this process. *We must promote equality and support the aspirations for a full life for all people, beyond economic and political power* (2001, italics added).

Thus, there are two dimensions of criticism regarding the relationships between Buddhism and market economy. The first one is against economic logics per se: that is, financial forms and productive processes. This is the "Buddhist" or Buddhist-inspired critique of the outcomes of global economy, and the likelihood of making industrial or postindustrial economy more "humanistic" and respectful of Man, Nature, and Society – a "Buddhist economy," as promoted by Schumacher. Buddhist or Buddhist-inspired critiques of the market consider that private accumulation – in the hands of elites – of industry and wealth runs contrary to "free-trade" logics, reclaim a change of mind or a change of cultural habits to rebalance the world economy (Simmer-Brown, 2002).

The second one is the switch from Buddhism as an ascetic way of living, based on the ethics of renunciation and salvation, to an instrumental technique of "well-being," which can "cure" or help people cope with the ailments of modern societies, that is, societies subjugated to economic logic (Obadia, 2008). Buddhist themes are available in a "cultural marketplace" as existential and identity resources (Matthews, 2000). Buddhist techniques such as meditation, mental quietness, or body control by breathing are "consumed" like any other "goods" for moral comfort or therapeutic relief (Obadia, 2008), and Buddhism is accommodating itself quite well to a "religious market" (Prebish & Tanaka, 1998, p. 10). Observers of such processes of "consumption" of Buddhism and Asian traditions have been highly critical of them. Harvey Cox denounced it in the 1970s as the alteration of "genuine Asian traditions" into secular and down-to-earth Western ideologies, and the superficial adoption of only the "ersatz" of "genuine" Asian tradition (Cox, 1977). Later, Lilian Silburn expressed the same views when she deplored the reshaping of Buddhism in the West as spiritual "merchandise" (1983, p. 9).

These critiques, however, rest on the image of "pure" and somewhat idealized Asian traditions, harmoniously living in premodern societies without being corrupted by economic influences, recently perverted by Western and global influences. They do not take into account the fact that all religions have always adapted to new conditions of living and new opportunities to spread, neither the technique of branding Buddhism is subjected to, in the context of globalization, especially in Western settings.

The diffusion of Buddhist ideas and practices indeed aligns with technological, human, and economic circuits and exemplifies a kind of "Dharma industry," to borrow the expression coined by Tibetologist Beatrice Miller, in another context, but here in the sense Theodor Adorno gave to the "culture industry" in the late 1940s: as "industrial" production and "standardization" of culture, where Buddhism is, along with other traditions, "merchandized" in (American) popular culture – even more particularly the case for Tibetan schools of Buddhism (Korom, 1997; Schell, 2000). It is dyed in the colours of humanism, secularism, esotericism, ecologism, scientism among other ideological layers by which it has been reinterpreted in the West, according to the ideological tendencies of the promoters of Buddhism, and the (alleged) preferences of the audiences it is targeting (Obadia, 2007). Douglas Padgett (2000) demonstrates that the westward expansion of Buddhism is (but did not actually *turn*) "mercantile" as he lists some of the material products and services labelled "Buddhist" that are available in the United States, and the marketing techniques (online) retailers use. Moreover, Buddhism also aligns with the values and ideals of "modern consumer culture" as is, for instance, the case for the Japanese Soka Gakkai movement in the United States. Hammond and Machacek (1999) have logically applied a "supply–demand" theory to the understanding of the workings of this. The two sociologists suggest that the appeal of Buddhism (at least for this modernized movement) lies in the ideological and practical adjustments that it has absorbed along with modern ideals (on the "supply-side") and the expectations of the audience (on the "demand-side"): techniques of well-being, inner-worldly ethics, and rationalism, among other items. But finally, it is as if Buddhism were torn between two opposite tendencies, and the dilemma of being both located *within* and *against* the market.

## CONSUMING BUDDHISM: "DHARMA SHOPPERS" AND OTHER CREATURES

Another major facet of contemporary Buddhism, especially in its westward, expanding form, is indeed the rise of these "economic" attitudes. In all the countries in the West where Buddhism has planted itself as a missionary religion, that is, in *all* the Western countries (where it has also established itself as a migrant religion), the figures of converts and of "sympathizers" are somewhat contrasted. In the case of France, for instance, the press and mass media estimate the number of Buddhist sympathizers at perhaps five million, but devoted practitioners, who have temporarily or more permanently joined a community, amount to less than 800,000 persons (Obadia, 2007). A similar discrepancy can be observed in the figures on sympathizers and practitioners in the United States (Seager, 1999).

Sociologists and anthropologists from both sides of the Atlantic (Étienne & Liogier, 1997; Obadia, 1999 on France, Coleman, 2001 on the United States) have witnessed the same twofold and interrelated processes: in the very heart of community life, Buddhist practitioners are "converts" and adopt more profoundly the norms and ethics of the congregation or movement they belong to (up to a full engagement in monasticism), and quite the reverse, the more distant they are from the institutional, ideological, and practical "core" of orthodox Buddhism, the more incompletely they adopt Buddhism, and mix it with other beliefs and practices, in a hybrid combination. If Buddhists from the first category are quite easy to locate (in communities or *sangha*) and to study (since they exhibit discursive and practical signs of belonging), those of the second category, who are not actually "Buddhists" in the canonical definition of the term, are more difficult to trace and to understand (except by quantitative methods, but little convincing research has yet been done, with the exception of some typologies). Still, their attitude toward Buddhism is far more interesting for economic theorization, since it exemplifies the locus where the processes of "consumption" (choosing, picking, and using selected aspects of Buddhism – existential ideas or meditation techniques for instrumental purpose) are the most salient.

In his reflection on the theoretical importance (beyond the demographic weight) of this group, aptly titled "Night-Stand Buddhists and Other Creatures," Thomas Tweed (1999) suggested adding a new category of (Western) Buddhists in the vocabulary of religious and Buddhist studies: the "Dharma Shoppers." Following Jan Nattier, who used an economic terminology to typify the categories of Buddhism, Tweed goes further, and attempts to bypass the vagueness of the category of "Dharma hoppers" (1998, p. 83):

> When it comes to the Dharma, there are not only baggage bearers, importers, and exporters, but *shoppers* as well. At least tens of thousands – and probably hundreds of thousands – of Americans have neither inherited the tradition from their parents nor bought it fully in the marketplace of U.S. religion. They shop – purchasing a bit of this and consuming a bit of that, but never buying it all.

Is Buddhism like a hamburger, then, that people should "consume" in an open marketplace, without any desire to become Buddhists? I deliberately employ this provocative allegory keeping in mind that other elliptic conceptualizations have given rise to bitter controversies in Buddhist studies – a recent, famous one being the "tomato controversy." In a 1994 article, Martin Baumann proposed a study of the rooting processes of

Buddhism in Germany with reference to the term "transplantation" (1994). Eva Neumaier-Dargyay contested vehemently the "horticultural" metaphor (1995), a "response" that brought about a "response to the response" (1996) and so the controversy continued ... To what extent actually, does this culinary metaphor exemplify the modern attitude toward globalized Buddhism? A very interesting anthropological fact is that the "consumerist" attitude toward Buddhism is not exclusively *cultural* (Western) but *sociological*, beyond contextual geographic and cultural settings. Indeed, in the context of globalization, "the West" is far from being the sole locus where these influences infuse and where attitudes toward Buddhism are reshaped by economic logics. Case studies recorded and analyzed in Asia reveal similar processes. For instance, the rise of new lay social strata, which have emerged from the industrialization of Asia, still, on the one hand, participate in the funding of monastic orders but, on the other hand (and according to an "orthodox" conception of Buddhist piety and loyalty), now "consume" sacred Buddhist symbols and techniques in accordance with their own social ethics and motivations (on Cambodia, see Kent, 2006, p. 355). Similarly, Jim Taylor's study of the Dhammakaya movement in Thailand argues that the adaptations of Theravada urban Buddhism to modernity involve the adoption of the principles and logics of market capitalism. Using Debord's views of the modern *Society of spectacle* and Baudrillard's *Simulacra and Simulation*, Taylor explores the new cultural economies of signs in Thailand, and concludes that the Dhammakaya Stupa (votive monument) illustrates a syncretic and fabricated "Disneyland" (-styled) modernity of contemporary Buddhism in Thailand (Taylor, 2007). This conclusion might be a bit crude, but besides this, all the religious and cultural landscapes of Asian societies (and societies engaged in globalization) are henceforth crossed and reshaped by the dynamics of competition and market logics (Delcore, 2004).

For Gordon Matthews, who has studied the cultural and religious changes under the impetus of globalization in several national contexts (Asian and Western), the theoretical framework of economics and especially the concept of "spiritual marketplace," is all but problematic: quite the opposite, actually, on condition that one distinguishes between *material* and *cultural* supermarkets, and assuming that only the latter provides meaningful "goods" that people can "consume" for existential purposes (2000, pp. 19–22). He thoughtfully spotlights the dialectics between "truth" and "taste" in the "consumption" of religious goods in both spiritual and cultural supermarkets (p. 82). Likewise, economics is not just a parabolic outline of the contemporary observable logics of "truth seekers" in the "spiritual supermarkets": it is also a discursive resource, by which social actors identify themselves, in a rather ironic way. Matthews indeed recalls that the promoters of Buddhism in the West saw (and still see) themselves as "peddlers" of a "product" (p. 79).

In France, and in many other countries, Buddhism is rarely practiced exclusively, or, more accurately, adopted as a whole (Obadia, 2007), and the larger part of Buddhist sympathizers do not join a cultic community, but simply "mix" Buddhist items (themes, values, beliefs, practices) to others, be they secular or religious. This process of "picking" and "blending" Buddhism can be regarded as "*bricolage*" (preferred in French and European sociology of religion) or "consuming" (more utilized in American sociology, although not substitutive to the former, since there exist semantic equivalents like "hydridization," "creolization," or *métissage*). "Bricolage" refers to the manners by which individuals arrange personal combinations between elements borrowed from different "stocks" of traditions – it relates to a new *sociology* of religious action (Hervieu-Léger, 2000). "Consuming" otherwise connotes a calculation of "costs and benefits" in the choice of religious preferences, in a market where religions are "branded" – it refers to the *economics* of religious action. Despite the theoretical differences, in both cases, actors are motivated by instrumental and utilitarian action, rather than by emotional or psychological motifs. The dichotomy between "Dharma hoppers" and "Dharma shoppers" corresponds to the models of the "seeker" and the "consumer," respectively.

Buddhist institutions and their representatives, however and rather surprisingly, do not subscribe to the idea of turning Buddhism into "merchandise" and to the logics of the market – if global capitalism can give birth to genuine new religiosities inspired by the values of market economy (Chidester, 2005), ancient and religious traditions, including Buddhism, might embrace the supermarket dynamics with reluctance (Harris, 1995, p. 199). But how can we anthropologists understand the place and meaning of economy in Buddhism (and in Western Buddhism, in this case) when, on the one side, official institutional discourses contest any kind of connivance with capitalism and denounce the "economization" of Buddhism, and, on the other side, the actors' behavior and even speech denote the influence of economic logics ("pick and choose" attitude) and sometimes declare explicitly that they are "shopping around in the 'spiritual supermarket'?" (Matthews, 2000, p. 104)

All things considered, it sounds like the Buddhist "problem" with economy is mainly with a particular (modern) conception of economy and certain (global) effects of capitalism. Indeed, Buddhism itself exemplifies a kind of "spiritual capitalism" *before* economic capitalism: Buddhist practices, be they ascetic (monastic) or devotional (popular), engage the Buddhist follower in the path of salvation (*bodhi*) or rebirth by means of accumulation of merits (*puña*) to increase the symbolic capital of sacredness (*karma*). This "pecuniary dimension" of Buddhism might have been one of the reasons of the success of Buddhism in ancient India (Paul Lévy quoted in De Berval, 1987, p. 25). Some Western supporters of Buddhism did not hesitate, hence, to imagine that the Buddhist *ethos* is exactly corresponding – or even similar in nature – to that of *homo economicus*, and therefore with modernity itself (Kolm, 1982). The symbolic economy of Buddhism is however not exactly similar to the influences of economy *in* Buddhism. These two models refer to economy as an empirical thing and illustrate a shift from *real* to *symbolic* economy. A third model, the economics *of* Buddhism – by which it is seen as "commodity" and "corporation," achieves this shift and opens a new perspective, considering economy as a *model of reality*.

## CONSUMERISM: COMMUNITY AND ORGANIZATIONS

What distinguishes the economics of religion from other sociological theories, and in particular the European ones, is the focus upon the individual, for the former, and the community, for the latter (especially in Emile Durkheim's views) (Warner, 1993). Beyond the epistemological status of these two conceptual entities, it is true that, on many occasions, the development of market economy and the infusion of the culture of capitalism in religions might have been seen as a threat to their integrity. About Buddhism, Peter Hershock maintained the "commodification focuses our attention on products rather than on conducts, on things rather than on relationships" (1999, p. 64) and he points out the threat to the (moral and social) Buddhist community. But things are not as simple as that. Indeed the cohorts of Buddhist sympathizers and seekers can be seen as "communities of consumption" (Padgett, 2000, p. 71), but the sense of community in the institutionalized monastic context (as I have studied it in Tibetan-oriented groups of converts in France, for instance) also depends on social bounds, identification with the religious school or lineage, and the symbolic "link" (*samaya*) the adherent is supposed to tie with the "three jewels" (*triratna*), that is, the *Buddha* (the prophet), the *Dharma* (his teaching), and the *Sangha* (the community) –especially with the master himself. Economy, however, is in every dimension of the *sanghas*' life. "Monks do not fly in the air by themselves" used to say the Buddhist followers in the temples. With this sentence, they underscored the need for Buddhism to rely upon *real* economy for the survival and development of the community, and very prosaically, the funding of their traveling religious masters from Asian countries to Western ones. Data about the economy of temples in the West is however scarce and at best conjectural – most of the research has been done on "ethnic" economies of Asian Buddhists (from migrant extraction) in the West (for more details see a list of works in Obadia, 2007). Economic behaviors have nonetheless been recorded in "white" or "convert" Buddhist temples: the factual economy of goods (buying books, cushions, artefacts), donations for the temple, and/or the community in France (Obadia, 1999), as in North America, Buddhist followers champion a rather immaterial view of their life and community – just as if they were in suspension of the material world (Padgett, 2000, p. 63). But the significant shift from economy in Buddhism and economics of Buddhism does not lie there, but in the interpretation of social dynamics in the prism of economic conceptualization. James V. Spickard (2008), who has also investigated relationships between (an Asian) religion and economy, has made a stimulating contribution to the emerging field of "economics of religion." Rather than focus solely on the impact of economic logic on the believers' or seekers' behavior, or on the "advertising" strategies of spreading religions, he has focused on the "economic-like" dynamics of religious organizations. Spickard is convinced , from his study of the transnational missionary activism of the Japanese sect Sekai Kyusei Kyo, that similarities between the global dynamics of enterprises and the global dissemination and reorganization of religions allow scholars to merge them into a single analytical model, based upon the *organizational* reshaping of religions in economic globalization. While Peter Berger, for instance, insisted upon the "institutional modelling" of religions in globalization, alongside the yardstick of (global) Christianity (2007), and other authors have maintained that *local* religions were adapting to secular global conditions or that globalizing religions were reshaped by local social and cultural settings (see, respectively, Rothstein, 1996; Warburg, 1999), Spickard puts emphasis upon the economic structure of the world, and recognizes the economic dynamics of international corporations in transnational religions (2008). Actually, the same can apply for Buddhist organizations that have turned international, and assume networked shapes, with "nodes" and cultic sites in many countries: the Japanese *Soka Gakkai International* and *Zen International Association*, the Tibetan *Foundation for the Preservation of the Mayahana Tradition*, and the *Theravada-oriented Friends of the Western Buddhist Order*, among others. These transnational Buddhist organizations, as noticed by Martin Baumann (1997) while they expand outside Asia, are in the unusual situation of coexisting in the same geographic area (*Tibetan*, *Japanese*, *Vietnamese*, *Chinese*, or *Korean* forms of Buddhism in the same countries in Europe or North America) while in Asia, most of them have had little, if any, chance to meet or confront one another. Moreover, globalization and the introduction to new audience has made their coexistence a context of competition; indeed, not only does Buddhism compete with other religions (especially Christianity and Judaism) in which it finds new converts or sympathizers, but Buddhist traditions also compete with each other in the race for expansion and recruitment – and in this context, the Soka Gakkai movement has distinguished itself by a striking sense of rivalry and exclusivism that has led to the marginalization of the movement. Another remarkable dynamic is the "concentration" of Buddhist groups or movements (of the same school and tradition) under the same umbrella organization: in this respect, the worldwide *Foundation for the Preservation of the Mayahana Tradition*, with 160 meditation centers or temples scattered throughout 40 countries, but united by the norms and values of a single institution, exemplifies such processes. Last, another economic phenomenon is the "cooperation" between these Buddhist "corporations." Competition is neither the only stance of Buddhist globalized traditions nor the process of concentration: they also attempt to create and maintain collaborative actions or structures, justified in the rationale of "dialogue" and "ecumenism," as it is the case for the *World Fellowship of Buddhists* (based in Asia), but also motivated in the West by the need to reduce the internal competition between traditions belonging to the same religious matrix (Freiberger 2001; Spuler, 2000). Corporations, competition, concentration, and cooperation – the "four-C" conceptual model demonstrates that, in principle, religious dynamics *can* (but by no means *must*) be interpreted in economic terms.

## A CONCLUSIVE REMARK: ECONOMICS, BETWEEN ANALOGIES AND REALITIES

Since the issues surrounding the application of economics of religion to Buddhism are still a work-in-progress, and considering that this chapter has attempted to portray some significant outlines of relevant developments, in conclusion I will limit myself to offering a short critical (but not unconstructive) appraisal of the limits of this framework. At first glance, the conceptual elements and empirical evidence covered here corroborate the relevance of applying the models and methods of the "economics of religion" to the case of globalized Buddhism. The interesting – and challenging – counterpoint to this analysis is challenging but requires further intellectual consideration. Actually, descriptive and analytical economic terminology certainly proves to be relevant to the case of Buddhism, as I have attempted to briefly demonstrate in this essay. Some of the cases mentioned here are more directly linked with economic issues than others: Schumacher's "Buddhist" economic reformation, organizational transformations of economic production in rural South and Southeast Asia, and anticapitalistic Buddhist discourses range among the most significant examples of "economy near concepts" (evoked in the introductory chapter of this volume). Other cases seem to bear much more similarity to "economy distant concepts" touching upon *metaphorical* references to economy, and one can wonder to what extent, the actual issue is a question of language or of terminological choices, and beyond, of interpretative schemes – and economic-inspired interpretation of religious behaviors, organizations, and dynamics.

Indeed, "exporting" Buddhism can also be called "missionization" (Nattier, 1998) and so can other concepts be expressed in noneconomic terms: "reception" instead of "importing," "appropriation" instead of "shopping," "diffusion" and "acclimation" instead of "branding," "bricolage" instead of "shopping," "international institutions" rather than "transnational corporations," "ecumenism" instead of "cooperation," etc. Similarly, the spread of the Soka Gakkai movement in the West has been interpreted in *economic* terms in the North-American context (Hammond & Machacek, 1999) and in *sociological* terms in Britain (Wilson & Dobbeleare, 1994). How shall we explain these differences? Do they originate in the "economic" and "social" shapes the Soka Gakkai movement assumes in these different countries? Or do they have to do with the perspectives scholars have chosen on the both sides of the Atlantic? If Buddhism, as this chapter has attempted to demonstrate, is to be a fascinating empirical object and methodological entry for the extension of economics of religion beyond the monotheistic focus it used to have, this new paradigm must solve the epistemological issue arising from the tension between the ontology of phenomena (religious symbols and practices *are* economic goods and therefore Buddhism *is* a "hamburger"(?)) and the metaphors used to describe them (religious symbols and practices are *like* economic goods and, therefore, Buddhism is *like* a "hamburger"(!)).

# REFERENCES


Badiner, A. (Ed.) (2002). *Mindfulness in the marketplace: Compassionate response to consumerism*. Berkeley, CA: Parallax Press.

Bailey, G., & Mabbett, I. (2003). *The sociology of early Buddhism*. Cambridge, MA: Cambridge University Press.

Banks, M. (2006). Moral economy and cultural work. *Sociology*, *40*(3), 455–472.

Batchelor, S. (1994). *The awakening of the West: The encounter of Buddhism and western culture*. London: Aquarian.

Baumann, M. (1994). The transplantation of Buddhism to Germany: Processive modes and strategies of adaptation. *Method & Theory in the Study of Religion*, *6*(1), 35–36.

Baumann, M. (1996). Methodological smugness and the transplantation of symbolic systems: A reply to Eva K. Neumaier-Dargyay. *Method & Theory in the Study of Religion*, *8*(4), 367–372.

Baumann, M. (1997). The Dharma has come west: A survey of recent studies and sources. *Critical Review of Books in Religion*, *10*, 1–14.

Bell, D. (1976). *The cultural contradictions of capitalism*. New York, NY: Basic Books.

Beyer, P. (2007). Globalization and the institutional modeling of religions. In: P. Beyer & L. G. Beaman (Eds.), *Religion, globalization and culture*. Boston, MA: Brill.

Bloom, A. (2001). Globalization and Buddhism. Retrieved from http://www.shindharmanet.com/writings/globalization.htm. Accessed on April 1, 2011.

Carrithers, M. (1983). *The Buddha: A very short introduction*. Oxford, MA: Oxford University Press.

Changkhwanyuen, P. (2004). Buddhist analysis of capitalism. *The Chulalongkorn Journal of Buddhist Studies*, *3*(2), 247–259. Retrieved from http://www.stc.arts.chula.ac.th/CJBS/Buddhist%20Analysis%20of%20Capitalism.pdf. Accessed on May 3, 2011.

Chidester, D. (2005). *Authentic fakes: Religion and American popular culture*. Berkeley, CA: University of California Press.

Coleman, J. W. (2001). *The new Buddhism: The western transformation of an ancient tradition*. Oxford, MA: Oxford University Press.

Cox, H. (1977). *Turning east: The promise and peril of the new orientalism*. New York, NY: Simon and Schuster.

Daniels, P. L. (2005). Economic systems and the Buddhist world view: The 21st century nexus. *Journal of Socioeconomics*, *34*, 245–268.

De Berval, R. (Ed.) (1987). *Présence du bouddhisme*. Paris: Gallimard.

Delcore, H. D. (2004). Symbolic politics or generification? The ambivalent implications of tree ordinations in the Thai environmental movement. *Journal of Political Ecology*, *11*(1), 1–30.

Étienne, B., & Liogier, R. (1997). *Être bouddhiste en France aujourd'hui*. Paris: Albin Michel.

Fields, R. (1992). *How the swans came to the lake: A narrative history of Buddhism in America* (3rd ed.). Boston, MA: Shambala.

Freiberger, O. (2001). The meeting of traditions: Inter-Buddhist and inter-religious relations in the west. *Journal of Global Buddhism*, *2*, 59–71.

Gombrich, R. F. (1988). *Theravada Buddhism: A social history from ancient Benares to modern Colombo*. London: Routledge and Kegan Paul.

Hammond, P., & Machacek, D. (1999). *Soka Gakkaï in America: Accommodation and conversion*. New York, NY: Oxford University Press.

Harris, I. (1995). Buddhist environmental ethics and detraditionalization: The case of ecoBuddhism. *Religion, 25*, 199–211.

Hershock, P. D. (1999). *Reinventing the wheel: A Buddhist response to the information age*. Albany, NY: SUNY Press.

Hervieu-Léger, D. (2000). *Religion as a chain of memory*. New Brunswick, NJ: Rutgers University Press.

Hoang, T. T. (2005). The essence of Buddhist ethics: Its value in tradition and in modern time. *Social Sciences, 1*, 27–39.

Hutanuwatr, P. (2000). Globalization for a Buddhist perspective. *Semper Reformanda. World alliance of reformed churches*. Reformed World (Vol. 50, Issue 2), Globalization and its consequences. Retrieved from http://www.warc.ch/pc/rw002/04.html. Accessed on April 1, 2011.

Kent, A. (2006). Reconfiguring security: Buddhism and moral legitimacy in Cambodia. *Security Dialogue, 37*(3), 343–361.

Kolm, S.-C. (1982). *Le Bonheur-liberté, bouddhisme profond et modernité*. Paris: Presses Universitaires de France.

Korom, F. (Ed.) (1997). *Constructing Tibetan culture: Contemporary perspective*. St-Hyacinthe: World Heritage Press.

Lamotte, E. (1976). *Histoire du Bouddhisme Indien, Tome I: Des Origines à l'Ere Saka*. Louvain-la-Neuve: Publications de l'Institut Orientaliste.

Liogier, R. (2004). *Le bouddhisme mondialisé. Une perspective sociologique sur la globalisation du religieux*. Paris: Ellipses.

Lopez, D., Jr. (1998). *Prisoners of Shangri-La. Tibetan Buddhism and the West*. Chicago, IL: University of Chicago Press.

Mathews, G. (2000). *Global culture/individual identity: Searching for home in the cultural supermarket*. New York, NY: Routledge.

Mullen, E. L. (1998). Orientalist commercializations: Tibetan Buddhism in American popular film. *Journal of Religion and Film, 2*(2). Retreived from http://www.unomaha.edu/jrf/OrientalMullen.htm. Accessed on July 1, 2011.

Nattier, J. (1998). Who is a Buddhist? Charting the landscape of Buddhist America. In: C. Prebish & K. Tanaka (Eds.), *The faces of Buddhism in America* (pp. 183–195). Berkeley, CA: University of California Press.

Neumaier-Dargyay, E. K. (1995). Is Buddhism like a tomato? Thoughts about the transplantation of Buddhism to Germany: A response to Martin Baumann. *Method & Theory in the Study of Religion, 7*(2), 185–194.

Nira, O. J. (2009). Buddhism. In: M. de la Torre (Ed.), *Hispanic American religious cultures* (vol. 1, pp. 89–93). Santa Barbara, CA: ABC-CLIO/Greenwood.

Norberg-Hodge, H. (1997). Buddhism in the global economy. *Resurgence, 181*. Retrieved from http://www.gn.apc.org/resurgence/articles/norberg_hodge_buddi.htm. Accessed on February 8, 2002.

Obadia, L. (1999). *Bouddhisme et Occident. La diffusion du bouddhisme tibétain en France*. Paris: L'Harmattan.

Obadia, L. (2007). *Le bouddhisme en Occident*. Paris: La Découverte.

Obadia, L. (2008). The economies of health in western Buddhism: A case study in a Tibetan group in France. *Research in Economic Anthropology, 26*, 227–259.

Obadia, L. (2011). *Buddhism and modernity*. Oxford: Wiley-Blackwell.

Padgett, D. M. (2000). Americans need something to sit on. *Journal of Global Buddhism, 1*, 61–81.

Pande, G. C. (1974). *Studies in the origins of Buddhism*. Delhi: Motilal Banarsidass.
Pardue, P. (1968). *Buddhism. A historical introduction to Buddhist values and the social and political forms they have assumed in Asia*. London: Collier McMillan.
Prebish, C., & Tanaka, K. (Eds.). (1998). *The faces of Buddhism in America*. Berkeley, CA: University of California Press.
Pryor, F. (1990). A Buddhist economic system – In principle. *American Journal of Economics & Sociology*, *49*(3), 339–349.
Pryor, F. (1991). A Buddhist economic system – In practice. *American Journal of Economics & Sociology*, *50*(1), 17–32.
Rothstein, M. (1996). Patterns of diffusion and religious globalization: An empirical survey of new religious movements. *Temenos*, *32*, 195–220.
Schell, O. (2000). *Virtual Tibet: Searching for Shangri-La from the Himalayas*. New York, NY: Metropolitan Books.
Schopen, G. (2004). *Buddhist monks and business matters: Still more papers on monastic Buddhism in India*. Honolulu, HI: University of Hawaii Press.
Schumacher, E. F. (1973). *Small is beautiful: Economics as if people mattered*. New York, NY: Harper Perennial.
Seager, R. H. (1999). *Buddhism in America*. New York, NY: Columbia University Press.
Silburn, L. (Ed.) (1983). *Le maître spiritual selon les traditions d'Occident et d'Orient, Hermès* (Vol. 3). Paris: Ed. des Deux Océans.
Simmer-Brown, J. (2002). Remedying globalization and consumerism: Joining the inner and outer journeys in 'perfect balance'. *Buddhist-Christian Studies*, *22*, 31–46.
Spickard, J. V. (2008). Organizational transformations in global religions: Rethinking the relationships between organization, culture and market. In: A. W. Geertz & M. Warburg (Eds.), *New religions and globalization* (pp. 109–127). Aarhus: Aarhus University Press.
Spuler, M. (2000). Characteristics of Buddhism in Australia. *Journal of Contemporary Religion*, *15*(1), 29–44.
Stanca, L. (2010). The geography of economics and happiness: Spatial patterns in the effects of economic conditions on well-being. *Social Indicators Research*, *99*(1), 115–133.
Taylor, J. (2007). Buddhism, copying, and the art of the imagination in Thailand. *Journal of Global Buddhism*, *8*, 1–19.
Tweed, T. A. (1999). Night-stand Buddhists and other creatures: Sympathizers, adherents and the study of religion. In: D. R. Williams & C. S. Queen (Eds.), *American Buddhism: Methods and findings in recent scholarship* (pp. 71–90). Richmond, VA: Curzon Press.
Vallet, O. (1995). *Les religions dans le monde*. Paris: Flammarion.
Varma, R. (2003). E.F. Schumacher: Changing the paradigm of bigger is better. *Bulletin of Science, Technology & Society*, *23*(2), 114–124.
Warburg, M. (1999). Baha'i: A religious approach to globalization. *Social Compass*, *46*, 47–56.
Warner, R. S. (1993). Work in progress toward a new paradigm for the sociological study of religion in the United States. *The American Journal of Sociology*, *98*(5), 1044–1093.
Weber, M. (1958). *The religion of India*. New York, NY: Free Press.
Wilson, B., & Dobbeleare, K. (1994). *A time to chant. The Soka Gakkai Buddhists in Britain*. Oxford, MA: Clarendon Press.
Zadek, S. (1993). The practice of Buddhist economics? Another view. *American Journal of Economics and Sociology*, *52*(4), 433–445.

# PART II
# EMPIRICAL EVIDENCE – GLEANINGS FROM "THE FIELD"

# SPIRITUAL CAPITAL: ON THE MATERIALITY AND IMMATERIALITY OF BLESSINGS IN PUERTO RICAN *BRUJERÍA*

Raquel Romberg


## ABSTRACT

*This essay situates the significance of "spiritual capital" within Puerto Rican* brujería *(witch-healing) in relation to re-enchantment theories of modernity. It argues that the merging of spiritual and economic values has engendered a form of "spiritualized materialism" that has turned sheer economic prosperity into spiritually wrought rewards. Within this moral economy, matter does not simply function as a conduit for the sacred; it actually constitutes the very idea of the sacred. In comparison to recent work on corporate attempts to fuse religious ethics with business, this essay is noteworthy in that it unravels the logic and effect of such fusions at the vernacular religious level.*


> The gods relate to and are activated by things that do not conform to cravings for purity or longings for transcendence.
> –Joan Dayan (1997, p. 18)

**The Economics of Religion: Anthropological Approaches**
**Research in Economic Anthropology, Volume 31, 123–156**

**ISSN: 0190-1281/doi:10.1108/S0190-1281(2011)0000031009**

## INTRODUCTION

It is quite remarkable that the anthropological investigation of the economic aspects of religion and the materiality of religion has attracted recently so much debate and scholarly interest. I am thinking about this volume as well as the various calls for panels and papers posted on anthropology websites, following the organization of conferences, around topics such as religion and the marketplace, religion and commodities, and matter and spirituality.[1] In a very general way, these efforts might reflect a renewed attempt to add a materialist perspective to what, for the most part, has been a mentalist approach to religion.[2] The exploration of the materiality of religion, however, could mean many things, from the materiality of ritual and religious commodities to the material basis of religious experiences. In such cases, matter is assumed as a "conduit" for the sacred. But to approach the materiality of religion could also mean the exploration of the material conditions of practitioners and their impact on the meaning and form of religious values and worship. I want to suggest here that both attempts at re-focusing on the material conduits for numinous experiences and the existential conditions of practitioners still leave untouched the implicit opposition between material and religious orientations to reality.

The divide between the material and spiritual worlds has acquired such a factual reality in the West – not just as a conscious worldview but also as an ingrained ethos – that it also constantly blotches other areas of social action outside of religion. Even when this divide is purposefully historicized and spatially circumscribed, its matter-of-factness makes these attempts seem futile. Obviously in religion and less obviously in the arts, the moral split of materiality and immateriality seems to be more acute than in other areas of human social action. It seems as if stories about starving artists and ascetic saints – more than telling us about specific trajectories and social processes – circulate as cautionary tales, as regimes of value, that shape how we make judgments about reality. I am always astonished to hear my very young students conform and reproduce almost exactly centuries-old discourses of nostalgia about the loss of aura of popular musicians who they see as regrettably losing their "authenticity" after gaining recognition and economic success. As if struggling musicians and visual artists or, for that matter, ascetic healers are guaranteed a purity and originality and effectiveness by their very lack of economic success. As if the "authenticity" and quality of their music, artwork, or spiritual work are irreversibly tainted by commodification processes, dismissing the very possibility of different forms of aura, authenticity, and spirituality that may emerge from commodification processes, and new regimes of value and evaluation.

One can argue that the current revisiting of the materiality of religion in its various forms, in academic and nonacademic circles, hints by negation to the success of the Reformation and the Enlightenment in separating religion from economy, and making that separation into an unquestionable truth in the West.[3] That "wherever there is money there could not be religious considerations" and "where there is religion there cannot be money involved" have been naturalized to the point of common sense. Put in a slightly different way, passions and belief have no place in economy, and economy trumps authentic soul searching and religious devotion.[4] And if economic issues are discussed together with religion in nonacademic circles, it is usually in a negative sense – as a contravention, showing that the basic ideas exposed in Max Weber's *The Protestant Ethic and the Spirit of Capitalism* (1958/1930), written more than a century ago, have remained as theoretical constructs confined to the academy. In this essay, I will reflect on the ways in which lay and academic orientations to social realities still tend to implicitly presume – with some remarkable exceptions, explored below – the separation between religion and economy.[5] It will proceed critically via a self-reflexive and case-based exploration of my ethnographic research of Puerto Rican *brujos* (witch-healers) and *brujería* (witch-healing).

As the title of my dissertation, "Spiritual Entrepreneurship: Puerto Rican Witch-Healing under Consumerism and the Welfare State" (1998a), suggests, it explored the merging of the worlds of economy and spirituality in the workings of urban *brujos*, and the changing faces of magic and healing practices in Puerto Rico within the context of consumerism and the welfare state. I remember the interest of various university press acquisition-editors when I described my manuscript in these terms. More than the methodological innovations, the historical account, or the ritual details of magic and divination, editors, referees, reviewers, and commentators of my manuscript (published thereafter as *Witchcraft and Welfare* in 2003) were all intrigued by the apparent crossing of borders of *brujos*, who intervened not only in spiritual matters but also in practical issues related to welfare agencies, legal matters, and unemployment. What impressed readers and commentators was the fusion of spiritual and economic motivations within *brujería*, as well as the unproblematic combination of spiritual and material goals directing the work of *brujos*.

In the context of an exacerbated politics of culture in the late 1990s, the ways in which the work of *brujos* and their spirits surpassed the exclusionary aspects of national identity, as well as categorical distinctions between religion and magic, and between economy and religion, felt liberating. Not less telling were the often amused reactions among members of the audience, during professional conference presentations, of photos and recordings from my fieldwork about Social Security applications blessed and placed under a Buddha, and Hail Marys prayed in litany during the making of a magic work. But perhaps, what was lost to the audience was that, rather than exemplifying the unusual merging of separate social worlds, clients who bring documents produced by welfare state agents to consultations with *brujos* are seeking to achieve the material benefits that might be garnered with the appropriate spiritual intervention. Similarly, rather than demonstrating the fusion between religion and magic, rituals in which Catholic prayers are performed by *brujos* during the making of magic works are tangible manifestations of past challenges to the exclusivity of the Catholic Church, and the illicit takeover of its most cherished symbols and gestures by popular devotees.[6] Retrospectively, I read the favorable reactions of readers and commentators to my ethnography of *brujería* as a symptom of the pervasive, ingrained paradox between materiality and immateriality, spirits and economy, and magic and state bureaucracy.

More than a decade later, as I was preparing my notes for a course on witchcraft, magic, and modernity, I re-read Stanley Tambiah's *Magic, Science and Religion* (1990). When I found E. B. Tylor's (1958/1873, 1871) characterization of sorcerers, magicians, and diviners as "impresarios," my knee-jerk reaction was to question the originality of my own characterization of *brujos* as "spiritual entrepreneurs." But then, upon reading further down, I realized that it was quite obvious that what the evolutionist Tylor meant was actually the very opposite of my take on spiritual entrepreneurship. Rather than highlighting the economic, pragmatic aspects of the spiritual labor of witches, Tylor meant impresarios as charlatans, as cunning artists, who are able to hide false, mistaken associations made between ideal and real connections, in making their predictions, via various forms of sleight of hand and rhetorical stratagems such as vagueness and ambiguity – all of which were meant to avoid the invalidation of their predictions and help them get away with it.[7] In the same vein, interpreters and scholars of religion, inspired by the Reformation's dictum that the world of God pertain to belief but not to matter, have established the assumed difference between magic and religion (both from evolutionist and formalist perspectives) on the basis of the immateriality of the first and the crude materiality of the second.[8] As if the assumed manifestation or objectification of the belief in God on earth was of an inherent different order from other embodied religious phenomena found in ritual practice, visions, miracles, or possession. Pertinently, Daniel Miller (2010, p. 71) references the ancient Egyptians' "faith in the potential of monumentality to express immateriality" in writing about the Western paradox between materiality and immateriality, in his *Stuff*. They had solved this paradox, Miller argues, through the construction of colossal pyramids and sculptures, and the development of unprecedented technologies of mummification for securing immortal transubstantiation – a far cry from the iconoclasm and asceticism demanded by the Reformation.

Part of the task of revising the opposition between matters related to matter and those pertaining to religion imply also a revision of such categories as superstition, animism, magic, and fetish. In addition, it will explain my purposeful indistinct use of "religion" and "magic" here. The legacy of the Enlightenment is obvious.[9] Encyclopedists established these categories and the distinctions between "superstition," "magic," and "enlightened" religions as a result of empirical "facts" about exotic others and ignorant folk, gathered by travelers and antiquarians, as well as their personal rejection of dogmatic religions and embrace of deism (Flaherty, 1992; Gay, 1977/1966, pp. 145–149).[10] Another well-known comparison that attracted extensive scholarly and theological debate was that between religious dogma (and/or magic) and science. In this framework, institutional dogmatic religions and magic were seen as opposed to the rule of reason and the practice of criticism, which Enlightenment philosophies constituted – not with little disregard for the scientific discoveries made by alchemists and astrologers – as the basis of modernity and progress.[11] With the development of science and the rule of rationality that it implied – the argument went – the detachment from the mystical worlds of magic and superstition (ruled by error) was to mark a new modern era.[12] This assumed separation between the worlds of faith and those of reason informs also Weber's "disenchantment" theory of modernity, which has been recently revisited not just by critical theorists of modernity but also by scholars addressing the recent flourishing of global religions and religious healing in so-called first world countries (Habermas, 2008; Landy & Saler, 2009).[13] Overall, this revision suggests the revisiting of the secularization thesis implied in modernization theories (Asad, 2003; P. L. Berger, 2001, 2006; Beyer, 1990, 1994; Casanova, 1994, 2001; Gillespie, 2009; Latour, 1993; Scott & Hirschkind, 2006; M. Taylor, 2007). If, in fact, the world has never ceased to be enchanted – as the assignation of spirit to things in, but not limited to, commodity fetishism à la Marx (1983/1867) – the idea of "re-enchantment" ceases to have real import in theorizing religious revivals in late modernity (Landy & Saler, 2009).

Rather than tracing the extensive polemics surrounding the moral divide established between material and immaterial worlds, and between religion and economy, I will proceed by reflexively using my research on Puerto Rican *brujería* as a stepping board to launch a cross-cultural reflection and critique of the assumed separation between the sacred and the profane, and between economy and religion. For that purpose, I will draw on the ideas of spiritual capital, spiritual entrepreneurship, spiritualized materialism and blessings, which I have developed as a result of my ethnographic research in Puerto Rico. But first, I will trace the macro processes that help situate Puerto Rican *brujería* in a temporal as well as global perspective.

## THE MORAL ECONOMY OF *BRUJERÍA*: SPIRITUALIZED MATERIALISM IN A TEMPORAL VEIN

For the last five centuries, extra- and intra-religious forms of power have shaped the moral economy of Puerto Rican *brujería*.[14] As many other noninstitutional vernacular religions, it has retained the symbols of hegemonic culture long after they have ceased to be relevant in the mainstream (Williams, 1980). In this sense, the moral economy of *brujería* has been shaped by what Anna Tsing terms the "margins": those "zones of unpredictability at the edges of discursive stability, where contradictory discourses overlap, and where discrepant kinds of meaning-making converge" (1994, p. 279). The resulting moral economy thereby encompasses apparently incongruous manifestations, such as the presence of the Catholic cross in the midst of African and Asian deities, the performance of Catholic and Protestant worship in the making of magic works, and the convergence of consumerist desires with the moral laws of Spiritism.

*Brujería* is the native term given in Puerto Rico by insiders to a variety of religious practices that have fused for five centuries, in the most unorthodox ways, the beliefs, the healing, magic, and divination rituals, and worship of popular Spanish Medieval Catholicism, a uniquely Puerto Rican blend of French Kardecean Spiritism (*Espiritismo*), U.S. Protestantism, and Cuban Santería.[15] Along these processes, *brujería* has responded successively to the political, economic, and social conditions of colonialism, slavery, nation building, consumer capitalism, and transnationalism. Each period presented new ideas and practices to be incorporated, as well as challenges to that incorporation.[16] In tracing this moral economy, even briefly, it is inevitable to address also the consequences of its tortuous history, which entails illicit appropriations of religious symbols and gestures, persecution, vilification, and misunderstanding. For example, as a result of colonial Spanish rule – and not without deadly consequences – *brujería* adopted the gestures of popular Catholicism, some of its saints, its healing rituals, and seasonal devotions. With the liberal period of the 1860s, Scientific Spiritism (Espiritismo Científico) enters the idiom of *brujería*, adding a more secular general theory of communication with the spiritual world, and reincarnation, which creole elites recruit in building a sense of progressive Puerto Rican civic identity (see Romberg, 2003a).

Most importantly, Spiritism adds a timeless and spaceless moral order that assumes that human beings are responsible for their actions in the past, present, and future. This moral order is encapsulated in a set of spiritual laws: the Law of Cause and Effect establishes that every action has its effect in this or other lives, the Law of Love means that the cosmos is inherently ruled by harmony and love, and the Law of Reincarnation suggests that we are given infinite opportunities to improve our karma through our free will. According to the ethos of Spiritism, thereby, it is not possible to separate between profane and sacred realms of action since both are integrated into one cosmic order.

In subsequent decades, very much to the dismay of *espiritistas científicos* who had defined Spiritism in philosophical – not religious – terms, popular practices of *Espiritismo* add an array of Latin American, African, and Asian entities such as *Indios, Gitanas, Madamas, Papa Candelos*, Buddhas, and *Arabes*. *Espiritistas científicos*, mostly of whom belonged to the ruling elites, launch a multi-prong war in the early decades of the twentieth century against "popular" Spiritists through the legal, medical, and media establishment for being "charlatans" or false Spiritists (see Romberg, 2003a, 1998b). Since the 1960s, as a result of Cuban, intra-Caribbean, and revolving-door migrations, certain iconic elements of Santería are also added to the practices of *brujería* in the form of "*collares*" (color-beaded necklaces representing seven deities of Santería), certain healing and magic procedures, and sacred music. These additions are kept in secret, away from public discussion, until roughly the late 1980s, when the ideologies of multiculturalism and cultural nationalism kick in (see Romberg, 2007).

The intense intra-Caribbean circulation of ritual specialists – of a free-flow migration of *espiritistas, santeros, brujos*, and New Age healers from Santo Domingo and Cuba – and the revolving-door migration of Puerto Ricans back and forth between the island and the mainland since the end of the twentieth century have contributed visibly to the internal dynamism of

Puerto Rican *brujería*. For example, in *botánicas* (stores that sell religious paraphernalia) and in private altars, one can see today icons representing various African, Asian, and Middle Eastern spirits – all of which arrived to the island as a result of the global circulation of ritual commodities.[17]

In response to the transnational expansion of ritual commodities and the idiom of consumerism, novelty becomes a new tradition within *brujería*. "New and improved" ritual commodities – from magical potions and healing emulsions, packaged in mass-produced bottles and aerosols, to an assortment of amulets, candles, magical perfumes, lotions, and figurines from all over the globe – are welcomed, following the logic of capitalist expansion, as signs of progress and improvement. My point here is that by keeping abreast with the novelties offered in the market of ritual goods, *brujos* demonstrate their high level of professionalism and entrepreneurship. For instance, during my fieldwork and apprenticeship with Haydée, a Spiritist *bruja*, she and I used to conduct multiple visits to *botánicas* on a regular basis. After one such visit, she said to me, "I always like to check out what's new here ... check out the latest novelty."

Contrary to assumptions about the "traditionality" of folk religions, that is, their fixity in some pristine time and space, *brujería* practices are as cosmopolitan and eclectic as its practitioners and clients. They are immersed – as the majority of Puerto Ricans – in moving in and out of the world of late capitalism and the realities of Puerto Rico's modern colonial relations with the United States, marked by the ethos of consumer and welfare capitalism.[18]

The American imposition of a capitalist economic system in combination with a welfare state (commonly referred to as welfare capitalism) produced a unique hybrid form of economic, political, and cultural colonial domination, characterized half ironically by Puerto Rican anthropologist Jorge Duany (2001, p. 6) as a "postcolonial colony" and by political scientist Ramón Grosfoguel (1997) as a "modern colony." Much like the French and Dutch colonies in the postwar Caribbean, what characterizes Puerto Rico as a modern colony (in contrast to neocolonial colonies) is that it is granted (1) annual transfers of billions of dollars in the form of food stamps, health, education, and unemployment benefits; (2) participation in metropolitan standards of mass consumption; (3) metropolitan citizenship and democratic/civil rights; (4) and the possibility of migration without the risks of illegality (*ibid.*). These politico-economic arrangements were established as a result of the American-sponsored economic boom of the island between World War II and the 1970s, which was strategically "showcased" as an American success story of development (especially in contrast to the involvement of the USSR in Cuba).[19] The U.S. welfare system was extended to Puerto Rico as a social and political buffer for its various massive postwar capitalist development programs, which included extending its food-stamp program to the island (Grosfoguel, 2003, pp. 57–66; Morrissey, 2006).[20]

In addition to transforming Puerto Rico into a modern colony, the Americanization of the island reconstituted not just the previous roles of *brujos* and the basis of their spiritual power but also the material desires and predicaments of their clients. New sites for economic mobility that had been opened up by U.S. federal welfare-state agencies and U.S.-based businesses, together with the alluring powers of the modern colony, of consumerism and fame, have reshaped again the moral economy of *brujería*, opening up new areas of intervention for *brujos*.

But this is only one side of the story of *brujería* under the modern colony. The expansion of *brujería* in ritual matters – promoted by the American spiritual laissez-faire ethos, consumerism, and welfare capitalism – acquires an added significance in relation to Puerto Rican ethnic politics of culture, which in turn provide a new public exposure and valuation of folk religions such as *brujería*. In light of the ambiguous status of Puerto Rico as a "free but associated state" (ELA) of the U.S. commonwealth, a unique form of cultural nationalism has emerged, since the 1980s, in which the notion of Puerto Ricanness is premised on its creole ethnic roots (Grosfoguel, Negrón-Muntaner, & Georas, 1997; Morris, 1995). In the field of vernacular religions, this has led to processes of revitalization and essentialism that constructed *brujos* as "our popular doctors," and *brujería* as a token of "our popular wisdom."[21] This trend has also reshaped the moral economy of *brujería* with a more inclusive and positive attitude toward people and things African (see Romberg, 2007). In line with this cultural nationalistic spirit, some *brujos* began to be featured in newspapers as heroes, as unique voices of Puerto Ricanness, and as saviors of ancient Taíno and African traditions. In this context, *brujos* were able to freely add and proudly show off "African"-based religious prayer songs (imported from Cuba or New York), and exhibit Santería and Vodou paraphernalia. Strategically thus appropriated, some key commercialized icons of Santería, such as the seven powers and the beaded necklaces of the orishas, became Creole symbols of an imagined, generalized notion of "African" ritual power (even without adopting the essential tenets of animal sacrifice and initiation rituals through which these symbols acquire their ritual power). Not playing into this cultural politics yet protected by its public force, *brujos* have been able to capitalize from this kind of cultural revitalization of Africanity, and boost their professionalization within the implicit idioms of heritage and multiculturalism, securing additional translocal spiritual powers to better serve their clients. Protected by these idioms, yet free of their constraints, *brujos* systematically have rejected any form of ethnic orthodoxy. The epigraph with which I began this chapter reflects this spirit.

The last point about the Americanization of the island and its impact on the moral economy of *brujería* I address here has to do with the separation – at least at an official level – of state and religion, and the subsequent opening up of the gates to religious eclecticism and competition. In contrast to Spanish rule, American Catholic and Protestant Churches mushroomed since the American invasion of 1898. And later on, with political exiles arriving to the island, following the Cuban revolution (1959), several Santería temples were established.[22] During the first decades of American rule, many families ended up being constituted by individuals affiliated to distinct religious traditions in unprecedented combinations.[23] It is in this eclectic religious atmosphere – with its various logics of practice – that many of the *brujos* I worked with were raised and later, as adults, developed their employment trajectories, shaping in great measure their individual ritual styles.

Tonio, a famous *brujo* in his nineties I met in Loíza in 1995, for instance, followed popular Catholicism, Spiritism, and creole reworkings of African-based magic practices. In the early decades of the twentieth century he used to work as an overseer in an American-owned sugar plantation, acquiring an insider's knowledge of the workings and effects of capitalist forms of management and employment. For 60 years (until his death in 1998), however, he dedicated himself fully to his *obra espiritual* (spiritual work). Haydée, whom I met through Tonio, followed Tonio's style with an added mode emerging from her upbringing as the daughter of a Catholic mother, who converted to the American Protestant Church, and a Spiritist father. She worked for many years as a legal secretary and then as the personnel manager of a state-run health-care clinic, before devoting herself fully to the *obra espiritual* after a series of health problems. The youngest of all the healers I met, Armando, was raised by an *espiritista* mother in New York, where he had the opportunity to expand his ritual knowledge among Cuban and Nuyorican *babalawos* as well as other healers from South and Central America, continuing his initiation in Santería under Ronny, an exiled Cuban *babalawo* in Puerto Rico.[24] Armando worked in an American-owned paper-goods factory in Puerto Rico, and as a healer after work and on weekends, with the intention of fully dedicating himself to the *obra espiritual* as soon as he could leave his in-laws' house. Basi, the owner of a *botánica*, was in her mid-sixties when I met her and lived with her during several months of my fieldwork. She was raised by a Spiritist grandmother, and since roughly the 1980s blended New Age versions of Spiritism with an ecumenical form of Christian religiosity in her *obra espiritual*. Reflecting her healing style, Basi's *botánica* was profusely supplied with the usual potions, icons, trinkets, herbs, candles, and books with added special sections for New Age and herbal medicine products.

Indeed, against assumptions held among outsiders, the social space in which *brujos* operate today is far from being situated on the margins of society, in the bush, or in communal settings. Surely its transmission does not depend solely on face-to-face interactions or on the existence of a preestablished local community. Individuality, technological innovation, extended services and choices, and the international circulation of ideas are some of the values directing both society and the practices of *brujería*. What this brief account about the moral economy of *brujería* in a temporal vein shows is that far from being a closed form that is centered in a locale or circumscribed to an ethnic group, *brujería* is an open form in constant change, its contours discontinuous and permeable. As a vernacular religion, *brujería* has transformed its practices through the centuries and has shaped its moral economy as a result of its various layers in a way that it enables its practitioners to be both modern and moral. That is, the moral or ethical codes of *brujería* far from rejecting the ethos of capitalist exchanges and consumerism transforms this ethos to fit its religious values into what I have called elsewhere a form of "spiritualized materialism" (Romberg, 2003b).

## THE MAGIC OF CONSUMER AND WELFARE CAPITALISM

Following my argument about the impact of the ethos of consumer and welfare capitalism on the ritual expansion and eclecticism of *brujería*, I propose to explore, in more detail, the constitutive role of economic realms in *brujería* practices. In particular, I develop the idea that in addition to the magic of commodities à la Marx (1983/1867), there is a spiritual, transformative meaning to the power of commodities and consumption within *brujería*. Many have related consumption to the self, in particular for giving material form to desired narratives of self-identity (Giddens, 1991). But what I find most relevant here is the work of some anthropologists who have recently connected magic with consumption, and spiritual power with commodities. I am thinking of the work by Vincanne Adams (1997) among the Sherpas. They mimic the attitudes and gear of Western climbers of the Everest not out of submission to foreigners or reverence for materialism but, paradoxically, as a result of the belief in the nonattachment to material things, and in the power of an ideal effigy of becoming – through appropriate ritual interventions – an extension of the self. Also, Jonathan Friedman (1991) addresses the belief in the cosmic relation between commodities and the self. He refers to *les sapeurs*, a name given to very poor young Congolese men who buy very expensive Parisian label-clothes, as a form of cargo, in order to illustrate how consumption becomes a vehicle through which powerful energies could be appropriated in generating a desired, more powerful self (cf. Sansi Roca, 2007).

In *Witchcraft and Welfare* (2003b) I show how the ethos of consumer and welfare capitalism has constituted the very practices of *brujería*, its rituals, the roles of *brujos*, and their general appeal in the field of spiritual healing. In a recent essay I focus on the selective ways in which capitalist welfare and consumer desires and opportunities have been reworked into the spiritual realm, arguing that they point to the emergence of an "alternative vernacular" – or even a "pirated" – "modernity" (Romberg, 2012).

I insist on the fact that *brujería* is a vernacular religion that unintentionally and unprogrammatically has incorporated consumer and welfare values in redefining the power of spirits, and the nature of their interventions in the everyday struggles of practitioners and followers. It is this particular quality which distinguishes *brujería* from current programmatic attempts at integrating religious values and economic projects in all sorts of management reforms. A case in point: workshops are run in Indonesia among business people for the purpose of connecting the values of Islam with neoliberal corporate entrepreneurship (Rudnyckyj, 2009). These workshops entail "inculcating the ethical dispositions conducive to market success," which include adopting an "ethics of work as worship, self-discipline, responsibility, and accountability to achieve worldly affluence and otherworldly salvation" (p. 130). On this account, Daromir Rudnyckyj distinguishes between these workshops as examples of "spiritual economies" and "prosperity religions," which "are premised on the notion that enhanced religious devotion will foster economic prosperity through divine intervention" (p. 129). It should be obvious at this point that a further distinction should be added between programmatic interventions that entail the spiritualizing of economic practices, and the spontaneous, noninstitutional spiritualized materialism of *brujería*. Within a broader context, presented in the introduction, all these attempts at making the economic, spiritual and vise versa – regardless of whether they are sponsored or spontaneous – demonstrate that the separation of the material and immaterial worlds, assumed by classic modernity theories, is nothing but one possibility for being modern.

Furthermore, unlike ethnographies that report on the negative effects of capitalist consumption and accumulation, which result, for instance, in "contracts with the devil,"[25] the surplus of "zombie laborers" working for "cannibalistic witches"[26] or in an "economy of the belly,"[27] economic prosperity marked by one's ability to consume luxury goods is not envisioned within the moral economy of *brujería* as "evil" or "the labor of the negative." Rather, it is viewed as a cosmic retribution for leading a moral life according to Spiritism. Indeed, the Americanization of the island opened up new economic opportunities, especially by U.S. federal welfare-state agencies and U.S.-based businesses, that have reconstituted not just the previous roles and power basis of *brujos* but also the material desires of their clients: the alluring powers of the modern colony, of consumerism and fame, now informing the practices of *brujería*.

In framing my discussion within "consumer capitalism" – and more broadly "consumerism" – I draw attention to the expansion of new capitalist modes of consumption under the modern colony as a critical site for the exploration of both the constitutive aspects of capitalist neocolonial forms of domination and the potential agency of consumers as producers of meaning – in particular within the practices of *brujería*. Here I follow the distinction made by Daniel Miller (1995) between a priori and a posteriori differences in the kinds of rupture that the consumption of commodities might entail. By focusing on the a posteriori effects of consumer capitalism, I can illuminate "the unprecedented diversity created by the differential consumption of what had once been thought to be global and homogenizing institutions" (p. 3). Rather than solve theoretical conundrums, it provides a lens to observe how people "commonly live out these contradictions in local practice" (p. 18).

Looking at the constitutive nature of consumption on Puerto Rican subjectivities, Ortiz-Negrón's study reveals that consumer culture offers an escape from the utilitarian spaces of everyday life; it signifies the participation in, not just the illusion of, equal access to goods and services, and allows for a nontraditional perception of commodities and social relations that stresses elements of desire and cultural capital (2007, pp. 41–42). This last part of the quote pertains to my essay here, suggesting that the nontraditional perception of commodities as cultural capital could be extended also to spiritual capital, as will be shown below.

The choices of lifestyle offered by consumerism in conditions of "high modernity" impart a more or less integral set of practices that an individual "is forced" to choose (we have no choice but to choose) "not only because such practices fulfill utilitarian needs, but because they give material form to a particular narrative of self-identity" (Giddens, 1991, p. 81). Acquisitiveness, as an endless process of materialization, satisfies at one and the same time the possibility of enhancing and renewing one's self according to ever-changing narratives of self-identity and lifestyles. The materiality of these lifestyles acquires yet an added value within *brujería*, following the idea of manifestations mentioned earlier: they become objectifications of the spiritual power of their owners. Consumerism, as a postmodern means of imagining and constructing self-images through the acquisition of commodities, hence, relates to the magic of commodities, in general, because of the transformative potential of commodities (as in the spirit of matter, e.g., in "commodity fetishism") and to *brujería* practices, more specifically, as one of the social arenas in which one's "blessings" could be attested and tested (I develop this idea below).

Stressing the opposition between commodification and the "true" self – reminiscent of other oppositions made in other epochs between materiality and immateriality – critics of the culture industry and mass consumption of the first half of the twentieth century saw commercial forces as the archenemies of authentic culture. If one would follow their vision today, the spiritual effectiveness of vernacular religions like *brujería* would have appeared as irremediably tainted by the commodification of its practices. Defying extra-religious considerations of authenticity, however, Puerto Rican *brujería* has transformed the values of consumerism, the welfare state, and heritage in accordance to the Spiritist ethos, conferring its own criteria of authenticity to its ritual practices: ritual efficacy measured by the improvement and expansion of one's *bendiciones* (blessings). Indeed, against the tropes of loss and spiritual maelstrom projected by critics of the culture industry, *brujería* promotes neither the "disembedding of social relations and a disregard for social responsibility" nor an "alienated individuation" (Giddens, 1991, pp. 172, 198). On the contrary, the ability to consume newer lifestyles in the present is perceived as a reward, as the fruit for having enjoyed propitious worldly and otherworldly relationships.

In sum, based on how *brujos* and their clients relate to the notion of blessings today, it is evident that material and spiritual progress not only are not at odds but are intimately connected. Especially in a world guided by capitalist modes of production and the sensuous insatiable consumption of lifestyles and self-images, *brujos* and their clients, more than endangered species, should be therefore seen as active participants in these mainstream forces, speaking to them in their own particular modern yet spiritual idiom.

## SPIRITUAL CAPITAL

Scholarship on the various forms of capital – such as human, economic, social, cultural, religious, and spiritual – is only tangentially relevant here, because it has used these concepts, for the most part, as variables within theoretical models aimed at explaining macro social processes, from social stratification and the reproduction of class inequalities to the connection between the rise of church attendance and economic crisis, and so forth.[28] In contrast, the reason I choose to characterize the spiritual power garnered by *brujos* as spiritual capital stems from the very ways in which practitioners and followers envision spiritual power within *brujería*. As a fluid, positive energy that could be enhanced and accumulated according to the Spiritist ethos through free will, spiritual power or spiritual capital always begets and is transformed into other forms of capital such as social power and material success.

A few more words that highlight the aptness of "spiritual capital" in relation to *brujería* are necessary. *Brujería* is the term given to a variety of vernacular religious practices shaped by the spiritual charisma of individual *brujos*, rather than by any form of religious organization, structure or hierarchy ruled by theological or initiation legitimation systems (as in Santería). As such, the ability of *brujos* to assert their spiritual power in competition with others depends solely on their spiritual capital, which needs to the be constantly enhanced, publicized, and proven – even if proofs are very malleable in the field of magic, divination, and healing. As in other areas of social action, the expansion and innovation of their spiritual capital are fundamental for competing, specifically, in the field of *brujería* practices and, more generally, in the field of spiritual healing.

Also in this respect, the way spiritual capital is addressed here differs essentially from the ways it has been addressed in others contexts. The recent adoption of terms such as "spiritual capital" and "spiritual economy," featured in contemporary economic and anthropological debates, seems to respond to the increasing global demands for social and economic justice, social innovation, and corporate social responsibility (see, e.g., Rudnyckyj, 2009; Rima, 2012). On a theoretical level, it seems to point to the cross-cutural revitalization of Weber's *The Protestant Ethic and the Spirit of Capitalism* (1958/1930) in the areas of economic policy and global economic corporate practice, in ways that transcend the Protestant ethic, and include Islam, New Age, and other types of religious or spiritual practice.[29]

In contrast, another scholarly corpus has emerged in the anthropology of Africa around the notion of "occult economies" and "predatory capitalist practices," which highlight the criminalization of non-Western forms of spiritual capital and spiritual economies (Comaroff & Comaroff, 1999, 2001). Under the negative umbrella of "magic," this scholarship points at the devastating social and moral costs of fusing local beliefs in spiritis and ancestors with global economic practices. If the economic scholarship mentioned above highlights the need for adding moral values to the amorality of capitalist corporate gains, the second highlights the tragic consequences of unattainable capitalist gains under neoliberalism.

A few ethnographic vignettes will illustrate, in contrast, the meaning of spiritual capital within *brujería,* by focusing on a number of its elements: miraculous beginnings, *pruebas* (tests), fame and success, and one's *cuadro* (spiritual power) and *protecciones* (protections).[30] All these elements are considered *manifestaciones* (manifestations), according to the premise that the spiritual world can be manifested in various, unpredictable ways in this world (see Romberg, 2009).

During the year and half that I worked with *brujos* in Puerto Rico, particularly with Haydée, with whom I worked most intensively, I have followed closely everyday rituals and consultations held in private *altares* (house temples). I have seen physicians, teachers, workers, business people, lawyers, and unemployed people come to consult with Haydée, saying, "*Vengo a resolver*" (I come to resolve). I have seen waiting rooms filled with clients coming to consult early in the morning, often making big sacrifices and waiting for several hours to be seen. I have heard *brujos* brag about the number of clients and the long distances they have to travel, often crossing the island, in order to come see them. But all this bragging had a purpose: to show how successful they were as *brujos* and the many sacrifices they had to make in order to fulfill their mission as healers. For example, "the waiting room is full ... I know when I go in my altar-room but don't ever know when I will leave it" pointed to the sacrifice that fame entails. In a unique way, a "celebrity" discourse (indexing fame, success, and public devotion) was fused with a "sacrifice" discourse (economic, physical, and emotional) in order to highlight the spiritual mission of *brujos*.

Miraculous encounters *brujos* usually report having had with God or a saint at an early age or at the outset of their *obra espiritual* confer to them a sense of mission and empowerment on earth, and most vividly manifest their godly calling.[31] Miraculous stories depicting in great detail the exact moment at which saints, God, or some other benevolent spirit bestowed spiritual powers on them reveal the enormous power these stories have in asserting that they had been summoned to a life of sacrifice and spiritual mission. To their miraculous beginnings *brujos* add the achievements and spiritual capital emanating from the daily physical, material, and emotional sacrifices (investments) they perform in their spiritual work. These sacrifices are framed as inevitable and as signs of their true spiritual calling, which usually begins after having to endure various "*pruebas*" or misfortunes, such as serious illness, divorce, and the loss of children. They are retrospectively framed as tests of their true devotion and dedication as healers, and as signs of their calling.[32]

In addition to asserting their spiritual capital through miraculous encounters and the endurance of *pruebas*, the spiritual capital of *brujos* increases in direct relation to the richness of their house temples, the amount of *santos* (figurines of the saints) and offerings, and the ability to throw lavish spiritual fiestas and coronations for their patron saints. These forms of conspicuous consumption (which also entail material sacrifices for the sake of their spiritual work) are public assertions of the success and prosperity of *brujos*. Like the aforementioned *sapeurs*, flashy clothes and the latest technological gadgets manifest the success and spiritual power of *brujos,* signifying the rewards for their sacrifice as healers – as will be shown in the section on blessings.

But what, if any, might be the cost of the recent incorporation of consumerism into the practices of *brujería*? Does it jeopardize the authenticity of its spirituality? Do the commercial forces incorporated into the practices of *brujería* taint its purity and diminish its effectiveness – following what critics of the culture industry saw as the dangers of mass consumption? Practitioners and followers of *brujería* would dismiss these questions altogether, emphasizing that material and spiritual progress not only are not at odds but are intimately connected. In fact, *brujos* enhance their spiritual capital by a combination of, and interrelation between, their material and spiritual success. To their material success they add their enlightened spirituality. It is publicly demonstrated through repeated references to their god-given gifts, the miraculous beginnings of their spiritual work, their charity, the tests (misfortunes) they had to undergo to become true healers, and the tremendous sacrifices they have to make, even of losing spouses or jobs, in order to pursue spiritual work. Haydée expressed poetically her mission as a *bruja* and her total commitment to helping others at the expense of all her other personal commitments, even her own well being, saying:

Whatever there's to eat we'll eat [*Lo que haya para comer, comeremos*]
Whatever we'll need to drink, we'll drink [*Lo que haya que tomar, tomaremos*]
Whatever we'll need to dance, we'll dance [*Lo que haya que bailar, bailaremos*]
And whatever we'll need to "witch," we'll "witch" [*Y lo que haya que brujear, brujearemos*].[33]

Far from being demands for asceticism, personal sacrifices of worldly goods, relationships, and well being are the ultimate expressions of being authentic *brujos* and recipients of God's grace. Essentially, like the sacrifices of Jesus – which many reference in their speech – the sacrifices of *brujos* assure that their spiritual healing powers will be multiplied as a result of the Spiritist laws of Cause and Effect and of Love, mentioned earlier. One of the ways in which they multiply is by the addition of new *protecciones* (protective spirits or guardian angels), who act as spiritual shields aimed at protecting *brujos* from all sorts of evil attacks. They form the personal *cuadro* of a person and inform the dynamic nature of spiritual power – powerful *brujos* having the stronger, most elaborate and enlightened *cuadros*.

Showing off what one has might promote the *envidia* (envy) of others – one of the most common motives behind *causas* (bewitchments) and *trabajos malos* (black magic) – and thus of misfortune. But unlike people in general, *brujos* would never feel intimidated by the threat of *envidia*. They have the power to *revocar*, deactivate it by all kinds of spiritual means. Exposing their material success regardless of the potential *envidia* it might create, *brujos* reassert that they are in control of their powers, and that spirits are in their favor. Material success indexes the blessings of *brujos*, which – the logic goes – they could not have been able to uphold had they not also been protected from evil attacks by their *cuadro* and *protecciones*, which had made them invulnerable to evil attacks. These are important messages that need to be conveyed not just to clients but also to other healers competing with them for fame and reputation. Pursuing fame and spiritual enlightenment through acts of charity and sacrifice are two essentially different yet related modes of "investment" in accumulating "spiritual capital." This double meaning of being "blessed" – as will be developed below – constitutes the core of *brujería* in its present phase, and defines it as a form of spiritualized materialism. It suggests that the quest for economic power acquires quasi-religious proportions, and that the roles of *brujos* shift on a continuum between being saints and brokers or spiritual entrepreneurs.

## SPIRITUAL ENTREPRENEURSHIP

If the material prosperity of *brujos* signals that they have been showered by the favor of spirits, to clients it assures that they have come to the right healer for help, because the same positive energies of that healer will eventually be transmitted to them. It is therefore imperative that everything indexes the financial and spiritual flow around *brujos*, who often appropriately often place continuously running fountains in their waiting rooms. Adding to the spiritual capital accumulated by *brujos*, new forms of social capital afforded by interventions in business and welfare agencies are also accumulated and redistributed by *brujos* to their clients. And again, being at the center of several commercial and bureaucratic circles, the number of influential clients they attract, and the possibility to redistribute whatever riches and connections they might have gathered through these networks beget and enlarge their spiritual capital. Depending on their relative fame, *brujos* are usually at the center of various social networks that might include members of the political, professional, and commercial elite. In this capacity they are able, for example, to recommend their unemployed clients to companies headed by their influential clients, and inform their needy ones of new welfare regulations that may become available. *Brujos*, thus, often find themselves at the crossroads of crucial channels of information. This pool of knowledge and connections gathered during consultation, and then exchanged in gossip among other *brujos*, comes in handy when informing their clients of how to apply – on time and in the right manner – for federal help, a job, housing, social security benefits, and the like. *Brujos* also provide assistance in more direct ways, for example, by putting managers and directors in touch with potential employees. *Brujos* hence become brokers between local and transnational corporations, redefining the locality and spirituality of their expertise in order to encompass global economic markets and federal agencies based elsewhere. Knowledge and control over the transcendental world is now complemented with knowledge and control of market opportunities and welfare-state policies.

As a result, the spiritual entrepreneurship of *brujos* has expanded their services to include those traditionally assigned not only to psychologists and social workers but also to officials of the labor, justice, and public health systems. For instance, after Hurricane Bertha hit the island in summer 1996, a subject that came up frequently in consultations was the Federal Emergency Management Agency (FEMA), which, among other things, deals with hurricane victims' complaints and demands. Federal funds allocated for these purposes were distributed according to the specifications and under the administration of the Puerto Rican government. Haydée, Basi, Tonio, and other *brujos* were well informed as to who was eligible to claim losses from FEMA and how, where, and when to file for them. Few knew that just by making a telephone call, a small but meaningful payment could be received without undergoing annoying appraisals. Because Haydée had an *ahijado* (spiritual protégé; lit., "godson") whose sole job responsibility was answering hurricane-related emergency telephone calls for the government, she was fully aware of this pool of easily available money that had recently arrived; she directed her clients who had suffered the aftermath of the hurricane to make the best of it. Many were encouraged to make the first move by Haydée's saying, as she read the cards, "You'll cry when you receive this gift from FEMA. The money will help you resolve many things."

Consequently, as will become evident below, the healing and magic styles of powerful *brujos* – those blessed by the spirits and influential clients – encompass not only the spiritual but also the material welfare of their clients. Interceding more directly in the material conditions of their clients, and no longer persecuted as heretics or vilified as charlatans, *brujos* have began to function implicitly as "spiritual entrepreneurs:" as brokers between state, business, and professional networks. As such, they are sought out when mainstream medicine, psychology, or social work fail to provide solutions to a variety of health, relationship, and economic problems, but more comprehensively, for promoting one's blessings or ultimate success in life. Legitimized by their spiritual power and charity, *brujos* assert their expertise as professionals who intercede between worldly and supernatural realms in order to help their clients maximize their worldly potentials in morally appropriate ways. When Nora, a young woman in her twenties, came for a consultation with Haydée with a health problem, aggravated by the refusal of Social Security to recognize it and grant her work compensation money, Haydée asked Nora to show her the official documents she had received. Attempting to obtain Social Security benefits can be a complicated and frustrating process, filled with long forms and red tape. Haydée knew that many of those who apply for Social Security Disability for the first time are denied until they can bring the necessary evidence. Numerous impairments could qualify as disabilities, and thus it is crucial to retain a knowledgeable attorney who can gather the necessary evidence and present it to the court. After carefully examining the reasons for the rejection and identifying the agent who signed it, Haydée advised her to go see a friend of hers who works in the local social security office, and (mentioning her commendation) ask for her help in reapplying for benefits. The consultation was not over until the power of spirits of prosperity and justice were summoned, the official documents were placed under an icon of San Judas Tadeo (the saint in change of difficult legal cases) and a lit candle was offered to him. As a final warning, Haydée said, "Remember that you can't work when you apply for disability."

Indeed, *brujos* look at misfortune as the result of a *sum* of causes. Treating all aspects of life simultaneously, *brujos* orchestrate solutions that integrate usually dissonant domains of human action – employment, education, medicine, the legal system, and so on. In more than one way, *brujos* provide clients with a holistic approach: just as the causes of misfortune are thus holistically diagnosed, so is the treatment holistically administered.[34] As spiritual entrepreneurs they constantly look for ways to improve their services, and this seems to be irresistible to anyone who comes into contact with them. Since the spiritual field of *brujería* is largely shaped (especially healer–client relationships) by free-market consumer considerations, intense competition, self-promotion, and specialization are essential. Understandably, in asserting their fame and powers as spiritual entrepreneurs, healers often define their expertise in relation to mainstream "cloak professions:" Armando, for example, defines himself as a "spiritual consultant," Haydée as a "doctor of the soul."

Besides encouraging assertiveness and alertness in the material sphere, *brujos* redirect their clients toward a morally oriented attitude in pursuing these very goals according to the Spiritist ethos encoded by Kardec. In line with the Spiritist Law of Cause and Effect and the notions of spiritual justice and reincarnation, the advice given by *brujos* can transform merely instrumental advantages into ones that are spiritually endowed – since every action in this world has an effect in the other and every action is an opportunity to pay spiritual debts acquired in previous lives. *Brujos* thereby provide not only the "eyes and ears" for clients in order to find possible resources in bureaucratic organizations and capitalist enterprises, but also the "soul" or moral charter behind the demands and profits that could be made.

In fact, unlike the bureaucratic nightmares involving sorcery, criminality, and terror in places such as Haiti and Castro's Cuba,[35] *brujos* and followers of *brujería* imagine the redistributive role of the Puerto Rican welfare state as potential sources for furthering one's blessings.[36] *Brujería* practices have hereby turned fame and success into rewards for leading a morally and civically responsible life: material and spiritual progress not only are not at odds but are indeed intimately connected.

## BLESSINGS

Within the current moral economy, material acquisitiveness and desire for success have been elevated to a higher moral and spiritual order of aspiration: *brujos* and their followers see material and spiritual progress as well as the attainment of high social status not only as morally legitimate quests but also as visible signs of being "blessed" by the spirits. This form of spiritualized materialism suggests that profit and success have become infused with an ultimate moral purpose, once spiritual forces are believed to have intervened in achieving these goals. Defined in terms of both material and spiritual progress, the quest for *bendiciones* has been molded recently by consumer and welfare capitalist values and sensibilities, adding to the hitherto exclusively Catholic and Spiritist spiritual understandings of *bendiciones* a concern for the material conditions of one's existence (similar to those promoted by charismatic Pentecostal churches).

A unique connection between spiritual and material blessings is hence established: material success – measured by one's acquisitive power, social status, and overall progress – attests to having been gifted with spiritual blessings (and vice versa). This redefinition of the meaning of *bendiciones* is embodied in rituals and orientations to reality that aim at achieving and explaining economic and social success. For instance, under the Spiritist Law of Love and Charity, one's *bendiciones* (in this case, one's *cuadro*, and the spiritual capital composed of protective spirits) have to be shared in order to multiply them: the more we share, the more blessings and prosperity we are given back in return.

As a regime of value that has emerged out of the ethos of consumer and welfare capitalism, the notion of blessings informs the content of desires and social action of followers; it works within but also adds new values and meaning to consumer and welfare capitalism. For example, if achieved, material success becomes a marker of one's *bendiciones* or spiritual powers; and if it has yet to be achieved, it becomes an endless motivational force that guides personal and social choices. If one's personal power (or *bendiciones*) becomes materialized and desired objects become spiritualized (when spirits are thought to be involved in achieving them), the moral economy of *brujería* today maneuvers murky sets of correspondences. Material consumption is simultaneously proof and reflection of having spiritual *bendiciones*; and having spiritual *bendiciones*, such as having a nice *cuadro* and a host of powerful *protecciones*, anticipates material blessings.

Botánicas, for example, have to have their shelves full, well-supplied, and have the latest innovations, with "New and improved," expensive items, in order to index they are "blessed by the spirits." A prosperous-looking botánica (like prosperous *brujos*) attracts clients with the hope that its good fortune will also affect them. But the sign of prosperity is not the size of the *botánica* but its displayed stock, in terms of both variety and quantity (the latter related to availability, the ongoing bountifulness of supply). The general advice, then: Never be put out of stock!

*Bendiciones* can take other forms and meanings, emerging from the interventions of *brujos* in commercial and bureaucratic matters. Thanks to Haydée's connections, for example, a young unemployed woman found a job with a restaurant chain, since the manager of one of these restaurants was one of Haydée's clients. Through another client, a manager of a hotel chain and car-rental agency, Haydée secured a receptionist job for a young Nuyorican man just arrived from the mainland. Interventions like these were public pledges to her power as a *bruja*, as well as a display of the *bendiciones* – acquired via her spiritual work – she was able to share with her clients.

The apparent contradiction of motives – of sacrifice and spirituality on the one hand, and lavishness, and material success on the other – will make more sense as new layers of the complex meaning of *bendiciones* are further unraveled. Similar to Calvinist belief, prosperity is a sign of being blessed by the spirits. But unlike the Calvinist concept of "election," one's cuadro (personal spiritual power) is not preordained. While considered to be a gift that is inherited, the *cuadro* lacks any deterministic feature. It has to be developed and nurtured throughout one's life – in this and later reincarnations on earth. This is why clients who show signs of being endowed with spiritual gifts and mediumship often hear: "*debes echar ese cuadro pa' delante*" (you need to push forward your *cuadro*), since only after they make good use of their *cuadro* by sharing it in spiritual work they would ripe the blessings that it can generate.

The quest for economic power acquires religious proportions and the taking up of a spiritual morality has its material rewards. Indeed, it reflects on the personal spiritual power of individuals, defined by the *cuadro* (spiritual frame) one is born with and acquire, and the battery of *protecciones* (spiritual shields) one is able to summon. On the other hand, *bendiciones* are signaled by the commodities one is able to consume, one's buying power, as well as the public visibility and influence one might be able to achieve. So, either as a potential force ready to be materialized or as an objectified reality that proves one's spiritual capital, *bendiciones* point to the ingrained desire to be economically and spiritually successful within *brujería* practices. Like the phantasmagoric nature of the fetish mentioned by Michael Taussig, *bendiciones* elucidate "a certain quality of ghostliness in objects in the modern world and an uncertain fluctuation between thinghood and spirit" (Taussig, 1993a, p. 217, 1993b). If both self and commodities become entangled in fetishist relations, one's personal power becomes materialized and desired objects become spiritualized. Acquiring and at the same time confounding their assumed qualities, the need to perceive one's personal power materialized in objects destabilizes both the self and the objects that are meant to embody it. Within this new moral economy, then, material acquisitiveness and desire for success have been elevated to a higher moral and spiritual order of aspiration: *brujos* and their followers see material and spiritual progress as well as the attainment of high social status as not only morally legitimate quests but also visible signs of being blessed by the spirits.

This sensuous moral economy fits well with the enticements and predicaments of consumer capitalism, acquiring a spiritual, cosmic meaning. Through a conflation of spiritual and social responsibility to others, it offers an unorthodox, individualistic form of spiritual guidance and religiosity in achieving material success.

## CONCLUDING REMARKS

In the preceding discussions I have tried to tease out the differences between materiality as the conduit for the sacred and materiality as the manifestation of the sacred. Analytical frameworks such as "occult economies," and "cargo cults," offer good examples to test these differences further, even though the first emerged out of the African context and the other the Melanesian. Ton Otto (2009), in his recent assessment of cargo cult frameworks, defends their relevance (in spite of the critiques launched against them) because they provide vantage points for advancing a cultural critique of Western society that challenges the sharp distinction between religious and economic values – a major obstacle, he argues, for understanding contemporary moral paradoxes wrought by global corporate capitalism. The anthropological use of these frameworks have been based on the general assumption that the emotional/spiritual attachment to commodities are the result of flawed types of causation, which connect the consumption of desired commodities with the expected intervention of spirits. They are erroneously believed to be the conduits for making these commodities available to those who worship them in the right manner. In these cases, consumer capitalism engenders unrealistic, ill-considered, and most surely un-rewarded magical rituals and ceremonies. In this capacity, they provide ample evidence for what evolutionist scholars established more than a century ago as the indisputable difference between magic and religion: "occult economies" and "cargo cults" acting as "gate keeping concepts" (Trouillot, 1992) that reinforce the temporal distance between traditional "magic" and modern "religions" (Asad, 1993). The opposition between the materiality and instrumentality of magic and the immateriality and lack of instrumentality of religion (mentioned in almost all introductory volumes on magic and religion) thereby acquire an empirical confirmation. The moral economy of *brujería* stands in stark contrast to these portrayals. What "occult economies" seem to help muster elsewhere, the modern colony provides for *brujería* practices in Puerto Rico. And what "cargo cults" seem to summon, contemporary *brujos* make available through combined spiritual and practical advice. The worlds that witchcraft and magic practices summon are not unlike the "invisible worlds" that inform the accumulation of wealth among the dynastic rich in the contemporary United States (Marcus, 1998) and, for that matter, also the "flexible" forms of capitalist accumulation under globalization (Harvey, 1991). Like these unseen worlds, the moral economy of *brujería* works not just to adapt to the modern colony but also to reproduce it, if unwillingly and in oblique ways. Similarly to the practices of Korean shamanism, which in the last twenty years increased the frequency of "prosperity rituals," rather than "ancestor rituals," in order to fit the capitalist needs of its practitioners (Kendall, 1996), the spiritual world of *brujería* and the cosmological morality it entails are summoned for *promoting* the necessary practical means to achieve mainstream goals, not for *substituting* them. Adding the ethical tenets of Spiritism to the spectral ethos and predicaments of consumer and welfare capitalism, the moral economy of *brujería* can therefore be seen as fusing the material and immaterial worlds of consumer capitalism, as in commodity fetishism, without assuming its alienating outcomes. This moral economy, as argued here, is the result of several layers of economic and religious meanings in the past and the present. As the current attempts to make the amorality of global capitalist projects more moral in corporate reform programs, the worlds of economy and religion or spirituality are not inherently incompatible. I do not mean to suggest that the enticements of the modern colony in Puerto Rico are such that they disavow the predicaments of consumer and welfare capitalism. As with fetishism, the fetishism of the modern colony involves a powerful fascination or desire that is both *indulged* and at the same time, *denied* (Hall, 1997, p. 267).

On this note, I can end with a play on Latour's *We Have Never Been Modern* (1993) and suggest, "we have never been disenchanted," or that religion and economy have never been separated.[37] Passions and commerce, magic and commodities and, more abstractly, immateriality and materiality have their own ways of operating without following necessarily the constitutive prognosis of the Reformation and Enlightenment, and the diagnosis of modernization theories – the current alleged re-enchantment of the world being just a phantom that covers up for its unfulfilled disenchantment.[38]

## NOTES

1. I am thinking of the themes of the 2011 biennial meeting of the Society for the Anthropological Study of Religion (SAR), and the sessions of this society proposed for the 2011 annual meeting of the American Anthropological Association.

2. Geertz's (1977) critique of mentalist approaches to culture in the 1970s could be regarded as a similar attempt at drawing attention to the materiality and public nature of culture.

3. A parallel argument has been made in the colonial context by Talal Asad (1993), who argues that labeling a ritual as magic – in contrast to religion or miracle – is already a constitutive act, geographically and historically defined by power relations.

4. Coincidentally, I found an online article, written by Rabbi Shmuley Boteach, where he calls on his own community to take a critical stand against the display of wealth and to remember the religious purpose of material wealth: "we must embrace the great Jewish philosopher Maimonides", articulation of the purpose of material wealth, namely, the facilitation of good deeds like charity, hospitality and the proper provision for one's family's needs (http://www.wnd.com/index.php/index.php?pageId=35865#ixzz1HoxtKJDu).

5. The title of one of the several books recently published on this topic, *Business and Religion: A Clash of Civilizations*? clearly captures the essence of this presumption.

6. I develop this idea in Romberg (2005, 2012).

7. The idea of magicians as dexterous performers of deception and concealment is revisited magisterially by Michael Taussig (1998) who reminds us that their dexterity often includes also the performance of rituals of revelation. See also Sharot (2001) and Weber (1960) on the differences between priests and popular healers.

8. Another comparison that attracted extensive scholarly and theological debate was that between religion (or magic) and science (discussed below).

9. According to historian Keith Thomas (1971) the distinction between religion and magic did not exist before the second half of the seventeenth century.

10. Most encyclopedists were deists who believed in the universal existence of a supreme creator of the world, which, after being created, functioned according to natural laws.

11. I am referring here to Giordano Bruno and other established scientists who made advances in science (according to modern definitions of science) based on what the Enlightenment might have viewed as esoteric, mambo-jumbo. Indeed, science and magic were united until the Enlightenment. For example, Tambiah notes (1990, p. 28), the background of Newton has been sanitized by the Enlightenment in order to constitute him as the icon of modern reason even though Newton gave equal importance to his work on astrology and alchemy as that on astronomy and mathematics.

12. In this case, I draw on the distinction between societal modernization and cultural modernity made by many – among them, Gaonkar (2001) and Trouillot (2002).

13. See the edited volumes by Barnes and Starr Sered (2004), Helen Berger (2006), and Csordas (2009) on the variety of current modes of religious healing in a global/transnational context in America and the Caribbean, as well as Lindquist (2006) for healing in contemporary Russia. In more general terms, see Huss (2007), Styers (2004), and Wexler (2007).

14. My use of "moral economy" addresses the emergence of vernacular (nonofficial) moral and religious beliefs and practices in various economic, political and institutional religious contexts. It differs from the works by James Scott (1977) and others such as E. P. Thompson (1971), where it refers to pre-capitalist strategies or local beliefs recruited by marginalized groups in order to deal with the injustices of capitalism.

15. Santería, also called *La Religión de los Orishas* or *La Regla de Ocha*, is an Afro-Cuban religion. *Ocha* in Spanish and *orisha* in English derive from the Yoruba word for deity, òrì\sà. *Espiritismo* refers to the belief in spirits as encoded by the French scientist and man of letters Allan Kardec (1804–1869). Its orthodox practice is referred to as *Espiritismo Científico* (Scientific Spiritism). Yet, any follower of *espiritismo*, whether in its orthodox or popular form, is generally called an *espiritista* – except orthodox practitioners who disparagingly call popular *espiritistas, espiriteros* (Romberg, 1998b).

16. In my previous work I have explored these issues extensively. See Romberg (1998b, 2003a, 2003b, 2005, 2007).

17. I am sure that those versed in Latin American popular culture will recognize, in various degrees, these trends in other parts of the Americas. Suffice to look at the works written on Brazilian Umbanda, Cuban and Venezuelan *Espiritismo*, and

Haitian and Dominican Vodou. Many are the parallels between the histories of these places and Puerto Rico.

18. I refer to "welfare- and consumer-capitalism" strategically in order to contextualize my discussion of the moral economy of Puerto Rican *brujería*. The theoretical-historical discussion about the emergence of these concepts and the differences and connections between the two are beyond the scope of my argument. The colonial relations tying the U.S. mainland with the island began with the U.S. invasion in 1898 and were consolidated under the commonwealth status in 1950.

19. For example, Operation Bootstrap ("industrialization by invitation") in the 1950s boosted labor-intensive industries and the infrastructure (Wagenheim & Wagenheim, 1994). The exemption from federal taxes granted to American companies on the island, under the 936 Law of 1976, propelled massive foreign and federal capital investments for capital-intensive industries on the island.

20. By the 1980s, it was used by approximately 60% of Puerto Rican families. Most analysts conclude that these economic changes had not only economic and social repercussions but also political and cultural. They contributed to the assimilation of, and dependence on, American consumerist and welfare values and practices, which eventually hindered the decolonization impetus of the island, and constituted a unique *boricua* everyday practice marked by political and cultural ambiguity (Negrón-Muntaner, 2007).

21. Since the 1980s, pride in folk religions replaced the criticism of the 1950s, when the same practices were framed by a development-inspired media as superstitious and as survivals of medieval beliefs (see Romberg, 2003a).

22. As a result, Puerto Rican *brujos* could be initiated into Santería without having to travel to Cuba. For the various religious movements arising during this pluralist period, see Agosto Cintrón (1996), Duany (1998), Hernández Hiraldo (2006), and J. Vidal (1994).

23. Trusting that the American presence would help modernize and bring prosperity to the Puerto Rican nation after centuries of declining Spanish colonial rule, many (rich and poor alike) began converting to the newly established American Catholic and Protestant Churches on the island. See Hernández Hiraldo (2006) and Silva Gotay (1985, 1997).

24. A *babalawo* is the highest priest in Santería.

25. See Taussig (1980, 1987, 1995) about the devil and its relation to commodities, colonialism, and exploitation.

26. For vivid depictions of the city of witches and their predatory nature, see Rosalind Shaw (2002a, 2002b).

27. Jean-François Bayart's notion, referenced in Peter Geschiere (1997, p. 7).

28. For a brief review, see Iannaccone and Klick (2003).

29. Also, several nonacademic books and blogs, couched in various human rights, environmental and corporate-culture discourses, highlight the need for a more moral form of capitalism across the globe. For an example of a corporate-culture approach to spiritual capital that draws on the basic human need for higher motivations, such as social justice, see the nonacademic book by Zohar and Marshall (2004).

30. For a more comprehensive account, see Romberg (2003b, 2009).

31. The convergence of these stories with those of Catholics and Protestants is striking. The interrelations are not casual. Most *brujos* have been educated in either Catholic schools or have participated as children in Protestant services. Some have experienced both, having born into a Catholic family that shifted to Protestantism in the early decades of the past century.

32. A more extensive ethnographic discussion about miraculous beginnings and *pruebas* can be found in Romberg (2003b).

33. Haydée invented a verb out of the noun *bruja* ("*brujear*"), which I translate as "to witch."

34. *Brujos* combine different types of healing techniques such as various forms of spiritual cleansing, divination, and herbal-based or purely spiritual healing rituals (see Romberg, 2009).

35. See Palmié (2002, 2004, 2006), Routon (2010), and Wedel (2004) for examples of the bureaucratic terror embodied in current "black" magic practices attributed to Palo in Cuba.

36. Except, of course, by the Puerto Rican Independentist movement, which sustains that these welfare benefits explain the reticence of the population from voting for the total separation between Puerto and the United States. Indeed, after decades of deferred controversies, visible in the enactment of endless plebiscites, the future of Puerto Rico's status is still entangled in irreconcilable options between the commonwealth status and complete annexation, leaving out completely the independence option, which in the 2004 election represented a meager 2.75% of the votes.

37. In this regard, the emergent "postsecularism" scholarship would have to be at least categorized if not relabeled.

38. See Meyer (2010), Meyer and Pels (2003), and Masquelier (2004) for anthropological discussions about the modernity of magic, and the magic in/of modernity. Compare with a political-science discussion of the secularization thesis, for example, in C. Taylor (2007).

# REFERENCES


Adams, V. (1997). Dreams of a final Sherpa. *American Anthropologist, 99*(1), 85–98.

Agosto Cintrón, N. (1996). *Religión y cambio social en Puerto Rico, 1898-1940.* Río Piedras, Puerto Rico: Ediciones Huracán.

Asad, T. (1993). *Genealogies of religion: Discipline and reasons of power in Christianity and Islam.* Baltimore, MD: The Johns Hopkins University Press.

Asad, T. (2003). *Formations of the secular: Christianity, Islam, modernity.* Stanford, CA: Stanford University Press.

Barnes, L. L., & Starr Sered, S. (Eds.) (2004). *Religion and healing in America.* Oxford, UK: Oxford University Press.

Berger, H. (Ed.) (2006). *Witchcraft and magic: Contemporary North America.* Philadelphia, PA: University of Pennsylvania Press.

Berger, P. L. (2001). Reflections on the sociology of religion today. *Sociology of Religion Special Issue: Religion and Globalization at the Turn of the Millennium, 62*(4), 443–454.

Berger, P. L. (2006). Religion in a globalizing world: Pluralism, not secularism is the dominant trend in an 'age of explosive, pervasive religiosity.' Pew Research Center Publications. Retrieved from http://pewresearch.org/pubs/share.php. Accessed on June 15 , 2011.

Beyer, P. F. (1990). Privatization and the public influence of religion in global society. *Theory Culture Society*, *7*(2), 373–395.

Beyer, P. F. (1994). *Religion and globalization*. London: Sage.

Casanova, J. (1994). *Public religions in the modern world*. Chicago, IL: University of Chicago Press.

Casanova, J. (2001). Religion, the new millennium, and globalization. *Sociology of Religion*, *62*(4), 415–441.

Comaroff, J., & Comaroff, J. (1999). Occult economies and the violence of abstraction: Notes from the South African postcolony. *American Ethnologist*, *26*(2), 279–303.

Comaroff, J., & Comaroff, J. (Eds.) (2001). *Millennial capitalism and the culture of neoliberalism*. Durham: Duke University Press.

Csordas, T. J. (Ed.) (2009). *Transnational transcendence: Essays on religion and globalization*. Berkeley, CA: University of California Press.

Dayan, J. (1997). Vodoun, or the voice of the gods. In: M. Fernandez-Olmos & L. Paravisini-Gebert (Eds.), *Sacred possessions, Vodou, Santería, Obeah and the Caribbean* (pp. 13–36). New Brunswick, NJ: Rutgers University Press.

Duany, J. (1998). La religiosidad popular en Puerto Rico: Una perspectiva antropológica. In: Á. Quintero Rivera (Ed.), *Vírgenes, magos y escapularios: imaginería, etnicidad y religiosidad popular en Puerto Rico* (pp. 163–185). San Juán, PR: Centro de Investigaciones Sociales de la Universidad de Puerto Rico.

Duany, J. (2001). Nation, migration, identity: Rethinking colonialism and transnationalism apropos the case of Puerto Rico. Invited lecture at the Department of Sociology and Anthropology, Swarthmore College, November 30.

Flaherty, G. (1992). *Shamanism and the eighteenth century*. Princeton, NJ: Princeton University Press.

Friedman, J. (1991). Consuming desires: Strategies of selfhood and appropriation. *Cultural Anthropology*, *6*(2), 154–163.

Gaonkar, D. P. (2001). On alternative modernities. In: D. P. Gaonkar (Ed.), *Alternative modernities* (pp. 1–23). Durham, NC: Duke University Press.

Gay, P. (1977/1966). *The Enlightenment: The rise of modern paganism*. New York, NY: W.W. Norton.

Geertz, C. (1977). Religion as a cultural system. In: C. Geertz (Ed.), *The interpretation of cultures* (pp. 87–125). New York, NY: Basic Books.

Geschiere, P. (1997/1995). *The modernity of witchcraft: Politics and the occult in postcolonial Africa*. P. Geschiere & J. Roitman (Trans.). Charlottesville, VA: University Press of Virginia.

Giddens, A. (1991). *Modernity and self-identity: Self and society in the late modern age*. Stanford, CA: Stanford University Press.

Gillespie, M. A. (2009). *The theological origins of modernity*. Chicago, IL: University of Chicago Press.

Grosfoguel, R. (1997). The divorce of nationalist discourses from the Puerto Rican people: A sociohistorical perspective. In: F. Negrón-Muntaner & R. Grosfoguel (Eds.), *Puerto Rican jam: Essays on culture and politics* (pp. 55–76). Minneapolis, MN: University of Minnesota Press.

Grosfoguel, R. (2003). *Colonial subjects: Puerto Ricans in a global perspective*. Berkeley, CA: University of California Press.

Grosfoguel, R., Negrón-Muntaner, F., & Georas, C. (1997). Beyond nationalist and colonialist discourses: The Jaiba politics of the Puerto Rican ethno-nation. In: F. Negrón-Muntaner & R. Grosfoguel (Eds.), *Puerto Rican jam: Essays on culture and politics* (pp. 1–38). Minneapolis, MN: University of Minnesota Press.

Habermas, J. (2008). Secularism's crisis of faith: Notes on post-secular society. *New Perspectives Quarterly*, *25*, 17–29.

Hall, S. (Ed.) (1997). *Representation: Cultural representations and signifying practices*. London: Sage.

Harvey, D. (1991). *The condition of postmodernity: An enquiry into the origins of cultural change*. Hoboken, NJ: Wiley-Blackwell.

Hernández Hiraldo, S. (2006). *Black Puerto Rican identity and religious experience*. Gainesville, FL: University Press of Florida.

Huss, B. (2007). The new age of Kabbalah and postmodern spirituality. *Journal of Modern Jewish Studies*, *6*(2), 107–125.

Iannaccone, L. R., & Klick, J. (2003). *Spiritual capital: An introduction and literature review*. Preliminary draft, prepared for the Spiritual Capital Planning Meeting, October 9–10, 2003, Cambridge, MA.

Kendall, L. (1996). Korean shamans and the spirits of capitalism. *American Anthropologist*, *98*, 512–527.

Landy, J., & Saler, M. (Eds.) (2009). *The re-enchantment of the world: Secular magic in a rational age*. Stanford, CA: Stanford University Press.

Latour, B. (1993). *We have never been modern* (C. Porter, Trans.). Cambridge, MA: Harvard University Press.

Lindquist, G. (2006). *Conjuring hope: Magic and healing in contemporary Russia*. New York, NY: Berghahn Books.

Marcus, G. E. (1998). The problem of the unseen world of wealth for the rich. In: G. E. Marcus (Ed.), *Ethnography through thick and thin* (pp. 152–160). Princeton, NJ: Princeton University Press.

Marx, K. (1983/1867). Commodities (Capital vol. 1). In: E. Kameka (Ed.), *The portable Karl Marx* (pp. 437–461). New York, NY: Penguin Books.

Masquelier, A. (2004). The return of magic. *Social Anthropology*, *12*(1), 95–102.

Meyer, B. (2010). "There is a spirit in that image": Mass-produced Jesus pictures and Protestant-Pentecostal animation in Ghana. *Comparative Studies in Society and History*, *52*, 100–130.

Meyer, B., & Pels, P. (Eds.) (2003). *Magic and modernity: Interfaces of revelation and concealment*. Stanford, CA: Stanford University Press.

Miller, D. (1995). Anthropology, modernity and consumption. In: D. Miller (Ed.), *Worlds apart: Modernity through the prism of the local* (pp. 1–22). London: Routledge.

Miller, D. (2010). *Stuff*. Malden, MA: Polity Press.

Morris, N. (1995). *Puerto Rico: Culture, politics, and identity*. Westport, CT: Praeger.

Morrissey, M. (2006). The making of a colonial welfare state: U.S. social insurance and public assistance in Puerto Rico. *Latin American Perspectives*, *33*(1), 23–41.

Negrón-Muntaner, F. (Ed.) (2007). *None of the above: Puerto Ricans in the global era*. New York, NY: Palgrave Macmillan.

Ortiz-Negrón, L. L. (2007). Space out of place: Consumer culture in Puerto Rico. In: F. Negrón-Muntaner (Ed.), *None of the above: Puerto Ricans in the global era* (pp. 39–50). New York, NY: Palgrave.

Otto, T. (2009). What happened to cargo cults? Material religions in Melanesia and the West. *Social Analysis*, *53*(1), 82–102.

Palmié, S. (2002). *Wizards and scientists: Explorations in Afro-Cuban modernity and tradition*. Durham, NC: Duke University Press.

Palmié, S. (2004). Fascinans or tremendum? Permutations of the state, the body, and the divine in late-twentieth century Havana. *New West Indian Guide*, *78*(3/4), 229–268.

Palmié, S. (2006). Thinking with Ngangas: Reflections on embodiment and the limits of "objectively necessary appearances". *Comparative Studies in Society and History*, *48*(4), 852–886.

Rima, S. D. (2012). *Spiritual capital and economic transformation: A US perspective*. Surrey, UK: Ashgate Publishing.

Romberg, R. (1998a). *Spiritual entrepreneurship: Puerto Rican witch-healing under consumerism and the welfare state*. Unpublished Ph.D. dissertation, University of Pennsylvania, Pennsylvania, PA.

Romberg, R. (1998b). Whose spirits are they? The political economy of syncretism and authenticity. *Journal of Folklore Research*, *35*(1), 69–82.

Romberg, R. (2003a). From charlatans to saviors: Espiritistas, curanderos, and brujos inscribed in discourses of progress and heritage. *Centro Journal*, *15*(2), 146–173.

Romberg, R. (2003b). *Witchcraft and welfare: Spiritual capital and the business of magic in modern Puerto Rico*. Austin, TX: University of Texas Press.

Romberg, R. (2005). Ritual piracy: Or creolization with an attitude. *New West Indian Guide*, *79*(3–4), 175–218.

Romberg, R. (2007). Today, Changó is Changó, or how Africanness becomes a ritual commodity in Puerto Rico. *Western Folklore Special Issue: Afro-Caribbean Religions, Culture, and Folklore*, *66*(1–2), 75–106.

Romberg, R. (2009). *Healing dramas: Divination and magic in modern Puerto Rico*. Austin, TX: University of Texas Press.

Romberg, R. (2012). The moral economy of *brujería* under the modern colony: A pirated modernity? In D. Paton (Ed.), *Obeah and other powers: The politics of Caribbean religion and healing*. Durham, NC: Duke University Press.

Routon, K. (2010). *Hidden powers of state in the Cuban imagination*. Gainesville, FL: University Press of Florida.

Rudnyckyj, D. (2009). Spiritual economies: Islam and neoliberalism in contemporary Indonesia. *Cultural Anthropology*, *24*(1), 104–141.

Sansi Roca, R. (2007). 'Dinheiro vivo': Money and religion in Brazil. *Critique of Anthropology*, *27*(3), 319–339.

Scott, D., & Hirschkind, C. (Eds.) (2006). *Powers of the secular modern: Talal Asad and his interlocutors*. Stanford, CA: Stanford University Press.

Scott, J. C. (1977). *The moral economy of the peasant: Rebellion and subsistence in Southeast Asia*. New Haven, NJ: Yale University Press.

Sharot, S. (2001). *A comparative sociology of world religions: Virtuosos, priests, and popular religion*. New York, NY: New York University Press.

Shaw, R. (2002a). The production of witchcraft/witchcraft as production. In: R. Shaw (Ed.), *Memories of the slave trade: Ritual and the historical imagination in Sierra Leone* (pp. 201–224). Chicago, IL: University of Chicago Press.

Shaw, R. (2002b). *Memories of the slave trade: Ritual and the historical imagination in Sierra Leone*. Chicago, IL: University of Chicago Press.

Silva Gotay, S. (1985). Social history of the churches in Puerto Rico, preliminary notes. In L. Vischer (Ed.), *Towards a history of the church in the third world*. Papers and reports about the issue of periodization, presented at the Ecumenical Association of Third World Theologians in Geneva, July 17–21, 1983.

Silva Gotay, S. (1997). *Protestantismo y política en Puerto Rico, 1898–1930*. Río Piedras: Editorial de la Universidad de Puerto Rico.

Styers, R. (2004). *Making magic: Religion, magic, and science in the modern world*. Oxford, UK: Oxford University Press.

Tambiah, S. J. (1990). *Magic, science, religion, and the scope of rationality*. Cambridge, UK: Cambridge University Press.

Taussig, M. (1980). *The devil and commodity fetishism in South America*. Chapel Hill, NC: The University of North Carolina Press.

Taussig, M. (1987). *Shamanism and colonialism and the wild man: A study of terror and healing*. Chicago, IL: The University of Chicago Press.

Taussig, M. (1993a). Maleficium: State fetishism. In: E. Apter & W. W. Pietz (Eds.), *Fetishism as cultural discourse* (pp. 217–247). Ithaca, NY: Cornell University Press.

Taussig, M. (1993b). *Mimesis and alterity: A particular history of the senses*. New York, NY: Routledge.

Taussig, M. (1995). The sun gives without receiving: An old story. *Comparative Studies in Society and History*, *37*(2), 368–398.

Taussig, M. (1998). Viscerality, faith, and skepticism: Another theory of magic. In: B. Nicholas Dirks (Ed.), *In near ruins: Cultural theory at the end of the century* (pp. 221–256). Minneapolis, MN: University of Minnesota Press.

Taylor, C. (2007). *A secular age*. Cambridge, MA: Belknap Press of Harvard University Press.

Taylor, M. C. (2007). *After God*. Chicago, IL: University of Chicago Press.

Thomas, K. (1971). *Religion and the decline of magic*. New York, NY: Scribners.

Thompson, E. P. (1971). The moral economy of the English crowd in the eighteenth century. *Past and Present*, *50*(1), 76–136.

Trouillot, M-R. (1992). The Caribbean region: An open frontier in anthropological theory. *Annual Review of Anthropology*, *21*, 19–42.

Trouillot, M-R. (2002). The otherwise modern: Caribbean lessons from the savage slot. In: B. M. Knauft (Ed.), *Critically modern: Alternatives, alterities, anthropologies* (pp. 220–237). Bloomington, IN: Indiana University Press.

Tsing, A. L. (1994). From the margins. *Cultural Anthropology*, *9*(3), 279–297.

Tylor, E. B. (1958/1873, 1871). *The origins of culture and religion in primitive culture* (Vols. 1 & 2 of 1873 edition of Primitive Culture). New York, NY: Harper & Brothers.

Vidal, J. R. (1994). Citizens yet strangers: The Puerto Rican experience. In: J. P. Dolan & J. R. Vidal (Eds.), *Puerto Rican and Cuban Catholics in the U.S., 1900–1965* (pp. 11–143). Notre Dame, IN: University of Notre Dame Press.

Wagenheim, K., & Wagenheim, O. J. (Eds.) (1994). *The Puerto Ricans: A documentary history* (updated ed.). Princeton, NJ: Markus Wiener.

Weber, M. (1958/1930). *The Protestant ethic and the spirit of capitalism*. T. Parsons (Trans). New York, NY: Charles Scribner's Sons.

Weber, M. (1960). Gods, magicians and priests. In: R. Robertson (Ed.), *From the sociology of religion* (pp. 407–418). New York, NY: Penguin.

Wedel, J. (2004). *Santería healing: A journey into the Afro-Cuban world of divinities, spirits, and sorcery*. Gainesville, FL: University Press of Florida.

Wexler, P. (2007). *The mystical society: An emerging social vision* (in Hebrew). Jerusalem: Carmel.

Williams, R. (1980). Base and superstructure in Marxist theory. In: K. Marx (Ed.), *Problems in materialism: Selected readings* (pp. 31–49). London: Verso.

Zohar, D., & Marshall, I. (2004). *Spiritual capital: Wealth we can live by*. San Francisco, CA: Berrett-Koehler Publishers.

# PROMISING AND ENGAGING THE FUTURE THROUGH RITUAL SPONSORSHIPS IN EASTERN YUCATAN, MEXICO

Andrés Dapuez, Andrés Dzib May and Sabrina Gavigan

## ABSTRACT

*In a village of Eastern Yucatan, Mexico, cargo or* kuuch *sponsors compare their ritual tasks to "buying life" from crosses, Catholic saints, and Mayan deities or "owners." The local notion of* compromiso, *engagement, or commitment, helps these festival participants express the condition of possibility to successfully perform such exchanges. Decisive for these life renewals, promises, and* compromisos *depend upon empathy to authorize ritualists and subsume social and natural phenomena under exchange paradigms. By defining, critiquing and using the concept of "disposition" as an inherently self-other stance through which economy transforms into religiosity and vice versa, this chapter analyzes this particular regime of engagement and the temporalities it implies. Through a commitment to the past and the practice of promissory exchange, sponsors develop a new perceptual scheme in which the ritual cultivation of discipline, awareness, expectation, and responsibility are expressed.*

**The Economics of Religion: Anthropological Approaches**
**Research in Economic Anthropology, Volume 31, 157–186**

**ISSN: 0190-1281/doi:10.1108/S0190-1281(2011)0000031010**

# INTRODUCTION

The village that I will refer to here as "Ixán," Yucatan, Mexico, was one of the places where the Caste Wars and the "new religion" (Bricker, 1981) of *Cruzo'ob* was initiated in the nineteenth century. Situated nine miles away from Valladolid, the second largest city of the Yucatan State, Ixán is a village of around 2,000 persons. Approximately 98% call themselves Catholic. Not until the late 1980s, when electricity and running water came to town, were Pentecostals, or *los hermanos*, also allowed by authorities to regularly visit Ixán. The conversion of the son of a *Comisario,* or communal mayor, marked this turning point in the village's relationship with *los hermanos*. However, the village's elite still openly resist and distrust Pentecostals. Guardians of the Cross, *Maestros Cantores*, shamans – ritual experts called "elders" – speak out against them because, according to the general opinion, *protestantes* endanger and deny local traditions. With no Catholic priests in the village, it is up to the *Maestros Cantores* to recite chants and prayers and perform novenaries. One *Maestro Cantor* insists that *los hermanos* make no promises and take no compromises; they only sing in the two temples and sometimes make "acción de gracias" in their field plots. This same *Maestro Cantor* explains that these *hermanos* expect the second coming of Jesus to occur within their lifetimes. In preparation for the Advent, one *hermano* even sold almost all of his possessions. Laughing, though, he admitted that there were already two Pentecostals dead and buried in the cemetery and Jesus did not come.

Authorities in Ixán include 15 *Sargentos Primeros* who lead opinions and make decisions in political matters. Among the political authorities there is also a *Comandante* who presides over meetings and assemblies, and takes care of various duties including writing acts, conducting hearings, and prosecuting ordinary crimes. Every male older than 18 must serve under one sergeant, or *Sargento Primero,* as a soldier or *soldado* on a rotating basis. *Soldados* clean up the main square, guard the main building, incarcerate wrongdoers, and perform other related tasks. This military-like system of local law enforcement seems to have resulted from the independence and Caste Wars (1847–1901)[1] and their aftermath. After their participation in the independence wars of 1812 and 1841, and since being organized as a regular army force with ranks and offices, some villagers have maintained their own police force. The systematic use of force it implies has sometimes collided with the state and federal systems, yet remains today as a method of handling the less important crimes and minor cases of delinquency. Furthermore, following the Mexican revolution, the office of *Comisario* was created under Mexican law. A *Comisario Comunal* intervenes in all political issues but his authority depends on *Sargentos Primeros* and, more formally, on the village's assemblies. He, most of all, represents the village in issues concerning the nearby Commune, or *Municipio,* of Valladolid. Under the Mexican constitution, there is also a *Comisario Ejidal* who oversees communal land issues.

Mesoamerican ritual sponsorships have been understood under exchange paradigms by numerous ethnographers and ritual practitioners. Most analysts, following Tax (1937), Wolf (1955, 1957, 1986), and Foster (1965, 1966, 1988), consider cargo and fiesta systems to be ideological manifestations of highly conservative economic structures – "closed corporate peasant communities" or "limited good models." Generations of analysts have interpreted cargo rituals in terms of their function within such economic structures (Cancian, 1965, 1967, 1992; Carrasco, 1961, 1990; Chance, 1990, 1994; Chance & Taylor, 1985; DeWalt, 1975; Dow 2001, 2005; Early, 1983; Friedlander (1981); Rus & Wasserstrom, 1980; Wasserstrom, 1980). Dependent on homeostatic schemas, ritual transactions are generally considered to be modes of economic redistribution (Polanyi, 1944). While such studies have significantly contributed to our understanding of ritual practitioners' symbolic political economies (including the redistribution of wealth, transformation of economic surplus into prestige or authority, etc.), many aspects of these complex transactions remain critically under-examined. To that end, we examine here the ontological transformation brought about by the cargoholders' dispositions. Ultimately, the process could be expressed as a simple question: What is considered engagement?

There are three main levels in the analysis. We refer to them in accordance with the classic scheme developed by C.S. Peirce of indexical, symbolic, and iconic aspects of human experience. For Peirce, even the most symbolic phenomenon necessarily entertains iconic and indexical aspects. Peirce's philosophical underpinnings allow us to understand ontological phenomena occluded by Christian semiotic ideology (Keane, 2007) in Manichean dichotomies such as thing and sign. Following Latour (1993) Keane has called this process the "work of purification" (2007, p. 80). In this sense, for the many authors that explain the underpinning logics of cargo systems, the taken-for-granted ontological categories of material wealth and symbolic prestige are considered to preexist to any posterior transformation they describe. For instance, Cancian (1967, 1992) among others, considers cargo rituals as a means of transforming material surplus into prestige and authority through maximizing schemata. However, the sharp and definitive line that segregates objects from signs, and wealth from prestige in

Zinancantán, Chiapas, does not resemble any indigenous ontology; instead, it presupposes that of United States secularizing protestant academia. This separation of concomitant phenomena, such as the above-mentioned wealth and prestige or flesh and the spirit, can be attributed to a gap that the current secular academia has inherited and reworked from preexistent Christian institutions and their disciplines. As it has been masterfully depicted by Fenella Cannell, Christian ascetic ideologies have "powerfully shaped the language and procedures of social science itself" (2005, p. 352). In the case I will analyze here, *compromiso,* a word also used to refer to matrimonial engagement, acts as a growing and living symbol of something else. God's indifference to what happens in this world has not been established as epistemic rule in Ixán, nor has redemption been procrastinated to any afterlife.

As Peirce (1998) showed some years ago, the continuity between conventional symbols, causal indexes, and likely icons cannot be reduced to a timeless relation of pairs. The development of any meaningful experience in a certain time span and in a certain place prevents us from conceiving the mirage of symbols that lack both iconic and indexical aspects. Following these logical and semiotic precautions could allow us to understand how authority and power are reproduced by the living resembling elders, by ritual practitioners indexically affecting their acquaintances with gestures, liquor, and food, and, finally, by making conventional agreements among themselves.

In this chapter I will focus in particular on how symbolic pacts unfold into indexical relations and develop in sponsors a special attentiveness to their milieu. I suggest that while cargoholders transact for life renewals, they also cultivate a particular religious disposition that empowers and authorizes them on the condition that they become more attentive to their changing landscape, their acquaintances, elders, and the village's religious traditions. In this sense, the term *compromiso*, which means both an agreement and commitment, should be understood as more than a contract-like relationship of trade between ritualists that is projected onto metaphorical relationships between persons and divinities, person and things, and persons and dead ancestors. More interestingly, this chapter considers *compromiso* as the affirmation of an ontological contiguity of beings taught through ritual tradition.

## ANNUAL FESTIVALS

In Ixán, this ritual tradition includes many annual festivals. Sometimes organized by political authorities – headed by the commandant, or *Comandante,* and the *Comisario* – these are public ceremonies for the well-being and, of course, entertainment of the people of Ixán. Nevertheless, at four calendric dates, select individuals organize and support feasts, dances, processions, and prayers with the help of acquaintances. Participants in these rituals are typically relatives and friends of the sponsors. The main sponsor is called *kuuch*,[2] cargoholder, *interesado* or *diputado*. Meaning burden, but also to carry or to hold up (Stross, 1988), the phrase *kuuch* is frequently used to say that a person is bearing the consequences of an illness or that a person has caught a spiritual force (*iík* or wind). According to Bolles (1997), however, another interpretation of the word *kuuch* is locus, "site, or the place of residence of an object." Sponsors bear the cost and the effort entailed in organizing a complex set of ceremonies (see also Eiss, 2002; Fernandez, 1994; Hervik, 1999; Loewe, 1995, 2003; Pohl, 1981; Price, 1974; Redfield, 1941, 1960, 1964; Redfield & Villa Rojas, 1967; Villa Rojas, 1987). *Kuuch* sponsorships in Yucatan have also been related to Wayeb ceremonies. Most particularly, in order to foresee and obtain the best upcoming year for their people, the year-bearer's impersonators must address different sets of ceremonial arrangements according to the year-commencement (e.g., Bill et al., 2000; Bricker & Miram, 2002; Bricker & Vail, 1997; Coe, 1965; Farriss, 1984; Love, 1986, 1991; León-Portilla, 1988; Taube, 1988; Thompson, 1934, 1958, 1970; Tozzer, 1941; Vail, 1997; Vogt, 1976).

In Ixán, *kuuch*-sponsored festivals take place on:

- May 3 and 4, *Fiesta de la Santísima Cruz Tun*, The Festival of the Sacred Cross Tun
- July 23 and 24, *Cambio de traje del Santo Cristo*, The change of the dress of the Christ
- July 31 to August 7, *Corridas* (bullfight) or *Fiesta del Pueblo*, the village festival (a new host everyday)
- February 14 to February 18, *Gremios* or Guilds (the "Agricultural Guild of Ixán" ceremonies are held, for example, on February 14, and they are sponsored by one *kuuch* and his helpers)

One characteristic of the village sponsorships is the biennial duties they engage. The cargoholder, or *nohoch kuuch* (*nohoch* means big and older), and his or her helpers, or *itsin kuucho'ob* (*itsin* means "minor," and is the plural form of *kuuch*), must support and organize ceremonies for two consecutive years. *Kuucho'ob* report that they sponsor and organize these celebrations "for their own benefit." They spend around 3,000 U.S. dollars to sponsor a day of *Corridas*, for example. These festivals are organized with the intent "to buy life and rain" for the sponsor's house and, in the case of the larger festivals (*Fiesta del Pueblo* and *Gremios*), for the whole village.

With a transactional logic represented in other ritual contexts as *loj naj*, *loj corral*, and *k'eex* (house redemption, farmyard redemption, and exchange) the arrangement is imagined as a promissory exchange between a person who makes the expenditure and some indexed but invisible powers. They are *Yuumtsilo'ob,* which means "lords" as well as "owners" or deities, and are mainly addressed though the iconic manifestations of Catholic saints and through the village's cross-shaped-idol called *Santísima Cruz Tun*. According to various elders, sponsors and *j meno'ob* in Ixán, many of these divine forms of life reside in the outer space, represented by the forest. Usually referred to as *kalano'ob k'áax* or forest guardians or *dueños del bosque* in Spanish – though sometimes also referred to as *Me'etan k'aáxo'ob* – they are thought to be able to take the form of serpents or other animals. Protecting the surroundings of the village and especially taking care of the *Santisima Cruz Tun*, are also the *Itzá maako'ob* or, literally, the Itzá people. The *Yuum Báalamo'ob o balames*, in the Spanish-like plural, see after the village and the field plots or *milpas*. There are also numerous *Cháako'ob* who are tasked with pouring water down over the fields (for a detailed description see Terán & Rasmussen, 2008). And, of course, the people in the village who keep bees must deal with *Yuum kaab*, the lord of bees. Entering into the domestic living space, we find ritual offerings addressed to *Wan Tul* who, after receiving the *loj corral* offerings, watches over the corral animals. *Kalan Yuum Wíiniko'ob*, on the other hand, is the "people's or family's chief guardian" (comparable to "*Nuchuch macob*" or "*nucuch uinicob*" in Redfield & Villa Rojas, 1967). *Me'etan lu'um* are also referred to as the *dueños del soolar*. Among these are the *Ah Kanulo'ob* and the *Kuuch kaabalo'on* who take care of the family inside the *soolar*, or domestic, living space, which encompasses both the inside and the outside of the house. Like many other deities in Ixán, they are invisible and thus compared to the wind. An old man serving as a helper in the first *Gremio* describes one of them as "like the wind, you cannot see him but he can see us."

While invisible, these divine powers do make their presence known in daily life. When animals die and people begin to fall ill, for instance: "when your head aches or your siblings are going to the doctor, it is the plot who is talking, he is asking for something, for doing a *loj soolar* for calming him." Correspondingly, every person is also protected and watched by a *Santo Wíinik*, a personal guardian who protects a person from the dangers she may face in life. A *k'eex*, or ritual exchange, is often prescribed when a person, typically a toddler, becomes injured or frequently ill. If, for instance, this toddler is known to be an *ikim* (an evil entity that drains the life from other family members), *j meno'ob* attempt to deceive the spirits who are hunting her. This deceit is usually accomplished by changing the name of the person to that of a baby chicken, which dies in the process, and then renaming her. It is also worth noting that many of these "lords" or "guardians" are commonly referred to as *dueños*, or owners, implying the existence of a sort of spiritual regime of property in almost all aspects of life. "Everything has an owner," says a *Maestro Cantor*, "they are like custom officers, and you have to pay for everything."

People from Ixán express these sacred transactions in the Catholic terminology of *promesas* or promises and *compromisos* or engagements. A person makes a promise to the cross, for instance, for the health of her animals. She pledges a novena to it, or some other service that implies an expenditure. However, if this person fails to fulfill her pledge, "the cross will remind her she has an unsettled *compromiso* with it." Frequently, this reminder will take the form of illness for her or her animals. If the person does not go to an *j men,* or medical and magical "doer," to "see" the reason for the illness, then she or her animals could die. The *j men* will give advice about how to pay the debt or comply with the *compromiso*. It is worth noting that the temporality of *promesas* and *compromisos* differs. The promise expresses a present orientation toward mainly the near future while an engagement usually unfolds past facts into the future with a normative character. In brief, a *compromiso* is the moral but actual consequence of having made a promise. Accordingly, *compromiso* cannot be directly translated into "obligation." Unlike an obligation, or any debt that can be balanced or canceled finitely, a *compromiso,* as engagement, entails an ongoing and long-term future relationship. Even when people "calm" spirits by "paying" them through due offerings, they are aware that any resulting prosperity and tranquility is only temporary. Indeed, the term *compromiso* serves as a reminder that the form of companionship it entails exceeds the people it involves. *Compromisos* always unfold in indexes that remind the offering givers that they are just a minor part of a more important association.

In a context in which life is considered extremely fragile, and threats to it are considered indices of divine "punishments," sponsors recurrently enact practical knowledge in order to regenerate, and appear as regenerators of, their families, plants, animals, friends, and field plots. Playing with the limits of human cognition, cargoholders, by giving and taking, interpret and prospectively engage themselves with the past, their peers, and the environment. They are, according to their own words, "doing the same their ancestors did before." Therefore, they also construct their leadership in the community by indexing a continuity of a past in the present. After their expenditures cargoholders expect a divine sanction, or what they call a "miracle." These expectations are made explicit. In the *Gremios* festival, for example, agriculturalists first ask for good rains, tranquility, and a prosperous harvest before they begin to cut down and burn the forest, or the old maize plants, and seed. Their expectation has a one-year-long term. If the expected miracle does not occur within one year and instead a *castigo* "comes down" and strikes the village, they can only hope that this punishment will not be harsh. For Ixán, 2008 was one such year of *castigo*. Due to drought, maize plants only reproduced for reseeding in 2009. However, Marcial, an *j men* who made the first fruit offering or *primicia* for the first guild in 2009, maintains that, unlike in other places, *castigos* in Ixán are mild: "here, *castigos* pass through without striking us too much because we perform our traditions."

In Ixán, as in other Yucatec communities, unfortunate events tend to be interpreted by eschatological narratives (Sullivan, 1990). The end of any life cycle is a reminder that "this world," too, will end soon. Hurricanes, illnesses, famines, and other personal misfortunes indicate "punishments" and reinforce the apprehension of the proximity of final decay. Consequently, many people in Ixán believe ritual sponsorships are fundamental to any effort to thrive and avoid "punishments." Through his or her dealings with numinous entities, one may reverse, at least for a while, the economic or natural decadence which their punishments imply. Future blessings and "miracles," or "punishments," then become logical outcomes of the sponsor's performances. *Interesados* or *kuucho'ob* try to secure divine favors by sponsoring ceremonies with "faith and commitment." With the help of ritual experts called *mayores* or *nohoch*, which means "elders," "ancestors," as well as "big" in Maya and in Spanish, they learn how to transact with the sacred-natural realm which such powerful forces inhabit, and, in the village, with the people who help them finance and sponsor these celebrations. The success of promises and engagements is then manifested in the productivity of field plots, in the wellness of the *kuuch'ob's* houses, and in the sufficiency of means of living. Thus, power and authority also unfold ontically not only intersubjetively (as, for instance, in Mahmood, 2005; Silverstein, 2008).

Health, wealth, and well-being can then be read as signs of a sponsor's authority insofar as they signal his mastery of the correct disposition and, consequently, his success in addressing the gods. On the other hand, "if you have made a promise and you do not fulfill it, you will get a warning," they say. The death of a pig before it can be slaughtered for the feasting, for example, is taken as a very bad omen for the sponsor. In other cases, illness, fever, or pain all index an unsettled *compromiso*. I was told by a sponsor that "if you cannot solve the problem with a physician you go with the *j men* and he will tell you: 'You have a *compromiso*, here. You must accomplish it. You promised – for example – a glorious mystery at the Santa Cruz chapel and you have not fulfilled it, yet.'"

## SUPPORTERS' RELIGIOUS DISPOSITIONS

Talal Asad (1993) reminds us that any universal anthropological definition of religion and its adjective "religious" should be suspected of being inflected by Christian traditions. Asad maintains that the idea of religion as a universal category of humankind, which he finds, for example, in the influential work of Clifford Geertz (1973), itself presupposes the assertion of seventeenth- and eighteenth-century Christian universalist premises. According to Asad (1993) "there cannot be a universal definition of religion, not only because its constitutive elements and relationships are historically specific, but because that definition is in itself the historical product of discursive processes" (p. 29).

To further his critique of any universal definition of religion, Asad challenges that which was put forth by Geertz. But when Geertz (1973) defines religion as "(1) a system of symbols which *acts* to (2) establish powerful, pervasive, and long lasting moods and motivations in men by (3) formulating conceptions of a general order of existence and (4) clothing these conceptions with such an *aura of factuality* that (5) the moods and motivations seem uniquely realistic" (p. 90, my emphasis), he does not deny the particularities of "a people's ethos – the tone, character, and quality of their life, its moral and aesthetic style and mood" (p. 90). Instead, Geertz focuses on describing how sacred symbols of a religion "synthesize" these particularities. Asad is less concerned with the historical particularities of religious facts than with the anthropological definition of religion that is in itself a historical product of Euro-Christian discursive processes. But on the same basis, why shouldn't the concept of "ethos" or the notion of "disposition" be the target of a similar critique of universality? Why not consider "ethos" or "disposition" universal byproducts of the Euro-Christian discursive processes?

In *Genealogies of Religion* Asad analyzes the historical formations and transformations of discourses, using a Foucaultian genealogical approach. However, he does not reflect on the immense synthetic power that rites and, in this case, a religious disposition may have for concrete ritual practitioners. Perhaps due to his inclination to examine the negative aspects of discipline and ascetics, he seems to disregard the exuberance and power the "faithful draw from the accomplished rite" (Durkheim, 1995, p. 386), or what Durkheim has called the "positive cult."

In Ixán, sponsors annually pay to anachronistic "owners" the right to exploit their lands and cattle through offerings that seek a prosperous future. The temporalities of the promissory exchanges I describe do not coincide with our understanding of a historical past segregated by a present time from an uncertain and open future (Koselleck, 2004). On the contrary, *Kuuch's* tribute to the tradition and sacred "owners" implies its own temporalities. Obviously this ritual tradition expresses knowledge of time and a lived history that we can only partially reconstruct here. In the regime of engagement performed by cargo rituals, death emerges as a source of power needed to reproduce life in the future. Mesoamerican *tanatofilia*, however, vivid and lucid, reminds people of how scarce a resource human time is. Recognizing this scarcity, cargoholders in Ixán continue to engage with the dead, gods, and ancestral spirits through offerings and gifts in exchange for a prosperous near future.

As a historical anthropologist of discourses, Asad rightly stresses the impossibility of a general category of religion for anthropologists. Nevertheless, this impossibility does not affect ritual practitioners who continue to perform their rites independently of the historicity of the discursive categories Asad critiques. Even when people engaged in ritual activity know the ephemeral character of their practices they always seem to assume they are situated in a tradition of practices. Overall, they are apposite for a purpose.

On the other hand, Asad is extremely sensitive to the symbolic imperialism Geertz's hermeneutic enterprise entails for anthropology. According to Asad (1993), Geertz's assumptions construct religion as a "matter of symbolic meanings linked to ideas of general order (expressed through either or both rite and doctrine)" (pp. 42–43). From Asad's point of view, Geertz's highly conceptual perspective for defining religion precludes the understanding of religion as a set of concrete practices. Moreover, Asad warns us against Geertz's conceptualization of religion and ritual as expressive and always meaningful. Instead, what most interests Asad is the historical importance of the "practical contexts" (Scott & Hirschkind, 2006, p. 7) by which the understanding of symbols is made possible in a given tradition. These practical contexts are closely related to the generative power of the body, gestures, "embodied aptitudes" (p. 8), discourses, and practices of argumentation, also called "authorizing processes."

Asad's notion of the authorizing process opens up new areas of inquiry. By relating any universal definition of religion to a determined tradition or, more specifically, to the use of these traditions, Asad objects to the subordination of dispositions to the power of concepts. At the same time, however, he gives priority to the practical constitution of religious phenomena:

> The argument that a particular disposition is religious partly because it occupies a conceptual place within a cosmic framework appears plausible, but only because it presupposes a question that must be made explicit: how do authorizing processes represent practices, utterances, or dispositions so that they can be discursively related to general (cosmic) ideas of order? In short, the question pertains to the authorizing process by which "religion" is created. (1993, pp. 36–37)

For Asad, a religious disposition is built up in relation to particular authorizing processes. Its main goal is to produce authorized subjects. While Asad's work does not universally define the notion of traditions, it does offer many explanatory possibilities as to how interpretations are crafted through the practice of authorizing processes. The specificity of Asad's notion of an "authorizing process" leaves aside all the aura of universality the notion of religion represents for Euro-Americans as an autonomous sphere of life.[3]

The issue now is not so much to identify and segregate diverse orders such as practice and theory (or ritual and theology), but to show how subjects are authorized through gift-giving. In our case, the engaged disposition could be preliminarily defined as a social mechanism interiorized in the self which, allowing further conceptualization, would produce prosperity. In the particular case of the Ixán sponsors, a specific regime of engagement is a condition of possibility for life renewal. *Kuuch* sponsorships cultivate a religious disposition that is expressed in a logic of burdensome commitment. Nevertheless, commitment does not end in self-discipline, trustworthiness, and humility but should be handsomely rewarded through worldly possessions. In other words, the ascetics of bearing the burden of sponsorship and paying attention to the land owners are considered a means of reproduction. Understandably, the reward is also considered to be economic proof of the existence of the other parties in the exchange.

## DISPOSITION AND DISPOSITIVES: HEXIS OR HABITUS

Aristotle has ascribed one of the first uses of "disposition" in the tradition we commonly define as "western" to Empedocles. The latter suggests that a "disposition" explains concomitant facts of the physical and the representational orders. According to Aristotle, "Empedocles says that when [human] dispositions change, [human] thoughts change" (1998, pp. 17–20). It is also Aristotle who defines "disposition" ("hexis") as a human tendency, induced by habits, to have appropriate or inappropriate feelings and, later, behaviors (1994, pp. 25–26). By considering ethical virtue as a disposition, Aristotle objectifies the foundations for Ethics, a new subdiscipline at the time (*ibid.*, pp. 1–2), in psychology. Only in Kant's (1785) foundation of metaphysics are nature and passions purely opposed and segregated from morals and ethics. In Aristotle's *Nicomachean Ethics* and *Eudemian Ethics*, "habits," "dispositions," and "emotions" relate to each other in a sort of intellectual expertise in which ethical virtue is an intermediate condition between two other states, one involving excess, and the other deficiency. In this sense, all of book IV of *Nicomachean Ethics* (Aristotle, 1994, p. 78) is dedicated to clarifying the importance of the right proportion in giving and taking. Aristotle portrays the prodigal as ruining himself by wasting "his own substance" (p. 193). Meanness, on the other hand, is applied to those who care more than is proper about wealth. However, he maintains that, "In crediting people with liberality their resources must be taken into account; for the liberality of a gift does not depend on its amount, but on the disposition of the giver, and a liberal disposition gives according to its substance" (*ibid.*).

The right disposition of material goods would be a condition of possibility for virtuous happiness (*eudaimonia*, translatable as "good-daimon-possession"). Carlo Natali (1995) has shown that an individual stable state of mind or "hexis" is considered to be an important part of Hellenistic economic knowledge (p. 103). An internal state of mind cannot, then, be entirely comparable to an external arrangement of property until we have those inward and outward spheres. The psychological, moral, economic, and political spheres do not refer to each other in a circular manner simply because they do not preexist separately and autonomously before being objectified by practices, in this case ritual practices. As in cargo festivals, the moral engagement of the ritualist is shown through a controlled expenditure of economic goods, at the same time that the old Christian semantic distinction between "outward sign" and "inward meaning" (Asad, 1993, p. 59) is reworked.

The fact that "hexis" stems from a verb related to possession and ownership, and is often translated as "having," should not be overlooked. As an administrative arrangement of property, "hexis" actively constitutes happiness or unhappiness and, as in the human body, the good or bad arrangement of its parts is reflected by health or illness. It should also be noted that "hexis" has been systematically translated into Latin as "habitus," which also comes from a verb that indicates the act of possession. In Hellenistic times, economics was not principally a discipline residing in a set of books but a permanent quality of the experts' minds, an expertise, "an intellectual virtue or excellency more than a moral virtue" (Carlo Natali, personal communication). It was not until well after Christianity that we had moral or unmoral economies and dispositions.

It was Agamben who noted that the Foucaultian rediscovery of the "*dispositif*" is related to the "theological trope of *dispositio*" (Hent de Vries, 2008, p. 75). According to Agamben (2006), dispositions designate the "historical element, with all the weight of rules, rites, and institutions" posited and imposed on individuals "due to an external force, but which also finds itself, as it were, interiorized in systems of belief and sentiments" (p. 75). Thus "disposition" also refers to a patristic trope. According to de Vries,

> Theologically, it involves the justification of the Trinity, of divine providence, and of Christ's incarnation. Suffice it to note that the Greek *oikonomia* was rendered by the Latin Fathers as *dispositio* and that, for Agamben, it inaugurates a distinction – indeed, nothing short of "schizophrenia" – between God's "being" in and for himself (his "nature" or "essence"), on the one hand, and his "action" in the world (his "operation," "governance," and "administration" of creaturely affairs), on the other, and hence between "ontology" and "praxis." (2008, p. 75)

As noted by de Vries, in the patristic lexicon disposition is equated to *oikonomia* as the "handling" or "management" of a set of things, usually assuming or implying *god's management* of this-worldly issues. One can also say that in the posterior God's abandonment of economy to economists She or He has followed the anti-essentialist and negative theology that dominates the academic milieu today. Perhaps influenced by a monastic division of labor, perfected through centuries, theologians have severed the disposition and management of economic issues from God's presence, with the clear aim of purifying theology from this-worldly concerns. According to Lossky, Clement of Alexandria's way of rendering God intelligible in the third century BCE had more to do with an "economic perspective" than a theological one (Lossky, 1985, p. 23). Lossky (1985) clarifies that in Clement's writings the human impossibility of knowing God is superseded by a "God-given-virtue." This gift is grace:

> Grace, for Clement, is above all a new aptitude for knowing an hexis gnostiké [εξις γνοςτικη] which obtains for the perfect Christian, for the Gnostic (today one would say for the "spiritual" or "contemplative") eternal contemplation (αιδιος θεορια), i.e. the capacity for seeing God-Pantokrator face to face. (V, 11) (p. 22)

Therefore, also according to Lossky, Clement's Trinitarian notion has nothing of theology "in the sense which the father of the fourth century will impart to the term. Rather all its merits [lie] in the economic perspective which is its own" (Lossky, 1985, p. 23).

Thus Lossky situates the difference and opposition between *oikonomia* and theology in the fourth century. Likewise, Lossky (1985, p. 15) proposes more of the later and less of the former,

> The distinction between οικονομια and θεολογια – which was for Origen a knowledge, a gnosis of God in the λογος – means in the fourth century everything which concerns Trinitarian doctrine, everything which can be said of God considered in Himself, outside of his creative and redemptive economy. In order to reach this "theology," properly so-called one therefore must go beyond the aspect under which we know God as Creator of the universe, in order to be able to extricate the notion of Trinity from the implications proper to the "economy." To the economy in which god reveals Himself in creating the world and in becoming incarnate, we must respond with theology, confessing the transcendent nature of the Trinity in an ascent of thought which necessarily has an apophatic thrust.

As a theologian who stresses the importance of the negative way of knowing god (apophasis) in almost every tradition, Lossky is of course interested in the historical process by which god is "decanted [and] stripped of all economic attribution" (1985, p. 24). Here, his investigations are useful in examining when and how "hexis," habitus, and disposition, too, are "stripped" and "decanted" of "all economic" connotations. It is worthwhile to refer to this notion of *dispositio* beyond its historicization of Foucault's and Asad's genealogical enterprises. Recognizing the theological underpinnings of Asad's and Foucault's works helps us to open up the understanding of religious technologies of the self toward godly possessions (in Aristotle "eudaimon") toward god-like and economic dispositions.

In other words, the virtuous disposition of property should also be considered a religious phenomenon before it is stripped of any meaning and considered a purely "inward" moral practice. In Ixán the ritual tradition teaches sponsors a divine art of administration. *J meno'ob* and *nohoch máako'ob* are obsessed with counting how many tortillas they offer to the saints and gods, for example. *Nohoch kuucho'ob* register in accountant books to what extent each *its'in kuucho'ob* contributed. However, this extreme form of accountability is not an end in itself. The lessons taught in divine management may make sponsors more prudent and disciplined, but liberals as well.

Leaving aside the way the *kuuch* disposition is seen or imagined thanks to aesthetic processes of fascination and how it is linguistically represented by pacts, in this chapter I aim to understand how this disposition burdens or affects *Kuucho'ob* with social responsibility or commitment. By isolating the *kuuch* disposition from the authorizing processes that produced it, however, I do not mean to remove it from its particular "history." My claim is that these dispositions are religious even though they go beyond simply conveying "symbolic meanings linked to ideas of general order" (Asad, 1993, p. 42). Here I am assuming Asad's critique of Geertz (1973). Instead of taking for granted that a set of symbols will unilaterally determine or modify a disposition, I am exploring the influence that supposedly meaningless dispositions have on symbols and conceptions or, in this case, how the miracle is socially authorized. Further following Asad, I also understand that the moral economy of the self in the cargo-sponsored ceremonies I am analyzing has less to do with their symbolic or ideological expressiveness than with the cargoholders' pursuit of ontological regeneration. However, I do not consider regeneration or "miracles" to be mere symbolic sanctions of correct ritual performances. Miracles and punishments are important because they index the copresence of saints, spiritual owners, and gods in an engagement.

Sponsors' practices enter into a constant relationship with symbols but they do not always depend on symbolic interpretations to be transmitted. In the case of the Yucatec commitments, the *kuuch* religious disposition should also be understood on an ontological level. Commitment and burden-like affection, in Spanish *compromiso*, is the pre-subjective stance that elders try to cultivate in festival sponsors. Cargoholders should be predisposed toward the past (invisible owners, ritual tradition, elders, and ancestors) in a certain manner that could assure a prosperous future for them and their village. The regeneration of maize, rain, and prosperity in general relates meaningfully to the individual who has sponsored the festival and engaged successfully with a hierarchy of seniority that ends with the dead. The acceptance or rejection of his or her offerings is read in natural signs; however, the signs that qualify the sponsorship do not socially affect the sponsor in a direct manner. In some communities in Chiapas, on the other hand, if it rains the cargoholder is jailed based on the assumption that he has been too drunk or that he lacks the proper dedication necessary for the ritual preparations. In Ixán the sanction of these complex gift-giving duties affects a person's relationship to others. Beyond cultivating a sort of religious neurosis or neurotic morality in elite individuals, sponsorships reveal ontological links between economy and religiosity. Also beyond any hermeneutical hypothesis which could pursue further meaningful explanations besides those given by participants – that is, asking for a miracle or for *la gracia* (harvest in its literal sense but also any divine return) through sacred duties and offerings – implies the exercise of an extreme sensibility. This is, I argue, the main purpose of inducing a disposition or, in this case, predisposing ritual sponsors in a certain manner.

## WHAT DOES A CARGOHOLDER HOLD?

In the process of learning how to successfully sponsor these annual festivals, sponsors assimilate with their ancestors in a tradition of ritual practices. Through ceremonial preparations and divine and solemn transactions, ritual experts or "elders" instruct the *kuuch* in the proper ritual manners. Preparations for the day-long rites start months ahead of time. Elders guide the *kuuch* and his partners through the various duties they must face. For example, a particular elder advises the *kuuch* as to whom he should approach for contributions of money, food, or service for the festival. In these cases, the elder also witnesses the arrangement between the two men, one asking for a contribution, the other either pledging himself, or *comprometiendose,* to give it or rejecting the request. In the process, let me say, of pledging or *comprometerse* with a potential helper the *kuuch* always pays his visit accompanied by an elder and a bottle of liquor. The elder testifies to and remembers the agreement reached by the *kuuch* and potential helper. A shot of liquor precedes the transaction. Ritual drinking predisposes everybody's mood. It also transforms *promesa*s into *compromisos*. Since alcohol affects both parts of the transaction, a positive inclination tends to arise. Once the *kuuch* has recruited his helpers, his involvement becomes, in Peirce's terminology, less symbolic and much more indexical.

Indications, or indices, "show something about things, on account of their being physically connected with them" (Peirce, 1998, p. 5). As Peirce puts it, an indexical sign stands in a relation of "dynamic coexistence" with its object. Copresence and contiguity are characteristics of indexical relationships, too. More often described using the language of cause and effect, indexical semiotics might be better expressed in terms of ontological affections. Peirce (1998) uses the extreme example of the sun and the sunflower; he considers the flower's phototropism to be indicative of a semiotic relationship (p. 273). As one is affecting the other, it follows that there is an object and a sign, in some sort of continuity or relationship. In another example he gives, the sound of thunder affects a person who does not know what is happening at that moment. After a while, the individual could associate the sound with a previous, perhaps unseen, flash of lightning and then the idea of the thunder arises in the person's mind. In both cases a conscious acknowledgment, or a conceptual representation, does not start or stop the indexical force. The person is affected by the sound of thunder; she reacts. Her idea of thunder comes later.

Contrariwise, contract-like agreements among ritual practitioners, elders, and helpers, in Ixán, are only the start of the *kuuch*-sponsored ceremonies. Pacts among men are merely the initial stages of a more profound understanding. *Compromisos* go from symbolic representations of exchange (e.g., how many pesos to contribute for the feasting) toward an indexical participation between partners. Later, on the festival day, elders supervise food preparation, serve ritual drink, or perform other duties that entail solemnity and right gestures.

Ritual experts or elders, therefore, possess know-how that is mainly transmitted by imitation. By performing different duties with the *kuuch*, the elders supervise and authorize him to transact with ancestors and partners "in the same way that their ancestors did it before." However, advice and imitation do not just transfer a discrete quantity of information from one set of individuals to others (or from one generation to another). In the process of imitating, both sponsors and ritual experts enact a scene in which empathy is a crucial element for the whole ritual. Ritual knowledge, along with the tradition in which it is embedded, is transmitted through nonverbal acts. It is my main hypothesis here that instead of a discrete transmission of information, the *kuuch* disposition articulates a particular self-other locus. Besides cultivating the ethical virtues that the cargo or *kuuch* disposition entails – endurance, measurement, frugality, and generosity, for instance – this self-other stance, often represented by the word *compromiso,* is considered a necessary condition for any future regeneration. The renewal of maize harvests, animals, even the bodies of the cargoholder and his family, is dependent on this stance. With this in mind, the main purpose behind the disciplined formation of selves may be restated, with important theoretical implications. Beyond monasticism, asceticism, the omnipresence of moral discipline, and the current anthropological retreat into the ethical self, or turn into the self (Agrama, 2010), these sponsorships return economic power to the analysis of ritual and religion as in the form of material grace.

From entering into sponsorship contracts to correctly executing dances and gestures, ritualists depend on the elders' advice. Elders are persons who have sponsored these ceremonies many times and know "how to do it." Elders serve alcohol, cook, witness economic transactions among helpers and cargoholders, and suggest who could help the cargoholder with music, bulls, and other items. But, more importantly, elders are there to be imitated in all of these tasks. In other words, the elder-like preparation of these festivals assures their success. As in many other human activities, elders cannot transmit their knowledge more successfully than by doing what they know how to do. Conceptually poor, the "right way" or the right manners must be learned by trial and error or, in Ixán's terms, by miracles and punishments. Authority comes at last when the sponsor becomes reliable, humble, and most of all committed to the village's traditions and its ancestors. This authority is felt more concretely, as well. In Ixán it is commonly understood that a man who has successfully sponsored a ceremony is also more capable of filling civic or political positions in the cargo system (including old positions like *comandante* and *comisario,* or relatively new ones such as *contralor de Procampo*, or the controller of the Cash Transfer Program for Agriculturalists, etc.).

In short, through advice and imitation, engagement arises as a distinct aspect of common action. From Mauss (2002 [1925]) we know that gifts engage. The most important issue here, however, is the need to engage in this form of discipline, to give. How, and to what extent, should gifts be controlled by practices aimed at producing such engagements? Nevertheless, before we address virtue or delve into the teleological reasons that virtue and its formations are considered necessary, we shall further examine the concept of disposition in its historical avatars. Otherwise, one would assume that an ascetically virtuous disposition, notwithstanding its "historical" and "cultural" context, could be a condition of possibility for any form of power.

## MATERIALIZATION OF POWER THROUGH SACRED DEALINGS AND PROPER ENGAGEMENTS

In their work, Asad and Bourdieu stress the capacity of rites to inscribe or automatize perceptions and thoughts in the practitioner's body for the consequential performance of significant practices. To shed light on the current anthropological definition of ritual practices at that time, Asad revisits an aspect of rites that he characterizes as a "pre-modern," "Christian," and "monastic" discipline. The symbolic imperialism of western discursive processes, then, has limited the definition of ritual to include

> Apt performance of what is prescribed, something that depends on intellectual and practical disciplines but does not itself require decoding. In other words, apt performance involves not symbols to be interpreted but abilities to be acquired according to rules that are sanctioned by those in authority: it presupposes no obscure meanings, but rather the formation of physical and linguistic skills. (Asad, 1993, p. 62)

Asad's insights denounce anthropology's expressive, symbolic, and ideological assumptions for taking part in a modern and secularized tradition of representational practices. As a consequence, the medieval Christian concept of moral discipline has, since Asad, been projected to interpret various situations as condition of possibility for further meanings. Bourdieu (1990) also defines ritual activity in opposition to meaning, conceptual expression and the mind:

> Rites, more than any other type of practice, serve to underline the mistake of enclosing in concepts a logic made to dispense with concepts; of treating movements of the body and practical manipulations as purely logical operations; of speaking of analogies and homologies (as one sometimes has to, in order to understand and to convey that understanding) when all that is involved is the practical transference of incorporated, quasi-postural schemes. (p. 116)

Both Asad and Bourdieu refer back to "Techniques of the Body" (Mauss, 1979), the text of a common ancestor. For the particular cargo system I am analyzing here it may be partially correct to stress that the "socio-psycho-biological" continuum of the burden is necessary for any entry into a purposeful "communion with god" (Mauss, 1979, p. 122). However, as I have already mentioned, these purposive rites anticipate material objectifications of power, miracle, and grace that cannot be depicted simply as a part of the "moral economy of the self" (Asad, 1993, p. 67). Instead, "miracles" and *gracia* prove to be ampler forms of commerce and communication with spiritual forces and gods that, by becoming material, evolve into affection with moral consequences. In what follows I will depict some of these embodiments of miracle and power that limit and serve as contexts for a pure sociology of the body (on their contraries, related with death and punishments, see Dapuez, 2010 on "antitotem"). The particular in this case is that instead of a state of grace produced by a virtuous disciplined manner, *gracia* and miracles materialize after the correct performance of these rites of renewal.

In Ixán, don Gustavo and I stop to drink beer on our way to the ceremonial center. Don Gustavo is one of the two *nohoch Mako'ob* of Ixán and the sponsor of the second Guild. Earlier this morning I paid a visit to his house accompanied by regular gifts of liquor and food. We have been eating ritual food, drinking, and praying for hours. He offered me some beer and I invited him and his *itsin kuucho'ob*. Everyone was happy, if not drunk. Even more prayers and chants commence upon our arrival at the ceremonial center. Candles were lit and food subsequently offered to the saints, crosses, and owners. We exit the church-like building in a specific order: first the *j men*, followed by the *nukuch* (plural of *nohoch*), then don Gustavo and me, and finally the *itsin kuucho'ob*. Many people are in attendance. In addition to the *Maestros Cantores* and people from other guilds, common people have gathered hoping for a bit of *relleno negro* in return for their services or for free. Many have come just to watch the pig's head dance, which seals the transfer of the *kuuch* sponsorship and assures the continuation of the festival for the following year. Once the prayers end, we begin to salute the images situated at the main altar. In the center of the altar, behind an arch constructed from *sipilche* leaves and branches, sits the axis mundi: *Santisima Cruz Tum* or "the three persons." To her left and right are virgins and crosses from the nearby villages. I recognize almost all of these images from the altar at don Gustavo's house this morning. There are also plenty of offerings – flowers and candles, both lit and unlit, surround the images. At each image don Gustavo pauses to say some words. Finally we come to the *Tres Personas* and stop. Usually kept in a crystal case, the *Tres Personas* are tree crosses dressed up in *hipiles* with mirrors hanging down around their necks. Here don Gustavo removes a flower from a floral offering and hands it to me. I thank him and, not knowing what to do with it, return it to the altar. Nodding, don Gustavo informs me that what he has given me has power, that I must keep it with me. It is like a talisman, he says, it has a miracle within and will not only keep my family healthy, but empower me as well.

The ascetic and symbolically poor model of ritual depicted by Asad and Bourdieu may apply perfectly well to the experience of practitioners whose only possessions are their bodies or, even better put, the emergent practices of their bodies. However, for those who posses land, or have acknowledged that the land could be possessed by spiritual owners, this model may fall short. For the latter, work and disciplined hexis are necessary but not sufficient conditions for harvest reproduction. From simple participants, to invited guests, *itsin kuucho'ob*, *nohoch kuuch*, musicians, elders, *Maestros Cantores*, and *j men*, we have a range of possible points of view from which we could choose to depict one of these *Kuuch*-sponsored ceremonies and the new materiality that they produce. These very different narratives would each stress different events as critically important while effacing, or ignoring, others.

For instance, a common *j meno'ob* description normally highlights the exchange between him, as the representative of the *kuucho'ob*, and the cross or the particular *Yuumtsilo'ob* involved. As I show below, they also explicitly mention the consecution of "power," *gracia* and "miracle" as a desired outcome of these ceremonies. On the other hand, the *Maestro Cantor's* typical narrative can be considered a more Catholic version of the event. In his recounts, a *Maestro Cantor* often purposefully effaces any mention of spirits or owners that are not completely Catholic. Instead, he describes the chant or novena performed by him and his colleagues. Unlike that of the *j men*, who focuses on the gift of power from owners, the *Maestro Cantor's* narrative describes the desire to avoid divine punishments and mentions God more frequently. In their turn, elders' accounts usually accentuate the traditional mode of ceremonial sponsorship and the fact that you learn it only by performing it many times. A *Kuuch*'s narrative usually refers to the help of elders, the previous work of getting the necessary resources to spend, the pacts he or she had to make with the *itsin kuucho'ob* and, overall, to the expectation of grace in return for their expenditures. Indeed, they express these sponsorships as a deal, as "buying the rain and buying life for their persons, families, cattle, and maize fields." Nevertheless, the roles I mention here are not static and only occasionally do they exist individually. Most of the time a *j men* or a *Maestro Cantor* has performed as *kuuch* in the past or the invited guests at one ceremony may help the following year by serving as *itsin kuuch*.

Marcial is an *j men* who happens to live in front of an old friend of mine in Ixán. I was introduced to Marcial by this friend at his house during a birthday party. As we drank beer together, Marcial told us that he had felt someone powerful had arrived at the village that day. It was me. I told him I was interested in researching the village traditions. Later, I saw him at the church and ceremonial center called the "Center of the world" during a sponsor house ceremony. Fulfilling his role as a *j men*, Marcial offered food to the *Santísima Cruz Tun*, oversaw the feastings and directed the preparation of sacred food such as *noj-wah* (big tortilla) and *relleno negro*. On another day I decided to drop by Marcial's house to talk. Our conversation turned toward his work and how he helps people in need.

Marcial portrays his role as an *j men* as dependent upon a gift from God, a gift of "power:"

> The kind of jobs we use to do you cannot learn from books. There is no way to learn it in schools. It is only the work of god. He *gave us the power* to save our fellows ("cheen u obra jajadios tu *tśaaj tóon u paajtalil* e k-meyajtik leeti yo'olale' pos to'one je'el e k-salvartik"). We are with god and he is with us always to help us to help other persons

and to perform the old traditions. Our grandfathers and ancestors use to do this. This is what we continue to do and this is why we cannot allow this to be forgotten.

For Marcial and many people in the village, "power" is something attained by trading with spirits and, overall, by their material representative, the *Santisima Cruz Tun* "the three persons." It is sometimes a gift, received from ancestral spirits or a more or less Christian god, that allows *j meno'ob* to give, to cure, and to make offerings. Being the recipient of *u poderil* or *u paajtalil*, however, is not always a desired position. In Ixán common people say that becoming a *j men* involves giving something in return; it is a sad commerce. Upon receiving his power, a *j men* is expected to give back the life of one of his family members to finish the deal. In other words, gifts only occur in a typical chain of gift-giving. When the *j men* represents himself as a giver, as someone able to give, he explains, first, that he has received a gift and he has given back before. To put it almost tautologically, any current gift exchange depends on the engagement of the exchangers. The more engaged the giver, the more effective the gift will be. As a temporal sequence, engagement represents the former facts of having received, the current process of giving back and the future return the giver can expect. Thus, for the engaged exchanger, any commonly imagined distinctions between these temporalities are blurred. They exist simultaneously.

For instance, it is his engagement that allows Marcial to cure and make promissory offerings. Referred to as the capacity and power to give, engagement is expressed through a gift-giving rhetoric. "Being with god, god being with us," "doing as our ancestors did before," etc., imply a sort of cancellation of time beyond the limits of our own regime of historicity. In our regime of historicity, the current present must be different from any other time, past or future. It is considered unique. On the other hand, as Hanks (2000) has shown, the copresence of ancestral gods and spirits in a local time makes it possible that the offerings will be effective.

In Ixán *u poderil* or *u paajtalil* as a desired outcome, as well as a condition of possibility for those expected returns to come, occurs concomitantly. Therefore, Marcial expresses engagement as not only a question of debt and obligation to the past but as a purposeful action oriented toward a promissory future. Immediately after the words quoted

For instance, the above, Marcial continues,food [offering] for the field plot (*janlil kool*), the food [offering] for the house-terrains (*janlil soolaro'ob*), the rain ceremonies (*ch'a' cháak*), etc., all of these we have the power to perform it (*yaanto'on u paajtalil k-meyajtik*). We know how to do it ... like the curing work, you have to know how to do it ... there are different ways ... like in the *Gremio's* festival we are going to have at the church in the center of the world (*chúumuk lu'um*). For instance this Sunday afternoon,

> I am going to be there to make a first fruits offering (*primicia*) in the advantage (*favor*) of the harvest (*gracia*), in the favor of the town, and for the *Gremio*. We do it like this in Ixán. For the needed people, for the workers, for the field plot-worker (*koolnáalo'ob*), for asking for maize (*gracia*) for the person (*u tia'l k-k'áatik u gracia wíinik*), this is why we perform the ceremony with the big tortilla (*x-noj-waj*). This is our custom since our ancestors.

With these words Marcial explained to me a characteristic of those exchanges that has been repeated hundreds of times by the sponsors, *j meno'ob*, helpers and common people in Ixán: its purposeful teleological action. It is future-oriented and produced for the well-being of the people. For me, it has taken years to understand the apparent paradox of this future-oriented tradition. The paradox vanishes, however, if we understand that *compromiso* or engagement ties up or replicates these three different temporalities we use to represent our experiences. Past, present, and future are only distinguished from each other if we consider the past and the future as ghostly imaginings. In Ixán engagements through gifts represent them otherwise. Past "punishments" and "miracles" continue to be felt by ritualists in Ixán while at the same time incoming "punishments" and "miracles" are feared or desired.

Clearly, moral discipline should not be considered an end in itself. To do so would be to take on the point of view of the extreme skeptic, looking for the construction of monastic-like institutions, or that of the believer, driving the practitioner closer to God. The reduction of religion into morals and ethics clearly resembles the Protestant practice of some American Ascetics Sects beautifully depicted by Weber in his 1904 essay, "Protestant Sects and the Spirit of Capitalism." Many of these sects first sprouted in American universities and now some anthropologists are furthering what can rightly be called "the negative theology of practice," not only purifying practice from any symbolic meaning but also considering any ritual practice as ascetic and self-centered.

Therefore, the regime of engagement these ritual activities produce can only be schematically described as payments to ancestral forces aimed toward "buying life." Instead of traditionalist payers or blind keepers of tradition, sponsors can be described as sacred entrepreneurs who, with the help of ritual specialists, regularly seek miracles. These miracles are not extraordinary events that defy natural laws. They are, to some extent, an expression of them. Among them is the Christian Grace of God – or *gracia*, a term appropriated from the Catechism by Mayan speaking peasants to refer to their holy maize and, metonymically, the harvest (which includes pumpkins, chilies, beans, etc.).

These sought-after gifts, if given, represent proper engagement. Ultimately, the gift is the engagement made present and not otherwise. Similarly, a negative engagement could also be represented by a punishment. If due duties are not attended, or when gifts and offerings are promised but not given, the slighted owners, or *Yuumtsilo'ob*, will "talk" to the people through punishments. In this context, in which older beings or spiritual owners are able to reward or punish attended or unattended commitments, discipline is only a part of the ritual exchange. More is at stake in these rituals for the people of Ixán, who speak, not of discipline, but of rewards and power. Perhaps due to academia's tendency toward ascetics, not by Asad but by Asadians, we have been unable to acknowledge the ways in which rewards, grace, and happiness produce hexis or dispositions.

## CONCLUSIONS

Less a phenomenological embodiment (Csordas, 1997), or habitus (Mauss, 1979; Bourdieu, 1990), sponsoring *kuuch* festivals through committed actions regulated by a tradition allows for the personal unfolding of a new sensibility of natural phenomena inhabited by ancestral forces, fellow ritualists, and the village tradition. This particular self-other disposition, which has to be learned and reproduced in order to maintain the continued development of authority, allows for transactions aimed toward life and the regeneration of transect bodies.

After some contract-like interactions, *kuucho'ob's* duties seem to replicate their ancestors' postures. To become an elder or *nohoch maak*, one must also be able to produce ancestor-like gestures and understand a hierarchy based on the logic of majority. *Compromiso*, then, seems to entail an involvement more complex than that of punctual deals. *Compromiso* implies an indexical participation, based on gestures, actions, affections, or what I call dispositions, into a time continuum. To some extent, these dispositions look like indexical bindings, not *symbola*. They aim to produce successful transactions with ancestors while at the same time they resituate the sponsor in a position of minority. The fact that there is no place outside the ritual tradition to objectify it as an ever-changing or discontinuous set of manners, practices and rites, produces a particular regime of historicity that also shapes the future in particular manners. Even if an anthropologist or historian could possibly historicize how these festivals change, how different families interpret and try to control the village politics through sponsorships, etc., without an understanding of the local ontology of reproduction and renewal cultivated in ritual modes, one would only ascribe external motives for their behavior. This lived and enacted ontology of responsiveness ritually states how things really are.

The task of ordering a conundrum of temporalities in past, present, and future is only the beginning for the sponsor. Working for resources, giving them away in feastings and offerings, and expecting a prosperous return does not exhaust the *kuuch's* duties. I would argue that the most important lesson the *kuuch* learns is that there is always someone else actively asking for something from him or her. As a result, the *kuuch* develops a new form of perception. This new sensitivity allows him or her to know with certainty that before the obligations to give, to receive and to give back there is a more important one: the obligation to ask. He or she must understand the preexistence of his or her elders' demands and respond. Imitation and the tasks imposed upon the *kuuch,* then, resituate him or her through a self-other standpoint that bridges the gap between the past and the future and transforms him or her into a person from whom something has been demanded. The committed dispositions of cargoholders, through their own generative powers, make particular futures possible and portray these futures as responses to previous human actions in a particular regime of engagement.

## NOTES

1. Yucatan declared its independence in 1841. In 1842 the Mexican government of Antonio López de Santa Anna invaded Yucatan. Frustrated in their attempts to take either Campeche or Mérida, the Mexican troops withdrew to Tampico. In 1833 the wealthiest Yucatecos started to cultivate henequen in large-scale plantations, which, along with sugar plantations, encroached on Maya communal land. The Maya workers recruited to work on these plantations were mistreated, underpaid, and kept in debt bondage. In 1847 a large force of armed Mayas gathered in a property owned by Jacinto Pat, the Maya *batab* (leader), near Valladolid. Fearing revolt, Yucatan governor Santiago Méndez Ibarra arrested Manual Antonio Ay, the principal Maya leader of Chichimilá accused of planning a revolt, and executed him at the town square of Valladolid. In the following months, several Maya towns were ransacked and many people were arbitrarily killed. In the spring of 1848, the Maya forces controlled most of the Yucatan territory, with the exception of the walled cities of Campeche and Mérida and the southwest coast. The reasons for their retreat are still debated. Nevertheless, a new cult of speaking crosses (Dumond, 1997; Reed, 1964; Rugeley, 1996, 2001) and an emergent political and military theology developed from those turbulent years.

2. There are many possible spellings for the Maya Yucatec language. For instance, "kuuch" can be found as "cuch" or "kuch." For the simplicity sake I follow the 1984's alphabet with the modifications produced in the 2006 in the Regional Forum of "Reglas gramaticales y homogeneización de la escritura de la lengua Maya en la Península de Yucatán," promoted by the National Institute of Indigenous Languages (Instituto Nacional de Lenguas Indígenas) and the Campeche Autonomous University (Universidad Autónoma de Campeche).

3. The keyword in Asad's denounce is "discipline." However, the Asadian and Foucaultian notion of discipline, borrowed mainly from Vernant's works (1962) on "melete" (discipline, attention, concern and not just "care"), cannot be directly exported from stoic texts for the analysis of all religious phenomena from a secular point of view. As Pierre Hadot has clearly noted Foucault's "souci de soi" takes only one part of the classics exercises, that one of interiorization and freeing oneself from the world, leaving aside the second, a more important movement of reengaging nature as a new being.

"To summarize: what Foucault calls "practices of the self" do indeed correspond, for the Platonists as well as for the Stoics, to a movement of conversion toward the self. One frees oneself from exteriority, from personal attachment to exterior objects, and from the pleasures they may provide. One observes oneself, to determine whether one has made progress in this exercise. One seeks to be one's own master, to possess oneself, and find one's happiness in freedom and inner independence. I concur on all these points. I do think, however, that this movement of interiorization is inseparably linked to another movement, whereby one rises to a higher psychic level, at which one encounters another kind of exteriorization, another relation with "the exterior." This is a new way of being-in-the-world, which consists in becoming aware of oneself as part of nature, and a portion of universal reason. At this point, one no longer lives in the usual, conventional human world, but in the world of nature". (Hadot, 1999, p. 211)

## ACKNOWLEDGMENTS

Andrés Dapuez wants to acknowledge that fieldwork research for this chapter was made possible by IIE-Fulbright, the Latin-American Program, National Science Foundation Research Improvement Award (BC0921235) and the Anthropology Department of the Johns Hopkins University. Andrés is also indebted to the people of Ixán, especially to the friendship of Honorio Nahuat, Lázaro Kuh Citul, and their extended family. Andrés's wife Laura Maccioni supported this long enterprise with enthusiasm and care. He hopes his children Angela, Eliseo, and Gracia learn the art of thoughtfulness easier than their father did. Jane Guyer, Veena Das, and Marcel Detienne were fundamental in this process. Carlo Natali was also very kind in responding some questions on Aristotle Ethics. Of course, any error is solely Dapuez's.

# REFERENCES


Agamben, G. (2006). *Qu'est-ce qu'un dispositive*. Paris: Rueff.

Agrama, H. A. (2010). Ethics, tradition, authority: Toward an anthropology of the fatwa. *American Ethnologist, 37*, 2–18.

Aristotle. (1994). *Nichomachean Ethics*. Cambridge, MA: Harvard University Press.

Aristotle. (1998). *The metaphysics*. New York, NY: Penguin.

Asad, T. (1993). *Genealogies of religion*. Baltimore, MD: Johns Hopkins University Press.

Bill, C. R., et al. (2000). The relationship between early colonial Maya New Year's ceremonies and some almanacs in the Madrid Codex. *Ancient Mesoamerica, 11*, 149–168.

Bolles, D. (1997). Combined dictionary-concordance of the Yucatecan Mayan language. Retrieved from http://www.famsi.org/. Accessed on August 2, 2008.

Bourdieu, P. (1990). *The logic of the practice*. Stanford, CA: Stanford University Press.

Bricker, V. R. (1981). *The Indian Christ, the Indian king*. Austin, TX: University of Texas Press.

Bricker, V. R., & Miram, H. M. (2002). *An encounter of two worlds: The book of Chilam Balam of Kaua* (Vol. 68). New Orleans, LA: Middle Atlantic Research Institute.

Bricker, V. R., & Vail, G. (1997). *Papers on the Madrid codex* (Vol. 64). New Orleans, LA: Middle American Research Institute, Tulane University.

Cancian, F. (1965). *Economics and prestige in a Maya community*. Stanford, CA: Stanford University Press.

Cancian, F. (1967). Political and religious organization. In: M. Nash (Ed.), *Handbook of Middle American Indians* (pp. 283–298). Austin, TX: University of Texas Press.

Cancian, F. (1992). *The decline of community in Zinacantán*. Stanford, CA: Stanford University Press.

Cannell, F. (2005). The Christianity of anthropology. *Journal of the Royal Anthropological Institute, 11*, 335–356.

Carrasco, P. (1961). The civil religious hierarchy in Mesoamerican communities: Pre-Hispanic background and colonial development. *American Anthropologist, 63*, 438–497.

Carrasco, P. (1990). Sobre el origen histórico de la jerarquía político-ceremonial de las comunidades indígenas. In: M. Suaréz (Ed.), *Historia, antropología y política: Homenaje a Ángel Palermo* (pp. 306–326). Mexico City: Alianza Editorial Mexicana.

Chance, J. K. (1990). Changes in twentieth-century cargo systems. In: L. Stephen & J. Dow (Eds.), *Class, politics, and popular religion in Mexico and Central America* (pp. 27–42). Washington, DC: Society for Latin American Anthropology; American Anthropological Association.

Chance, J. K. (1994). Indian elites in late colonial Mesoamerica. In: J. Marcus & J. Francis Zeitlin (Eds.), *Caciques and their people: A volume in honor of Ronald Spores* (pp. 45–65). Anthropological Papers, No. 89. Ann Arbor, MI: University of Michigan, Museum of Anthropology.

Chance, J. K., & Taylor, W. B. (1985). Cofradias and cargos: An historical perspective on Mesoamerican civil-religious hierarchy. *American Ethnologist, 12*(1), 1–26.

Coe, M. D. (1965). A model of ancient community structure in the Maya lowlands. *Southwestern Journal of Anthropology, 21*, 97–114.

Csordas, T. (1997). *The sacred self: A cultural phenomenology of charismatic healing*. Berkeley, CA: University of California Press.

Dapuez, A. (2010). Una historia imposible de la muerte en el Oriente de Yucatán. *Temas Antropológicos. Revista Científica de la Universidad Autónoma de Yucatán, 32*(2), 23–42.

De Vries, H. (2008). *Religion: Beyond a concept*. New York, NY: Fordham University Press.

DeWalt, B. R. (1975). Changes in the cargo system of Mesoamerica. *Anthropological Quarterly*, *48*, 87–105.

Dow, J. (2005). The expansion of Protestantism in Mexico: An anthropological view. *Anthropological Quarterly*, *4*, 827–850.

Dumond, D. E. (1997). *The machete and the cross: Campesino rebellion in Yucatan*. Lincoln, NE: University of Nebraska Press.

Durkheim, E. (1995/1912). *The elementary forms of religious life*. New York: The Free Press.

Early, J. D. (1983). Some ethnographic implications of an ethnohistorical perspective on the civil-religious hierarchy among the highland Maya. *Ethnohistory*, *30*, 185–202.

Eiss, P. K. (2002). Hunting for the Virgin: Meat, money, and memory in Tetiz Yucatan. *Cultural Anthropology*, *17*(3), 291–330.

Farriss, N. M. (1984). *Maya society under colonial rule: The collective enterprise of survival*. Princeton, NJ: Princeton University Press.

Fernandez, F. J. (1994). *Fiesta system in Yucatán: Popular religion, and socioeconomic organization*. Unpublished Ph.D. dissertation, Department of Anthropology, University of Florida, Gainsville, FL.

Foster, G. (1965). Peasant society and the image of limited good. *American Anthropologist*, *67*, 293–315.

Foster, G. (1966). Foster's reply to Kaplan, Saler, and Bennett. *American Anthropologist*, *66*, 210–214.

Foster, G. (1988). *Tzintzuntzan: Mexican peasants in a changing world*. Prospect Heights, IL: Waveland Press.

Friedlander, J. (1981). The secularization of the cargo system: An example from post-revolutionary central Mexico. *Latin American Research Review*, *16*, 132–143.

Geertz, C. (1973). *The interpretation of cultures*. New York, NY: Basic.

Hadot, P. (1995). *Philosophy as a way of life. Spiritual exercises from Socrates to Foucault*. Oxford, UK: Blackwell.

Hanks, W. F. (2000). *Intertexts: Writing on language, utterance, and context*. Lahnam, MD: Rowman & Littlefield.

Hervik, P. (1999). *Mayan people within and beyond boundaries: Social categories and lived identity in Yucatán*. Amsterdam: Harwood Academic.

Kant, I. (1997/1785). *Groundwork of the metaphysics of morals*. Cambridge: Cambridge University Press.

Keane, W. (2007). *Christian moderns. Freedom and fetish in the mission encounter*. Berkeley, CA: University of California Press.

Koselleck, R. (2004/1979). *Futures past: On the semantics of historical time*. New York, NY: Columbia University Press.

Latour, B. (1993/1991). *We have never been modern*. Cambridge: Harvard University Press.

León Portilla, M. (1988). *Time and reality in the thought of the Maya*. Norman, OK: University of Oklahoma Press.

Loewe, R. (1995). *Ambiguity and order in Yucatán: Identity and power at the Mexican periphery*. Unpublished Ph.D. dissertation. University of Chicago, Chicago, IL.

Loewe, R. (2003). Yucatán's dancing pig's head (cuch): Icon, carnival, and commodity. *Journal of American Folklore*, *462*, 420–443.

Lossky, V. (1985/1967). *In the image and likeness of God*. Crestwood, NY: St. Vladimir's.

Love, B. (1986). *Yucatec Maya ritual: A diachronic perspective*. Unpublished PhD Dissertation, University of California, Los Angeles, CA.

Love, B. (1991). A text from the Dresden new year pages. In: M. G. Robertson & V. M. Fields (Eds.), *Sixth Palenque Round Table, 1986* (pp. 293–302). Norman, OK: University of Oklahoma Press.

Mahmood, S. (2005). *Politics of piety: The islamic revival and the feminist subject*. Princeton, NJ: Princeton University Press.

Mauss, M. (2002/1995). *The Gift: the form and reason for exchange in archaic societies*. London: Routledge.

Mauss, M. (1979/1934). Techniques of the body. In *Sociology and psychology: Essays* (pp. 95–123). London: Routledge.

Natali, C. (1995/1992). *Oikonomia* in Hellenistic political thought. In A. Laks, & M. Schofield (Eds.), *Justice and generosity: Studies in Hellenistic social and political philosophy* (pp. 95–128). Cambridge; Cambridge University Press.

Peirce, C. S. (1998). *The essential Peirce. Selected philosophical writings. Volume 2 (1893–1913)*. Edited by the Peirce Edition Project, Bloomington, IN: Indiana University Press.

Pohl, M. (1981). Ritual continuity and transformation in Mesoamerica: Reconstructing the ancient Maya cuch ritual. *American Antiquity, 46*(3), 513–529.

Polanyi, K. (1944). *The great transformation. The political and economic origins of our time*. New York, NY: Rinehart and Co.

Price, B. (1974). The burden of the cargo: Ethnographic models and archaeological inference. In: N. Hammond (Ed.), *Mesoamerican archaeology – new approaches: Proceedings of a symposium on Mesoamerican archaeology* (pp. 445–465). Austin, TX: University of Texas Press.

Redfield, R. (1941). *The folk culture of Yucatan*. Chicago, IL: Chicago University Press.

Redfield, R. (1960). *The little community and peasant society and culture*. Chicago, IL: Chicago University Press.

Redfield, R. (1964/1950). *A village that chose progress: Chan Kom revisited*. Chicago, IL: University of Chicago Press.

Redfield, R., & Villa Rojas, A. (1967/1934). *Chan Kom*. Chicago, IL: University of Chicago Press.

Reed, N. (1964). *The caste war of Yucatan*. Palo Alto, CA: Stanford University Press.

Rugeley, T. (1996). *Yucatan's Maya peasantry and the origins of the caste war*. Austin, TX: University of Texas Press.

Rugeley, T. (Ed.) (2001). *Maya wars: Ethnographic accounts from nineteenth-century Yucatan*. Norman, OK: University of Oklahoma Press.

Rus, J., & Wasserstrom, R. (1980). Civil-religious hierarchies in central Chiapas: A critical perspective. *American Ethnologist, 7*(3), 466–478.

Scott, D., & Hirschkind, C. (2006). Introduction: The anthropological skepticism of Talal Asad. In: D. Scott & C. Hirschkind (Eds.), *Powers of the secular modern. Talal Asad and his interlocutors*. Stanford, CA: Stanford University Press.

Silverstein, B. (2008). Disciplines of Presence in Modern Turkey: Discourse, Companionship and the mass mediation of Islamic practice. *Cultural Anthropology, 23*(1), 118–153.

Stross, B. (1988). Burden of office: A reading. *Mexicon, 10*(6), 118.

Sullivan, P. (1990). *Unfinished conversations: Mayas and foreigners between two wars*. New York, NY: Knopf.

Taube, K. A. (1988). *The ancient Yucatec new year festival: The liminal period in Maya ritual and cosmology*. Unpublished PhD thesis. New Haven, CT: Yale University.

Tax, S. (1937). The municipios of the midwestern highland of Guatemala. *American Anthropologist, 39*, 423–444.

Terán, S., & Rasmussen, C. (2008). *Jinetes del cielo maya: dioses y diosas de la lluvia en Xocén.* Mérida: Ediciones de la Universidad Autónoma de Yucatán.

Thompson, J. E. S. (1934). Sky bearers, colors, and directions in Maya and Mexican religions. *Contributions to American Archaeology*, Pub. 436, No. 10: 209–242. Carnegie Institution of Washington, Washington, DC.

Thompson, J. E. S. (1958). Symbols, glyphs, and divinatory almanacs for diseases in the Maya dresden and madrid codices. *American Antiquity, 23*(3), 297–308.

Thompson, J. E. S. (1970). *Maya history and religion.* Norman, OK: University of Oklahoma Press.

Tozzer, A. M. (1941). Landa's Relación de las cosas de Yucatán. Papers of the Peabody Museum of American Archaeology and Ethnology, Vol. 18. Harvard University, Cambridge, MA.

Vail, G. (1997). The yearbearer gods in the madrid codex. In: S. Rueda Smithers, et al. (Eds), *Códices y Documentos sobre México. Segundo Simposio* (Vol. I, pp. 81–106). Mexico, D.F.: Instituto Nacional de Antropología e Historia/Dirección General de Publicaciones. Comisión Nacional de Cultura y Artes.

Vernant, J.-P. (1962). *Les origines de la penseé grecque.* Paris: Press Universitaires de France.

Villa Rojas, A. (1987). *Los elegidos de dios: Etnografía de los Mayas de Quintana Roo.* México D.F.: Instituto Nacional Indigenista.

Vogt, E. Z. (1976). *Tortillas for the gods: A symbolic analysis of Zinacanteco rituals.* Cambridge: Harvard University Press.

Wasserstrom, R. (1980). Exchange of Saints in Zinancantan: The socioeconomic bases of religious change in southern Mexico. *Ethnology, 17*, 197–210.

Weber, M. (2008/1904). *The Protestant ethic and the spirit of capitalism.* Oxford: Oxford University Press.

Wolf, E. R. (1955). Types of Latin American peasantry: A preliminary discussion. *American Anthropologist, 57*, 452–471.

Wolf, E. R. (1957). Closed corporate peasant communities in Mesoamerica and central Java. *Southwestern Journal of Anthropology, 13*, 1–18.

Wolf, E. R. (1986). The vicissitudes of the closed corporate peasant community. *American Ethnologist, 13*(2), 325–329.

# GOD UNLIMITED: ECONOMIC TRANSFORMATIONS OF CONTEMPORARY NIGERIAN PENTECOSTALISM

Asonzeh Ukah

## ABSTRACT

*The last three decades of the 20th century was a period of momentous social, economic, political and religious turmoil in many African societies. Nigeria is a prime example. Although the economic transformations of this period were perhaps bigger than other kinds of change, religious shifts probably had more remarkable social effects. One particularly noticeable development was the emergence of a new strand of Pentecostalism that serves as a source of political power and as a vehicle for economic mobilisation. Embedded in a theology of materialism and a redefinition of 'money', this new ideology found a fertile ground among local and global corporations struggling to cope with problems such as a devalued currency and political corruption and instability. Using data from ethnographic research on the Redeemed Christian Church of God (RCCG), with more than 10,000 congregations worldwide, this chapter shows how the near economic meltdown of the last decades of the 20th century precipitated a massive religious (re)engagement with economic structures and practices in Nigeria.*

**The Economics of Religion: Anthropological Approaches**
**Research in Economic Anthropology, Volume 31, 187–216**

**ISSN: 0190-1281/doi:10.1108/S0190-1281(2011)0000031011**

## INTRODUCTION

Religion is on the loose in Nigeria. Any first-time visitor to the country will be impressed by the social vitality of a plethora of religious groups and activities. 'Unlimited God' was the title of a recent (April 2004) Pentecostal revival programme in southern Nigeria that promised people abundant wealth from the unlimited treasures of God. This event, with its catchy and attractive caption, is characteristic of many similar events staged at numerous Pentecostal and charismatic churches and ministries, each promising attendees unprecedented wealth, success and a super-healthy life, all made possible by believing in an infinitely rich God and by giving financially to the (wo)man of God hosting the event. A new form of Pentecostalism emerged in the late 1970s and 1980s to rejuvenate social and economic activities in a country under the heavy yoke of economic liberalisation and structural adjustment programmes. Particularly in urban centres, these diverse groups engage in various activities such as crusades, vigils, prayer meetings, retreats, conventions and healing and deliverance services. In addition, there is a vast range of activities that are not directly related to the business of religion, such as the provision of social services like schools, hospitals, maternities, orphanages as well as the running of financial enterprises like banks, insurance companies, bookshops, hotels and the like. In the face of this obvious multiplex role of contemporary religion in Nigeria, it is surprising that scholars have not yet produced a descriptive analysis in which money and Nigerian Pentecostalism factor large.[1] While few Nigerian scholars of religion will contest the claim that money has come very close to the heart of most urban religious revivalism, many still find it difficult or shy away from engaging with the obvious but intractable study of the increasing monitisation of religiosity. As one Nigerian Pentecostal pastor, John Moyibi Amoda, recently put it, 'the merchandising of the Gospel of the Lord Jesus Christ' is 'the primary source of all the problems enervating the spiritual life of the church' (Amoda, 1997, p. vii). He laments that leaders and owner-founders of Pentecostal churches and ministries 'rule over their congregation as captains of industries oversee business empires' and pastors administer their congregations 'as fiefdoms and principalities' (Amoda, 1997, p. xi, x).

Generally, scholars of religion in Africa are consistently reluctant to investigate Pentecostal fiscal activities partly because of the implicit belief that religion primarily concerns a supra-human realm and has little to do with mundane concerns, and partly because of the fear of being considered as scandal mongers eager to cause disaffection among church leader-owners and their followers. Further, most Nigerian-founded pentecostal organisations are run as family estates with a rigid code of secrecy put in place by the founder-leader. In the organisations established according to the structure of family firms, the owner-founders, together with their spouses, control all financial dealings and records and consequently administer these churches as financial empires. These records, where they are kept at all, are never made accessible to either the members of the church or the public. In a survey of more than 500 pentecostal churches and ministries in Ibadan in 1998–1999, no pastor agreed to release the financial records of his organisation. One of the reasons given for this refusal was that it would create suspicion among church members should the wealth or financial standing of the church be made public. Church leaders actively discourage any attempts on the part of members to demand fiscal accountability of them, and sometimes threaten to curse them.

Historically, religion has been a formidable force for political and economic change but never before has Nigeria witnessed such a massive surge of religionisation of patterns and structures of social, economic and political life. While Muslims in the predominantly Islamic northern states have consolidated their grip on social, economic and political structures through the expansion of the Shari'a code of law, Christians in the South, particularly those affiliated with Pentecostal-charismatic churches, have not left anyone in doubt about their real intention in pentecostalising principal economic formations and practices. What has characterised the two major religious traditions has been more of competition than cooperation. This competition is for greater spheres of influence and power through the control of major political positions since these directly translate into economic advantages for their followers and various associates.

Among Christians, however, a different pattern of competition has emerged over time. While the Christian community is immensely variegated, the groups that most strongly and forcefully represent the new culture of economic competition have been the neo-Pentecostal churches and ministries. Pentecostalism is not altogether new in Nigeria, as it has emerged through a complex interaction of both local and foreign elements of Christian practice in the first three decades of the twentieth century (Ayegboyin & Ukah, 2002; Peel, 1968, 2000; Turner, 1979). Some Pentecostal groups were founded by Nigerians who broke away from mission churches, but others were established through the direct missionary activities of western Pentecostal associations such as the Four Square Gospel Church and the Assemblies of God Church. Over a period of more than half a century, these diverse Pentecostal groups have grown and consolidated on the local turf, responding in various ways to local religious experiences and needs.

Following Nigeria's political independence in 1960 and the expansion of educational institutions in the country in the post-war period of the 1970s and 1980s, a new form of Christianity emerged and took root within the proliferating tertiary institutions. Headed by educated young men and women, this brand of 'Campus Christianity' negotiated its identity through a copious consumption of literature mainly from the United Kingdom and north America (Ojo, 1986). Printed materials such as tracts, magazines and free bible study texts, and also recorded audio and video cassettes of sermons and religious messages became very popular among the members of this new class of young religious proselytisers. Many of these Pentecostal proselytisers were recent graduates of various institutions of higher learning in the country. Quite a few of these educated young men and women soon established their own independent Pentecostal churches and ministries, then deepen and enlarge their circles of friends, associates and followers.

Propelled by a combination of historical, social and economic processes occurring in the country in the late 1970s and early 1980s, what originally appeared as a slow, gradual and largely ignored process of growth, has blossomed into a dizzying frenzy of divisions and subdivisions within the 'Pentecostal-charismatic' fold. In a related development, the experience of the civil war (1967–1970), which resulted in the death of several thousand people, produced among many Nigerians a sense of sombre reflection and a desire to be closer to God in order to avert a similar disaster. The new-found income from high crude oil prices in the 1970s produced a new class of wealthy Nigerians who indulged in massive importation of consumer goods from abroad while a profligate military – conniving with a thieving political class – expropriated the nation of huge oil revenues. The new religious groups of this period were mainly of the Holiness type. These not only frowned at what was going on, they engaged in anti-government rhetoric and aggressively condemned the political class. The Deeper Life Bible Church, founded about this time, exemplified this Holiness trend and the anti-government, other-worldly orientations of this period (Ojo, 1992). Deeper Life's orientation to the world as a corrupting sphere of life which could distract from the attention to the things of heaven as well as a negative reaction to material accumulation as exemplified in the lives of the new elite – made possible by Nigeria's new-found oil wealth – were some of the reasons for its other-worldly focus.

The crash of oil prices in 1981 and the subsequent imposition of the IMF-World Bank negotiated Structural Adjustment Policy (SAP), with its attendant austerity measures in 1986, brought far-reaching changes to Nigerian society, in the form of currency devaluation, massive retrenchment of workers, fold-ups of companies and factories, and also a high graduate unemployment rate. In the midst of legitimacy crises of a bankrupt military leadership, social decay, state failure, massive corruption, endemic graduate unemployment, environmental degradation in the Niger Delta region, unprecedented abuse of human rights and crippling poverty of many set against the scandalous wealth of a few, new churches and ministries proliferated. Among the masses in southern Nigeria, religion became the answer to the negative consequences of economic liberalisation and marginalisation.

A significant feature of the new churches was its leadership – made up of university- and college-educated young men – and in a few cases, women – who were self-assertive, upwardly mobile, and articulate individuals. They were also well versed in the use of modern mass media technology. These leaders liberally injected a massive dose of secular learning acquired in such disciplines as economics, business management, political science, marketing and advertising into church teachings, practices, organisation and administration. An influx of audio tapes, video cassettes, magazines and books written by both American and local Pentecostal leaders on 'church marketing', prosperity, wealth, deliverance techniques and other 'techniques of the self' (in the elegant phrase of Michel Foucault, quoted in Ellis & ter Haar, 2004, p. 166) and the spirit inaugurated an era of prosperity and popular Pentecostalism. As the influence of the state dwindled, the new brand of popular religion sought to help its adherents negotiate the massive social, political and economic transformations going on in the country.

As Nigeria's political and economic environment deteriorated further in the 1990s, more ministries and churches sprang up – particularly in urban centres – all contesting for the souls and pockets of the suffering urban masses. As large businesses and factories folded up because of the high cost of doing business, a general lack of electrical power and massive importation of finished goods from abroad, new churches took over the vacated office spaces and warehouses, erected massive billboards, printed glossy, high-quality wall-size posters of their leaders, and embarked on an enterprise of proselytisation of the economic frontiers. The popularity of the new Pentecostal groups became infectious as older Pentecostal churches renegotiated their public and doctrinal identity by incorporating new doctrines and grafting new practices onto their organisational behaviour in order to compete effectively in the emergent religious market. One group that effectively reconstructed its identity in the 1980s is the Redeemed

Christian Church of God (RCCG). As fully detailed elsewhere (see Ukah, 2008), the importance of RCCG in the sacred market of Nigeria is that it redefined what a successful religious group has to be, introduced new trends and religio-economic products that other lesser-known churches have followed or emulate.

## RCCG: HISTORY OF A 'TRIBAL CHURCH'

The Reverend Josiah Akindayomi, an estranged prophet and Apostle in the Cherubim and Seraphim (C&S) church, founded the RCCG. Born Ogunribido Ogundolie (Ogunribido means 'Ogun has found a dwelling place') in 1909 in Ondo in Yorubaland into a family of adherents of Ogun, the Yoruba deity of war and iron, Josiah became a traditional healer (*onisegun* in Yoruba) before converting to the Church Missionary Society (CMS) in 1927, where he took the Christian name Josiah. After only four years in the CMS, he joined the just established C&S movement in 1931 (see Peel, 1968). Josiah was literate in Yoruba but not in English. He quickly rose to the rank of prophet and Apostle in the C&S, and formed a small band of followers around himself called *Egbe Ogo Oluwa*, the 'Glory of God Fellowship'. In 1952, he clashed with the leadership of the C&S movement and was consequently ex-communicated for insubordination. He transformed his small band into a church and changed the name to 'The Redeemed Christian Church of God' claiming it was a name divinely revealed to him. For four years (1956–1960), this church was affiliated with the Apostolic Faith Mission of South Africa, a relationship that was terminated after Nigeria gained political independence. The church grew slowly and when Josiah died in November 1980, there were 39 parishes or separate congregations all in Lagos and its environs with a membership of less than a thousand.

Just before the founder of the church died, he nominated Enoch Adejare Adeboye, a university lecturer with a doctorate degree in mathematics, as his successor. Adeboye had spent only seven years as a member of this church, and was himself only 39 years old when he took over the reins of power in January 1981. After an initial period of bitter fighting over the leadership that saw the church splintered into three factions, Adeboye set himself to the task of turning around the fortunes of a church that was aptly described by one of its provincial pastors as 'a tribal church'. One of the faction leaders had earlier described the church as 'a muddy pool of water that would soon dry up'. Adeboye did not want this gloomy prophecy come to fruition.

In order to underscore the importance of the transformations that Adeboye brought to the church, it is necessary to describe the type of congregations he inherited. The parishes of the RCCG in the 1970s and early 1980s, later called the Classical Parishes, were the Holiness type of congregations, with the posture of a pietistic movement. Because of the founder's literalist interpretation of the bible, it was forbidden for women to wear trousers, earrings or make-ups or visit the salons to fix their hair; they had to cover their hair during services or whenever they were on the church premises. In addition, they were not allowed to ride on motorcycles, for this was adjudged inappropriate of a 'Christian sister'. The founder of the church had also considered it unworthy of a Christian sister to indulge in any of these activities. The congregations of the church were very small and located at the back streets of Lagos and its environs. Services were conducted in Yoruba with translations into English in some parishes, and electronic instruments and bands, as well as the clapping of hands, were forbidden in the church. Virtually all the members of the church were Yoruba. Grave seriousness marked worship services as 'worshippers [were] wrapped ... in tears, groaning in prayer' (Akinremi, 2002, p. 33). The weekly crying service sessions earned the church the nickname of '*Ijo elekun*', meaning, 'the weeping church'.

Another significant feature of the pre-1980 RCCG was the church's attitude towards money: there was no collection of offerings during services. The leader-founder of the church believed that 'money should not separate people from God' (Akinremi, 2002, p. 33). In an interview in 2001 with Ifeoluwa Akindayomi, the son of the founder, the principal source of its revenue was the collection of tithes or gifts from church members and well-wishers. As if to deal with the problem of free-riders, there was a strict dress code for all who entered the church's premises. These parishes represented an apocalyptical, or rather prophetic, movement as they prepared and waited for the coming of the end of the world that the Parousia will supposedly herald. Made up mainly of disempowered and uneducated members, the church saw itself as a pilgrim movement. According to 'RCCG at 50', a document produced by the church in 2002 to mark its golden jubilee, the pre-1980 church members were taught to perceive themselves as just passing through this world – which was regarded as a vale of tears – but not of the world, and so, not loving the things of this world for they all pass away whereas the love of God is considered to last forever (1 Jn 2:15,17).

Aside from the schisms that the RCCG suffered because of the appointment of Adeboye as leader, the new leader faced other serious challenges. First, the doctrines and practices of the church alienated the youth. Hence, the church became, in the words of Johnson Funso Odesola, a senior pastor, 'a church of elderly people, a bundle of people who were in the main illiterates, people who were not educated in a modern way'. Second, the church was poor and for many years could hardly raise enough money to pay the meagre salaries of its clergy. Third, the church was seen as socially unprogressive, particularly concerning the prohibition of members from working in tobacco or alcohol producing, distributing and marketing enterprises. Further, members were prohibited from working in the armed forces or the police as these professions were, according to J. H. Abiona (2000, p. 6), the church's Deputy General Overseer, considered 'at variance with the doctrines of the church'. Fourth, because of all the above, the church was having difficulty attracting and keeping well-educated, young, upwardly mobile professionals.

## DIVERSIFICATION OF RELIGIOSITY

In response to the above situation, the new leader set out to alter the structures and social character of the church. However, because he was young and relatively a newcomer to the church, he met with entrenched resistance from an older group of pastors and members who held rigid views on church life. Rather than risk a possible rebellion from both his pastors and followers, Adeboye created a new type of parish and called it the Model Parish in 1988. The new parishes, in contrast to the older ones which he now christened the 'Classical Parishes', permitted all the things that were previously outlawed, in addition to being located at such strategic but 'profane' places as hotels, nightclubs, cinema halls, highbrow city centres and other places where 'worldly people' are found. In the words of the Assistant General Overseer (AGO) in charge of Administration in the church, prospective members were instructed:

> to come as you are, for the Lord will touch you as we minister to you. Let them come to Jesus as they are. Whatever the painting on their heads or faces or on their hair; whatever the disposition or garments they are putting on. At the end of the day when God is through with them, their lives would be changed rather than say they should not enter the church.

Unlike the Classical Parishes with their apocalyptic attitudes, services in the Model Parishes were – and still are – conducted in English with no translation into Yoruba, accompanied with electric musical instruments and western drums and bands. Headed by professionals – the first three by a lawyer, a banker and a medical doctor respectively – the Model Parishes set out to redefine the Pentecostal self-perception and identity in urban southern Nigeria. The vision behind the Model Parishes, according to a senior pastor of the church, 'was to reach the younger folks, graduates, upwardly mobile executives, which the older folks [in the Classical Parishes] could not have done due to a lot of limitations' (Pitan Adeboye, 2001, p. 23). Through the Model Parishes, the collection of money as offerings during liturgical events was introduced in the church. Gradually, the church was monetised through increased financial demands on its members in the form of tithes, fees and levies, offerings of many kinds (thanksgiving, freewill, seeds offering, smiling offering, rejoicing offering, etc.) and donations. At root, however, a more radical change was taking place: religious demands or obligations were being monetised such that money replaced certain pietistic demands within the church.

The two types of parishes still coexist. (There is a third strand of parishes, called Unity Parishes, which was initiated in 1997 to harmonise the social and religious features of the first two strands. However, this latest addition has not met with much success as did the Model parishes.) While Classical Parishes emphasise holiness, Model Parishes emphasise modernity, prosperity and flaunt images of wealth as an index of grace and salvation. They symbolise what is best in the material world, bring home to people such icons of high modernity as new media and global consumption appetites. The Model Parishes quickly became very successful in attracting young, educated people from different ethnic and economic backgrounds. Through their rapid proliferation, they introduced trans-cultural elements from outside the Yoruba cultural milieu into the church. Among other things, the 'success' of the Model Parishes resulted from a lowering of the strict standards that governed the conduct of personal life in the Classical Parishes. Removing restrictions over membership is like a discount on a purchase; it stimulates and sustains demand. The people who trooped into the Model Parishes were taught to increase their expenditure, time, conviction and commitment in the cause of the church. Financial giving to the church soon became a significant index of commitment and public piety. Members of the Model Parishes are in the main influential, border-spanning networkers, mobile middle class men and women who criss-cross Nigerian society and try to extend their connections all over Africa and the world. The rapid increase and expansion of the Model Parishes soon became the driving force for the local multiplication of parishes as well as the founding of parishes in Europe and North America. The dynamics generated through the Model Parishes aptly captures Kanter's (1995) four trends of the processes of globalisation: mobility, simultaneity, bypass and pluralism. The new parishes are pragmatic and cosmopolitan in outlook, emphasising product packaging, re-branding, powerful delivery of the message, astute salesmanship and creative media use.

By redefining the 'cost' of belonging to the church through the creation of Model Parishes, Adeboye stimulated religious demand, making the church attractive to many educated and upwardly mobile urban dwellers. More significantly, he permanently changed the social, economic and demographic structures of the church. From 39 parishes in 1981, the RCCG has, as of August 2009, grown to 12,000 parishes in more than 90 countries, more than 70 per cent of which is of the Model Parish variety. This is a marked case of religious engineering.

## CAMPUS NICHE

In September 1988, the same year that the Model Parishes were established, the new leader invited 18 young undergraduates from some universities in the Southwest to his office. These young men and women received a mandate to go back to their campuses and start fellowship groups, to be collectively known as Redeemed Campus Fellowship (RCF). The undergraduates obeyed and got all the support they needed from the church. The groups they founded blossomed as young students put their minds and energy into proselytising campus frontiers for the church. From the ranks of university graduates the church recruited its pastors and created new cadres of ministers such as deacons, assistant pastors, unordained ministers and church workers.

Over the years, members of these groups have scattered all over Nigeria, and some have travelled outside the country as well. Wherever they went, they carried with them the teachings of their new leader – to establish new parishes wherever they resided or worked. Many assumed managerial roles and positions in corporate Nigeria, thus placing the church and its concern on the corridors of social and economic power in the country. The wealth of the church increased as the number of quality persons affiliated to it increased.

### *A Special Purpose Group: The CRFU*

In order to consolidate its improving fortunes, in January of 1990 the new leader created an interdenominational elite group called Christ the Redeemer's Friends Universal (CRFU). Membership in CRFU is narrow and elitist in orientation although it claims to embrace all persons 'who are born again and profess the Lordship of our Lord Jesus Christ'. According to the Constitution of the group, members must not be less than 18 years old with an academic qualification of at least a National Certificate of Education (NCE) or not less than 30 years of age with at least an NCE qualification or 'without any educational qualification at all but who have distinguished themselves in their career or profession'.[2] According to the a flier produced by the CRFU in 2001, the group's primary responsibility is to proselytise 'the people in the upper echelons of society for Christ', and through them mobilise money, trained personnel, technical skills and publicity within the corridors of social, political and economic power in the country. Members of CRFU are mainly accomplished executives as well as professionals: lawyers, bankers, accountants, medical doctors, architects, engineers, pharmacists, estate and land surveyors and academics. The CRFU is a ready source of personnel, sponsors and financiers of the RCCG activities. The RCCG's strategy is to target 'those people in positions of authority who invariably are rich and affluent' (Bankole, 1999, p. 62). The RCCG, much like many other Pentecostal groups in the country, deliberately and systematically skims 'more of the cream of society than the dregs' (Stark & Bainbridge, 1985, p. 395). Through this category of persons in CRFU, the church aims at the social and economic conversion of Nigeria.

## TOWARDS AN ECONOMIC THEOLOGY OF WEALTH

According to Keister (2003), religious beliefs and practices influence a person's wealth ownership because they shape values and priorities, contribute 'to the set of competencies from which action is constructed, and may provide important social contacts' (p. 176). Significantly, the quality of persons drawn into CRFU, many of whom have become pastors and assistant pastors of the church, have in diverse ways modified the teachings and practices of the church. This is easily noticeable in the way the church has come to embrace market practices and given overt support to a highly corrupt political class in the country. The theological orientation of the church markedly changed following the influx of businesspersons and educated elite through the Model Parish programme. The CRFU is the church's most aggressively proselytising and revenue machine.

According to the son of the founder of RCCG, Ifeoluwa Akindayomi, his father preached against wealth and prosperity because he thought it was a corrupting influence for Christians in general and for members of his church in particular. However, following the downturn in the Nigerian economy in the mid-1980s and the need to bring people of influence and affluence into the church, the new leader imbibed the prosperity teachings that were first popularised in the country by Archbishop Benson Idahosa (1938–1998) of Church of God Mission, Benin City, Nigeria. Idahosa's teaching was directly related to his training in North America (Hackett, 1995), and was to alter church behaviour. Significantly, religious behaviour for the new cadre of leadership was not confined to church rituals, but also involved economic practice: these new churches were not simply interested in teaching their members how to behave on earth in order to merit heaven but how to conquer, subdue and succeed in this world and turn it into a sort of 'heaven on earth'. Such reorientation set a new order of priority for the RCCG's economy that greatly enhanced its capacity for competition and survival.

The central pillar of the new theology that emerged in the mid-1980s is the teaching on 'exchange'. Richard R. Lee (1992, p. 26) has examined religion as a form of social exchange, concluding that '[r]eligious behaviour follows the same principles as economic behaviour'. According to Adeboye, 'God is a God of exchange' and he can do nothing for you if you have done nothing for him. God involves human beings in a range of exchange activities either as individuals or as groups. In this exchange relationship, God gives, or rather, rewards, his votaries with wealth that is essentially money and material things that money can purchase. Adeboye describes material comfort and wellbeing in line with Deuteronomy 28:11 to mean 'cars, houses, clothes, land, anything money can buy – material things!' (Adeboye, 1989, p. 7). Those who intend to relate with God must also understand the nature and character of God, Adeboye teaches. For him,

> God is not poor at all by any standard. Furthermore, the closest friends of God [in the Bible] were wealthy people [...] God is the God of the rich, and his closest friends are very wealthy [...]. The rich are friends of the rich, and the poor are friends of the poor. Therefore God decided to befriend the rich. (Adeboye, 1989, pp. 2–3)

To be poor, according to this strand of thought, completely excludes one from the friendship of God since '[b]irds of the same [*sic*] feather flock together' and poverty is an evil as well as a curse that brings hatred and destruction in its wake (Adeboye, 1989, p. 6). According to this new teaching,

> Those who will get blessing from God will have to go beyond ordinary giving of offering or paying of tithes. Daily they [should] look for an opportunity to do something special to God that will compel Him to do more than what He wanted to do for them. Those who trade with God never lose. (Adeboye, 1989, p. 29)

## TRADING WITH GOD: FORMS AND SCOPE

The leader of the RCCG, Enoch Adeboye, as the chief theologian of the church, has worked out this theology of 'trading with God' into practical behaviour for both individuals and groups. For the church, it is the bedrock of economic transformation and divinely ordained social change.

### *Individual Exchange*

The theology of wealth and success is the operating system on which many Nigerian Pentecostal churches run. Obviously, it is a soothing theology for the rich and powerful, although it is by no means a consolation for the poor who may be encouraged, cajoled – or even blackmailed – to try to join the rich people's club by becoming rich through giving generously to the church. For individuals, there exists different forms of giving to God through the church such as tithe – which is the obligatory giving of ten per cent of one's income, profit on business transactions and gifts to the church – and thanksgiving offerings, 'love offerings', Sunday offerings and voluntary offerings. It is not uncommon to hear about 'smiling offering' or 'rejoicing offering' in the church as separate forms of financial collections taken during Sunday worship services. As well, different types of cash offerings are taken during such weekday programmes such as bible study, choir practice, healing service and prayer meetings. The logic of the different offerings is exchange: if a person gives to God, s/he will receive in return. Adeboye reinforces this doctrine by insisting that '[w]hen you begin to give extraordinarily, you will begin to receive extraordinarily ... It is a key that opens the door of abundance. ... When you are giving you are loading your cloud and when the cloud is full then it is going to fall down as rain [of abundance]'.[3] Some forms of giving are called 'sowing', in relation to the law of harvest. Sowing is defined as something such as money given by a person to a pastor for a particular purpose: 'You sow specifically in order to reap specifically'. This law, for Adeboye, enables a person to control his/her future. 'We can become the controller of the wealth of this nation if we just ... sow aggressively... sow consistently ... [and] sow as if something is wrong with us'.[4] The harvest is proportional to the seed cultivated.

> If you want a double portion of wealth, you have to do something greater than what Solomon did. You have to give an offering the kind that you had never given before. God is a God of principles: Do what nobody had done before; He will respond by giving you something that nobody had ever got before.[5]

A unique character of this teaching is that it is not directed to Christians or born-again believers or even members of the church: Adeboye encourages anyone to give whether or not they are believers. '[E]veryone who sows would reap'.[6]

The teaching on giving as investment was put to test recently. During a monthly religious event held on 1 March 2002, Adeboye announced that God instructed him to set up four groups of people in the church who would carry out four different tasks for the RCCG in exchange for divine favours. The first group of individuals would be a thousand people who would be willing to fast for 60 days a year for the next 10 years, with half of this fasting period being continuous. For this cohort, their reward would be any gift of the Holy Spirit they should desire, such as the gift of healing, or of working miracles, or of prophecy. Those who wished to belong to this group but could not endure the rigours of fasting were invited to make a payment of 60,000 naira (ca. US$390.00/€285.00) yearly in exchange. The second group also consisted of 1,000 persons who would volunteer to do manual work for 60 days a year for 10 years at the church's Redemption Camp free of charge. As their recompense, God would enable anyone in this group to enjoy divine health for 10 years. Similarly, the third group consisted of 1,000 people who would be willing and able to give God one million naira (ca. $6,500.00/€4,700) a year for 10 years. God would reward these generous donors by showing them the true meaning of prosperity. As if one million naira was an insignificant amount in a country where more than 70 per cent of the 160 million people live on less than US$1 a day, Adeboye's fourth group consisted of 100 people willing and able to give 10 million naira (ca. US$65,000.00/€47,500.00) each year to the church for the next 10 years. Their reward would be that God would quietly transfer the wealth of nations to them. In addition, all participants in the different groups were guaranteed being alive for the duration of the participation period, regardless of how hard any enemies may try to harm them.[7] Moreover, for maximum effect, an individual could choose to belong to more than one group, which would only help to concentrate the person's rewards. For the many individuals who volunteered to give money to the church, no questions were asked about the sources of their wealth and their intentions for giving. The persons who responded to the call to donation were later called 'covenant partners'; the four groups formed in 2002 have increased to five in 2004 and by 2005 have grown to seven different groups of covenant partners who continuously make monthly and yearly donations of time, material and money to the church. These specialised groups are still existing and increasing in number.

Underpinning this theology of monetised piety is the neatly formulated maxim: 'He who cannot be generous with money, surely will not be generous with anointing' (Adeboye, 1999, p. 47). Adeboye articulates three kinds of blessings that individuals receive in return for what they give to God: 'double blessings', 'compound blessing' and 'concentrated blessing'. It is difficult to determine any difference between these, but for greedy and corrupt politicians, businessmen, contractors and corporate executives who are willing to oblige Adeboye's demands, they are appealing – they are a form of religious identity mark, the consumption of which will guarantee them security and continued success. States Adeboye: 'There is only one way by which you can get this greater blessing. It is by doing something special that will move God and cause him to bless you more than he intended' (Adeboye, 1989, p. 24). RCCG's economy of grace is tightly linked to the amount of money a person gives to the church; the degree of anointing one gets is correlated with the amount of money one gives.[8] According to Adeboye, there is a form of giving which is the 'principle of the first fruits'. This is giving to God the first fruits of one's increase:

> If you get a job, the first salary is called the first fruit. If you are a contractor, you register a company and that company gets a contract, the profit on that contract is a first fruit. Or at the beginning of the year, there is an increment on your salary – the increment on the first month is first fruit.[9]

## *Corporate Trading*

Having reformulated its doctrines of God and wealth, the RCCG was able from the late 1980s onward to attract upwardly mobile, university educated and ambitious young men and women. In 1986, Adeboye instituted a monthly prayer vigil called Holy Ghost Service,[10] and in 1998, he started an annual prayer festival called Holy Ghost Festival which was renamed Holy Ghost Congress in 2001. Both events attract thousands of people. The church's annual convention week, held in August, brings large numbers of people together for several days and nights. These are not just religious events – they are also media and economic events for different companies. For these events, the church actively employs the finest corporate marketers to sell advertising and marketing or sponsorship rights to corporate organisations. Because some of these corporate marketers have brought such large amounts of revenue to the church, they have been elevated in the church's hierarchy to the position of elders and assistant elders, demonstrating the fact that even for promotion to ritual roles in the church depends on some form of resource exchange.

In the mid-1990s, a novel practice became noticeable in the church. The aggressive policy of proselytising the upper middle class of the society paid off with managers and corporate heads of many companies, particularly in the southwest of the country, joining the church or one of its elite para-church groups. These organisations have been encouraged, or cajoled, to go into partnership with the church by sponsoring the church's activities. Such corporate sponsorship of religious events in the church comes in different forms. Some of the companies make financial commitments to the church in the form of 'donations' by issuing promissory notes or cheques, and some provide equipment such as electricity generating plants, communication gadgets, trucks and vans, or even construct buildings for the church. Furthermore, some companies, in addition to one or two of the above, provide personnel, logistics and expertise for hosting large congregations.

Many companies are now involved in sponsoring RCCG events, an act that comes with specific economic benefit for the firms, as they use the events to create PR opportunities as well as product visibility. More importantly, by affiliating with the church, the companies demonstrate much needed corporate piety that helps them to gloss over corporate malfeasance. The first company that made the headlines in national dailies regarding this practice was the Nigerian Brewery Plc (NB), the largest producer of a range of alcoholic beverages such as beer and malt drinks in the country. In 1997, the NB gave the church 20 million naira as a 'donation' towards the hosting of the church's annual programme at Lekki Beach in Lagos. In exchange for this donation, the NB got the sole right to market its soft drink products. By prohibiting the sale of any other brand of soft drinks during the event, the church made it possible for NB to recoup its 'investment' in the sponsorship deal. In a similar way, other corporate entities manufacturing household products have scrambled into the sponsors' club in order to have their wares displayed and marketed during the church's numerous events. A certain advertisement for a Unilever line of laundry detergent, published in a brochure of the RCCG, depicts boxes of the product with rays of light emanating from behind and fanning out to the sides (a reproduction of the actual box illustration). This is typical of the kind of advertisements that may follow the granting of such sponsorships and marketing rights to commercial entities. The anchoring text of the advert, 'Neither sin nor stain shall have dominion over you' is a deliberate misquotation of Romans 6:14: 'For sin shall not have dominion over you … '. Putting the text in quotation marks, as is done in the advertisement, is likewise a deliberate ploy or a commercial gimmick to deceive or confuse readers into assuming that it is a direct quotation from the Bible. Other than Unilever, international corporations that engage in this sort of practice in Nigeria include Procter & Gamble, Nestlé Foods, Coca-Cola, 7-Up, and many banks, insurance companies and cellular telephone providers as well (see Ukah, 2005).

Similarly, the church is in economic partnership with travel agencies or holiday companies for which it recruits customers and parts with a share of the profit. For an example, the RCCG in conjunction with Cloud 7 Cruises, a London-based company, organised what it called the 'Heaven on the Seas Conference' from 19 to 24 June 2004 on HMS Wonderland, sailing from Miami, Florida, to the Port of Nassau, Bahamas, and then back to Miami. For religious tourists interested in the cruise, a non-refundable deposit of US$500 or £350 or ₦68,500 was demanded. The rates of the cruise ranged from US$5,000 to US$2,250. Although the cruise was advertised as a 'holiday', it was also said that Adeboye would be teaching during the seven days and seven nights of the journey. Such tourist trips and events are organised annually, taking participants to places such as Israel, and of course, they are mainly for the rich and powerful members of Nigerian society.

Financial institutions such as banks, insurance providers, savings and loans companies, estate developers, and manufacturers of household products, are all designing special products and services for the church, targeting both individuals and para-church groups, but particularly the very rich who openly fraternise with the leadership of the church. City Express Bank, for example, has put forward a range of 'mission products' that include the Church Remittance Account Scheme (CREMAS), Church, Cheques and Cash collections (4cs), the Church Asset Acquisition and Development Scheme (CAADs), and the Church Planting and Missions Account (CHURPMAS).[11] The bank claims to be a partner with the church in fulfilling its missionary dream and expanding its missionary work. There is rabid competition between these banks to control RCCG's purse, and also to woo the money class who are now attracted by the theology and practices of the church regarding wealth creation and the religious significance of money.

For the church and these companies, 'God' is not just a theological or metaphysical idea but an economic one, since it can be presented and utilised in attracting and maintaining a niche, and in marketing specific products and services to this group. Because of the economic functions of RCCG's theology and ritual events, commercial entities unabashedly embark on aggressive advertising of the church's programmes and leaders. They put out advertorials in the national media (newspapers, radio and television), erect countless numbers of impressive and expensive billboards, and print posters, car bumper stickers and banners announcing the church's programmes and inviting the public to come and participate. In return, the leader of the church, like the media celebrity that he actually is, endorses the companies and their products and directs his audiences to patronise the goods and services of the church's corporate sponsors (see Ukah, 2003, p. 251f). For the commercial firms, the church is an economic asset; the leader positively identifies with their practices and products, and his followers are turned into loyal consumers. The church earns endorsement fees in return.

### *Exchange with the Political Class*

Since before colonial times, and during colonial rule, religion has consistently played important roles in the politics of Nigeria. However, never before has this intersection between politics and religion been more forceful and undisguised as since the Fourth Republic, which started in May 1999 (Adekunle, 2009). Since that year, the RCCG has shown strong connections to the political ruling elite in the country. Because of its nonadversarial posture towards politicians – who are particularly responsible for the dysfunctional character of the country through corruption and misrule – and as a result of its ability to gather huge crowds during some of its programmes, politicians have found it expedient to fraternise with the church in the hope of getting political support, particularly during elections. The church also functions as an image-laundry mechanism or PR platform for corrupt politicians who seek to be positively perceived by the public. The country's former president, Olusegun Obasanjo, is a friend of Adeboye, the church's General Overseer.[12] As a sitting president, Obasanjo often attended the church's services or sent official representatives. Adeboye also was a frequent guest of the president at the State House in Abuja, where he conducted special prayers and deliverance services – he was the unofficial chaplain to the president. For all his support for the political establishment, and through its relationship with the Obasanjo administration, the RCCG received import tax waivers amounting to more than 20 billion naira in 2006 and 2007. The church imported 300 luxury cars, 100 SUVs (Jeeps), plastic chair moulds, video recording equipment and building materials worth more than 100 billion naira.[13]

Several sitting governors also visit the church's expansive 12,000 acres Redemption Camp. Frequently, to demonstrate its influence, the church displays photographs of politicians on the cover pages of its official newsmagazine, the *Redemption Light*. Top political officers of the state, who may not even be Christian, often visit the church's Redemption Camp. According to a former official of the church, Tai Adetoye, these politicians donate to the church, manifestly as a show of goodwill but latently as an exchange instrument. It is also known that the leader of the church openly told his followers to vote for a particular political party (Erinoso, 1999, p. 47) during the transition to civilian rule in 1999. Political candidates all visit the camp and its leaders in the hope of securing political allegiance. On 17 December 2010, Goodluck Jonathan, the incumbent president of Nigeria, visited the RCCG Camp for a religious event and knelt down before Adeboye for prayers, an act that many commentators saw as a political stratagem to demonstrate divine endorsement amidst the ongoing electoral campaign. This type of political behaviour is also seen as a form of trading with God: paying one's dues to God through the church secures for the person positions of power and privilege in society. In turn, the church admonishes that 'All Christians are to obey the law of the country, obey the government and authority' for 'All authority that exists is established by God' (Romans 13:1b).[14]

One other way the RCCG has pandered to the political class is the studied silence of its leaders in the face of national confusion and distress. During the failed attempt of former president Olusegun Obasanjo to amend the Constitution so he could contest for a third term in office as president, Adeboye never uttered a single word of protest or condemnation. Similarly, during the prolonged absence of the late president Umaru Musa Yar'Adua from the country because of ill health without a proper transfer of power to the vice president – an action that precipitated a constitutional crisis and a near national meltdown – Adeboye never aired his voice among those who called for the rule of law and respect of the Constitution of the Federal Republic. The leadership of the church generally believes that the prolonged social, economic and political crises facing Nigerians are caused by the devil, who does not want Nigeria to achieve its destined position in history as the nation to lead the global community to God. For all existing problems in Nigeria, Adeboye has specific prescriptions for the country, such as: every Nigerian should constantly and continuously be thanking God; all Nigerians should uphold the vows and pledges that they made to God at the beginning of the struggle for political deliverance, and finally, Nigerians should call on God on the day of trouble. One example which Adeboye gives about how God is supposedly going to solve all the problems of Nigerians has to do with food: he claims that God, and not economists and politicians, will resolve the escalating cost of foodstuff and the perennial problem of electricity power shortages: 'God who made the mouth of a fish a bank, can heal our economy[...]We cannot solve our problems by human wisdom; not by legislation, except we go back to God'.[15]

## BIBLICAL ECONOMICS

The RCCG provides a range of varied religious products such as monthly, annual and weekly vigils, and revivals and crusades or deliverance services, which are – in themselves – huge money-spinners in addition to sponsorship and marketing deals from global and local companies. The church is also a trendsetter in the production of religious material culture in the country. The leader's sermons are routinely commodified in several forms such as audio and video tapes, compact discs (CDs) video compact discs (VCDs) and DVDs. Transerve Digital Technologies Limited, a company founded by the church and headed by one of its senior pastors, distributes and markets these items. The same sermons are edited, published, distributed and marketed by Christ the Redeemer's Press, owned by Christ the Redeemer's Ministry (CRM), a sister organisation of RCCG. In addition, the RCCG is into purely economic enterprises designed, according to its International Directory (1999, p. 19), to 'declare the Lordship of Jesus Christ over every sphere of life particularly the marketplace'. It runs two large business schools: the Redeemer's Business Academy (RBA), which is the 'Biblical management training arm' of the church, and the International Bible Institute and Leadership Training School (IBI&LTS), which was established in 1994. Through the IBI&LTS, the RCCG disseminates its ideas about 'biblical economics' meant to produce 'well-rounded, well-equipped, efficient and effective ministers/leaders in the body of Christ and in various areas of human endeavour'.[16] Both schools train elite personnel who exercise influence beyond the pulpit as well as – in the views of the church – become God's instruments to effect spiritual and economic transformation of the society.

In addition to these two main business schools of the church, there are numerous other 'business academies' and forums established by parishes of the RCCG to teach members and other born-again Christians how to conduct and regulate their mundane activities, especially those relating to economic practice. Attendance at these business schools requires the payment of various fees, which are sometimes higher than fees charged in similar schools run by professional associations. These schools teach church members about 'strategies for a successful business'. One of the schools claims to teach its students and church members how to tend, keep and guard their businesses on five grounds: packaging a proposal, being positive about projects by believing and trusting God to deliver, ensuring security of office by sanctifying it, having a good corporate image, and finally, investing in the name of Jesus. (An example given by the church of having a good corporate image is not to wear traditional attires during business hours and dressing better than the unbeliever-businessperson.) As one pastor said:

> A businessman who wants to be successful must not be without prayer and fasting. He should be able to fix a daily appointment with God and keep it and must learn to praise God in everything[...]With these strategies, a businessman will always be victorious in business.[17]

The RCCG is not so much concerned with teaching people what to believe but how to prosper economically. An example: the leader of the church established the Jubilee Development Foundation (JDF) in 2002, the year of the church's jubilee celebration, in order, according to Akin Akinwande – a pastor and project member – to enlighten and mobilise its members for economic empowerment and development. Nominally, the JDF exists 'because the church has an enduring concern and a continuing interest in the overall development and welfare of people and society: spiritual, economic, educational, social and emotional'.[18] To reconcile the interest of the church in people's economic development and its spiritual concern, the church set up the Jubilee Cooperative Society (JCS) exclusively for its members under the JDF. The church describes the objectives of the JDF as follows: the eradication of poverty in the church, the promotion of education, training and human development, the ensuring of availability of capital for viable projects of credible church members, and assisting the wealthy to continue to prosper. To be seen to be interested in the welfare of ordinary church adherents is important for the leadership of the RCCG, which is decidedly pro-establishment and supportive of the status-quo. Consequently, the church advises its followers to participate in the JCS scheme because it is part of the 'law of harvest': 'When you minister to someone's needs, God will also send someone to minister to your needs'. The church leadership sees the JDF as 'a catalyst for the prosperity of all members' of the church. JCS resources are used for equity stocks and other fiscal arrangements that will yield dividends for members who may also be entitled to soft loans for setting up personal businesses.

The RCCG operates four community banks: Haggai Community Bank Limited, (established in 1994[19]), New Life Community Bank Ltd., Ore-Ofe Community Bank Ltd. and Sunrise Community Bank Ltd. In addition, the church owns Haggai Savings and Loans Ltd., a firm initially established as a microfinance group in 1994 and transformed into a mortgage bank in 2008. The managements of these financial institutions believe in the prosperity of the church and work to help RCCG parishes 'attract worshippers'.[20] The vision of Haggai, according to its managers, 'is to carry on the business of banking and provide financial services in a manner that glorifies God, tapping into God's capacity in business and finance, and bringing the awareness of these resources to our clientele'.[21] Haggai Community Bank is arguably the strongest community bank with the largest assets base in Nigeria. Its business slogan is '... so choose now this day, what your money will answer', an adaptation from Joshua 24:15 and Ecclesiastes 10:19.[22] The bank's manifesto states: 'we are on a God-given mission to finance God-given dreams/vision of individuals and corporate institutions. We are resolute in our determination to bring them to manifestation to the glory of God'. One of its missions is directed towards 'Sanitizing the market place by financing churches[...]'.[23] This bank also runs the Haggai Business School (HBS), in Lagos. According to the church, because '[g]lobal business values have failed the Christian in achieving plenty; there is need for a Christian Business School'.[24] This institute offers training in talent trading, 'Foundation to Christian Business', 'Leadership in the Marketplace' and the Business School Ministry (BSM) for churches. The HBS premises its activities with the question 'What would Jesus do if He were to run your business?'[25] The responsibility of the school, according to the management, is to provide valid answers to this question as well as creating what it terms God's kingdom's value – which is a system of values opposite to what is found in this material world – and principles for modern business.

As a matter of policy and discretion the church does not disclose the full list of all its business enterprises but these include hotels and accommodation houses, bakeries, restaurants, bookshops, a university, computer schools, supermarkets, nursery, primary and secondary schools. There are also smaller firms such as Covenant Guaranty Trucks Ltd., established in 1999. It imports and markets popular brands of used trucks and their spare parts. Prior to this, the church established Sharon Consultancy and Research Management (SCRM), a firm that claims to constitute a team of 'multi-disciplinary professionals committed to mobilising capital, technology and management resources for economic progress' of members of the church and the larger society.[26] The church owns and operates two security firms: Dominion Guards, and Prime Guards Nigeria Limited. One of the wealthiest of all RCCG parishes in Lagos established the Dominion Guards in 1994 with the help of an Assistant Commissioner of Police who was also an assistant pastor of the church (Ukah, 2003). The firm now supplies security personnel to companies and firms within and outside Lagos on a commercial basis. The Prime Guards claims to be 'a realistic attempt by a Christian [firm] to check the rapid decay in the security service industry [in Nigeria]' and boasts of using 'a combination of both spiritual and physical measures to achieve the tenets of security'.[27] In other words, rather than agitate for the Nigerian state – whose top officials patronise the church – to perform its statutory duties to its citizens, the RCCG establishes a form of disaster capitalism through which it effectively exploits the current national situation of a failed state that cannot effectively protect its citizens to make profit.

However, the aggressive pro-capital, pro-establishment theologies of the church have not paid off in transforming corporate behaviour in Nigeria, not even of those within the church. The manifest public intention of the church and its financial institutions to introduce Christian values of probity, transparency and accountability has not been met in reality. Many business executives, particularly in the financial sector, who are associated with the church, or are *bona fide* members of the church, have in recent times been indicted for fraud or are under prosecution for fraudulent conduct of public businesses. Two examples will suffice here. Cecilia Ibru was the former managing director/chief executive officer of Oceanic Bank International; she is a strong member of the RCCG and a close confidant of Adeboye and a major financier of RCCG. In October 2010, she was convicted on three counts of fraud for embezzling 160 billion naira of bank depositors' funds. As part of the plea bargain she reached with the Central Bank of Nigeria and the Economic and Financial Crimes Commission (EFCC), the court ordered her to refund or forfeit assets worth 191 billion naira (US$1.2bn). She was also ordered to forfeit shares in 80 listed companies on the Nigeria Stock Exchange and 20 unlisted companies. Rather than serve the four-year prison term her convictions carried, she is now serving a six-month prison term at the time of this writing. Similarly, Festus Akingbola, former CEO of Intercontinental Bank plc and a pastor of RCCG, is now standing trial for bank fraud. He initially fled the country to London but later surrendered to the EFCC officials for prosecution. He, too, was one of the arrowheads of RCCG's economic theology and practices who preached God as an economic and market concept. Yet, he wound up being accused by the Central Bank of Nigeria officials of misappropriating bank investors' funds. The activities and conducts of many church officials who have spearheaded different versions of the church's economic theologies have failed to conform to the church's so-called 'kingdom values'; in fact, they have fallen grossly short of best corporate practices. However, because these theologies are functional as rationalisation of aggressive accumulations, they are still being preached and reinforced by church officials.

## CONCLUSIONS

In Nigeria, Pentecostal churches are indiscriminately drawing upon the social and commercial culture of the society as well from the United States to fashion what is often hard-nosed, exploitative and profit-orientated narratives and practices. The sale of religious services as marketing opportunities to both global and local companies is a significant development in the relationship between Pentecostals, money and the market in Nigeria. The RCCG set the trend in the 1990s and many other churches are following the example. Since companies patronise only churches that can mobilise large crowds and are not antagonistic to market ideology or the creation of wealth, the present trend is creating a *brand wagon* effect. Churches mimic the successful ones in the hope of achieving similar success. Consequently, many churches jostle for state patronage and recognition as well as corporate funding (Ukah, 2002).

The RCCG is arguably the richest Pentecostal church in Nigeria, with more than 10,000 branches in and outside the country. With the magnitude of wealth it has amassed over the years, it is rightly considered to be the most economically fashionable Pentecostal church in Nigeria. As one of its pastors modestly says, 'RCCG is one of the richest churches in Nigeria today'.[28] Ezekiel Adeyemi, senior pastor says in an interview, 'a church that could not raise four hundred naira twenty years ago is now budgeting and spending four hundred million naira for a programme of three days'.

With the ascension of a new leader in the 1980s who assiduously reconstructed its doctrinal and social identity, religious doctrines and rituals became the driving impulse for economic accumulation. The RCCG is market-friendly and compliant; it encourages conspicuous consumption and builds social, political and religious networks upon contract and commerce (cf. Weller, 2000). In RCCG, as in other Pentecostal groups in Nigeria, there exists the uncanny juxtaposition of commercial shrewdness and popular religiosity. Increasingly, Pentecostal churches are boldly demonstrating an unusual ability to mix business and the gospel. The emphasis on giving and money-economy provides avenues for both old and newly-rich politicians and business people to give and identify with a 'noble' cause and thus justify or legitimise their wealth irrespective of how it is made. The appeal of the RCCG and the 'New Pentecostalism' that it represents to the rich is that it provides an answer to the moral problems associated with new, sudden, unexplainable wealth (Meyer, 2004, p. 460).

Some church owners who are in the forefront of this practice try to defend the new economic Pentecostalism by citing Martin Luther King Jr's statement: 'Any religion that claims to be concerned about people without addressing the economic conditions that strangle them is a dry and useless religion' (cited in Ashimolowo, 2003). For Pastor Matthew Ashimolowo, a former pastor of Four Square Gospel Church who later founded his own church, Kingsway Christian Centre (KCC), in London, born-again Christians should maximise the days and opportunities God has given them by creating wealth and living in wealthy places. Such mixture is the outcome of careful, or rather creative, reading and interpretation of social trends, economic vicissitudes, and popular tastes and desires. On the one hand, the teachings and practices described above may be considered a crafty exploitation of public sentiments and piety; on the other hand, it may be seen as a creative inventiveness that transforms religion into a useful tool for coping with contemporary uncertainties in the era of oppressive globalisation for some sections of the world. Although some pastors of the church decry what is happening as 'commercialisation of religion' and call it 'a cankerworm' eating deep into the church (Adekola, 1989, p. 291), it is also plausible to consider 'fee-for-service religion' as a transformation that makes religion relevant in a free market as well as to its social, economic and political context (Ukah, 2003). The popularity of the RCCG shows the general comfort of much of the Nigerian middle class with market relationship beyond the market, a point that is neither peculiar to Nigeria nor to Pentecostalism, as Weller (2000) shows regarding Taiwan. One can relate what is happening in Nigeria to the general appeal and resurgence of an 'occult economy' to cushion the effect of the distortions of globalisation and 'millennial capitalism' (J. Comaroff & Comaroff, 1999, 2000, 2001, 2002).

Underlying such practices of RCCG is the belief, according to Ellis and ter Haar (2004, p. 125) that 'prosperity flows from a good relationship with the invisible world'. Beyond this, however, is the fact that religion is the fastest growing industry in contemporary Nigeria. It is perhaps second only to the exportation of crude oil and the importation of refined petroleum products, or in the current political dispensation, politics. Karl Maier (2000, p. 263) writes that 'religion is a thriving business in Nigeria'; however, to say that does not rule out the equally legitimate assertion that it is also a genuinely deep spiritual engagement for many people. As an industry, it generates huge turnover 'far in excess of some multinationals',[29] a fact that has compelled the Nigerian government to initiate a legal bill in the country's national assembly that – if passed into law – will make it necessary for religious organisations to pay taxes to the state.[30] These churches operate economic enterprises whose primary objective is to make profit. Furthermore, because the churches charge very exorbitant fees for their schools, maternities and hospitals, these facilities cease being charity organisations. However, through its numerous businesses, bookshops, schools, etc., the Pentecostal industry also employs large numbers of persons thrown out into the labour market by the capricious deregulation and liberalisation policy of the government.

Nigeria is considered the most religious country in the world partly because the government is resolutely laissez-faire in religious matters and partly because religious entrepreneurs have found numerous ways to compete effectively with secular products or state services such as politics, economics, popular culture, education. Above all, religion has embraced the market and now aims at economic, social and physical conversion of the society. Even while the churches deny this and many scholars of religion may debate it, a major driving force for the expansion of Nigerian Pentecostal missions into African countries, Europe and North America in recent times is arguably to secure the flow of hard currencies to parent churches in Nigeria. The interpenetration of the sacred and the market, religion and money, Pentecostal revival and revenue, the prophet and profit makes contemporary Nigerian Pentecostalism unique and vibrant. Research in this aspect of popular, economic religiosity in the country is only beginning.

## NOTES

1. I use the phrase 'Nigerian Pentecostalism' deliberately rather than 'Pentecostalism in Nigeria'. The first phrase underscores the unique features of this religion that have made it the fastest growing religion in the country. Significantly, some features of Pentecostal practices in Nigeria are nowhere replicated and even in those African countries where some Nigerian churches have established branches, the host communities identify these features as uniquely Nigerian.

2. CRFU Rules and Regulation, clause 3, p. 3.

3. Pastor E. A. Adeboye, 'Keys to Prosperity', text of sermon delivered at the monthly Holy Ghost Service at the Redemption Camp, Ogun State, Nigeria, 6 July 2001, http://www.rccg.org/Holy_Ghost_Service/Monthly_Holy_Ghosat%20Service/jul2001.htm (accessed on 14 September 2001), pp. 6–7.

4. Adeboye, 'What happens when…?' sermon preached at the Holy Ghost Service, Redemption Camp, 1 February 2002, http://www.rccg.org/Holy_Ghost_Service/Monthly_Holy_Ghost%20Service/feb2002.htm. Accessed on 6 April 2002.

5. Adeboye, 'God of double portion', sermon preached at the HGS, Redemption Camp, 1 March 2002, http://www.rccg.org/Holy_Ghost_Service/Monthly_Holy_Ghost%20Service/mar2002.htm. Accessed on 21 May 2002. Interestingly, this sermon was delivered to mark Adeboye's 60th birthday. (He was born on 2 March 1942.)

6. Adeboye, *Congress News/People* (Lagos), vol. 1, no. 2 (2005), p. 7.

7. 'God of Double Portion'. At the time of delivering the sermon, the exchange rate of the naira to the US dollar was circa $1:N125. When the demand for money was made, many of Adeboye's followers came out of their seats to give their names, addresses and indicate which group they would belong. At each anniversary of the delivery of this sermon, the groups were expanded to five and again to seven in 2004 with some minor modifications! See, http://www.rccg.org/Pastor_E_A_Adeboye/covenant_partnership_group_with_.htm, accessed on 24 October 2004.

8. There is a form posted on the church's website titled 'Partnership Pledge with Daddy G.O.' with which interested people in submitting money or credit card details could do so with the assurance at the bottom of the form 'All donations will be acknowledged and all partnership pledges will be delivered directly to Daddy G.O.', see http://www.rccg.org/Resource_Form/donation-form-rccg-GO.htm. Accessed on 22 October 2004.

9. Adeboye, '*Keys to prosperity*', p. 10.

10. This programme holds every first Friday of the month. According to the church's website (www.rccg.org), the programme has an average attendance of between 200,000 and 300,000 persons. The first weekend of the month is the busiest weekend in any urban city in southern Nigeria when several pentecostal events are held across cities. Part of the reason for hosting these events at this time of the month is that it is the week closest to when wage earners are paid their salaries and these churches expect to collect tithes from members of their congregations as well as the general public before they channel their earnings to other uses.

11. See 'City Express Launches Special Mission Products', *Redemption Light*, vol. 7, no. 8, September 2002, p. 33.

12. *Redemption Light*, vol. 7, no, June 2002, p. 27. See also 'Comments of his Excellency the President of the Federal Republic of Nigeria' in Ojo (2001: 1–2).

13. See Ikenna Emewu, 'Holy Scam: Obasanjo's Church in N20b Import Waiver Deals', *Saturday Sun* (Lagos), 3 November 2007, http://sunnewsonline/webpages/features/newsonthehour/2007/nov/03. Accessed on 3 November 2007.

14. *The RCCG: Our Fundamental Beliefs in the Bible*, (1999) art. 13.

15. Adeboye, 'What Obasanjo must urgently do to succeed', *Redemption Light*, vol. 6, no. 5, June 2001, p. 6.

16. *International Directory of RCCG*, 3rd ed. 2000–2001 (Lagos: The Directory of Missions, 2001), p. 21.

17. Pastor Ogba Omagbemi, 'Strategies for a Successful Business', *Redemption Light*, vol. 4, no.2, March 1999, p. 41.

18. 'Cooperation: The Key to Every One's Welfare', RCCG Welfare Weekend Brochure (Thursday 7–Sunday 10 November 2002), p. 8.

19. The choice of name is based on Haggai 2:7 'And I will shake all the nations and the treasures of all nations shall come in, and I will fill this house with glory, says the Lord Almighty' (*The New American Bible* translation, 1970). It started as Haggai Investment Trust Company in 1994 'upon the mandate of the General Overseer' of RCCG and was upgraded to a full-fledged bank in 1998. 'A group of enablers [...] run [the bank] on behalf of what GOD has purposed to do with the financial empire of this nation'. See, http://haggaibank.com/About%20Us.htm. Accessed on 24 October 2004).

20. The chairman of Sunrise Community Bank is RCCG Pastor S. Biyi Owolabi, the past president of CRFU, see 'Community Bank Teams up with churches for souls', *Redemption Light*, vol. 8, no. 5, June 2003, p. 28.

21. http://haggaibank.com/about.htm. Accessed on 22 January 2011.

22. RCCG 2003 Annual Convention brochure, p. 2. The text of Joshua 24:15 reads 'Choose you this day whom ye will serve... ' while Ecclesiastes 10:19 reads 'A feast is made for laughter, and wine maketh merry; but money answereth all things'.

23. http://haggaibank.com/Mission%20&%20Vision.htm. Accessed on 24 October 2004.

24. *Redemption Light*, vol. 7, no. 10, November 2002, p. 23.

25. *Redemption Light*, vol. 7, no. 2, March 1999, p. 21.

26. *Redemption Light*, vol. 4, no 2, March 1999, p. 45.

27. *Redemption Light*, vol. 6, no. 6, July 2001, p. 35.

28. Pastor Joel Oke, 'Tragedies of the Mission Opportunities', *Catalyst* magazine vol. 1, no. 3 (October 2002), p. 27. RCCG's Directorate of Missions publishes the *Catalyst*.

29. *TheWeek Magazine* (Lagos), July 5, 2004, p. 10.

30. See 'A Due to Caesar', pp. 9–16.

## ACKNOWLEDGMENTS

This chapter was first presented at the Conference on African Christianity in the 21st Century held at the Nordic Africa Institute, Uppsala, in October 2004. I also thank Paul Gifford and David Maxwell for their comments. An in-depth ethnographic study of the national church was conducted from 2000 until early 2004. Fieldwork was carried out in Nigeria between April and July 2001 and again between July and November 2003 and data were updated in 2005 and 2010. The research was part of a larger study carried out under a collaborative research project on 'Local Action in the Context of Global Influences in Africa' based at the University of Bayreuth, Germany. I acknowledge the support of Professor Dr. Ulrich Berner and that of *Sonderforschungsbereich/Forschungskolleg 560*. I thank the editors of REA and the anonymous reviewers for their comments; the usual caveat holds.

# REFERENCES


Abiona, J. H. (2000). Interview. *Redemption Light*, *5*(10), p. 6.

Adeboye, E. A. (1989). *Turning your austerity to prosperity*. Lagos: CRM Press.

Adeboye, E. A. (1999). *The holy spirit in the life of Peter*, Part 1, Lagos: CRM Press.

Adeboye, P. (2001). No contest between classical and model parishes. *Lifeway*, *1*(3), 23.

Adekola, M. A. (1989). *The Redeemed Christian Church of God: A study of an indigenous Pentecostal Church in Nigeria*. Ph.D. thesis, Department of Religious Studies, Obafemi Awolowo University, Ile-Ife, Nigeria.

Adekunle, J. O. (Ed.) (2009). *Religion in politics: Secularism and national integration in modern Nigeria*. Trenton, NJ: Africa World Press.

Akinremi, A. (2002). Some old landmarks. *Redemption Light*, *7*(7), 23.

Amoda, J. M. (1997). *Pentecostalism in chains: The merchandising of the gospel of the Lord Jesus Christ*. New York, NY: Civiletis International.

Ashimolowo, M. (2003). *The 10 Ms of money*. London: Matthew Ashimolowo Media Ministries.

Ayegboyin, D., & Ukah, A. (2002). Taxonomy of churches in Nigeria: A historical perspective. *Orita: Ibadan Journal of Religious Studies*, *34*(1–2), 68–86.

Bankole, O. (1999). *Trees clap their hands: A photobook on the Redeemed Christian Church of God*. Lagos: El-Shalom Publishers.

Comaroff, J., & Comaroff, J. L. (1999). Occult economies and the violence of abstraction: Notes from the South African postcolony. *American Ethnologist*, *26*(2), 279–303.

Comaroff, J., & Comaroff, J. L. (2000). Millennial capitalism: First thoughts on a second coming. *Public Culture*, *12*(2), 291–343.

Comaroff, J., & Comaroff, J. L. (Eds.). (2001). *Millennial capitalism and the culture of neo-liberalism*. Durham, NC: Duke University Press.

Comaroff, J., & Comaroff, J. L. (2002). Privatizing the millennium: New Protestant ethics and spirits of capitalism in Africa, and elsewhere. *Journal for the Study of Religion*, *15*(2), 15–37.

Ellis, S., & ter Haar, G. (2004). *Worlds of power: Religious thought and political practice in Africa*. London: Hurst & Company.

Erinoso, K. J. (1999). The life and ministry of pastor Adeboye, the general overseer of the Redeemed Christian Church of God. B.A Long Essay, Dept. of Religions, Lagos State University, Nigeria.

Hackett, R. I. J. (1995). The prosperity gospel in West Africa. In: R. Roberts (Ed.), *Religion and the transformation of capitalism* (pp. 199–214). London: Routledge.

*International Directory of the RCCG*. (1999). Lagos: The Directorate of Missions.

Kanter, R. M. (1995). *World class: Thriving locally in the global economy*. New York, NY: Simon and Schuster.

Keister, L. A. (2003). Religion and wealth: The role of religious affiliation and participation in early adult asset accumulation. *Social Force*, *82*(1), 175–207.

Lee, R. R. (1992). Religious practice as social exchange. *Sociological Analysis*, *53*(1), 1–35.

Maier, K. (2000). *This house has fallen: Nigeria in crisis*. London: Penguin Books.

Meyer, B. (2004). Christianity in Africa: From African independent to Pentecostal-charismatic churches. *Annual Review of Anthropology*, *33*, 447–474.

Ojo, M. A. (1986). *The growth of campus Christianity and charismatic movements in Western Nigeria*. Ph.D. dissertation, University of London, London.

Ojo, M. A. (1992). Deeper Life Bible Church of Nigeria. In: P. Gifford (Ed.), *New dimensions in African Christianity* (pp. 135–153). Ibadan: Sefer Publications.

Ojo, T. (2001). *Let somebody shout Hallelujah! The life and ministry of pastor Enoch Adejare Adeboye*. Lagos: Honeycombs Cards and Prints.

Peel, J. D. Y. (1968). *Aladura: A religious movement among the Yoruba*. Oxford: Oxford University Press.

Peel, J. D. Y. (2000). *Religious encounter and the making of the Yoruba*. Bloomington, IN: Indiana University Press.

Stark, R., & Bainbridge, W. S. (1985). *The future of religion: Secularization, revival, and cult formation*. Berkeley, CA: University of California Press.

Turner, H. (1979). *Religious innovations in Africa: collected essays o new religious movements*. Boston, MA: G.K. Hall & Co.

Ukah, A. (2002). Reklame für Gott: Religiöse Werbung in Nigeria. In: T. Wendl (Ed.), *Afrikanishe Reklamekunst* (pp. 148–153). Wuppertal: Peter Hammer Verlag GmbH.

Ukah, A. (2003). *The Redeemed Christian Church of God (RCCG), Nigeria. local identities and global processes in African Pentecostalism*. Ph.D. dissertation, University of Bayreuth/ Germany. Retrieved from http://opus.ub.uni-bayreuth.de/volltexte/2004/73/pdf/ Ukah.pdf

Ukah, A. (2005). 'Those who trade with god never lose': The Economics of Pentecostal activism in Nigeria. In: T. Falola (Ed.), *Christianity and social change in Africa: Essays in honor of John Peel* (pp. 251–274). Carolina: Carolina Academic Press.

Ukah, A. (2008). *A new paradigm of Pentecostal power: A study of the Redeemed Christian Church of God in Nigeria*. Trenton, NJ: Africa World Press.

Weller, R. P. (2000). Living at the edge: Religion, capitalism, and the end of the nation-state in Taiwan. *Public Culture*, *12*(2), 477–498.

# MULTI-LEVEL MARKETING: AT THE CROSSROADS OF ECONOMY AND RELIGION

Nathalie Luca

## ABSTRACT

*This chapter focuses on the changing relationship between multi-level marketing (MLM) and religion. MLM originated in the 1950s in the United States out of a desire to make capitalism more humane. It was initially based on Protestant networks linked to prosperity theology, which among other things enabled it to grow internationally. Yet, comparing how MLM adapted to conditions in three different countries (South Korea, Haiti, and France) shows that its ability to break away from this controversial theology was crucial to its international development. It was then able to approach other religious movements, and even to secularize its values.*

## INTRODUCTION

For some time, at least in France, certain economists who were until recently little sensitized to religious issues have been appealing to sociologists of religion, puzzled by a new fact not clearly identified: the

**The Economics of Religion: Anthropological Approaches**
**Research in Economic Anthropology, Volume 31, 217–239**

**ISSN: 0190-1281/doi:10.1108/S0190-1281(2011)0000031012**

close ties between, on the one hand, certain corporate cultures and, on the other hand, values, philosophy, ethics, and even emotional practices borrowed from religion. Admittedly, there are well-known business trends and banking systems whose links with Islam or with Protestantism in particular are clearly asserted. Furthermore, we all know that no religious institution can do without any relationship with the economic world. On the other hand, what is new is the idea that companies too can feel the need to reconnect to religion, even though this link had been broken. Indeed, some companies incorporate elements from one or several religious cultures, depending on the kind of identity they seek to assert and on the country in which they are implemented. The peculiarity of this link questions afresh the secularization of institutions. Just as this process seemed to lead religious institutions to completely break away from the business world and its independent values and ends, some companies have decided, in a renewed and innovative way, to approach *such and such* religious or spiritual movements. This rapprochement is more or less conspicuous. It is characteristic of multi-level marketing (MLM). What is this all about?

MLM, also known as relationship marketing or network marketing, is a direct selling method (generally involving in-home selling situations) that comes from the United States. It is nowadays quite popular throughout the world, in the so-called North (Northern Asia, North America, and Europe) as well as in the so-called South (sub-Saharan Africa, Latin America, and Southeastern Asia). Since the fall of the Berlin Wall, it has also been experiencing a significant growth in Russia and even in China and in Vietnam. I have endeavored to observe it mainly in Metropolitan France, in the French Antilles, in French Guiana, in Haiti, and in South Korea.

MLM can be traced back to manufacturers of a quite varied range of goods (household cleaning products, high-tech products, telecom services, clothes, jewelry, cosmetics, housing, well-being – very much in vogue nowadays, and so forth) designed to appeal to a wide set of potential customers from various social backgrounds. To sell their products, these manufacturers opt for networks of independent contractors, which are formed as follows: a distributor A grows his/her own business by fostering customer loyalty and by recruiting new salespeople. The latter are the distributor's "downlines," also known as his/her "direct downline sponsored salespeople."[1] Each downline in turn sponsors other distributors. This repeated pattern forms the length of each network chain (Fig. 1). When introducing him/herself, a distributor says that he/she belongs to A's network and to the Nth generation of chain A1.

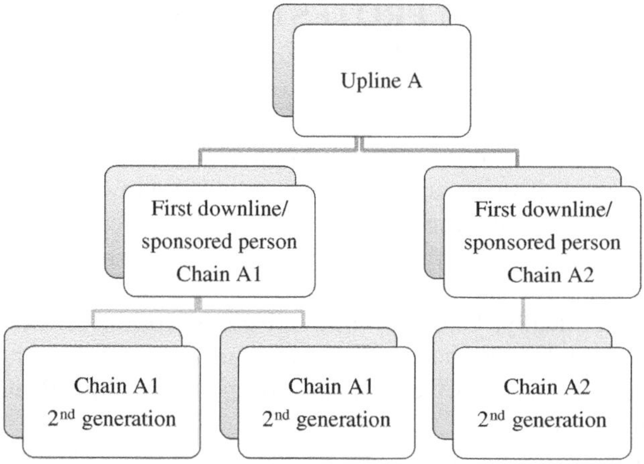


*Fig. 1.* Multi-Level Marketing – Basic Network Structure.

A company usually has several "uplines." The more the downlines there are corresponding to each upline, the more the chains, and the more these networks can expect to grow, locally, nationally, and internationally. A distributor earns income from his/her own retail sales and from his/her downlines' retail sales, either directly (when these recruits are the distributor's downlines) or indirectly (in the case of later generations). The perceived percentage out of which the distributor is paid decreases as the chain length increases.

I will focus here in particular on three points, which explain how I came to be interested in this topic, as an anthropologist specializing in religious issues and, more specifically, in controversial groups, commonly known in France as "sects." The first point deals with the kinds of links that possibly exist between MLM companies and religion, based on the understanding that these links can evolve; they can equally subside, disappear, or become stronger, depending on the context in which they develop. The second point deals with the transnational development of these companies, which rests on cross-border networks. I will limit myself here to showing that religion is not unrelated to network expansion. Ultimately, the final line of thought refers to the criticism regularly aimed at MLM, namely it's being akin to sects, which is very often related to the two other points previously mentioned.

## FROM THE PROTESTANT ETHIC TO COMPASSIONATE CAPITALISM

The occasional rejection of relationship marketing is not unrelated to its ambiguous connection to religion. This link can seem incompatible with the logical economic involvement of this activity. However, it is not as incongruous as it first seems. Max Weber associates modern capitalist economy, as developed in the West, with the protestant reformation that occurred in the 16th century (1964, p. 50). According to him, reformers' (and, more specifically, Calvin's) innovative conception of the relationship between Man and God had unforeseen consequences on the economic sphere. Thus, the "spirit of capitalism" originated in the Protestant ethic (other among things).

This "spirit" is reflected in some well-known adages: "Time is money", "Credit is money," "The good paymaster is lord of another man's purse," "Money is of the prolific, generating nature" [that] Weber comes across particularly in Benjamin Franklin's writings. Thereby, he eventually pinpoints the work ethic peculiar to capitalism: honesty, punctuality, diligence, and frugality far removed from any hedonistic conception of life. Man's salvation, always uncertain, requires his labor, success being a sign of his election. According to Weber, this search for signs partly accounts for dedication to work, redefined as calling (*Beruf*). Behind the Protestant ethic, there is indeed Calvin's distressing doctrine of predestination, according to which God preordained Man's destiny once and for all. Man's deeds cannot revoke God's final and infallible decision; man is either an elect or a reprobate, depending on God's choice. Only God, in His transcendence, knows the rationale for this choice.

But who could passively accept predestination? Something must somehow distinguish the elect from the reprobate. There must be some reassuring signs of one's election. Insofar as reformers considered monastic life worthless and as professional labor had become central to Christian life, professional skills, the ability to distinguish oneself as a dedicated worker, and finally financial success in this earthly existence became hints that one was indeed an elect. Therefore, capitalism would be the unforeseen result of an attitude consisting in believing in one's election. This would involve developing one's self-esteem, which only dedication to work and its positive effects seemed able to reinforce. This attitude created a new kind of entrepreneurs, very determined and dauntless. They developed self-confidence because they believed and claimed to be part of the elect. Self-confidence enabled them to overcome all the difficulties likely to prevent them from standing out.

However, capitalist economy does not elude the secularization process. Soon, the fear of both predestination and its consequences on labor would slacken the spirit of capitalism. Soon, the link with the Protestant ethic would be broken. Soon, economy would suddenly seem out of control. This contributed to the creation of an extremely precarious world, ruthless and exposed to financial crises (Stiglitz, 2002). As Bourdieu states, it is only very gradually "that its specific *nomos* was asserted, as expressed in the tautology 'business is business'; that economic transactions ceased to be modeled on domestic exchanges and therefore to depend on family or social obligations [...]; and that personal profit, thus financial interest, emerged as the dominant principle" (2000, p. 17). As burdensome sources of individual and collective misfortunes, crises are an additional cause for concern. The will to instill values and to enforce ethical behaviors on a deregulated business world permeates society, which tries to curb this tendency, in a desperate attempt to center capitalist conscience back on man.

There are, of course, several forms of resistance to this capitalism deemed inhumane. We focus here on the form of resistance on which MLM is based. It is characterized by the fact that it does not question the economic system, but endeavors to instill in it the values it gradually relinquished (Biggart, 1989). Therefore, it is no coincidence that this particular form of resistance comes from the United States, where Protestantism has never ceased to be a social cement. Nor is it a coincidence that this attempt to reintroduce certain values appealed, at least for some time, to some updated Protestant precepts (Bromley, 1995). The latter were considered able to contribute to a revised capitalism some would then call "compassionate capitalism."

Compassionate capitalism was championed by Rich DeVos, the cofounder of a leading relationship marketing company (among the most controversial ones). The notion is defined in his book titled precisely *Compassionate Capitalism: People Helping People Help Themselves* (1993). He first defines capitalism (which he equates with material welfare) as follows:

$$\text{Material Welfare} = \text{Natural Resources} + \text{Human Energy} \times \text{Tools}$$

According to him, capitalism races out of control because its tools only aim at profitability, with no respect for nature or human beings. He finds it unacceptable and believes that this trend can be reversed. Therefore, natural resources, human energy, and the tools of capitalism have to be infused with compassion. This will restore nature and the individual to the center of capitalism. He then suggests tools able to respect both. Thus, he explains that "[c]ompassionate capitalists still want to make a profit, but they are determined that real profits come when the good of people and the planet comes first. 'Profit' made at the expense of human or planetary suffering is not profit at all" (p. 10). The following equation illustrates his statement:

$$\text{Material Welfare} = (\text{Natural Resources} + \text{Human Energy} + \text{Tools}) \times \text{Compassion}$$

To infuse this compassion, DeVos resorts to a line of thought peculiar to prosperity theology, which is generally associated with what is called neo-Pentecostalism. Thus, the beginnings of MLM cannot be understood without discussing Pentecostalism. The latter was crucial in the sense that it enabled MLM to reach many Christian countries of the so-called South (sub-Saharan Africa, Latin America), but not exclusively (Corten, 1995; Corten & Mary, 2000; Corten, Dozon, & Oro, 2003; Fourchard, Mary, & Otayek, 2005; Luca, 2008).

Protestants saw financial success as a sign of election, a sign that could alleviate the anguish caused by the doctrine of predestination. On the other hand, Pentecostals found another way, apparently an even more definite one, to have proof of this and therefore to be reassured – the experience of God. Thus, believers can personally and emotionally experience the presence of God: as a result of the Pentecost experience, the faithful directly feel the presence of the Holy Spirit and receives baptism with him (also known as "baptism of fire"). Furthermore, various spiritual gifts are bestowed on them (such as, for instance, the gift of healing or the gifts of speech), which are concrete manifestations of the Holy Spirit. Thus, the faithful can ensure that God dwells in them. This explains why Pentecostals say, "I know God exists" (meaning "I sensed God's presence") instead of "I believe in God."

Prosperity theology does not directly pertain to Pentecostalism. Many churches even object to what they view as a manifestation of Satan. This is why prosperity theology is associated with the so-called neo-Pentecostal movement. However, it is directly linked to this notion of experience of God's almighty power. While the elect can directly sense it (through speaking in tongues or through healing), it can also be observed through the blessings God grants to His children. God is not an unworthy Father and would not let His loved ones live in misery. Let us highlight here a change compared with the Protestant ethic: at the core of this matter of experience and proof no longer lies work, but the very fact of being rich instead of being healed or experiencing the Holy Spirit's presence. Somehow, prosperity theology considers wealth to be one of God's blessings. This is why, when this belief is carried to extremes, some churches that have fallen into disrepute hold that those who do not become rich cannot view themselves as part of the elect. Thus, in contrast to puritan Protestants' austerity, it is recommended that one show off one's wealth.

It becomes easy to understand that prosperity theology has had economic effects as unforeseen as those of the doctrine of predestination. It is actually extremely distressing for those who do not succeed in becoming rich. Therefore, they need to find something that helps them get by, something that elevates their lives in order to ensure that God is still there. But, most of the time, these churches reach out to the most deprived social classes, and even to the most deprived within these particular social classes. The latter no longer expect anything from the traditional economic system, whose inhumanity they experience on a daily basis and which they view as a manifestation of Satan. Their salvations cannot come from there. This is obvious to them. They are left out of the system. Therefore, they need something else; something that will enable them to experience God's presence. They look for the hand of God, which will elevate them. And MLM is the hand of God.

At least, this is how DeVos approaches the religious sphere. Thereby – and this is important – he also underlines the value of work; he never claims that money is easy to earn. His writings do not imply that money grows on trees. Nevertheless, his compassionate capitalism is based on prosperity theology. Somehow, MLM is seen by the believers as the hand with which God reaches out to His creatures and blesses them – and this goes far beyond his own company.

I do not intend here to summarize *Compassionate Capitalism*, but only to outline some of its essential ideas. First of all, DeVos acknowledges that capitalism has sometimes failed and that these failures should be remedied. Thus, what is wrong is not so much capitalism itself as what it became, or to be more accurate, what it has become since it dismissed its ethics and its Christian values. He explains:

> What we think about people matters a great deal. If we think of them as children of God, possessing a divine spark and having God-given worth, it follows that we ought to treat all people with respect and dignity. But if we think of people in a strictly material sense, devoid of any spirituality and gaining worth only through the State, then what happens? We need only to look at communist history to answer that question. (pp. 5–6)

Capitalism should not follow this lead! Hence a watchword: love. That is, God's love for Man, in whom He placed His own dreams. Man's aims consist in achieving these dreams, and not to forget or to gloss over them.

> God is waiting patiently for you to come home, to receive His gifts, and to take your place at your Creator's beautiful table. We are created to dream. Our dreams, too, are created in the image of God's dreams. Imagine what it will mean for you to begin to have the same kinds of dreams that your Creator dreams for you and for the planet[...]Your dreams determine who you are and what you care about. The size of them determines the size of your soul. (p. 22)

And he continues: "We are loved by God and empowered by our Creator to see our dreams come true" (p. 23).

We do not only have to achieve these dreams (provided that, he specifies, they be not totally unrealistic and obsessive), but also have to take into account that the achievement of others' dreams (also instilled by God) matters as much as our own. We will then know how to effectively love and help one another. Here compassionate capitalism meets prosperity theology. Together, DeVos claims, we can change and achieve all the dreams God places in us. MLM is, therefore, just a way of attaining love and mutual aid, as well as making our dreams come true (Bromley, 1998). Considering this link, it is not surprising that MLM networks first developed among Protestants and above all among neo-Pentecostals. MLM surfed on the Pentecostal wave, wherever it was (Zúñiga, 2005).

## THE ROLE OF PENTACOSTALISM IN THE RISE OF – AND LATER ON THE CHALLENGE TO – MLM IN SOUTH KOREA

Western tourists who visit South Korea are often surprised by the Christian crosses that are to be found in every street of Seoul and in every town of Korea. More than 30% of South Koreans have supposedly become Christians between 1950 and 2000. The fact that Christianity – in particular the different forms of Protestantism – has become so popular in this country is surprising. It is surprising, especially, as the two superpowers surrounding it, China and Japan, have remained rather indifferent to this religion. The success of Christianity was initially linked to the need to rebuild a national identity widely challenged by forty years of Japanese colonialism, immediately followed by a war that divided the country. It was then necessary to make sense of this rift. South Korean churches, like the

American ones, did so by creating a founding myth. According to this myth, South Korea was the chosen land, where the ultimate battle against Satan – represented by communism and North Korea – was taking place. God's victory would be achieved through the fall of North Korean leaders and through the subsequent reunification of the two Koreas into one capitalist country. There was this national need to prove that South Korea was indeed the chosen land. This evidence would ease the pain endured by the families divided both by a war to which they did not subscribe as and by international political and economic interests that were far beyond them. Here again, hard work provided the sought-after evidence. To economically surpass North Korea, to become recognized as an Asian Tiger, to overcome poverty: all this proved that God was at work in this part of Korea. In this context, Protestantism offered South Koreans a way of making sense of the situation and being reassured, which helped them come together around new national borders (Luca, 2000). South Korea emerged as a US-inspired Christian state (Chung, 2001). The founding myth of the United States and their fight against communism permeated the Republican values and practices that developed in those days in South Korea. Ultimately, the churches were able to convince South Koreans to accept the sacrifices entailed by the recovery process. Undoubtedly, this contributed to its spectacular rise: its economy grew by more than 8% per year from 1960 to 1980 (Lanzarroti, 1992).

Thus, Protestant churches partook in the modernization of South Korea. But what was most remarkable was the zeal of one particular Pentecostal church, one of the largest in the world. The Yoido Full Gospel Church gained international recognition and a strong reputation, especially throughout Christianized countries of Latin America and sub-Saharan Africa. Indeed, it motivated Koreans to overcome poverty and enthusiastically supported the government's capitalist and anticommunist values. It also championed pro-Americanism. According to this church, the promise of success applied as much to the country as to the individual. Those who eagerly went to church were supposed to become rich quickly. There was prosperity theology, which more or less pervaded South Korean Protestant churches, most fervently preached. This church turned out to be a major support to the South Korean State and to its political and economic dynamics, enabling it to strategically take up residence in the political and financial district of Seoul (Luca, 2004a). It was in this church that MLM was most successful, although MLM companies are ubiquitous in Christian networks.

Since women had little access to the professional world, they became heavily involved in MLM, which they discovered through their Christian networks and which was primarily aimed at them. In addition, the methods of proselytizing used by Pentecostal churches were very similar to the business methods suggested to these women: handing out fliers and magazines, talking about it on every occasion and everywhere, on subways, going from door to door, and being close to one's neighbors. Thus, people could engage simultaneously in proselytizing and MLM, holding the Bible in one hand and the products in the other. This was not an issue for Koreans, let alone for the State. Koreans are all aware of this kind of company. Each of them bought some products and associated at some point with a Protestant distributor. MLM networks were widely based on preexisting Christian networks. They could spread quickly within the Full Gospel Church owing to the variety of weekly activities where the believers met and, above all, owing to "home cells": female members gathered at a member's home in a very friendly and relaxed atmosphere. Owing to these home cells, network meetings (as well as sales) could easily be carried out. Thus, the organization of the Full Gospel Church greatly contributed to the growth of MLM. The housewives were pleased to be involved in a profitable activity compatible with their faith in God's blessings. Building these networks sometimes had negative consequences for a woman's marriage, however – as soon as she started to enjoy it too much or to earn too much money. Such a situation was sometimes enough to hurt her husband and therefore lead to divorce. However, in most cases, the amount earned remained modest enough to financially relieve the husbands without hurting their feelings.

Yet, a particular event would deeply change the situation: the Asian financial crisis of 1997 (Stiglitz, 2002, p. 127). This had an enormous impact on South Korea; everything in which many had believed for nearly 50 years suddenly fell apart. It fueled the challenge to the American capitalist model and questioned the rightfulness of the US involvement in Korean domestic affairs, whether military or economic (Badie, 1999, p. 135). Anti-American demonstrations became quite widespread – and even more so when South Korea got involved in the Iraq War, to which South Koreans were generally opposed. This was harmful to the image of Christianity insofar as it was then viewed as a burdensome legacy of US involvement.

Furthermore, this crisis posed a challenge to the North/South duality postulate. Insofar as the proof of God's election of the South was entirely based on financial success, this crisis suddenly shattered the ability of prosperity theology to make sense of the situation. Korea suddenly lost the beliefs that had contributed to its self-confidence and to its people's motivation to strive for its economic success. Due to the crisis, South Korea could no longer claim to be the chosen land. Consequently, proselytizing has become so discreet that Protestants, until recently so ubiquitous, deserted the streets.

This is not unrelated to what would occur to the first MLM companies so closely linked to Pentecostalism and to prosperity theology. They fell apart along with the Christian networks on which their businesses were based. Even worse, like prosperity theology, they were rejected. From then on, MLM was regarded as a sect insofar as it was accused of promising easy money. This is all the more remarkable as South Korea, unlike France, is quite reluctant to use this term. But it quite accurately expressed one's disappointment. Unable to start over elsewhere, uplines were ruined; they were shut out. This chapter of history was closed.

Trapped companies did everything they could to break free from the Christian hold. They radically changed their approach to the network, and they have been trying since then to start over. In fact, I attended the most ostensibly nonreligious meetings in South Korea. No more thanking God, no more crying nor displaying strong emotions that could remind one of the Pentecostal services. Self-control and professionalism are now crucial to proving that MLM companies serve economy rather than religion.

In 2009, I had the opportunity to attend a congress. There was a striking contrast between this congress and what used to happen before the crisis: no speaker used the term "dream," nor did anyone give an extraordinary account of his/her success. One could feel how difficult it was to adapt to the new speech style. The speakers no longer had anything to talk about! Due to the detachment from Pentecostalism, nothing helped hold the audience's attention. It was almost boring. Monotonous speeches were lulling the audience into sleep. This I had never experienced elsewhere. We should not hastily generalize this to all MLM companies. Yet, they may have forgotten, as they professionalized, that distributors were not regular employees and needed, therefore, to be motivated in order to remain loyal. Companies faced a new problem: What should they rely on? Who should they target? What should they rebuild their networks on? The solution is still pending. To date, one cannot be sure that they will be able to recover, even though the crisis is over now and business is on again. A distributor told me that, in the course of the three years she had been involved in network marketing, she sponsored only one distributor. According to the accounts I gathered, this is why women end up quitting this activity; it has become too difficult.

However, it is interesting to point out that other MLM companies, until then much less well known in Korea and therefore less criticized, are taking over quite successfully. They rely on new networks, more in tune with the current spiritual sensibilities of Koreans, in relation to New Age and Buddhism. But Koreans are much less aware of them. It takes more time to build these new networks. It seems that people still have trouble trusting this kind of system.

I cannot detail here the South Korean situation, but it helps me establish a general framework in order to understand how MLM evolves. The facts that (1) Korean distributors now suffer from being identified as a sect; whereas they had enjoyed a very good reputation for a long time, (2) that some of them were ruined overnight, not because of the economic crisis but because of the impact the crisis had on how people perceived both prosperity theology and the religious networks on which their businesses were based, and finally that (3) the companies that are now recovering or being implemented not only dismiss the Protestant network within which distributors were initially recruited, but also look for alternative and less controversial networks show how important it is to contextualize the situation. Indeed, it enables us not only to understand the periods during which MLM developed and then weakened, but also to realize how flexible these companies are. Their links with religion depend on the situation, which means that these links cannot be broken once and for all. Furthermore, people are not necessarily shocked by them, nor do they mind them. They are not necessarily subjected to criticism. But when they start being criticized, the situation of MLM companies becomes more precarious for a certain time, a time during which they have to start over again, with new networks to rely on. They have to be able to adapt, by destroying, by reducing, or by altering their links with religion. We will see that this is currently occurring in Europe, and especially in France. Yet it is not always possible. The exceptional case of Haiti, where I went twice prior to the earthquake of January 2010, also helps understand the link between MLM and Pentecostal networks.

## MLM IMPORTED TO HAITI: A STORY OF FAILURE

In South Korea like in the United States, American MLM companies emerged, at least initially, as the manifestation of the hand of God, with which He provided wealth to the faithful. From the start, the situation of relationship marketing was more difficult in Haiti, precisely because it did not succeed in partnering up with the local Pentecostal movements. Thus, it tempted the faithful away and ended up taking the place of religion, professing highly controversial prosperity doctrines. Consequently, after a spectacular rise (still difficult to quantify), MLM encountered some serious difficulties. During my survey in Port-au-Prince in 2008, hardly more than fifty people attended the meetings. This still gives an idea of how it was when the network was blooming.

I tried to reconstruct the various evolution stages of relationship marketing in Port-au-Prince by studying in particular the religious and economic conditions in Haiti. Several points immediately appeared. None of the Protestant churches I visited, none of the ministers I interviewed, and none of the faithful I met identified with prosperity theology. It is difficult to say whether this is a sign of the French influence on this part of the island, but it seems that churches devalue money in their discourses. On the contrary, Protestants Haitians see the poverty and the suffering endured by their country as the very sign of God's election. Whereas (like the United States) South Korea is based on a free-market economy, capitalism, and prosperity theology, the Protestant and Pentecostal churches in Haiti, on the other hand, disparage "material blessings." None of the numerous parishes in Haiti seem to belong to neo-Pentecostalism (Corten, 2001; Hurbon, 2004). Those I observed explain that ecological, social, and political misfortunes are God's blessings, reminding that Jesus was crushed before being sanctified:

> There is no fulfillment without wrench, [...] After humiliation comes sanctification, [...] Let's cheer this harsh world, because it enables us to open up our hearts and listen to His words![2]

These parishes also see misfortune as a sign of the end of time and therefore encourage believers to await – more or less resignedly – the advent of the new millennium. "I would rather suffer more than lose my soul," as a prayer goes. This mindset is also to be found in the limits of economic growth: entrepreneurs are not ready to take too many risks. One should not be overzealous. One should not draw too much attention to oneself. One should not try to have more than necessary, this could only bring bad luck. Now, this inertia is precisely what the distributors in Haiti apparently want to oppose. An upline relied on a book by Haitian author Lionel Benjamin (*Haïti 2004: La Révolution mentale, révolution finale*) which was quite meaningful in this respect. It begins as follows: "Think and speak nicely of Haiti. Haiti shall be a paradise." On the back cover, the following prediction: "The time of mental revolution, for Haiti, has come." Finally, there is also the comment:

Lionel Benjamin puts forth a brilliant solution, peaceful and humane, in order to halt the decline of the first black republic in the world:

> Change yourself
> To change Haiti
> To change the world.

The content of this book, as well as the Sunday meetings of distributors' networks, are quite a watershed. They are diametrically opposed to the discourses of Pentecostal ministers. The latter encourage people to remain poor and resigned, as well as to turn to God, from whom they should expect everything. A religion of prosperity is actually being created here, a religion totally linked to US positivism and based in particular on Christian values. Before discussing products and network building, people pray and fervently thank God: "Make us successful, Lord. Here, in Haiti, there is a lot of misfortune, but we want to overcome it, we want to achieve this dream of a better country."

An upper class Haitian distributor, who built a network based on a spirit of mutual assistance, told me:

> I took interest in this form of marketing because it's the only way to show people that they can change their levels of conscience and change their lives. Their social conditions aren't determined once and for all at birth. Some people who start with nothing can actually earn money. People aren't aware of the power of the mind. It's not only about education. It's about what you have in there and what you believe in.

MLM started in the 1980s and managed to gather more than a thousand distributors whose daily lives radically changed. A florist told me:

> Thanks to this new job, young people learned to speak, to express themselves, to dress. Society doesn't teach them that. It made them subscribe to certain values, without which this system does not work. Many of them, it's true, didn't make much money, but they would fight for something since they don't have anything! They would wake up in the morning with a glimmer of hope nothing else had given them. That's no small thing!

This glimmer of hope died out due to internal splits (between an upline and his/her network) and to external reasons, the main one being a sudden reform and its immediate effect on customs duties. Distributors used to import goods from the United States. With the reform, customs held up their orders. The expiration date of certain goods expired; refunds had to be issued to the customers who did not receive their orders. Distributors ran into debt since they had to pay for the products that could not be delivered. This undermined the trust needed for MLM to work. Although later on the situation would be regulated, the networks had fallen apart and the customs duties had become too high for the business to remain profitable. In short, with this reform, MLM lost its momentum.

Yet the accounts show that some people are still willing to get involved in MLM, just because they miss the "magic" of the meetings so much. There is still a will and there is still hope. Yet, these networks are widely criticized within Protestant circles, including sometimes directly during religious service. A pastor explained to me:

> Some see these networks as a manifestation of Satan trying to seduce you, to lure you into sin, into a system that doesn't care about you. This is the evil of the Beast. It's all illusion, naivety, and deceitfulness. Many people were very optimistic at first, but as time went by they became disappointed and hostile to it. They came back to us.

For a short amount of time at least, Pentecostal pastors sensed that relationship marketing involved a serious risk in terms of competition. It is worth pointing out that not only were pastors approached, but they were also advised to "find new followers" ... quite a misleading turn of phrase! Another Pentecostal pastor told me that some of his colleagues chose to join MLM and were sometimes followed by their entire communities. He had also been tempted, but stood fast. Certain pastors even banned distributors from their churches. One of the ministers I interviewed concluded: "We were born in poverty, we grew up in poverty, and we shall die in poverty." An upline replied to this, saying: "MLM's message is that poverty isn't a condition. It isn't a disease."

Relationship marketing experienced a short-lived boom, but was mainly considered a sectarian activity, due to the importance granted to accumulation of wealth. Customs obstacles implemented by the State curbed this boom. The earthquake of January 2010 stopped it.

## THE PROFESSIONALIZATION STAGES OF MLM IN FRANCE: FROM BEING ROOTED IN RELIGION TO BEING ROOTED IN SPORTS

The growth of MLM in Metropolitan France and in the French overseas departments was similar to what had occurred in the United States, in South Korea, or in Haiti; at least initially, the companies tried to surf the wave of Pentecostal networks. It worked out in Guadeloupe, in Martinique, or in French Guiana, where there are many Pentecostal and Evangelical followers. Networks of distributors quickly found success there. On the other hand, they made a bad start in metropolitan France, where people do not go much to Pentecostal and neo-Pentecostal churches, which are contested, criticized, and disliked.

Yet, in the 1980s, in France, as in the United States, in Haiti, and in South Korea, relationship marketing Sunday meetings could start with a prayer. MLM did not necessarily encourage conversions in neo-Pentecostal churches, but it made distributors aware of prosperity theology. It should be noted that the concern over the link between prosperity theology and relationship marketing called forth (and continues to call forth) the same kind of aversion as in Haiti. This is quite obvious in the criticism it attracted. They are similar to those leveled by Haitian Pentecostal pastors. The latter were mainly afraid that the followers would desert their churches in order to join these devilish networks. The use of a religious discourse to deter candidates from swelling the ranks of distributors shows that MLM networks are based, at least in part, on a link with Evangelical and Pentecostal networks in France as in Haiti. The first ones recruit where the latter are most successful in proselytizing. Either they are powerful allies and strengthen one another, or they compete and weaken one another. Examples of anti-MLM network messages taken from two different French evangelical web sites show how distressing these supposedly evil offers are. One offers a cartoon showing Satan, engulfed in flames, explaining the workings of MLM arrangements to two anxious recruits. The caption reads: "It's a very good product. You'll love it! First, sell me your soul. Then, go find five distributors who'll send me their souls. And then, they find five distributors each ..." (Blogedei.com, 2007). The other posts a scan of a (watercolor?) painting depicting several people wearing sorrowful expressions and tattered robes, their hands bound by rope – evoking images of early Christians being persecuted for their faith. The text accompanying the figure asks: "Why do pastors use their religious files to contact people to sell 'under' them? Why indeed?" (d'Astier de la Vigerie, 2008). However, criticism has not come only from these evangelical circles. French society has been widely suspicious of these companies, insofar as they questioned the values related to laicism (*laïcité*). In France, people will hardly stand a secular sphere of activity being closely linked to religion (Luca, 2004b, 2008). This confusion immediately stirs up suspicions and rejection. From this perspective, it is not surprising that one of the most publicized scandals in France dealt with the conversion of French distributors to Pentecostalism. In 1994, the media reported on baptismal immersions performed on distributors in Arizona, in a Pentecostal church affiliated to the Assemblies of God in Phoenix. These distributors' trip to the United States was meant as a reward for their excellent sales figures. The pastor who officiated over the baptisms was the network founder's own brother! The scandal drew attention to a company that was also criticized for its ethical, fiscal, and financial ground attitudes, and which actually led to its dissolution. What sensitized the French public opinion was the denunciation of the religious link, rather than the presumed tax frauds, which speaks volumes.

Thus, the French newspaper *L'Express* published the following speech, given by a distributor high up in the network hierarchy at a congress of the accused company, as a proof of sectarianism:

> We were bound to meet again in this room – since long before we were even born! I know there are people here who suffer because they don't know how to clear their debts. They think the Business is taking too long. But Joan of Arc once said: "Only God will give victory!" God will help you cope with this, shoulder the burden. Let's entrust Him with all our dreams! Let's hold hands now and receive Communion all together. Lord, please, bless our organization. Amen! (Koch & Leblond, 1994, p. 80)

Belief in predestination, faith in God's will to deliver the elect from poverty, belief that our dreams were placed in us by God: Rich DeVos's influence on this speech is striking. This scandal tarnished the reputation of all the MLM companies and had a huge impact on their later growth in France. Legislators had already looked into the legality of this system. Laws had been passed so that the profession could be better supervised and, as a result, it could enjoy better recognition. But the whole profession actually realized how important it is to strengthen both its ethics and its professionalism to avoid falling into disrepute again. We can say, eventually, that this scandal gave fresh impetus to MLM. Providing a detailed account of the steps through which relationship marketing was ultimately able to grow in metropolitan France is beyond the scope of this essay, but one step in particular is quite important.

We saw that, in order to silence rumors of sectarianism, South Korean companies broke their links with Pentecostalism. But without a belief that could back up the faith in success, it was difficult for them to address distributors appropriately. The mere professionalization of the system is obviously not enough for the business to work. However, in France, relationship marketing found a discerning support perfectly suited to the French and European contexts: sportsmanship.

Thus, MLM now assumes a position within the more general context of "sportivization" of the Western way of life. At first, when religion ceased to oversee all fields of activities, due to secularization, science took over. This was then referred to as a transfer of transcendence. Later on, science ended up being attacked from several sides. It was the beginning of the counterculture movement. Ultimately, according to sociologist Alain Erhenberg's analysis (1999), sports have apparently supplanted science in regards to its capacity to affect all fields of activity.

Indeed, Ehrenberg observes that sports have become an object of exceptional interest. He associates it with their ability to embody, for the majority, the democratic ideals of equality and justice: no more class-based differences and no more privileges of birth. We all start from scratch and are offered a chance, even if not necessarily in the same sport. We can all find a sport that fulfils us, provided we try hard enough. The moves to learn, the efforts and the constraints, the qualities and the attitudes to develop are the same for all of us. Sports are considered to be "the school of life" (p. 39), able to impart us with the mindset that will lead to success, in our professional as well as social and private lives. Indeed, this mindset goes far beyond the mere practice of sports. It is prized in all fields of activity, for it holds the values based on which action is possible. Between individual sports, extreme sports, combat sports, and team sports ... There is a whole range of merits to acquire, which can easily be mobilized, even only metaphorically, to describe the kind of attitude that fosters individual or collective progress and that improves individual or collective skills. Companies realized that they could turn sportsmanship into a tremendous ally. Indeed, MLM is not alone in resorting to its potentialities.

Thus, catchy sports references now supplant religious references in the various congresses I have attended, thereby motivating distributors. Most companies I have visited have their own "sports representatives." Top-level athletes' involvement is even presented as a sign of their ethical strength. One of the members of the French soccer team that participated in the 1998 World Championship explained at a congress: "our dreams are our goals: I have dreams, we all have dreams. Let's remember that. Let's not be afraid of show off. More leads to more." Indeed, how can one become a champion if one did not dream about it, if one did not believe it? Even once prosperity theology has been rejected, the reference to dreams does not disappear. It is now simply based on something else. There are many more examples, such as a very famous French rugby player who broke his knee and had to start again from scratch. He learned to walk again and later on to jog. Eventually, he learned to run again. There is also a much-renowned one-legged rock climber.

After hearing such accounts, how can one claim that success does not depend on will and persistence? Such examples immediately empower people to claim their destinies. Unable to seek God's blessings and having renounced the welfare state, we still have to discover the god who is supposed to dwell in us, whatever his name may be. We want to believe that a full success kit is nestled within each of us. It is entirely up to us to use it, up to us and to the group which shares the same values, and symbols, and the will to win, and above all which also places a high priority on facing problems together, reaching out to the weak, and helping them get back on their feet so as to move on together. It is beautiful. It is powerful. Yet such a responsibility is quite something. It is even likely to be a burden ... But unity makes it seem less burdensome. Undoubtedly, these are very convincing arguments – arguments that can spur on the energy necessary to start MLM entrepreneurial businesses and keep them going.

In my nearly three years of survey work in Metropolitan France and in the French Antilles, I did not notice at the meetings any direct comment on religion, like those Rich DeVos's followers would make. People do still thank God, which reminds one what the networks are based on – I would not go as far as to say that religion is now totally absent from the motivation system used in Metropolitan France. However, people do not speak of it and yet one can sense it. MLM did not completely rid itself from religious references within compassionate capitalism, but it relinquished the religious institutions and the theologies to which it was originally attached. It has assumed its independence, perhaps has even found its cruising speed.

An evangelical distributor from French Guiana, originally from metropolitan France, who had joined a French MLM company, told me that she had deeply felt this link with religion during two congresses she had attended and during which, however, no religious or Christian references had been made. The link with religion can only be sensed by those who can recognize it thanks to their cultures or thanks to their personal religious affiliations:

> When I attended the congress, the first year, I said: "Well, well! This sounds familiar!" And since this year, I'm sure of it. There's this sentence, which I'm going to quote, that comes directly from the Bible: "The Lord said that you are the light of the world. You do not light a lamp and put it under the table. You put it on a bushel so that it gives light to all in the house." This year, at the congress, I hear: "There's no point in shining unless you brighten someone up." It means exactly the same thing! Today the sick no longer needs to be sick. He doesn't need to live in misery. No! Jesus died for this! He came to save the world. The first time I made the connection, last year, I was a young evangelist. I said to myself: "No, stop it, you see God everywhere." But this year, I'm sure of it.

Breaking this link with religion was a deliberate and political move, orchestrated both by the leaders of MLM companies and by the French direct-selling federation. The latter considers it an absolute prerequisite for approving a company's membership application. Thereby, the institutional leaders jointly contribute to the professionalization of what had trouble being recognized as an actual profession. Ethical codes and a restrictive normative system are nationally implemented and start to impact on the stances taken by European federations. MLM is changing so as to fit the French secular context. It associates the distributors' attitudes to a new content of belief that amounts to the cult of performance embodied by sportsmanship.

## CONCLUSION

In the United States, South Korean, Haitian, and French cases, the growth of MLM companies resulted – at least in part – from local beliefs. The trust in this business model depended on the context, the content, and the attitudes of local beliefs. To understand how the reception of MLM has varied from one country to another, we had to make a distinction between these three levels and to determine their degree of compatibility and how this compatibility evolved.

The *context of belief* represents the way in which a country sees and defines itself: what it wants or believes at a certain point: what its citizens identify with. It corresponds to a set of shared values: a founding myth, a political ideology, a relationship to religion, a sense of belonging to a chosen or a damned land ... All this makes up the belief context. It corresponds to the symbolic borders of a country. Due to their globalization policies, MLM companies are faced (1) at the synchronic level with different national contexts (Protestant land, secular land, and so forth), and (2) at the diachronic level with the evolution of national symbolic borders (for instance, a shift from pro-Americanism to anti-Americanism).

As for the *content of belief*, it varies of course with the context. As a result, content tolerated in a capitalist, Protestant, pro-American country will have trouble getting implemented in a communist, anti-American, or secular context ... They can be incompatible, in which case beliefs seem sectarian. To avoid this stigmatization, MLM companies have to adapt and adjust to the country and to the time frame.

Finally, *belief attitudes* are what is most stable. In each country, the same rules are taught. This is even referred to as duplication. For a business to be successful, one has to assume the right attitude, perform the right actions, make the right speeches ... This is why people can have the impression that relationship marketing creates standardized individuals. But it is a misconception, for their acts are related to specific belief contents, depending on *particular* belief contexts. Distributors cannot necessarily understand one another from one country to another. What motivates a sponsored distributor in France might prove inefficient in another country.

The following equation should be taken into account to calculate MLM companies' growth potential:

$$\begin{aligned}\text{National growth potential of MLM}\\ &= \text{National context of belief}\\ &\quad + \text{Tolerated collection(or contents)of belief}\\ &\quad + \text{Usual attitudes(or acts)beliefs}\end{aligned}$$

In the US Protestant *context*, these companies want to embrace a new spirit of capitalism that shifts to religion. This shift involved adopting a *collection* of beliefs related to prosperity theology, which associated the distributors' material success with an *attitude* of trust in God and later on in one's sponsor, an attitude of love and emotional generosity, integrity, effort, and persistence in one's work as well as resistance to ordeals. All this worked out quite well in South Korea too, until the Asian crisis called the pro-American and anti-communist *context* favorable to Protestantism – and in particular to Pentecostalism – into question. This change of context involved invalidating the *collection* of beliefs in God's election of the South, based on which distributors could believe in their material success, which therefore rendered incongruous the attitude based on which they developed their networks. An adjustment period was necessary so that the belief attitude characteristic of this kind of company could again rest on new belief contents related to a new belief context. Indeed, South Koreans are nowadays very attracted to the religious movements coming from Northern Asia, which are rooted in their history and which focus more on a Buddhist philosophy of life. Thus, when the belief context is no longer suited to Christianity, these companies have to borrow from the religious sphere a collection of beliefs more suitable. In France, the secular *context* forced companies to leave the religious sphere and to rest on a new belief *content*. The latter rested, *in fine*, on the cult of performance that derives from sportsmanship and that professes the importance of dreams to success. In the end, it seems that MLM is based on a set of attitudes, acts, or practices identical everywhere, but that both its survival and its potential growth depend at least in part on how well it links these practices to collections of beliefs that vary with the national cultural contexts in question.

To conclude, what can we learn from MLM about the potential link between economy and religion? We learn that this link is made up of times of exhaustion, pause, slowdown, and then acceleration or reversal of the shift between the two spheres of activity: it is made of fluctuations and adjustments. It is never set. This link can only be defined by observing this movement, which varies in particular with the social environment. It can therefore not be defined once and for all.

## NOTES

1. The French term for "sponsored person" (*filleul*) is very interesting because it can also be translated as "godchild."
2. This was part of a minister's speech.

## ACKNOWLEDGMENTS

This study was carried out thanks to the financial support of the *Agence nationale de recherche* on two projects: "Religious Plurality as a Source of Conflict: From Competing Memories to the New Uses of Identities" (CONFLIREL, 1997–2010) and "Transnational Religions in the South: Between Ethnicization and Universalization" (RELITRANS, 2008–2011). It was also supported by the *Fédération française de la vente directe*.

## REFERENCES

Badie, B. (1999). *Un monde sans souveraineté. Les Etats entre ruse et responsabilité*. Paris: Fayard.

Biggart, N. W. (1989). *Charismatic capitalism: Direct selling organizations in America*. Chicago, IL: University of Chicago Press.

Blogdei.com. (2007). *Purquoi les Chrétiens évangéliques devraient refuser de pratiquer la vente multiniveau*. Retrieved from http://www.blogdei.com. Accessed on June 24, 2011.

Bourdieu, P. (2000). *Les structures sociales de l'économie*. Paris: Seuil (Liber).

Bromley, D. G. (1995). Quasi-religious corporations: A new integration of religion and capitalism? In: R. H. Roberts (Ed.), *Religion and the transformation of capitalism: Comparative approaches* (pp. 135–160). London: Routledge.

Bromley, D. G. (1998). Transformative movements and quasi-religious corporations: The case of Amway. In: N. J. Demerath, et al. (Eds), *Sacred companies: Organizational aspects of religion and religious aspects of organizations* (pp. 349–363). New York, NY: Oxford University Press.

Chung, B. (2001). Politique et religion en Corée du Sud. *Revue d'études contemporaines Est-Ouest*, *32*(1), 85–110.

Corten, A. (1995). *Le pentecôtisme au Brésil. Emotion du pauvre et romantisme théologique*. Paris: Karthala.

Corten, A. (2001). *Misère, religion et politique en Haïti. Diabolisation et mal politique*. Paris: Karthala.

Corten, A., Dozon, J. P., & Oro, A. P. (Eds.). (2003). *Les nouveaux conquérants de la foi. L'Eglise universelle du royaume de Dieu (Brésil)*. Paris: Karthala.

Corten, A., & Mary, A. (Eds.). (2000). *Imaginaires politiques et pentecôtismes. Afrique/Amérique latine*. Paris: Karthala.

d'Astier de la Vigerie, M. (2008). Les dégâts de la théologie de la prospérité, par le pasteur Gilles Boucomont. Retrieved from http://www.michelledastier.org/index.php/2008/05/24/1136-acn-ou-les-degats-de-la-theologie-de-la-prosperite. Accessed on June 24, 2011.

Erhenberg, A. (1999). *Le culte de la performance*. Paris: Hachette littératures.

Fourchard, L., Mary, A., & Otayek, R. (Eds.). (2005). *Entreprises religieuses transnationales en Afrique de l'Ouest*. Paris: Ifra et Karthala.

Hurbon, L. (2004). *Religions et lien social. L'Eglise et l'Etat moderne en Haïti*. Paris: Cerf.

Koch, F., & Leblond, R. (1994). L'échappée belle du gourou. *L'Express*, September 8–14, pp. 78–80.

Lanzarroti, M. (1992). *La Corée du Sud: une sortie du sous-développement*. Institut d'étude du développement économique et social de l'université Paris I, Collection (Tiers Monde). Paris: PUF.

Luca, N. (2000). La conquête de la modernité par les nouveaux mouvements chrétiens coréens. *Social Compass*, *47*(4), 525–540.

Luca, N. (2004a). L'évolution des protestantismes en Corée du Sud: Un rapport ambigu à la modernité. *Critique internationale*, *22*, 111–124.

Luca, N. (2004b). *Les sectes: Que sais-je?* Paris: PUF.

Luca, N. (2008). *Individus et pouvoirs face aux sectes*. Paris: Armand Colin "Sociétales".

Stiglitz, J. E. (2002). *La grande désillusion*. Paris: Fayard.

Weber, M. (1964). *L'éthique protestante et l'esprit du capitalisme*. Paris: Plon.

Zúñiga, C. G. (2005). Congregaciones del èxito: Interpretación socio-religiosa de las redes de mercadeo en Guadalajara. Universidad de Guadalajara, El Colegio de Jalisco.

# ECONOMIC, RELIGIOUS, AND SOCIAL PRACTICE OF GIVING: A MICROANALYSIS OF DONATING IN THE KINGDOM OF TONGA

Natsuko Higa


## ABSTRACT

*This chapter focuses on donating to the church on the part of Wesleyan Methodists in the Kingdom of Tonga. It illuminates the dynamism and tension emerging between religious faith and economic practice. Quantitative analysis of income and expenditures are combined with qualitative observations of villagers' actions and discourse in this microanalysis of donating events, which seeks to comprehend the situation from point of view of the local adherents. It concludes that what might appear in Tonga on the surface to be a purely competitive practice is actually a complex blend of competition and cooperation, with the latter probably having a larger role than the former in these transactions.*


**The Economics of Religion: Anthropological Approaches**
**Research in Economic Anthropology, Volume 31, 241–263**

**ISSN: 0190-1281/doi:10.1108/S0190-1281(2011)0000031013**

## INTRODUCTION: RELIGIOUS PRACTICE AS A PART OF ECONOMIC ACTIVITY

Gifting practice has long played a vital role in the society of the Kingdom of Tonga in Polynesia, the South Pacific. This can be characterized by a great flow of materials ranging from traditional goods such as bark cloth to more modern ones – money in an envelope being perhaps the most extreme example. Many of the ceremonial occasions in Tongan society, from that focused on regular life events to more formal civic events involving the nobility, monarchy, or government (Evans, 2001), are marked by different kinds of gifting.

The heavy influence of gifting practice on the Tongan economy is visible in government statistics. According to the *Report on the Household Income and Expenditure Survey 2000/01*, the most important form of Tongan gift is "remittance" (Kingdom of Tonga, 2002). Remittance can be considered a kind of transnational gift; it helps to confirm ties between emigrants living overseas and their families in the homeland. Like other South Pacific countries, the national economy of Tonga has grown largely dependent on remittances from overseas since the 1960s, when Tongan emigration – particularly to New Zealand, Australia, and the United States – came to be particularly notable.

According to the survey, 75% of households polled were receiving remittances from relatives overseas – remittances amounting to some 20% of their annual cash income. Although the impact and importance of remittances on the economy of Tonga has been emphasized in economic studies of the Pacific region, and the motivations for migration much discussed (Brown & Leeves, 2007; Cowling, 2002; Lee, 2006), little attention has been paid to exactly how remitted money was spent inside the kingdom.

However, the fact that contributing to the church plays a large role in the household economy is clarified by the 2000–2001 government survey, mentioned above. Average total annual household expenditure in Tonga in 2000–2001 was TOP16,300 (11,000 cash and 5,300 non-cash).[1] Notably, about one-tenth of the total amount of annual non-food cash expenditures (TOP6,050) goes to the church – roughly TOP650 – and about TOP200 are spent per year on feasts (*ibid.*). In other words, church contribution is widely recognized as one of the most important economic activities in Tonga, and it can be assumed that such huge expenses are largely covered by remitted money. How, then, can we understand why such "gifts to God" practices have flourished in Tongan society – entangled with the modern phenomenon of migration and its deeply-rooted gift economy?

Regarding this issue, Gregory (1980) identifies structural differences between "gifts to God" and "gifts to man." Analyzing the relationships between amounts donated to the church and traditional clan structures in Papua New Guinea (PNG), Gregory argues that the "gifts to God" system in Melanesia exhibits structural resemblances to the "destruction" system of potlatch gift exchange. According to Gregory, this "gifts to man" system has been replaced by a "gifts to God" system of the classic potlatch type, with the difference being that the gifts take the form of money and are appropriated by the church instead of being destroyed (Gregory, 1980, p. 630). In the potlatch case, the intermediary is fire, and this destroys the gifts. But in the Papuan case, the intermediary is the Church, and it symbolically destroys the money by ensuring that it does not get back to the donors. Thus, the Church, by modifying the traditional gift exchanging system, has perpetuated a ranking system of clans and men that enables it to accumulate assets for the Church without incurring liabilities – to accumulate capital. Paradoxically, it is the "destruction" element of the "gifts to God" system that enables this accumulation to take place (*ibid.*).

Gregory's focus on the structural similarity of the potlatch system with Papuan gifting to the Church in terms of economic flow of properties provides a valuable clue to understanding the implicit structure underlying religious gifting practices in Tongan Christianity as well. His indication that the destruction of wealth seen in the potlatch in turn enables the accumulation of capital through Christian practice can be applicable in a sense to the Tongan case that I discuss here. In a society where gifts are actively circulated among the people, what is critical for them is to perpetuate the circulation flow, which tends to oppose the accumulation of personal wealth.

However, my analysis[2] sheds light on another aspect of religious gifting that is not explicable by Gregory's model. Compared with the social background of PNG of Melanesia – a ranking system of clans that informs gifting practice in a competitive atmosphere – Tongan Methodists are hierarchically differentiated into royalty, nobles, and commoners. Related to this, Barker (1990, p.8) discusses the general differences between the system of Christianity in Polynesia and Melanesia: "Many scholars … have contrasted the hierarchical nature of Polynesian church organization, in which village pastors often enjoy the respect and prerogatives of traditional chiefs, with the much more egalitarian ambience of Melanesian village

Christianity." With respect to Tongan Christianity in relation to traditional hierarchy, in particular, Marcus (1980, p.104) explains as follows:

> Money and labor contributions from the *kainga lotu* "congregation" pass up the hierarchy of church administration several times a year, while every tribute made to the chief (except when destined for the King) is offered by the people with a good deal of reluctance. In the provision of goods and services to the church, the minister, as manager of these activities, stands in a position presumably analogous to the local chief in old Tonga and has partially replaced him.

Such an analogy between Tongan social structure and the typical system of local Christianity has often been used to explain gifting practices of Tongan Christians (e.g., van der Grijp, 1993). However, at the same time, in order to explain the very active – or sometimes even aggressive – act of giving to the church, some scholars have acknowledged its competitive atmosphere as well (Decktor Korn, 1978; James, 1998).

Here, I attempt to resolve these different types of explanations of economic practices of Tongan Methodists, especially Wesleyans, from a village-centered point of view. "The donating ceremony focused here is called *misinale* and derived from the English work 'missionary.' This type of donating system is said to have started as early as the 1830s, right after the Wesleyan Mission arrived at Tonga and was accepted by influential chiefs of the time." By looking closely at the process and the results of an annual donating ceremony for the church and its historical and cultural background, I analyze how the Tongan "gifts to God" practice can be reconsidered.

## CHRISTIANITY AND ECONOMY IN TONGA

About 98% of the whole population (101,991 in the 2006 census) of the Kingdom of Tonga is nominally Christian, the religion having spread quickly after missionaries arrived and started proselytizing in the early nineteenth century (Kingdom of Tonga, 2008). It is so deeply ingrained today that Tongans are prohibited from working on Sundays, with few exceptions, by the Sunday Law. Furthermore, Methodist churches have been socially dominant in Tonga ever since the powerful early leader (and eventual first King of Tonga) Tāufa'āhau converted to the Wesleyan Church (Lātūkefu, 1974). Today, the Free Wesleyan Church (hereafter, FWC) claims about 40% of the population, with the Catholic Church in second place with about 16% (Fig. 1).

As mentioned above, gifting is a key to understanding the Tongan economy, from the personal level (giving a portion of food to one's neighbor) to the community or regional level (making huge contributions to

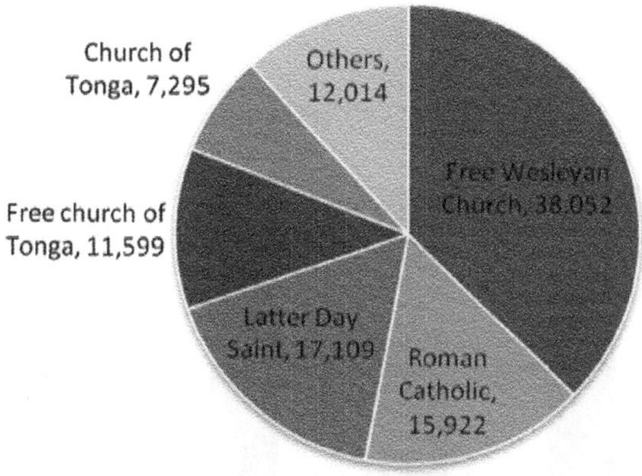


*Fig. 1.* Tongan population by religion in 2006 (Kingdom of Tonga, 2008).

the King). Above all, Christianity as a whole is deeply involved in the Tongan gift economy, even though expected donation size per member depends on the denomination. Focusing particularly on the religious-economic practices of the adherents of the FWC in Tonga, in the following sections I examine annual donating ceremonies in order to illustrate the ways in which their Christian ways of living are closely interwoven with their economic lives.

## *MISINALE* AS RELIGIOUS, ECONOMIC AND SOCIAL PRACTICE

### *Overview of* Misinale

On the day of *misinale* in 2004, the total amount of donations collected across the country exceeded US$3 million. This is a surprising amount, given that the Tongan national GDP for that year was estimated as US$178.5 million (CIA, 2007). In other words, money donated to the church only on one day accounted for more than 1.5% of the GDP. Furthermore, the total amount of money donated to the FWC is steadily increasing year by year (Fig. 2). This phenomenon clearly shows how tightly Tongan religious activities[3] are intertwined with economic ones.

Many recent studies have discussed the impact and importance of donating activities in Tonga from a socioeconomic point of view (e.g., Evans

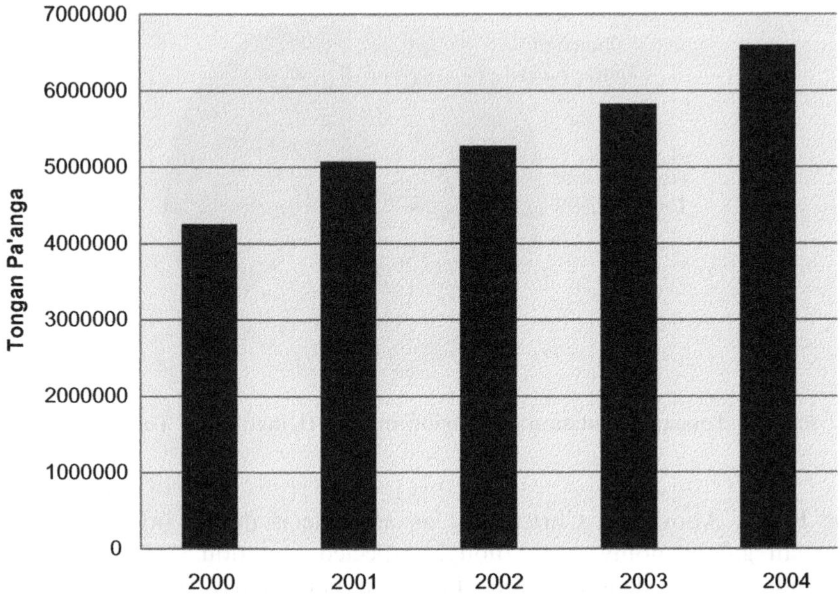


*Fig. 2.* *Misinale* donation to FWC from 2000 to 2004 (Siasi Uesiliana Tau'atāina 'o Tonga, 2005).

2001; James 1998), but most of their analyses have focused on the intensiveness of contribution, or only on collection activities. Therefore, how money is used afterwards inside the church organization remains unclear. However, by focusing on this issue from the viewpoint of adherent villagers and of the church as a part of social organization within the microcosm of a single village, we can help to fill this gap in knowledge.

The village called *Matangi*[4] is located on the main island of Tongatapu, about 20 kilometers from the capital. At the time of my visit in 2005, there were 68 households in the village and five churches – three Methodist (Free Wesleyan, Free Church of Tonga, and Church of Tonga), one Catholic, and the other Mormon (Church of Jesus Christ of Latter Day Saints, or LDS). The members of the FWC are the most numerous: 29 (42.6%) of 68 households. Yet, many members of the FWC have recently been moving to other churches, such as the LDS church (Decktor Korn, 1978; Gordon, 1990), and it appears to be accelerating. Such conversion is considered a reflection of rapid and drastic social change from traditional toward modern ways of living, seen in various aspects of Tongan society. This movement can also be interpreted as an indication of a shift in Tongan social structure from a rigidly hierarchical one to a more egalitarian one. However, such a movement is more apparent in urban areas than in rural villages like the one I focus on here, which is still permeated by a relatively conservative atmosphere.

*Misinale* is usually held on the last Sunday of November, on a church or village basis. In one specific year, the total amount of contributions made on the day of *misinale* in the village church (in *Matangi*) reached to TOP27,173.30. Based essentially on kinship structure, the members of the 29 households in the village church are divided into seven groups (I to VII). Each group consists of five to seven households – except Group VII, which consists of the minister, the steward, and the Youth Group of the village church. In addition, the two other Methodist churches in the village also made some contributions for subsidiary help, TOP50 and TOP100, respectively, and the steward of the neighboring village offered TOP50 as well.

### *The Day Before* Misinale*: Mutual Cooperation of Members*

On the day before the *misinale* event I witnessed in 2004, donation money was collected by each group. Each group has a household head that plays the role of leader, and group members brought money to the leading household. Therefore, the members of the group know from the start the amount of their contribution brought by other members. In this sense, even though they will eventually know the amounts of other members' donations, this will not affect individual decisions regarding personal donations. That is, it is not exactly competition among those in the same group, but rather that between groups, that really matters. Here, a group serves more as a unit of cooperation.

Much preparation has been made for the day of *misinale*, and the main concern of the church members is collecting enough money to reach the amount set in advance. Within a household, all family members have tried to save as much money as possible from their incomes, or tried to obtain what they could from relatives living overseas (or both). But their concerns are not only about money – they also must think about the feast to be held following the donating ceremony. Among the many ways for adherents to show their dedication and devotion to the church, giving feasts or offering food to church authorities is the most frequently employed, and people usually take turns for such food preparation duties. Needless to say, this requires much time and effort, and plenty of advance planning. People in charge of putting on a feast purchase a large amount of food, and ask friends and relatives for help with the cooking – friends who belong to other denominations, as *misinale* usually takes place on the same day among all of the villages.

Taking a close look at Table 1, which shows donation amounts, it becomes apparent that the sum given by Group VII stands out from the others by more than TOP7,000, which owes to large donations from the church authorities and the youth group. The members of the youth group usually take responsibility for voluntary work such as farming the land of the church or fixing the church building. The more than TOP7,000 donated by them was gathered in various ways, mainly through fundraising concerts (*koniseti*) or kava drinking events (*kalapu*) held in the village under the name of the group. These two forms of fundraising are very popular among Tongan people, regardless of the type of funding bodies or purposes. In 2006, the group held their final fundraising concert and kava-drinking event on the evening before the day of *misinale*.

*The Day of* Misinale*: The Donating Ceremony for the Church*

On the day of *misinale* in 2006, the donating ceremony began at 10 a.m. in the church building. Unexpectedly, not very many people attended the ceremony, since most were still busy preparing food for the feasts that would take place after the ceremony. Inside the church were about 15 men, 7 women, and 15 children, as well as a few others, such as ministers and secretaries from other villages. The master of ceremonies (MC) and the secretaries had been appointed in advance. Also, during the ceremony, the names of members were called according to group, the composition of which I discuss below.

When the MC called out the name of a group and its members, the head of the group would take the members' donation, consisting of a bundle of bills, to the secretaries. During this time, the MC encouraged the rest of the

***Table 1.*** Amount Donated by Group From 2005 to 2009 in FWC in *Matangi* (Compiled from Author's Field Notes, 2010).

| | Group I (5 Families) | Group II (5 Families) | Group III (6 Families) | Group IV (7 Families) | Group V (5 Families) | Group VI (6 Families) | Group VII (Minister etc.) | Total (36 Families) |
|---|---|---|---|---|---|---|---|---|
| **2005** | T$2,433 | T$2,262 | T$2,312 | T$4,730 | T$4,824 | T$2,004 | T$8,398.3 | T$26,963.3 |
| **2006** | T$12,943 | T$12,058 | T$5,319 | T$4,788 | T$1,902 | T$2,415 | T$8412.7 | T$47,837.7 |
| **2007** | T$3,211 | T$4,049 | T$5,205 | T$4,222 | T$3,060 | T$3,023 | T$8,366.2 | T$31,136.2 |
| **2008** | T$3,822 | T$4,305 | T$6,053 | T$5,916.2 | T$2,122 | T$2,426 | T$9,212.5 | T$33,956.7 |
| **2009** | T$4,434 | T$3,867 | T$10,586 | T$12,822 | T$13,600 | T$3,106 | T$8,077 | T$56,492 |
| **Total** | T$26,843 | T$26,541 | T$29,475 | T$32,478.2 | T$25,508 | T$12,974 | T$42,466.7 | T$196,385.9 |

members that were inside the church to help (*tokoni*), and some people responded by taking money directly to the secretaries, while others put money into the plastic basin carried around by one of the group members. All the money collected from that particular group was immediately counted by the secretaries, and then the MC read out the amount, how much the group had donated, how much the people from other groups donated, and how much was donated in total.

Most of the process of collecting money from the groups proceeded in this way. However, some variation existed within certain groups that had lost members due to death in the preceding year. In such cases, the family of the deceased had prepared a woven mat and a basket filled with perfumes and bottles of the same kind. The head and some other members of the group walked in line to the front of the church, offering these gifts to the church along with a bundle of money. Through this gesture, they made an offering on behalf of the person who had passed away, showing their respect for the deceased, an act called *fakamanatu* in Tonga. While the gifts were brought to the front, other members sang hymns. Then the ministers from other villages responded with short speeches. In such cases of *fakamanatu*, each group tended to donate much more than usual in memory of the deceased. A detailed analysis of the amount of the donations is given below.

When all the groups had finished giving money, it was immediately counted and the final result was announced. After the whole process of money offerings was completed (about one hour), the members who had attended the ceremony moved to the hall next to the church building, where the food had been laid out – ready for the *misinale* feast. People enjoyed the feast while listening to the speeches of the ministers or the secretaries of the church, and after all the speeches had finished they went back to their homes with leftover foods. In this way *misinale*, one of the busiest days of the year for the adherents, was performed and completed.

## RATIONALE BEHIND LARGE DONATIONS: INDICATORS OF GIVING

Table 1 shows the amount contributed by each group for *misinale* for each year from 2005 to 2009 and also illustrates the fact that the 29 FWC member households in *Matangi* are divided into six groups of five to seven households. These six groups are mainly structured according to kin relations, except the one that consists of the minister, the secretary, and the members of the youth group of the village. For example, among the five households of Group I, three of the household heads are brothers. Also, three household heads of Group II are brothers as well, and two heads of the same group are a mother and her son each. Table 1 also shows that the total amounts for each year is not increasing annually, but an increase is apparent in these five years, as the total amount for 2009 was more than twice that for 2005.

Why does the amount show gradual increase even though the amount is so large as to be very difficult for the members to collect every year? To understand this phenomenon, it must be noted that there exist certain standards of giving set by the church – standards that are shared among the members themselves. The two categories of standards are *faka'amu* and *fakamanatu*, the former set by the central church office and the latter a conventional part of local religious practice. Both of these work as economic standards and as norms of conduct in Tongan religious performance.

## *MISINALE*: AN ELABORATED SYSTEM OF RELIGIOUS GIVING

### Faka'amu*: Wished Amount of Money*

Church authorities and its adherents always emphasize that *misinale* is "voluntary" gifting on behalf of God. A church brochure declares: "Tongans love to give and giving is what makes a good Christian Tongan!" (Puloka, n.d.). Wesleyan adherents are generally most likely to live up to this admonishment in Tonga. However, it is incorrect to assume that the donated money is simply given "voluntarily" or "independently." By analyzing the actual process in detail, one can draw a different picture: the central church sets in advance a certain amount of money as donating target. Called *faka'amu* in Tongan, this apportion budget represents a wished or desired amount requested by the General Conference of every member.[5] The conventional formula for calculating *faka'amu* for each local church is total membership multiplied by each estimated individual member's contribution (*ibid.*).

For example, Table 2 shows how the *faka'amu* of the village church was formulated. There are five ranks or categories, from the top rank A (TOP39) to the bottom rank E (TOP26). The central church office examines and decides the rank of each local church, taking into consideration factors such as member numbers and previous donation amounts. The rank of the village church that year was D, meaning TOP31 for each person. In addition to

***Table 2.*** Ranks of *Faka'amu* (Apportionment Budget) and Formula of the Village Church (Compiled from Author's Field Notes, 2005).

| (Target by Rank | + | Other Needs) | × | Number of Members in the Village | = | Total |
|---|---|---|---|---|---|---|
| A: TOP39<br>B: TOP37<br>C: TOP35<br>D: TOP31<br>E: TOP26 | | For workers: TOP16<br>For buildings: TOP3<br>For district: TOP1 | | | | |
| (TOP31 | + | TOP20) | × | 149 | = | TOP7,599 |

*faka'amu*, there are three additional target figures. The first is for payments to people working in the church organization (TOP16 for each), which includes office workers and school teachers. The second is for construction or reconstruction of the church buildings (TOP3 for each), and the third is for the budget of the regional central office to which local village churches belong (TOP1 for each). Therefore, the sum total of these amounts (TOP31 + 16 + 3 + 1 = TOP51) is multiplied by 149, the total membership of the village church, and the product of TOP7,599 is considered the target amount of that year's *misinale*, expected by the head office.

The reach of the FWC in members' everyday lives goes far and deep, and is not restricted to massive church attendance on Sundays. Even regarding secondary education, it now plays an even more major role than the Tongan government. Throughout the kingdom, the FWC runs seven primary schools, three middle schools, three district schools, five large secondary schools, and an agricultural college (Grace, 2003). In this sense, education in Tonga is supported by the churches and that is another reason for the huge influence of Christianity on Tongan social values – "The church became the community and the community the church" (Taumoepeau, n.d.). In the past, when I visited the central church office located in the capital and asked workers about donating practices in Tonga, they usually said something along the lines of the following comment:

> Sometimes people coming from overseas are surprised by the large scale of donation and contribution to churches in Tonga, and then assume that we (churches) are exploiting people. But that is far from true. In Tonga, the church is playing many vital social roles, as a government or a company does. We collect money from the people, and we distribute it again to the people. It is like a bank. (Interview with an FWC office worker, 2006)

Fakamanatu:[6] *Commemorating the Deceased*

Except for the five outstanding cases of donating over TOP10,000 at one time (columns shaded in Table 1), amounts donated are basically the same across time for each group. In addition, in the five cases where more than TOP10,000 was donated, there was a substantial reason for each group to give such a large amount, an amount that dramatically exceeded the amount given in other years. In each of the five cases of massive giving shown in Table 1 (shaded), the large amounts were due to *fakamanatu*, because someone from each of those groups had passed away within the year preceding the relevant *misinale*. For example, Group I collected TOP12,943 in 2006 as follows: TOP10,000 from household one, TOP700 each from households two, three, and four (the heads of which were all brothers); TOP800 from household five; and the remaining TOP43 from other people who helped this group (friends or other members of the FWC). Therefore, almost 77% of the amount collected by Group I was provided from just one household, the head of which had passed away during the preceding year. As this household head had worked for more than 30 years as an FWC minister, even after retiring he and his family were known as some of the most dedicated members in the church. They voluntarily gave a large feast for the church members three times a year,[7] and actively participated in all church events.

Tongan funerals in general, and other ceremonial occasions such as weddings, are massive in scale, held not only for the relatives but also for many other people. Many types of food are provided for all guests by the family of the deceased, and traditional wealth in the form of mats is extensively exchanged among the people. Accordingly, families of the deceased face huge expenses. The scale of a funeral depends on the social status of the deceased or the family's financial situation, but in most cases they cost thousands of Tongan pa'anga. In Tonga, such huge and unforeseen expenses are usually met by family members living overseas, since most of the families living in Tonga cannot afford such an expense out of their limited earnings. Taking out a loan or hawking items at a pawn shop would be among the few ways for a family in Tonga to finance such a ceremony.

On the day of *misinale*, TOP10,000 from Household I was collected as follows: TOP3,000 from the eldest son who lives in the United States, TOP2,000 each from the second and the fourth sons who also live in the United States, and another TOP2,000 from the fifth and youngest son who lives in Tonga but spends most months of the year working overseas. They are the ones who always finance the needs of this Tongan family – in this case, the funeral and *misinale*. Of course, how much they give depends on the situation and how much they can afford at each occasion. Finally, the other four cases of giving in excess of TOP10,000 were also for *fakamanatu* – mourning the deceased. I did not get a detailed account of the other four cases but can estimate that from about TOP5,000 to TOP10,000 was given by each family that had suffered the recent loss of a member. Indeed, Puloka (n.d.) – a church minister – writes, "Families with recent deaths contribute large sums of money (TOP5,000–10,000) in memory of their loved ones who have recently moved on to Heaven. It is a very special time of remembering and rededication of the lives of the living." When I asked the family members of Household I about their extra giving on the day of *misinale*, or even when I asked others about it, I usually received almost the same explanation as Puloka's: to show their love and respect for the deceased, for God, and for the church. While a certain standard exists with regard to the amount, there is an acceptable range. As the case of *misinale* in *Matangi* clearly shows, the amount of money donated from a family of the deceased well matches Puloka's estimate – a "large amount" meaning somewhere between TOP5,000 and TOP10,000.

While all the cases discussed here involved an extra amount being given on behalf of the deceased, there were other situations (in other denominations in the same village) in which more than the usual amount was given on the day of *misinale*. These situations included the year of the birth of a child or his or her first birthday celebration, or of celebrating the 70th or 80th birthday of the head of the household. In general, families may make large contributions after an important family affair, whether as part of a celebration or mourning. The act of giving a large donation is done in order to show respect or love for both the family member in charge and God, and not vice versa. Or, in other words, the giving is after the fact and is not done with the expectation of receiving something in return from God.

Another important point is that Group VII's giving was much larger than that of other groups, except in cases of *fakamanatu*. Group VII, as mentioned earlier, is composed of the households of the minister, the secretary, and the youth group of this church, the members of which are also included in other groups.

*Faka'amu*, the apportionment budget of this church discussed above (TOP7,599 – see Table 2), was achieved as a result of the donation of Group VII alone. Consequently, the actual giving of the members of this church is well over the apportionment budget. Also, the average of total giving considered for five years was TOP39,277.18, which far exceeds TOP31,678.18 for *fakamanatu*. The question of why there is such excess giving then arises. The motivation of the members could be explained in many ways, such as in terms of faith or love, or in a more practical sense, because of their acknowledgment that the surplus of donation is to be accumulated in their village church.

*Historical Background of* Misinale

Although there are many ways of showing individual dedication to the Church, and a variety of other donation occasions such as special Sundays, or quarterly donating events called *faka kuata* held through the year, *misinale* is broadly recognized as one of the most important activities for all the members of the FWC in Tonga, as described above. It is an annual event, centering about donating to God and the Church, and the members spend much time and energy collecting money in preparation for the day's arrival far in advance.

In terms of introduction of such religious donating system to Tonga, it was one of the most significant missionaries in Tonga, Shirley Baker, who later had a tremendous influence on establishing the system of Tongan Christianity that had innovated the system of collecting money into a more efficient one by 1875 (Rutherford, 1996).

The structure or strategies of efficient collection innovated at Baker's time enabled the church to collect more money, encouraging active giving and generating a competitive mood among the members. In those days, modern currency had just started to flow into Tonga as a result of contact with foreigners – or more specifically, foreign traders – who bought coconut oil from the people. At that time, therefore, in order to make a donation to the church, people had to earn money by manufacturing coconut oil.

> Tongans manufactured coconut oil at collection time with more zeal than at any other time in the year, but many found, when the day arrived, that they had not sufficient to provide the sum which, under the stress of the occasion, they felt impelled to give. To these people Baker was prepared to allow credit; their promises were recorded as a gift, and they could subsequently make oil to cover the amount. ... Tonga's contribution was received by the Missionary Committee in Sydney with unbounded enthusiasm. (*ibid.* p. 45)

In this way, from the time of introducing the system of Christian giving to Tonga, making a generous donation to the church was not only highly encouraged among individual adherents but also thoroughly organized by the missionaries themselves, as a kind of elaborate apparatus. By constructing such a system of lending cash through coconut oil, or reorganizing people into groups in order to generate a competitive atmosphere, the church established the current system of *misinale* in Tonga under which the adherents are quite eager to give.

On the other hand, tracing back through history to the pre-contact period, this massive economic event – which now occurs on a nationwide scale – can be considered a reproduction or a revival of hierarchical structures that are comparable with the existing social system in the kingdom. *Misinale* is said to have originated from a Tongan traditional ceremony, *inasi*, of giving the first fruits of the land and the ocean to the gods out of appreciation. Van der Grijp (1993, p.214) relates this to Tongan gifting to the church or to the king seen nowadays, and explains it with a theoretical model of reciprocity:

> The annual donations of money to the church (*misinale*), the annual conference (*konifelenisi*) of the (national) Methodist Church, which is held by rotation on different island groups, and the extension of this institution to the other churches of Tonga, can all be seen as historical variations on the *inasi* theme. … But far more than these activities related to the king, the visits by, and gifts to, the church dignitaries (who include the king in case of national religion) have not only a political character but also an explicitly religious character, which brings them very close to *inasi*.

*Misinale* in Tonga was therefore introduced and later innovated into an elaborate system of collecting money by missionaries, which can be seen as having been established on the basis of traditional offerings seen in the pre-contact period. In this sense, it is a highly institutionalized way of giving, as we have seen above, with certain standards or goals of donating amount called *faka'amu* or *fakamanatu*. However, even under this elaborate system of religious giving, the adherents are not simply donating an amount of money as told but have various intentions and motivations that affect their giving practices as well.

### *Expecting Feedback from Others*

In the last section, I have discussed how the system of donation has been well structured in the historical context and the way it even generates a competitive mood to accelerate religious giving among the adherents. However, it is not enough to say that FWC members are making donations defined only by the hierarchical system of the church. As the data of donated amount shows, there is room for them to decide how much to donate, and it is apparent that not only did they achieve the goal or standard set in advance, but also that generally the amount goes well over the expected level.

I have often heard the church members talking about their contribution, saying, "Once we give, we forget about what was given." or "The most important thing is the act of giving itself." This mode of giving can be defined as an "act of love" in the context of Tongan Christianity. It is true that the enormous contributions made by adherents are truly motivated by their willingness to manifest "love for God" and that they are rooted in an intention to express their faith in a definite form. However, at the same time, no matter how much they emphasize that their contribution is only for the sake of God, given in religious faith, their donations of wealth are never free from the possibility of being evaluated by other people in the community.

When I visited *Matangi* again in 2006, I heard that the church members had collected more than TOP30,000 on the day of *misinale* held that year. They seemed very satisfied with their achievement; they compared it with the donating amount of the previous year, celebrating the increase of more than TOP4,000. Each year's achievement is, in a way, taken into account when setting the target figure for the following year. Although people claim to care little about what they give, some trace of reflection or feedback among the members would be expected. How do they think about their achievements, reflecting upon themselves?

In December 2006, I joined a church service, and just at that time the members were starting to prepare for *uike lotu*, the New Year's praying week, which is one of the most important ceremonies for the church. On the last day of the year (*pō lotu*) and the first week of the New Year (*uike lotu*), special services are held and certain guest preachers are invited. For the service of the last day of the year (*pō lotu*), *the village church* invites 10 people to recite a prayer – the number being different for each church. For *pō lotu* in 2005, among the 10 preachers, 4 came from a neighboring village and the rest were selected from the residents of *Matangi*.

I joined a circle of ladies who were chatting and gossiping as usual after the church service, and the topic had just shifted to the identities of the preachers for the coming *pō lotu*. There were six women – one the wife of the minister of the village church – and all were very serious about attending church services or other related activities. Their conversation was as follows (letters L, M, and N refer to three different women, age 50–70):

L: See the members of people coming to preach in our village, there's no one who comes from other large villages.

M: It is very strange that they do not send us some from Church Z (which serves as a district center, including *Matangi*) or any larger church, although we have contributed so much on the day of *misinale* this year.

N: I hear that Church U (the church of one of the neighboring village, in the same district as *Matangi*) will invite some people from Church Z, but I suppose their contributions were almost as same as ours, more than TOP30,000.

L: But you know, the number of members of Church U is much larger, so why not us (since we collected so much money with a smaller number of members)?

M: It really is strange.

Others: Yes, yes …

All the women joining the conversation nodded with serious expressions, but the discussion ended at that point. During my fieldwork, this was the only time I was able to directly observe firsthand reactions to achievements on the day of *misinale*.

Even though their complaints did not exactly amount to aggressive criticism against the decisions of the central church but rather merely expressed – most informally and vaguely – a lack of full satisfaction, the members of the village church did expect some people to come from much larger villages or some other major churches (because of their achievements). Given this hope, they were somewhat disappointed at the decision made by the district central office. Here is another reason why *misinale* is regarded as an extremely important ceremony for adherents; *misinale* is one of the few occasions that enables them to testify to the unity of their local church. And in the units of local churches, the members express their dedication to the central church office by means of donating money.

Under such an elaborate apparatus of religious giving, adherents in a sense become conscious of the assessment of their achievement, expecting more tangible and practical feedback from the central church office. In the next section, another rationale of the large excess in giving is discussed, considering the Tongan cultural norms shared by the people.

## TONGAN CULTURAL CONTEXTS IN THE ACT OF GIVING

### *The Economic or Cultural Norm of "Expected Redundancy"*

What is most striking in Tongan ceremonies in general, whether for church or family occasions or other kinds of events, is the size and extravagance of the things given or consumed at the site. In gift-exchange ceremonies, people often make a display of bark cloths, woven mats, and other gifts, commonly piling them up in front of the audience/participants. Feasts are held on many occasions, and tables are always full of food, gorgeously decorated with colorful refreshments, and the roasted pigs have a strong presence at the center of each of the table. The amount of food on display always far exceeds the needs of the guests, as is evident from the food left over at the end of each feast. In other words, no feast (*kai pola*) can be moderate in Tonga.

At first glance, this intended creation of excess could be seen as a part of competitive practice among feast-givers. However, the words of Decktor Korn (1978, p. 407) are important to recall here: "A feast-giver has the opportunity for a status-enhancing display and for having people acknowledge his status by the fact of their presence as guests at his feast. Nevertheless, there is no formal requirement to make a big display at a congregational feast." Even though this is true, all feasts in Tonga are big displays – without exception. Although there is flexibility around whether a feast will be held on each occasion, once the decision is made to hold one, there is no room for moderation. Such "expected redundancy" can be seen in everyday practice, such as when serving food to guests, giving gifts to friends, and so on.

In *Matangi*, TOP27,173.3 were actually collected on the day of *misinale* by the village church, meaning that the target amount of TOP7,599 was exceeded by a figure of TOP19,574.3, or 72%. This surplus amount was deposited into the account of the church. This happened even though it was recognized by all that there would be a large excess amount, for all are informed of the target amount in advance of *misinale* each year. Furthermore, this was not an isolated incident – it occurs across Tonga regularly, sometimes with massive surplus amounts of money being collected. Fig. 3 illustrates this by comparing the differences between target amounts set in advance by the central office (*faka'amu*) and the actual amounts collected for the entire district and the whole island of Tongatapu. The range of distribution of excess amount concentrates around 60–90%, with a mean of 65%, of the total amount donated by the members. Donors are clearly quite keen on generating a surplus, and intentionally try to maximize their contributions. Why, then, is the target intentionally exceeded – especially by such a large amount – even though people generally have to struggle to collect money?

According to James (1998), especially among people of lower formal education levels, remnants of older superstitions persist in the belief that gifts of money to God ensure a return gift of prosperity: "the more you give, the more you will be blessed" remains a popular belief in Tonga. On the other hand, defiance of church authority is considered to invite bad fortune and harm to one's family. Based on this, James concludes that the intensive Tongan gifting practice is supported by the notion of a reciprocal

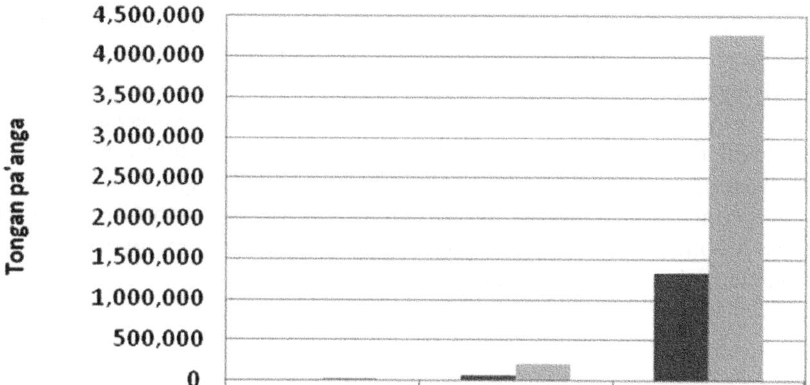


| | Village X | District X | Tongatapu Island |
|---|---|---|---|
| Faka'amu | 7,599 | 58,597 | 1334690 |
| Actual Amount | 27,173.30 | 217,175.30 | 4279711.68 |

*Fig. 3.* Comparison of *faka'amu* (apportionment budget) and actual donated amount (Siasi Uesiliana Tau'atāina 'o Tonga, 2005).

relationship between humans and God (*ibid.*). It is true that people sometimes express these beliefs outright. The distinction made by James between uneducated/educated could also be made in other ways, such as between elderly and young residents, or those of rural or urban areas, but after spending much time in Tonga it seems safe to say that this belief persists. This was reflected in the words of an elderly woman, an active member of the village church, when talking about the feasts prepared for *uike lotu* (week-long prayer events):

> See, this is how we Tongans do it. We do our best to offer great feasts and make generous donations. If I just keep all the money only for myself and I die, what does it mean? Saving money for my children? No, I don't want to do that. That's why I spend money for God and the Church. This is my way of showing my love for God. This is the Tongan way (*anga-fakatonga*) and it's very different from foreigners' ways (*anga-fakapalangi*), isn't it?[8]

When explaining her beliefs and the meanings of her religious donations, she used the terms "we Wesleyans" as "we Christians" and "we Tongans," which implies that in her mind the FWC's way is the Tongan way, which is different from foreigners' ways. This kind of speech is commonly heard among the Tongan people, most of whom are devout Christians who freely express their love. In this discourse, the virtue of dedicating one's possessions, being "full of love for others" and "devout Christians," and the "Tongan way" are thoroughly entangled with one another.[9] As the words of the elderly woman suggest, exhibiting a desire to possess money or goods will invite accusations of stinginess in Tonga, while donating – or even wasting – one's possessions brings praise. Although this reflects the Tongan concern in building an individual relationship with God, they also possess a concern for social relations with other church members, and also for secular relations with other people in general.

## CONCLUSION: WHAT UNDERLIES THE RELIGIOUS GIVING?

As has been explained here, under an elaborate system of raising funds managed by the central church office, FWC adherents are strongly motivated to collect as much money as possible and even to generate a huge surplus over the amount requested in advance by the church. In the context of gifting to the church by FWC adherents in the Kingdom of Tonga, the members are aware of how donated money is to be spent by the church organization afterwards: on the one hand, most of the money collected goes directly to the church and then is used for operating the institution or its schools, and on the other hand, the rest (the extra money local members have eagerly generated) is held by each church fund and put into their local assets. Therefore, in the long run, the adherents are eager to generate the surplus "for their own community" or, in other words, they create common property through gifting to God. This is the most conspicuously different point from a truly competitive case; the gift, or the donation, is not alienated or "destructed" by the church, but rather flows back to the local people themselves.

Inter-rivalry, or competitive relations, is the term often used to explain the driving force of people and societies maintaining a gift economy. Comparing the social structure of Tonga with that of PNG, however, the question is clearly much more subtle and obscure in the case of the former: what actually is the purpose of rivalry or competition? Thus, even though the arena of donating is pervaded by a sort of competitive atmosphere on an account of the "competitive" structure set by the church organization, it is not appropriate to simply conclude that Tongan gifting for the church is a competitive practice in the same sense of other cases, even in the Pacific region.

In conclusion, when we examine the donating activities of Tongan FWC adherents to the church, fulfilling the obligation of the community comes first in their consciousness. However, at the same time, each participant tries to create his or her own relationship between God not only by being faithful but also through such actual and salient acts of gifting. Thus, *misinale*, one of the largest economic activities endowed with religious meanings in Tonga, enables donors to accomplish the two purposes concurrently: to embody the relationship between themselves and God by fulfilling certain demands, on the one hand, and to create and confirm bonds among the members within a community, on the other. What Evans (2001, p. 137) has held up as ambivalent characteristics of Tongan local feasts can also be applied to these religious/economic activities: "First ... groups and group boundaries are formed. Secondly ... relationships within groups are defined in terms of interrelationship and mutual responsibility." This also in a sense conforms to the argument of Parry and Bloch (1989), which compares long-term cycles of money to short-term ones – the former restorative or orderly, and the latter individualistic and competitive.

To accomplish the goal amount set in advance, people cooperatively do their best to collect the money, but it always generates a surplus. Distinctive competitiveness arises between different local communities centered upon each church: the donation being well organized under the plan and the structure of the church. It cannot be denied that this institutional arrangement motivates the villagers to put themselves in a competitive mood, especially between the members of larger communities. However, at the same time, this arrangement also provides the adherents with an incomparable arena for exposing themselves not only to the imaginary "gaze" of God but also to the practical public gaze from their comembers. It is this second aspect of donation that confirms the adherents' sense of communality, which in turn is maintained and enhanced by secular practices of gift exchange in various spheres of everyday life activity. Thus, continuing such enthusiastic religious donations, Tongan FWC adherents, as has been shown earlier in this chapter, offer both their faith to God and their practical – or even pragmatic – response to the world around them through this religious, economic, and social practice.

## NOTES

1. One Tongan pa'anga (TOP) is almost equal to 0.58 US dollar (the exchange rate in June 2011).
2. Primary data for this chapter come from the author's original field research in the Kingdom of Tonga, conducted intermittently from 2005 to 2010.

3. Other significant religious activities for Tongan Methodists include (1) *Uike Lotu* (a week of prayer), the first week of every year, (2) *Toetu'u* (Easter weekend), (3) *Katoanga Misinale* (stewardship or mission giving Sunday), and (4) *Pō Le'o* (New Year's Eve) (Taumoepeau, n.d.).

4. The name of the village, *Matangi*, used in this chapter is a pseudonym selected by the author for protecting the privacy of the informants.

5. The General Conference of the FWC is held once a year. In it, the administrative performance of all member churches is reported and evaluated.

6. As with all conversations quoted in this chapter, the original words were spoken in Tongan and translated by the author.

7. Referring to the Tongan concept of *kole* (asking for favors), van der Grijp (2004, p. 164) notes: "The practice of requesting and giving *kole* is a kind of cement which keeps the members of the extended family (*kainga*) together. … Since the second half of the nineteenth century in Tonga, churches are the main demanders of *kole*."

8. The term *fakamanatu* means "to be remembered or commemorated" (Government of Tonga, 1959, p. 127).

9. There are many occasions for feasting according to the church calendar, and the family in charge of each feast is decided voluntarily.

## ACKNOWLEDGMENTS

I would like to thank all the people who helped me in Tonga with my fieldwork, the government of Tonga for permission to conduct research, and the Japan Society for the Promotion of Science (Grant-in-Aid for JSPS Fellows), the Shibusawa Fund for Ethnological Studies (Research Fund for Graduate Students), and the Resona Foundation of Asia and Oceania (Research Fund) for their generous financial support. I also want to thank the anonymous reviewers for their valuable comments and suggestions on quality improvement. Finally, this chapter would not have been accomplished without the continuous and warm support of the editor, Dr Donald Wood.

## REFERENCES

Barker, J. (Ed.). (1990). *Christianity in Oceania: Ethnographic perspectives*. ASAO monograph No. 12. London: University Press of America.

Brown, R. P. C., & Leeves, G. (2007). *Impacts of international migration and remittances on source country household incomes in small island states: Fiji and Tonga*. ESA Working Paper No. 07-13, FAO. Available at http://www.fao.org/es/esa/en/pubs_wp.htm. Retrieved on February 12, 2008.

CIA. (2007). *The world factbook*. Available at http://www.umsl.edu/services/govdocs/wofact2007/index.html. Retrieved on February 12, 2008.

Cowling, W. E. (2002). Motivations for contemporary Tongan migration. In: P. Spickard, J.L. Rondilla & D. H. Wright (Eds.), *Pacific diaspora: Island peoples in the United States and Across the Pacific* (pp. 99–117). Honolulu, HI: University of Hawai'i Press.

Decktor Korn, S. R. (1978). After the missionaries came: Denominational diversity in the Tonga Islands. In: J. A. Boutilier, D. T. Hughes & S. W. Tiffany (Eds.), *Mission, church, and sect in Oceania* (pp. 395–422). Ann Arbor, MI: University of Michigan Press.

Evans, M. (2001). *Persistence of the gift: Tongan tradition in transnational context*. Waterloo: Wilfrid Laurier University Press.

Gordon, T. (1990). Inventing the Mormon Tongan family. In: J. Barker (Ed.), *Christianity in Oceania: Ethnographic perspectives* (pp. 197–219). Lanham, MD: University Press of America.

Government of Tonga. (1959). *Dictionary: Tongan-English/English-Tongan*. Nuku'alofa: The Government Printing Press.

Grace, G. (2003). *Visit to the Free Wesleyan Church in Tonga: Report by Gabrielle Grace*, Overseas Service Secretary, January 2003. Available at www.methodist.org.uk/downloads/wc_tonga03.pdf. Retrieved on February 12, 2008.

Gregory, C. A. (1980). Gifts to men and gifts to God: Gift exchange and capital accumulation in contemporary Papua. *Man*, *15*(4), 626–652.

James, K. (1998). *Pacific Islands stakeholder participation in development: Tonga*. Washington, DC: World Bank.

Kingdom of Tonga. (2002). *Report on the household income and expenditure survey 2000/01*. Nuku'alofa: Statistics Department.

Kingdom of Tonga. (2008). *Tonga 2006 census of population and housing, Vol. 1: Administrative report and basic tables*. Statistics Department, Nuku'alofa.

Lātūkefu, S. (1974). *Church and state in Tonga: The Wesleyan Methodist missionaries and political development, 1822–1875*. Canberra: Australian National University Press.

Lee, H. (2006). 'Tonga only wants our money': The children of Tongan migrants. In: S. Firth (Ed.), *Globalization, governance and the Pacific Islands*. Canberra: ANU E Press. Available at: http://epress.anu.edu.au/ssgm/global_gov/pdf_instructions.html. Retrieved on February 12, 2008.

Parry, J., & Bloch, M. (Eds.). (1989). *Money and the morality of exchange*. Cambridge, NY: Cambridge University Press.

Puloka, T. T. M. (n.d.). Theory and practice of Misinale in the Free Wesleyan Church of Tonga. Available at http://www.gbod.org/stewardship/articles/tonga.pdf. Retrieved on February 12, 2008.

Rutherford, N. (1996). *Shirley Baker and the king of Tonga*. Honolulu, HI: University of Hawai'i Press.

Siasi Uesiliana Tau'atāina 'o Tonga. (2005). Ko e Fakamatala Pa'anga 'a e Konifelenisi Valungofulu ma Ua. Nuku'alofa.

Taumoepeau, R.'A. (n.d.). The worship life of the Tongan people. Available at http://www.une.edu.au/chaplaincy/uniting/finding_god/tongan.pdf. Retrieved on February 12, 2008.

van der Grijp, P. (1993). *Islanders of the south: Production, kinship and ideology in the Polynesian kingdom of Tonga*. Leiden: KITLV Press.

van der Grijp, P. (2004). *Identity and development: Tongan culture, agriculture, and the perenniality of gift*. Leiden: KITLV Press.

# PART III
# EXPERIMENTAL STUDIES – BEHAVIOR UNDER CONTROLLED CONDITIONS

# ARE RELIGIOUS INDIVIDUALS MORE GENEROUS, TRUSTING, AND COOPERATIVE? AN EXPERIMENTAL TEST OF THE EFFECT OF RELIGION ON PROSOCIALITY

Brian Paciotti, Peter Richerson, Billy Baum, Mark Lubell, Tim Waring, Richard McElreath, Charles Efferson and Ed Edsten

## ABSTRACT

*We investigated the effect of religion on generosity, interpersonal trust, and cooperation by using games developed by experimental economists (Dictator, Trust, and Public Goods). In these experiments, individuals were paired or grouped with unknown strangers to test the degree to which religion promotes prosocial behavior. We evaluated group- and individual-level effects of religion on prosocial behavior across the three games. Although playing the games in a religious setting showed no overall difference as compared to a secular setting, we did find a weak association*

**The Economics of Religion: Anthropological Approaches**
**Research in Economic Anthropology, Volume 31, 267–305**

**ISSN: 0190-1281/doi:10.1108/S0190-1281(2011)0000031014**

*between some individual-level dimensions of religiosity and behavior in some of the games. The weak association between religion and behavior is consistent with theory and empirical studies using similar measures – the anonymous pairing and grouping of the economic games may moderate individual-level effects of religion. Our research is a strong complement to the empirical literature because the three studies involved a large and diverse sample and used sensitive instruments that have been found to reliably measure prosocial behavior.*

## INTRODUCTION

Humans are often generous, trusting, and cooperative within large groups. Although folk sociology attributes much of prosocial behavior to religion, divergent research perspectives exist today. Dawkins (2006) believes that religion satisfies some individual cognitive problems, but he/she generally believes that religion is a source of conflict. Numerous researchers, however, argue that religious experience, participation, and belief function to promote prosocial behavior (Batson, Schoenrade, & Ventis, 1993; Beit-Hallahmi & Argyle, 1997; Momen, 1999). Some highlight the importance of religious morality and note that versions of the Golden Rule, "Do unto others as you would have others do unto you," are part of all major religions (Batson et al., 1993, p. 331; Wilson, 2002). Other researchers argue that religion mainly promotes cooperation and prosocial behavior within culturally defined in-groups (Iannaccone & Berman, 2006; Ruffle & Sosis, 2006) rather than supporting an indiscriminant propensity to behave prosocially.

The purpose of this study is to evaluate the degree to which religion promotes generosity, trust, and cooperation between anonymously paired strangers. We evaluated: (1) if individuals playing the games after a religious meeting were more prosocial than individuals playing the games after a secular meeting, (2) the degree to which individual-level religiosity measures correlate with prosocial gameplay, and (3) how much in-group boundaries influence the willingness to share with and trust a person with different religious beliefs. To measure prosocial behavior, we paired strangers with each other to play one of three types of games. The Dictator game measures generosity; the first player is given the opportunity to send some, part, or all of a 10 dollars windfall to an anonymous second player. The second player is later given any money that was sent to them. In the Trust game, the first player can send some portion of 10 dollars to a second player. This amount is doubled by the experimenter and allocated to the second player. Without knowing what amount was sent, the second player then decides how much they want to return to the first player for all of the possible amounts that might have been sent to them (Camerer, 2003; Kagel & Roth, 1995). Finally, the Public Goods game is a well-known game to measure cooperation. In this game, players can contribute money to a public fund; contributions are doubled and distributed equally among all of the players regardless of their individual contribution. After completing the games, participants filled out a detailed questionnaire that included demographic information such as age and gender. In addition, the survey incorporated numerous scales designed to measure various dimensions of religiosity, as well as personality constructs such as the "Machiavellian Personality" scale that measures a propensity toward self-serving behavior (Christie & Geis, 1970). We had a great deal of empirical leverage to evaluate the association between religion and prosocial behavior; participants contributed varying amounts in the games, and scored differently on a variety of personality and religiosity scales.

## *The Origin and Evolution of Religious Prosociality*

Early theorists from anthropology, sociology, and psychology had strong interests in religion (Durkheim, 1915; James, 1902; Tylor, 1871). Much work on the topic of religion and morality has been conducted since then (Batson et al., 1993), yet diverse perspectives remain. Social psychologists have conducted empirical research to understand the diverse social and psychological dimensions of religion. For example, Batson et al. (1993) evaluate if religion, like empathy, promotes altruistic behavior, and conclude that certain expressions of religious behavior may promote prosocial behavior. They argue that the motives leading to altruism, however, are likely to be egoistic. Researchers have also studied religion from the perspective of rational choice theory developed by economists (Stark & Bainbridge, 1997; Stark & Finke, 2000). This approach assumes that religion involves cost-benefit reasoning in which people make rational exchanges with imagined supernatural agents for scarce or unobtainable resources. Although religious participation offers benefits, the costs of ritual and other religious activities are substantial. The rational choice perspective posits that nonmaterial and humanistic rewards could maintain prosocial behavior, but does not fully account for the origins of such rewards. Finally, Durkheim (1915) favored a functionalist perspective in which prosocial behavior and cooperation were a fundamental problem for people to resolve. In this view, religion is a crucial mechanism to allow humans to function in harmonious and coordinated units (Wilson, 2002). However, like rational choice theory, functionalist theory was vague about the origins of the institutions capable of maintaining prosocial behavior.

Whereas most of the theory from social psychology, economics, and sociology is proximate in origin, evolutionary theory seeks explanations about the ultimate origins of behavior and social institutions. For example, if religious beliefs and moral systems are assumed to generate cooperative behavior, this begs the ultimate question of how such moral systems emerged. Evolutionists seek to discover the processes by which genes, culture, or gene-culture coevolution could possibly favor prosocial psychological dispositions and adherence to prosocial norms and institutions. Darwin (1874) suggested that selection at the level of tribes during primeval times had been responsible for prosocial "instincts" such as sympathy and loyalty to the tribe. But he thought that education, public opinion, religious institutions and the like had made the most important contributions to moral advancement in more recent times. Darwin, and more recent evolutionary theorists (Alexander, 1987) generally accorded religion an important, but proximate, role in the evolution of moral systems.

Wilson (2002) reviews several evolutionary hypotheses that might account for religious behavior. The clearest division is between adaptive and nonadaptive approaches. Adaptationists assume that religion evolved because the costs of religious behavior were outweighed by the benefits. Nonadaptative approaches do not presuppose that religion offers any substantial benefits in current times – some evolutionary psychologists (Atran, 2002; Boyer, 1994; Dawkins, 2006) stress that religion is likely a by-product of other evolved cognitive processes. For example, it is plausible that human self-awareness evolved because it gave individuals a survival advantage, yet such an adaptation allowed people to worry about their own deaths. Wilson (2002) suggests that from this perspective religion might have evolved to help people deal with such fears.

Norenzayan and Shariff (2008) summarize the literature related to the origins of prosocial behavior in terms of two theoretical approaches: religion as a cultural by-product and cultural group selection. First, the cultural by-product theory posits that human psychology evolved in the Pleistocene to solve problems such as inferring the thoughts of others and having sensitivity to one's prosocial reputation within the social group. Cultural beliefs associated with religion, if compatible with this evolved psychology, could then spread via social learning mechanisms. Second, cultural group selection[1] is a process that created religious cultural norms that encouraged prosocial behavior within the group, and prevented the group's public goods from being exploited by free riders.[2] This theory posits that religious institutions evolve to promote cooperation and sharing among in-group members more than people in out-groups (Paciotti & Hadley, 2003; Ruffle & Sosis, 2006). One reason to suspect that institutions will not evolve to favor out-group members is that it can be risky for individuals to advertise their prosocial intentions outside of their local group. Evolutionary theorists have discovered that advertising prosocial behavior can make an individual a victim of exploiters (McElreath, Boyd, & Richerson, 2003), and advertising antisocial behavior makes you a target for group-level punishment (Boyd, Gintis, Bowles, & Richerson, 2003). Thus, it is likely that people signal their intentions to be altruistic, trusting, and cooperative *within* an institutional setting, yet are cautious about this behavior when interacting with outsiders. As a result, even though a group may share common religious beliefs or experiences, they are unlikely to advertise these preferences to strangers who are outside of social networks capable of effective social control.

## BEHAVIORAL STUDIES OF RELIGION AND PROSOCIAL BEHAVIOR

There is empirical support for a link between prosocial behavior and religion. People who report being more religious also report stringent moral standards (Batson et al., 1993). There is also evidence that religion tends to reduce criminal behavior (Stark & Bainbridge, 1997). Nearly all of 60 studies published on the topic of religion and crime have found strong to moderate negative relationships (Baier & Wright, 2001) – the pattern holds at the regional level in the U.S. (Stark & Bainbridge, 1997) and among a sample of 13 industrial nations (Ellis & Peterson, 1996). The experimental evidence is less clear. Batson et al. (1993) reviewed nine studies and found positive, albeit weak, correlations between self-reports of helping a stranger and involvement with religion. When behavioral measures of helping were used, however, only one in five studies was significant.

### *Dimensions of Religiosity: Intrinsic, Extrinsic, Quest*

Social psychologists have produced an extensive literature addressing how religion and prosocial behavior interact with various dimensions of religiosity. Batson et al. (1993) used three dimensions of religiosity – *intrinsic, extrinsic*, and *quest* – to predict altruism and prejudice. The intrinsic dimension relates to religions as ends in themselves. Intrinsically motivated individuals are thus thought to have a closer relationship to "God" or their version of the Divine. In addition, they adhere most closely to prosocial religious doctrines, and thus are expected to be the most helpful or cooperative. Individuals measuring high on the quest dimension of religiosity (religion as a source of ongoing exploration) are predicted to have the most universal prosocial attitudes (Ibid.). Using six clever experiments, Batson et al. (1993) concluded, like other researchers, that intrinsic religion is associated with helping behavior. They suspected, however, that the behavior is not a source of true compassion that leads to altruism as scholars had previously suggested (Allport & Ross, 1967). Although the intrinsic types often behave in a more helpful manner, they seem to be motivated by their own need to *appear* helpful; these participants stop and help a stooge even when that person denies needing help (Batson & Gray, 1981). This may explain why studies using self-reports of helping behavior are stronger than behavioral studies. Finally, Batson et al. (1993) argue that individuals scoring higher on the quest dimension may be the most helpful and have motivations that are truly "other-regarding."

Other researchers have stressed the linkage between religious and antisocial behavior such as prejudice and extremism (Allport & Ross, 1967; Dawkins, 2006; Iannaccone & Berman, 2006). This view highlights how within-group religious boundaries can promote between-group conflicts. Some evidence supports this view. Some individuals scoring low on intrinsic and quest religiosity fit into the extrinsic dimension of religiosity – religion is a means. For example, extrinsic individuals likely attend religious services or meetings for personal or social goals (i.e., babysitting services, enjoyment of singing and socializing) rather than to be closer to God. Batson et al. (1993), like many others, found that individuals scoring high on the extrinsic dimension are *less* helpful. As discussed above, organizations that provide public goods to their members are at risk of being exploited by individuals who do not contribute to the group, yet take advantage of the benefits. Individuals need not believe in their religion, as long as they display correct behavior and signal their commitment to the group. This view may explain the existence of the extrinsic dimension of religion; people see the value of displaying religious signals even if they do not really believe in them.

### *Evidence from Experimental Economics*

Experimental economists have developed games to test the assumptions about human motivations built into economic models. A wide variety of games have revealed a substantial amount of individual variation in strategies adopted. The use of the Ultimatum game to test whether people behave as selfish rationalists is a classic example (Kagel & Roth, 1995). Although some skepticism about the use of experimental games is warranted (Hagen & Hammerstein, 2006; Sosis, 2005), the methodology holds promise for untangling the mechanisms of prosocial behavior because the games often result in considerable individual- and group-level variation in how participants play the games. Moreover, experimental economists are devising experimental designs to explore what types of individual-level traits (e.g., personality) are associated with this individual variation.[3]

Religion has been measured in a variety of experimental games, and some authors have found religion to predict game behavior. Henrich et al. (2010) incorporated religion into a follow-up study among 15 culturally diverse populations using three experimental games (Dictator, Ultimatum, and Third-Party Punishment). The authors evaluated the impact of market integration (percentage of household calories from markets) and religion (Christianity/Islam vs. other tribal religions) on how people played the games, after controlling for other individual- and group-level factors. Similar to their previous study (Henrich et al., 2005), they found a strong positive relationship between market integration and behavioral fairness as measured by the games. In addition, religion had a substantial effect. Participation in Christianity or Islam on average increased offers in Dictator and Ultimatum between 6% and 10%. Another study explored the degree to which implicitly activated God concepts influenced prosocial behavior in an anonymous Dictator game. Shariff and Norenzayan (2007) presented participants with scrambled-sentence tasks; those in the priming condition had religious target words (e.g., God, spirit, divine, sacred). They found that participants in the priming condition gave more than twice the amount of money in the Dictator game as compared to participants in the nonpriming treatment. In a follow-up study, they added an additional priming treatment that contained words related to secular moral institutions; the secular priming had nearly the same effect as the religious priming.

Another set of studies have not found a strong association between religion and behavior in the Dictator and Ultimatum games. Ben-Ner, Putterman, Kong, and Magan (2004) found that a history of religious training leads to greater offers in a two-part Dictator game, but is not associated with reciprocation by the other player. Tan (2006), using Dictator and Ultimatum games among German participants, found that his overall measure of religiosity that combined various dimensions (belief, experience, and ritual) was not predictive of gameplay. He argued that the different dimensions of religiosity produce counteracting effects that cancel out; offers in the Dictator game are positively associated with having a religious belief, but are negatively associated with participation in church-related activities. These results mirror the intrinsic and extrinsic dimensions described above. Using a setting similar to the Dictator game, Eckel and Grossman (2003, 2004) did not find a significant difference in the contributions to secular charities among participants who do or do not attend church services regularly.

A growing number of studies have evaluated the effect of religion on trust and cooperation. One of the first studies was conducted by Orbell, Goldman, Mulford, and Dawes (1992). They used a multiperson Prisoners' Dilemma game among participants from Logan, Utah, but did not find that religious subjects, in general, were more cooperative. Mormons with greater self-reported church attendance, however, were more cooperative. Sosis and Ruffle (2003) administered a two-person common pool resource experiment among secular and religious Israeli kibbutzim. They found that Orthodox males that went to synagogue daily were more likely than non-Orthodox members to behave cooperatively by making smaller claims on the common pool. This effect was not found among female participants, and the authors argue that this is likely the result of females having a less prominent role in the Orthodox rituals. The authors conclude that participation in religious ritual increases in-group cooperation. Tan and Vogel (2008) investigated the relationship between individual religiosity and trust. Assuming that religion is multidimensional, they used a survey instrument developed by De Jong, Faulkner, and Warland (1976) to measure three core dimensions (belief, experience, and ritual). Using a variation of the Trust game, they tested if religious people are trusted more, and if religious people are more trustworthy. A proposer was given the opportunity to send an unknown responder money, and once tripled by the experimenter, the responder could return any amount to the proposer. Proposers sent more money to responders whom they perceived to be more religious. Moreover, the effect was greater when proposers reported being religious. Religion also promoted trustworthiness; religious responders were more likely to send money back to proposers. In contrast to Tan and Vogel (2008), Anderson, Mellor, and Milyo (2010) found self-identified religious affiliation to be unrelated to behavior in Trust games, but found a weak association between church attendance and contributions in the Public Goods game. Participants who reported higher attendance of religious services offered 30% more, on average, than participants reporting lower church attendance. Contrary to the folk sociology claims of religion causing more prosocial behavior, they argue that their findings, in general, do not provide strong evidence that religion makes people more cooperative, trusting, or trustworthy.

Johansson-Stenman, Mahmud, and Martinsson (2009) conducted a two-person Trust game to evaluate if social distance would influence trust between Hindus and Muslims in rural Bangladesh. Although there appeared to be an in-group effect associated with trust in their survey questions, in the Trust game they did not find that participants were more trusting of partners from their own groups. Finally, although religion was not the focus of their study, Fehr, Fischbacher, von Rosenbladt, Schupp, and Wagner (2002) used a bilateral Trust game among German subjects and found Catholics to be more trusting than non-Catholics.

## PREDICTIONS

Norenzayan and Shariff (2008) offer three predictions relevant to this research. First, individuals who worship vigilant moral deities will have greater concerns about their prosocial reputation. Second, religious situations should activate or "prime" thoughts of moral deities, and thus increase prosocial behavior. Third, reliable signals of religious behavior and devotion should promote trust and cooperation. We agree that these are plausible predictions, but stress that these effects will be the strongest within religious groups. Thus, if religion does promote prosocial behavior such as that exemplified by the golden rule, any such effects will operate, at best, within the religious group. This thesis may help explain why in general, experiments conducted by social psychologists show a moderate effect of religion on prosocial behavior (Batson et al., 1993), whereas experimental games evidence mixed results. A general difference between these traditions is that the experiments conducted by social psychologists did not involve anonymous interactions, and often were conducted in the context of religious universities in which participants interacted with their peers. We suspect that the greater variability in results from the experimental economic studies is influenced by the anonymous pairing used in most experimental games, which causes individuals often to be paired with people from out-group populations such as different universities or villages.

In our research design people interact with strangers, and religious belief and practice should have little or no effect on prosocial behavior in our economic games. To whatever extent people are prosocial, that behavior is expected to be the outcome of innate prosocial instincts plus *nonreligious* institutions that govern prosocial expectations and behavior in our population.

## STUDY 1: DICTATOR GAME AMONG UNIVERSITY STUDENTS

The first study involved university students who played a version of Dictator in which neither the researcher nor the recipient would be able to match the identity of the proposer with their decision. The group of participants played the Dictator game among strangers in a neutral university setting. Given the strong context in this design to prevent even the researcher from knowing participants' decisions, we expected to find little or no association between gameplay and religiosity measures. As discussed by Norenzayan and Shariff (2008), we expected that individual religiosity variables would be important only when an individual's reputation could be influenced as a result of others knowing their game decision. Like the general findings from Batson et al. (1993), prosocial behavior should be uncommon among religious individuals when the social context does not allow them to gain prosocial recognition.

### *Participants*

Seventy-five participants were recruited through the UC Davis psychology department subject pool (see Table 1, second column). Students were given class credit for participating, but were not informed about the possibility of obtaining money until after the experiment had begun.

### *Design*

Upon completing consent forms, all participants were seated around a large table in an on-campus room. Participants played the Dictator game following the elaborate double-blind procedures pioneered by Hoffman, McCabe, Shachat, and Smith (1994) and modified by Ben-Ner et al. (2004). This procedure gives individuals complete privacy when making their decision, and gives them almost complete anonymity from the experimenter.[4] The experimenter first explained the rules of the game by reading word

***Table 1.*** Summary Statistics for Study 1 and Study 2.

| | Study 1 | Study 2 | | |
|---|---|---|---|---|
| | | Aggregate | Secular | Religious |
| N | 75 | 183 | 73 | 110 |
| Dictator amount | 2.3 (2.5) | 4.8 (3.1) | 3.6 (2.5) | 5.5 (3.1) |
| Trust amount | | | 2.4 (1.6) | 3.5 (1.6) |
| Age | 20.9 (4.6) | 38.9 (22.3) | 41.7 (26.8) | 37.1 (18.7) |
| Post-game | 14.0 (2.7) | 14.7 (2.4) | 14.4 (2.7) | 15.0 (2.1) |
| Intrinsic | 13.8 (4.5) | 16.1 (4.3) | 13.0 (4.2) | 18.2 (2.9) |
| Extrinsic | 17.1 (4.6) | 15.8 (3.6) | 15.6 (3.7) | 15.9 (3.6) |
| Quest | 17.6 (4.2) | 18.8 (4.5) | 17.2 (4.7) | 19.9 (4.1) |
| Mach | 79.2 (6.3) | 79.3 (6.4) | 81.2 (7.1) | 78.0 (5.6) |
| Female/Male (#) | 42/33 | 97/86 | 34/39 | 63/47 |
| White/Asian/Hispanic (#) | 33/35/7 | 146/25/12 | 170/9/4 | 159/16/8 |

Mean (standard deviation).

for word from a script. Participants were informed that they had been paired with an anonymous stranger so that they could play a game with them. It was made clear that both they and the other player would receive 10 dollars as a show-up fee regardless of their decisions in the games. No information other than that given on the script was given to the participants. Second, participants were given an envelope with 10 one-dollar bills and 10 slips of paper cut in the size of bills. A "student assistant," who was chosen at random from the group, then instructed individuals to go one by one to a privacy station. Having the student assistant run the experiment was designed to minimize participants' suspicion that the experimenters might be manipulating the procedures. At the privacy station, participants had the opportunity to take any number of dollar bills that they wanted to keep for themselves by putting these in an envelope, and then in their pocket or purse. Any money sent to the recipient was put in a separate envelope, along with slips of paper, so that there was a total of 10 slips: dollars, paper, or some combination. The student assistant then directed the participants to put their envelopes in a box. When all the envelopes were collected, he or she brought the box to another assistant hired by the experimenters who was waiting outside of the room. The student assistant and hired assistant then opened the envelopes and recorded the amount sent. After documenting the decisions, both assistants walked to a neighboring campus building to deliver the envelopes to the recipients waiting in another room.

### *Results*

To reduce the problem of colinearity among our numerous independent variables we conducted a cluster analysis.[5] Table 2 provides definitions and references for the questionnaire items considered in the analysis. Like previous researchers, we found that dimensions of religiosity (intrinsic, extrinsic, and quest) were both orthogonal and reliable. A large and clearly defined cluster included intrinsic religion, early religion, religious participation, orthodox religion, and current religious category. Based on statistical and theoretical criteria, we chose intrinsic religion as the variable that best represented of all these measures. Social desirability as measured by the Marlowe–Crowne scale clustered with the Machiavellian scale. We deemed the latter scale to be the best statistical choice and the most closely associated with theory.

Because contributions were limited to amounts between 0 and 10 dollars in the Dictator game, we adopted a Tobit regression model.[6] We also fitted Tobit models with participants entered as random effects to capture unmeasured individual heterogeneity. Finally, as a method to identify the robustness of our results, we fit OLS regression models. To limit spurious results that occur when fitting many models, we adopted the information-theoretical approach advocated by Burnham and Anderson (2002). This paradigm posits the need to select a priori a subset of models based on theory and experience from prior research. Once candidate models are selected, Akaiki statistics (or other post-estimation measures) can be used to compare models. Because our samples were small, we fit the $AIC_c$ statistic, and from this value calculated the difference between each $AIC_c$ value and the "best" model $AIC_c$ value, or the $\Delta AIC_c$. AIC statistics penalize models with more parameters based on information-theoretic reasoning. Next, we calculated the relative likelihood for every model – given our data – with an Akaiki weight ($w_i$). Of course, the method provides no way of knowing which model might be a true model; the weighted values simply provide a probability that some models are more likely than other models to explain the data. Finally, we also assessed the model assumptions and goodness of fit for all candidate models.

Like other researchers, we find that a large proportion of participants sent at least some money in the Dictator game, even though the game was anonymous between participants and even the experimenter. Fig. 1 illustrates that although 25 subjects contributed no money, the majority of participants sent a substantial amount of money to their paired partner. We fitted a full model with all of the independent variables as well as two

***Table 2.*** Candidate and Final Variables (Bold) Selected for Models.

| Variable | Definition | Items in Scale | Reference |
|---|---|---|---|
| **Age** | Age in years | | |
| **Gender** | Male/Female | | |
| Secular participation (Study 1 only) | Number of secular groups participated in: (1) high school and (2) at present | | |
| Economic classes (Study 1 only) | Number of economics courses taken | | Frank, Gilovich, and Regan (1993) |
| **Intrinsic religion** | Religiosity measure: religion is an ends in itself (e.g., get close to "God") | 9 items; Yes, No, Uncertain | Maltby and Lewis (1996); Revised Age-Universal Scale |
| **Extrinsic religion** | Religiosity measure: religion is a means (e.g., attend church to meet people or get social support) | 11 items; Yes, No, Uncertain | Maltby and Lewis (1996); Revised Age-Universal Scale |
| **Quest religion** | Religiosity measure: religion as a source of ongoing exploration | 12 items; Yes, No, Uncertain | Batson, Schoenrade, and Ventis (1993) |
| Early religion (Intrinsic cluster, dropped) | When growing up, how often did you: (1) attend religious training (2) think about God (3) say grace (4) pray (5) attend religious services | 8-point scale | |
| Religious participation (Intrinsic cluster, dropped) | During the past year, how often did you: (1) attend religious services (2) attend religious meetings (3) read or study holy writings (4) make financial contributions to a religious organization | 8-point scale | |
| Orthodox religion (Intrinsic cluster, dropped) | (1) Views of religious texts (2) Degree to which prayer is "speaking to God," directing thoughts to higher power, meditation, self-help, or not meaningful | 10 items; 5-point Likert scale | |

***Table 2.*** *(Continued)*

| Variable | Definition | Items in Scale | Reference |
|---|---|---|---|
| Religious category today (Intrinsic cluster, dropped) | Category the best describes my religion today | 6 categories | |
| **Machiavellian** | Tendency to deceive and manipulate others for personal gain | 20 items; 5-point Likert scale | Christie and Geis (1970) |
| Marlowe–Crowne scale of social desirability (Mach Cluster, dropped) | Tendency of participant to project favorable images of oneself | 13 items; Yes, No | Reynolds (1982) |
| **Post-game** (Dictator and Trust games) | Degree to which participant self-reports to understand directions, and trusted that the experimenter would preserve anonymity and send money to other participant | 5 items; 5-point Likert scale | Eckel and Grossman (2000) |
| **Religious/Secular group [Rel/Sec]** (Study 2 only ) | Participant was recruited and participated with a: (1) religious or (2) secular group | | |
| **In-group** (Study 2 only) | Participants given information about the religious beliefs of the person whom they were paired with | | |

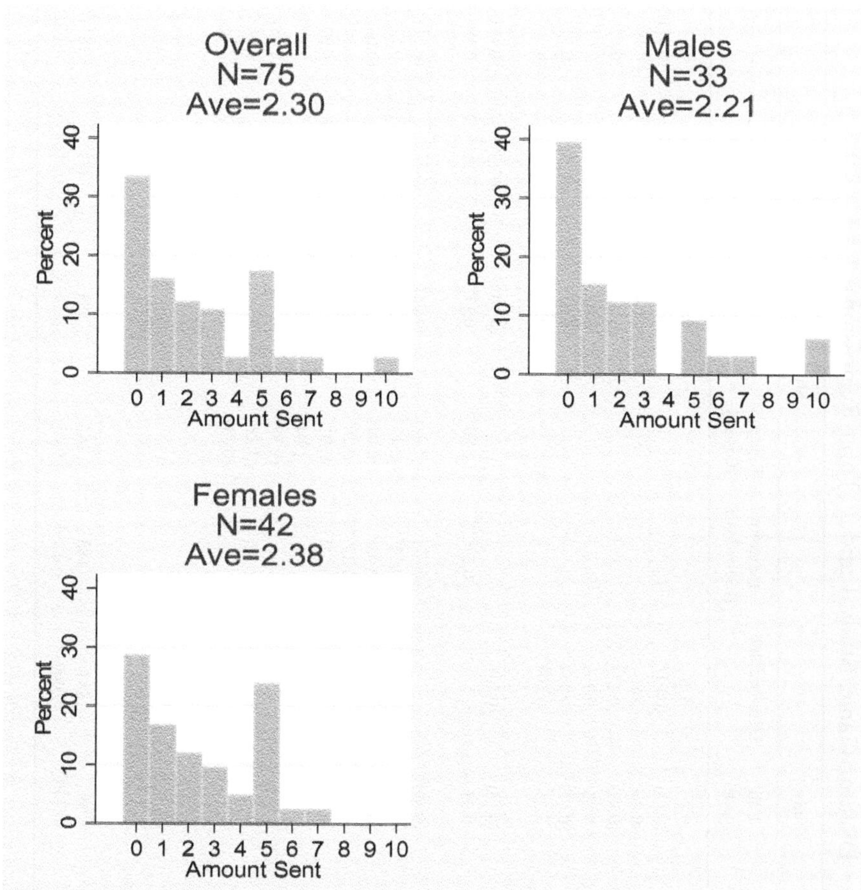


*Fig. 1.* Study 1 – Dictator Game.

additional models that included only demographic variables or only religious variables. Akaiki weights and goodness of fit statistics indicated that none of the models fitted the data well. Table 3 (third column) presents the results of the full Tobit regression model. We obtained similar results in both the random effects model and the OLS model. In this model, as well as other submodels (e.g., demographic only, religious only), none of the variables reached statistical significance. Since the sample is relatively small, it is worth noting that some of the variables are associated with the Dictator

**Table 3.** Dictator Game, Study 1 and 2 (Tobit Regression).

| Variable Types | Variables | Study 1 | Study 2 | | | | | |
|---|---|---|---|---|---|---|---|---|
| | | Full model | Demographic | Religion (Individual) | Religion (Group) | Demographic + Religion | Interaction 1 | Interaction 2 |
| Demographic | Age | 0.2 | 0.01 | | | 0.01 | 0.01 | 0.01 |
| | | (0.1) | (0.01) | | | (0.01) | (0.01) | (0.01) |
| | Gender | −0.28 | −0.25 | | | −0.14 | −0.13 | −0.13 |
| | | (0.83) | (0.67) | | | (0.62) | (0.62) | (0.62) |
| | Machiavellian | 0.02 | −0.06 | | | 0.02 | 0.02 | 0.01 |
| | | (0.07) | (0.05) | | | (0.05) | (0.05) | (0.05) |
| Demand characteristics | Post-game | 0.25 | 0.40** | | | 0.28* | 0.28* | 0.28* |
| | | (0.15) | (0.13) | | | (0.13) | (0.13) | (0.13) |
| Religion (Individual) | Intrinsic | 0.08 | | 0.27*** | 0.20* | 0.17* | 0.15 | 0.18 |
| | | (0.09) | | (0.07) | (0.08) | (0.08) | (0.11) | (0.11) |
| | Extrinsic | −0.07 | | −0.20* | −0.17* | −0.17* | −0.17* | −0.17* |
| | | (0.1) | | (0.08) | (0.08) | (0.08) | (0.08) | (0.08) |
| | Quest | −0.11 | | 0.23*** | 0.20** | 0.18** | 0.18** | 0.18** |
| | | 0.11 | | (0.07) | (0.07) | (0.07) | (0.07) | (0.07) |
| Religion (group) | In-group pairing | | | | 1.04 | 1.18* | 0.5 | 1.17* |
| | | | | | (0.58) | (0.58) | (2.31) | (0.58) |
| | Rel/Sec group | | | | 1.28 | 1.34 | 1.36 | 1.66 |
| | | | | | (0.74) | (0.75) | (0.75) | (2.83) |
| Interaction effects | In-group pairing × intrinsic | | | | | | 0.04 | |
| | | | | | | | (0.14) | |
| | Rel/Sec group × intrinsic | | | | | | −0.02 | |
| | *N* | **75** | **183** | **183** | **183** | **181** | **181** | **181** |
| | Akaiki weight ($w_i$) | 0.1492 | 0.000 | 0.0220 | 0.05 | 0.5614 | 0.1864 | 0.1791 |

$^{*}p<0.05$; $^{**}p<0.01$; $^{***}p<0.001$. Standard errors in parentheses.

game in predicted ways. The intrinsic dimension is positive and the extrinsic dimension is negative. However, unexpectedly, we find a negative, albeit nonsignificant effect for quest.

## STUDY 2: DICTATOR AND TRUST GAMES IN AN ORGANIZATIONAL SETTING

This study involved groups of organizational members ranging from 6 to 14 people and was conducted in organizational settings. This study had three important features: (1) all of the groups were recruited through an organization in which they held membership (either religious or secular); (2) the experiment was conducted immediately *after* an organization service or meeting; and (3) the sample included a large number of nonstudents. Our objective with this study was, first, to prime religious versus secular organizational doctrines and values and, second, to invoke any desires people had to maintain the reputation of their group. This priming ought to increase the effects of religious and secular culture on play in the games. Similar to Norenzayan and Shariff (2008), we posit that the link between religion and prosocial behavior is context sensitive. To evaluate the degree to which religious organizations can promote prosocial behavior beyond secular ones, we played the games after an organizational meeting among comembers. We did not expect participants in the religious context to be more prosocial than participants in a secular context.

A second important aspect of this study is that we purposely gave participants information about the religious beliefs of their paired partners in an attempt to test the hypothesis that religion can promote prosocial behavior between different religious populations or out-groups. We predicted that people would be more generous and trusting to paired partners that had similar beliefs about religion.

### *Participants*

One hundred and eighty three participants were recruited by contacting leaders of religious and secular groups (see Table 1). About half of the groups were UC Davis student organizations (churches: 5 groups, $N = 49$; secular clubs: 5 groups, $N = 41$) and the others were community organizations from Davis, CA (churches: 6 groups, $N = 62$; secular clubs: 4 groups, $N = 31$). We explained to the leaders the general goals of our experiment, and asked them for help recruiting about a dozen of their members following an organizational meeting or service. We did not provide any particular information about our theoretical motives, and stressed that we would give all of the groups a debriefing after they had participated.

### *Design*

Participants played the Dictator game by circling a number on a sheet of paper to instruct the experimenter how much they wanted to send the other player. After making a decision in this game, participants played the Trust game – the first player has the opportunity to send some portion of 10 dollars to a second player. This amount was doubled by the experimenter, and allocated to the second player. Without knowing what amount was sent, the second player then decided how much they wanted to return to the first player for all of the possible amounts that might have been sent to them. The Trust game may measure a tolerance for risk, but likely reflects the degree to which the first player expects the second player to be trustworthy, and return a fair portion. To facilitate a questionnaire-style of administration, a set of recipients for the Dictator and Trust games had already filled out a questionnaire and given us a mailing address so that we could send them money at a later time. These "second-movers" had no decision to make in the Dictator game (they simply received whatever money, if any, was sent to them). However, in the Trust game, these players had to provide amounts that they wanted to *return* to the first player, for all of the possible amounts (0–5 dollars in 50-cent increments) that this person might send at a later time. Using this protocol adapted from Fehr et al. (2002), we were able to immediately pay the Dictators and the first players in the Trust games, and send in the mail any money that their paired partner had received.

This study also included an in-group framing treatment. Half of the participants in each group were given a sentence in their instructions stating that their paired partner had "Religious beliefs and a relationship with God." The other half of the participants read a statement saying that their paired partner had "No religious beliefs and no relationship with God." We acknowledge that this treatment is a simplistic way to manipulate the scope of in-group boundaries; people may be concerned about the type of religion a person is from (i.e., denominations of Christianity or Islam), or how they personally approach their religion. This treatment, however, was designed to evaluate the degree to which prosocial behavior is influenced by a general religious category that extends beyond personal social networks.

After the games were completed, participants were instructed to complete the questionnaire (averaging about 45 minutes). Each subject was then paid in cash and reminded that no deception was used in the study.

## *Results*

Although there were no overall mean differences between the Dictator offers in the two groups, it is unusual that a large proportion of participants from the religious organizations gave away the full 10-dollar amount in the Dictator game (see Fig. 2). In the Trust game, participants from religious organizations sent slightly more money on average than those from the secular organizations (see Fig. 3).

For Dictator and Trust, we used similar statistical methods as described above to fit the full model, and a small set of demographic and religious submodels. We found that only a handful of models had a strong likelihood of being a good model. We were surprised to find that only models with religious variables had high likelihood values and associated Akaiki weights. Table 4 presents the full model that included all of the independent variables. This full model was clearly the best in the post-estimation analysis. The other models presented had small weights and are thus not plausible candidates to explain the data. The results concerning religiosity are highly consistent with Batson et al. (1993). Intrinsic and quest are fairly strong and significant predictors of Dictator gameplay, whereas extrinsic religion is negatively associated with Dictator (see Fig. 4 for bivariate correlations). These variables are consistent across all of the models. In the model that includes demographic measures and both types of religious variables, in-group pairing is also positive, reflecting that individuals who were paired with a religious person sent more money. However, we were surprised that the interaction between intrinsic religiosity and in-group pairing was not significant (Interaction 1). Thus, we found no evidence of an in-group effect; people who were more religious did not seem to favor sending more (or less) money to another religious (or nonreligious) individual. In addition, the interaction between intrinsic religion and the type of group that the respondent participated in was also not significant (Interaction 2). Finally, our "post-game" questions that controlled for the demand characteristics of the experiment are positive and significant. These questions measure the degree to which participants self-reported to understand the game instructions and trust that the experimenter would preserve personal anonymity and send money to other participant.

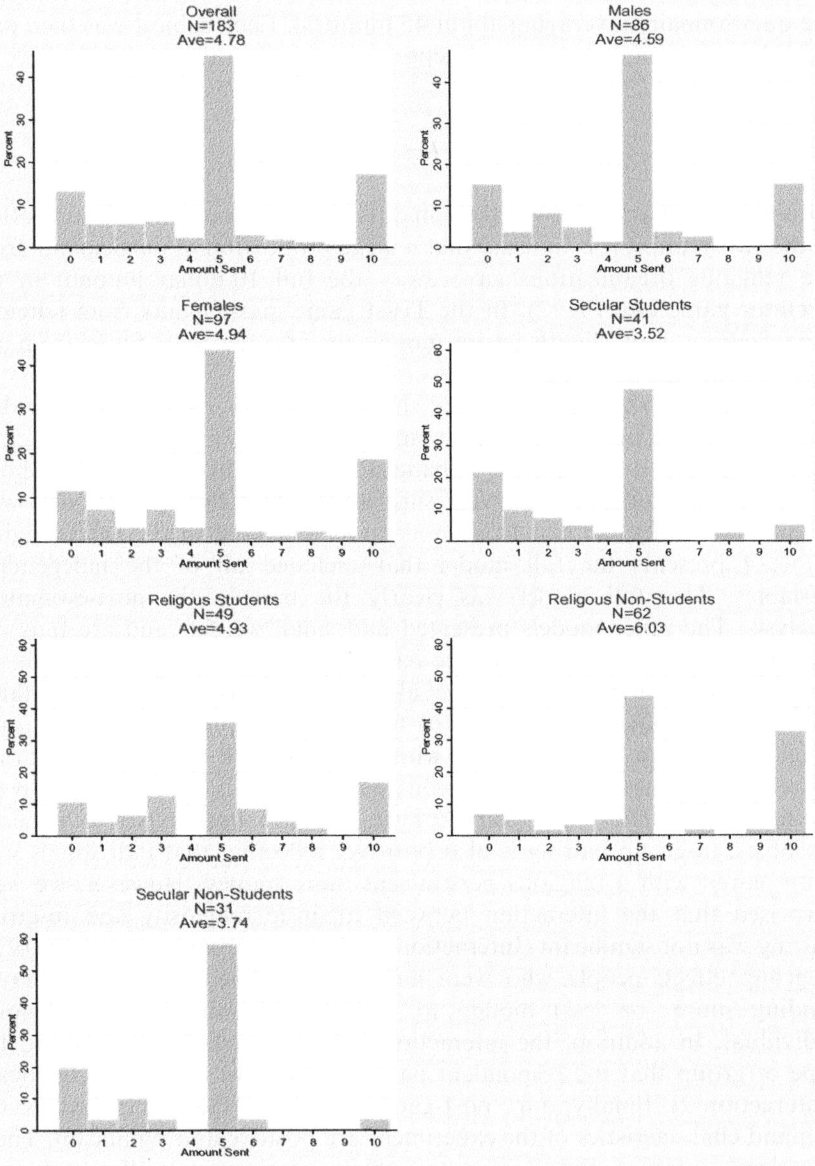


*Fig. 2.* Study 2 – Dictator Game.

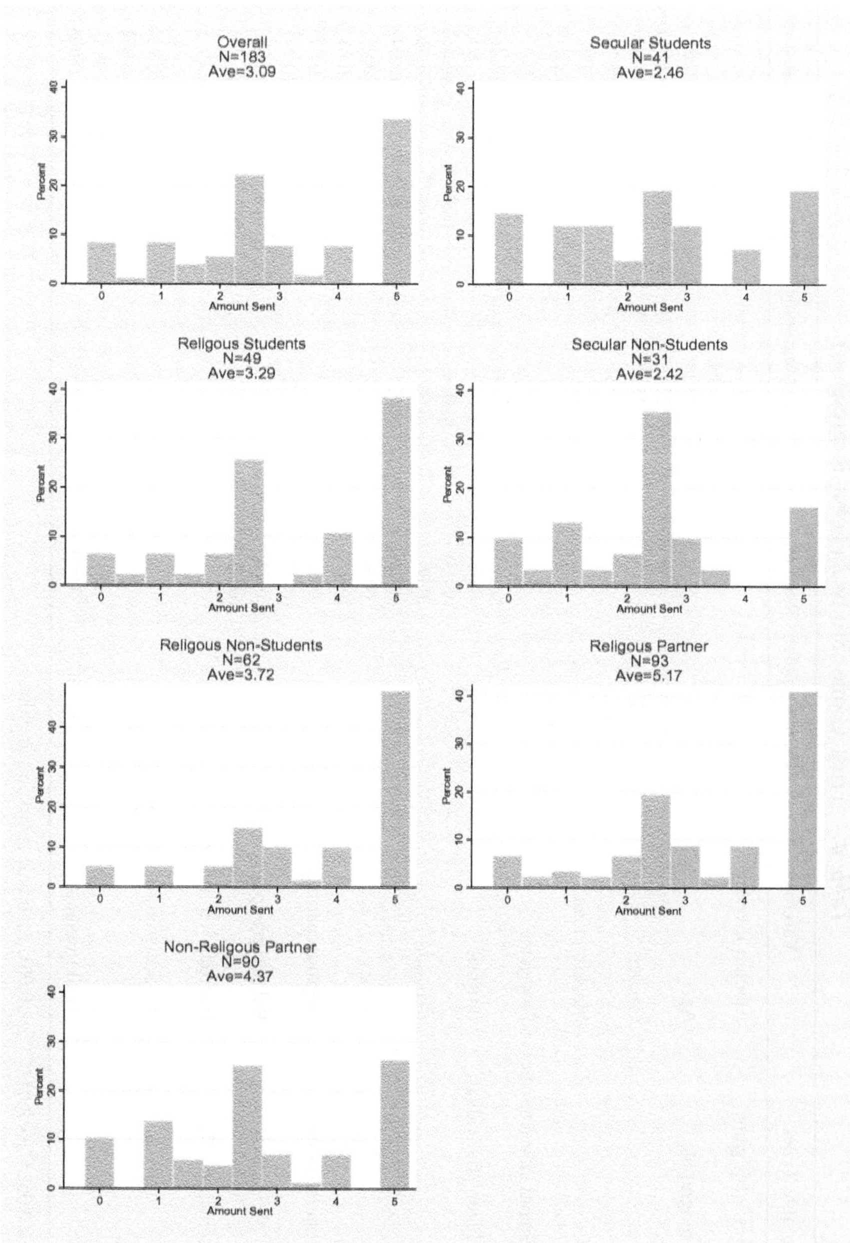


*Fig. 3.* Study 2 – Trust Game.

**Table 4.** Trust Game, Study 2 (Tobit Regression).

| Variable Types | Variables | Demographic | Religion | Religion + Demographic | Interaction 1 | Interaction 2 |
|---|---|---|---|---|---|---|
| Investment game | Amount invested | 0.18 | | 0.16 | | |
| | | (0.10) | | (0.09) | | |
| Demographic | Age | 0.0 | | 0.01 | 0.01 | 0.01 |
| | | (0.0) | | (0.01) | (0.01) | (0.01) |
| | Gender | 0.15 | | 0.18 | 0.14 | 0.09 |
| | | (0.27) | | (0.25) | (0.26) | (0.26) |
| | Machiavellian | 0.0 | | 0.03 | 0.03 | 0.04 |
| | | (0.02) | | (0.02) | (0.02) | (0.02) |
| Demand characteristics | Post-game | 0.12 | | 0.08 | 0.08 | 0.07 |
| | | (0.06) | | (0.07) | (0.07) | (0.07) |
| Religion (Individual) | Intrinsic | | 0.06 | 0.05 | 0.08 | 0.01 |
| | | | (0.03) | (0.03) | (0.05) | (0.05) |
| | Extrinsic | | −0.06 | −0.06 | −0.07* | −0.06 |
| | | | (0.03) | (0.03) | (0.03) | (0.04) |
| | Quest | | 0.06 | 0.04 | 0.05 | 0.05 |
| | | | (0.03) | (0.03) | (0.03) | (0.03) |
| Religion (Group) | In-group pairing | | 0.66** | 0.71** | 1.24 | 0.67** |
| | | | (0.25) | (0.24) | (0.95) | (0.24) |
| | Rel/Sec group | | 0.74* | 0.86** | 0.86** | −0.88 |
| | | | (0.32) | (0.31) | (0.32) | (1.20) |
| Interaction effects | In-group × intrinsic | | | | −0.04 | |
| | | | | | (0.06) | |
| | Rel/Sec group × intrinsic | | | | | 0.11 |
| | | | | | | (0.07) |
| | *N* | | 181 | 179 | 181 | 181 |
| | Akaiki weight ($w_i$) | 0.000 | 0.000 | 0.9885 | 0.0030 | 0.0082 |

$^{*}p<0.05$; $^{**}p<0.01$; $^{***}p<0.001$. Standard errors in parentheses.

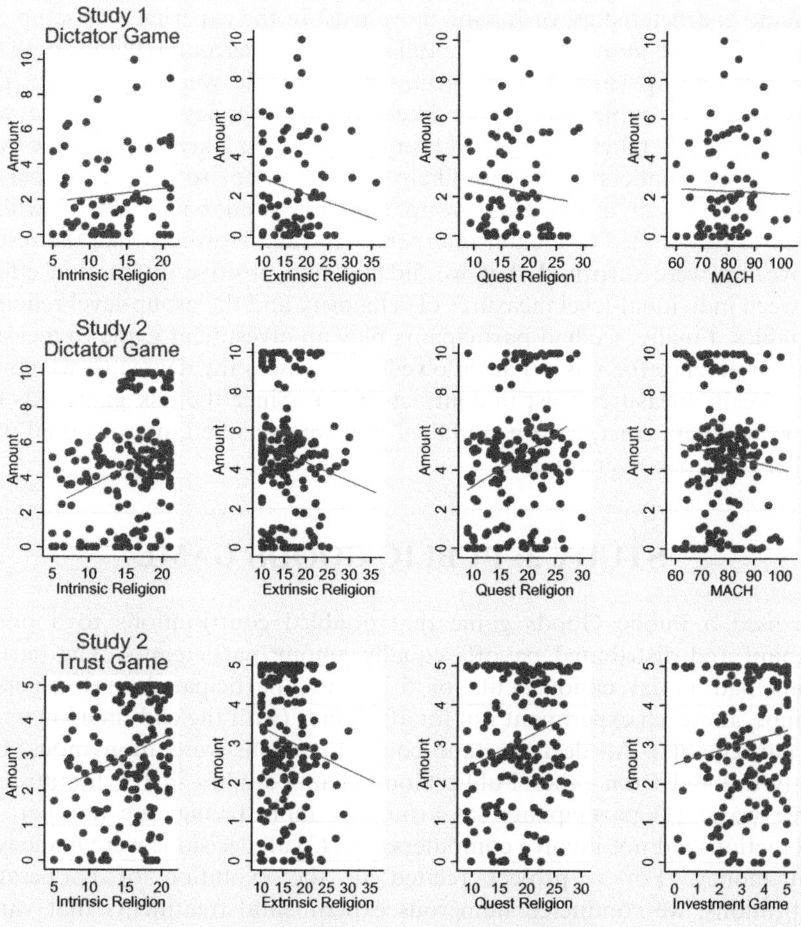


*Fig. 4.* Studies 1 and 2 – Summary Scatter Plots.

We interpret this to mean that individuals who think the games are easy to understand, and who trust that the experimenter will do as he or she said, send more money in the Dictator game.

The Trust game results differ substantially. The parameter estimates in Table 4 show that no individual-level variables were associated with Trust, even when the full model was the winner of the post-estimation process. The demand characteristics, or having more trust in the experimental setup, led to slightly more money sent in the full model. Concerning religion, both the in-group pairing variable and group-level variable were significant. This suggests that people were more likely to send money to someone who reported to be religious. In addition, people who played the game with religious comembers were more likely to send money to the second player. Overall, being in a religious group situation, and being paired with a religious person, led to greater interpersonal trust. However, like the results above, we were surprised that we did not find positive interaction effects between individual-level measures of religiosity and the group-level religious variables. Finally, we had participants play an investment game to measure their preference for risk.[7] This allowed us to assess the degree to which the game really measures trust in contrast to risk. Since the risk game was not associated with trust, we are confident that we measured interpersonal trust rather than risk aversion.

## STUDY 3: PUBLIC GOODS GAME

We used a Public Goods game that doubled contributions to a public account and distributed payoffs equally among participants. The participants had initial endowments of 5 dollars, participated in five-person groups, and each experiment ran for 10 rounds (with the end time known to all participants). All decisions and communications were anonymous. Our study differed from other Public Goods game studies in the literature in three ways: (1) participants sat around a table facing one another; (2) interactions did not involve computers; and (3) all decisions were made with real money. For a project related to the evolution of cooperative institutions, we conducted numerous experimental treatments that varied the context of the Public Goods game. In general, we varied the opportunity to (1) communicate with written messages; (2) reward and punish with two types of sanctions; and (3) obtain written advice from a previous group. Although the experimental treatments are complex and multifaceted, the experiments are general enough to be analyzed together in this chapter to evaluate the degree to which religious and personality variables are associated with cooperative behavior. Given the anonymity of decisions in this experiment, and few social cues to prime religious or secular institutions, we did not expect to find any strong relationship between religiosity and cooperation.

***Table 5.*** Summary Statistics for Study 3.

| | Aggregate | Baseline | Communication | Positive Sanctions | Neutral Sanctions | Advice |
|---|---|---|---|---|---|---|
| *N* | 255 | 35 | 30 | 75 | 60 | 55 |
| Contribution | 7.3 (3.5) | 5.6 (3.7) | 7.9 (3.2) | 7.2 (3.5) | 7.3 (3.5) | 8.3 (3.3) |
| Age | 19.6 (2.3) | 19.3 (1.2) | 19.6 (1.3) | 19.5 (1.8) | 20.1 (3.6) | 19.4 (1.5) |
| Intrinsic | 15.0 (4.4) | 15.0 (4.1) | 15.2 (4.4) | 14.1 (4.6) | 15.4 (4.2) | 15.8 (4.4) |
| Extrinsic | 21.0 (4.1) | 21.0 (3.5) | 20.8 (3.9) | 20.0 (4.2) | 21.8 (4.4) | 21.3 (4.1) |
| Quest | 20.8 (4.3) | 21.5 (4.5) | 20.2 (3.8) | 20.7 (4.2) | 20.8 (4.4) | 20.6 (4.3) |
| Mach | 75.0 (8.3) | 74.8 (6.2) | 75.3 (8.6) | 76.3 (7.8) | 73.8 (9.0) | 74.3 (8.7) |
| Female/Male (#) | 159/96 | 24/11 | 21/9 | 44/31 | 35/25 | 35/20 |

Mean (standard deviation).

### *Participants*

Two hundred and fifty-five participants were recruited from a subject pool operated by the Department of Psychology at the University of California, Davis (see Table 5). Each student received one experimental credit used toward his or her class, as well as any money in cash earned in the experiment. Similar to Study 1, participants were not told that they might earn money in the study until after they had arrived.

### *Design*

Participants sat around an 8-foot square table. Each was seated in front of cardboard box to conceal his or her choices and messages during the course of the experiment. To prevent suspicions that real money was not involved, we created "transaction boxes" for the subjects that allowed them to transfer real nickels in each experimental round while hiding their decisions from other subjects. These were constructed using plastic boxes with foam inserts. Inside the lid of the box was a map to illustrate how nickels should be moved to transfer money to the public account and how nickels would be returned from the public account. The subject placed nickels into a row of slots cut into the foam for "Contributions to the Public Account," and, when sanctions were included, into another row of slots labeled "Option Payments" to pay for the use of an option. Finally, when options were included, an additional row was filled with an initial endowment of 20 nickels from the individual's private account before the start of the game.

*Fig. 5.* Study 3 – Experimental Setup.

These allowed the researcher to subtract nickels from the subject if another participant's rule specified subtraction. Two small bins were cut out of the foam and labeled, "Public Account Returns" and "Returns from Additions," respectively. Any money earned from the public account or from the reward option was returned to the subject in these bins. In this way, each subject would be able to count the number of nickels received each round from the public account and from the option producing additions to other people's accounts. The researcher carefully showed each participant how to use the box, and any errors were quietly corrected when the researcher collected the boxes (see Fig. 5).

Each participant also had a manila "communication folder" that contained pages with numbered spaces to allow the writing of a message after each round. In the treatments with advice, the last page included instructions and a full page of space to leave advice for the next group about how to play the game. In the treatments with sanctions, each subject also had a stack of option sheets on which he or she checked one of three options: subtraction (punishment), addition (reward), or neither. The boxes for punishment and reward included space for indicating the contributions below or above which sanction should occur.

### *Public Goods Game*

After giving consent, five participants sat around the table, each in front of a cardboard box. To explain the game, the experimenter read word for word from a script. The script pointed out that each participant's cardboard box contained four plastic trays labeled "Private Account" and that two of these held nickels totaling 5 dollars. The script emphasized that this was their money and that this fund could either grow or diminish depending on the decisions made by them and the other participants. Next, they were told that the experiment involved no deception; all of the information was true, and they would receive in cash their final amount at the end of the experiment.

Participants were told to consider making a contribution to the pubic account. They were to take between 0 and 10 nickels from their "Private Account," and place them in the transaction box slots labeled "Contribution to Public Account." The script read: "At end of each round, the researcher will sum all of the public account contributions, double this amount, and then distribute it equally to each individual." The researchers displayed on a chalkboard the aggregate results of the round [total contribution to the public account (*n*), double that amount, the share that each individual received (*n*/5), and the total number of individuals that chose each option]. Finally, individuals were asked to open up their "communication folder" and write a message to the other participants "concerning how decisions should be made in this experiment." If they had nothing to say, they were asked to write "no message" to help preserve anonymity in the event that only a few people chose to write messages. When complete, the researcher gathered the folders from participants, shuffled the folders to preserve anonymity, and read aloud word for word all of the messages. As discussed below, in some of the treatments, participants had the opportunity to use "options" in which they could reward and punish other players.

### *Experimental Treatments*

There were five types of treatments (number of 5-person sessions in parentheses): Baseline (7), Communication (6), Positive Sanctions (12), Neutral Sanctions (15), and Advice (11). First, in the *Baseline* treatment, groups were not allowed to communicate, and did not have any options to influence the payoffs of other participants. All of the other treatments allowed participants to communicate with written messages. In the treatment called *Communication*, participants only had the option to communicate with written messages, and could not use any sanctions. We created two treatments that varied the costs and types of rewards and punishments that participants could use. In the *Positive Sanctions* treatment, participants could earn revenue directly from the reward system. In the

*Neutral Sanctions* treatment, the sanctions offered the opportunity to increase levels of cooperation, but participants could not gain money by rewarding one another. In both of these treatments, individuals had the opportunity to add, subtract, or take no action. The options labeled "Subtract" and "Add" stated that the participant could pay a specific number of nickels to have the researcher take away (or add) money to individuals' accounts who contributed less (or more) than a specific amount to the public account. Finally, in the *Advice* treatment, we gave groups the opportunity to transmit advice to another group about how the game should be played. After a group had participated in 10 rounds, they were instructed to write a message in their communication folder that would be read aloud to a future group of participants. Except for the first (progenitor) generation, each group heard all five pieces of advice from the previous generation read aloud before the first round.

## *Results*

A participant's contribution in round $T+1$ is likely influenced by a number of factors that occurred in round $T$ (and possibly earlier rounds). For example, it is possible that contributions by other players in previous rounds might lead a participant to contribute more or less in the following round. Our design adds the additional complexity of experiencing communication, rewards, and punishments in each round. Thus, it is also plausible that communication and various sanctions in previous rounds influence future decisions. To understand the role of these forces, we adopted a panel data regression design (Ashley, Ball, & Eckel, 2003). Random-effects Tobit models were used to predict the degree to which contributions were influenced by a variety of variables that were lagged to account for behavior in the previous rounds ($T-1$, $T-2$, $T-3$). These include (1) a participant's own contribution in earlier rounds; (2) the deviation of a player's contribution from the group average; (3) the amount and type of messages; and (4) the amount and type of sanctions administered. The models accounted for numerous "nuisance" variables such as round, overall contributions in early rounds, and dummy variables to control for all of the various treatments involving communication and sanctions. The individual-level questionnaire data were then treated as static trait variables for each subject, and allowed us to explore the degree to which such factors contribute to game dynamics.

Scatter plots (not shown) did not evidence any strong relationship between individual-level variables and contributions to the public fund. Because the Public Goods game involves interdependent decision-making processes, it is important to evaluate the degree to which such forces influence behavior after controlling for the behavior and decisions of others in the group. Table 6 shows the results from the Tobit regression models. The model labeled "Aggregate" contains all of the treatments in one model. With 2,550 total decisions, the model illustrates that intrinsic religion and Machiavellian personality have marginally significant, and very small, positive associations with contributions to the public account controlling for the decisions of others in the game. The other models are stratifications of the treatments. The Baseline model is the most interesting in that all three of the religion variables are significant, yet not in the directions expected by previous research. Batson et al. (1993) and many others show that extrinsic religion is negatively associated with prosocial behavior, whereas quest is found to be positive. The other models differ with regard to effect sizes and significance, thus it is plausible that sampling error is partly driving the results. The strongest effects occur in the Baseline treatment where the individual-level variables are less constrained by the institutional forces added in the other treatments. Overall, the effects are small and inconsistent, and we conclude that personality and religious variables are not strongly associated with contributions in the Public Goods game.

## DISCUSSION

### *Group-Level Effects: Religious versus Secular Institutions*

Like Darwin (1874), we suspect that secular institutions can promote prosocial behavior just as well as religious institutions. The effect of Christianity and Islam beyond tribal religions in the study by Henrich et al. (2010) might be related to the weaker secular institutions in many of these societies. To test this idea among Western participants, in Study 2 we purposely primed participants from both religious and secular organizations by having them play the games directly after one of their organizational meetings. For the Dictator game, as expected, we found no striking difference between these groups, although more participants offered the full 10-dollar amount following a religious meeting. Similar to the findings of Shariff and Norenzayan (2007), the priming of secular institutions seems to promote prosocial behavior equally well as the priming of religious

***Table 6.*** Public Goods Game, Study 3 (Tobit Regression).

| Variable Types | Variables | Aggregate | Baseline | Communication | Positive Sanctions | Neutral Sanctions | Advice |
|---|---|---|---|---|---|---|---|
| Game rounds | Time | −5.60*** | −1.37 | −6.55*** | −7.44*** | −7.21*** | −6.00** |
| | | (0.47) | (0.78) | (1.41) | (0.97) | (0.82) | (1.91) |
| PG contributions | Deviance from group (Lag 1 round) | 0.59*** | 0.51*** | 0.68* | 0.58*** | 0.52*** | 0.53 |
| | | (0.07) | (0.12) | (0.27) | (0.15) | (0.13) | (0.37) |
| | Own contribution (Lag 1 round) | 1.74*** | 1.25*** | 2.02*** | 1.58*** | 1.55*** | 2.56*** |
| | | (0.06) | (0.1) | (0.25) | (0.13) | (0.11) | (0.37) |
| Religiosity | Intrinsic | 0.07* | 0.20*** | 0.12 | −0.12 | −0.04 | 0.24 |
| | | (0.03) | (0.06) | (0.09) | (0.08) | (0.06) | (0.16) |
| | Extrinsic | 0.04 | 0.16* | 0.07 | 0 | 0.08 | 0.1 |
| | | (0.03) | (0.07) | (0.11) | (0.07) | (0.06) | (0.15) |
| | Quest | −0.05 | −0.20*** | −0.15 | 0.19** | −0.02 | −0.27 |
| | | (0.03) | (0.05) | (0.12) | (0.07) | (0.05) | (0.15) |
| Personality | Machiavellian | 0.03* | 0.06 | 0.11* | 0.02 | 0.02 | −0.02 |
| | | (0.02) | (0.04) | (0.05) | (0.03) | (0.03) | (0.08) |
| | Constant | −3.80* | −6.61 | −10.72 | −2.71 | −1.24 | −1.37 |
| | | (1.66) | (3.63) | (5.91) | (2.96) | (2.89) | (7.6) |
| | Sigma constant | 5.40*** | 3.65*** | 5.17*** | 5.40*** | 5.06*** | 8.98*** |
| | | (0.15) | (0.19) | (0.43) | (0.3) | (0.24) | (0.8) |
| | *N* | 2550 | 350 | 300 | 600 | 750 | 550 |

*$p<0.05$, **$p<0.01$, ***$p<0.001$. Standard errors in parentheses.

institutions. In contrast, greater interpersonal trust was found among participants in the religious group situation, and when people were told that they had been paired with a responder who reported to be religious. Thus, we have some evidence that group- or institution-level forces influence trust.

### *Weak Effect of Religiosity Measures on Prosocial Behavior*

In general, our religiosity measures are not consistently associated with behavior in the games, and when they are, the effect sizes are small. Indeed, behavior in the Trust game was not associated with individual-level variables at all. Thus, after holding constant other demographic forces, religiosity is not a strong predictor of gameplay among strangers. It is also important to note the lack of strong explanatory power among the demographic and personality variables. We did not find age or gender to be a significant factor in our experiments. From our theoretical perspective these results make sense; visible personal traits such as gender or religion would make people vulnerable to exploitation and punishment for prosocial or antisocial behaviors. Concerning personality, a substantial literature suggests that Machiavellian personality traits may associate with antisocial behavior (Wilson, Near, & Miller, 1996). However, similar to Gunnthorsdottir, McCabe, and Smith (2002), we find no evidence of this in either of our experiments. This is surprising since this scale intuitively ought to predict behavior in the Dictator game; people sending a small amount of money would seemingly rationalize their behavior with the constructs specified in the Machiavellian scale.

Although we believe that our main result is that the association between religiosity and prosocial behavior is weak, it is important to note that in the experiments that included organizational context (Study 2), we did find some small effects of religiosity. Using the Dictator game, we found like others (Batson et al., 1993), intrinsic and quest dimensions are positive predictors of Dictator gameplay, whereas extrinsic is negatively associated with Dictator. In contrast, these variables were not significant in Study 1. We conducted a power analysis for the multiple regression coefficients to identify what power we had to detect a 0.27 correlation for intrinsic religion as was found in Study 2. Given our models and sample size of 75, we have a power of about 0.60 to detect this effect – it is unlikely that we are missing strong real effects of religiosity in Study 1.

Although our research designs in Study 1 and Study 2 differ substantially, we cautiously compare the results between the studies.[8] Given that participants played the games in the context of their organization, Study 2 conforms to Norenzayan and Shariff's (2008) prediction that people who have immediate access to their religious thoughts are more prosocial. Moreover, when playing the games with organizational members, participants may have behaved more in congruence with how they really behave within their churches and secular clubs; intrinsics give more, whereas extrinsics give less. When framed in the perspective of one's organizational history, participants might have been less wary of displaying their real prosocial and antisocial markers. This follows the game theoretic assumption that displaying group affiliations and associated traits such as being generous (or stingy) can leave a person vulnerable to exploitation or punishment. As a result, when people are outside of known social networks, their religious traits are not expected to be associated with prosocial behavior.

### *Effect of In-Group Pairing*

We expected to find evidence that giving players information about the religious beliefs of their paired partners would affect gameplay in Dictator and Trust. However, there was no significant interaction between a player's reported religion and who they were paired with in the Dictator game. Yet in the Trust game, only group-level variables seemed to have any influence: trust in the experimental setup, being in a religious group while participating, and being paired with someone religious. Since we found no evidence of an in-group effect (i.e., sending more money to someone with similar beliefs as your own), we interpret the results to mean that both religious and secular people trust religious people, and people who are around their religious peers feel more trusting. Once again, the effects are weak, but it is plausible that religious (and nonreligious) people have experienced the cooperative nature of religious individuals, and are thus more likely to trust them. Overall, the effect of religious pairing is inconsistent and likely complex, yet the results do not allow us to reject the theoretical assertion that religion generates patterns of prosocial behavior among people from similar cultural in-groups. Our results are consistent with Anderson et al. (2010) who found no association between religiosity measures and the Trust game. In contrast, Tan and Vogel (2008) did find a significant relationship between religiosity and trust. Their design gave information about the level of religiosity of the other players using a 5-point scale. This information, as well as other subtle characteristics of their study design, may have reduced the effects of anonymity found in our study design. More research will be required to fully understand how the context of study designs influences the effect of religion on trust.

## CONCLUSIONS

We administered the Dictator, Trust, and Public Goods games to a large and diverse sample of participants. Like many other researchers, we found that many people are prosocial; participants share money in the Dictator game, are trusting in Trust, and are often very cooperative in the Public Goods game. In this research, we conducted three studies. First, we were interested in evaluating how individuals' religiosity impacts generosity. We used a double-blind Dictator game in which neither players nor the researcher knows game decisions. This design reduces the reputation-effects as stressed Norenzayan and Shariff (2008), but also provides little real-world context; student participants play the game among strangers in a neutral university setting, and have no information about their paired partners. Given this design, we were not surprised that religious variables were not associated with Dictator game offers. In our second study, individuals played the Dictator and Trust game with comembers following a religious or secular organizational meeting. Secular and religious participants were about equally prosocial in the Dictator game, thus we find little evidence that religious institutions promote more generosity as compared to secular institutions. We did, however, find that participants who played the Trust game in a religious setting or who were paired with a religious person were slightly more trusting. In this study, we also included an in-group treatment in which we provided information about the religious beliefs of the paired partners. We found no evidence of an in-group effect – religious participants were not more generous or trusting of paired partners with similar beliefs. Although it is difficult to compare our results to our first study, we did find that individual religiosity variables were associated in predicted ways with gameplay. It is possible that religiosity dimensions are mainly important when people are within the context of religious organizations, and our experiment provided some of this context. Finally, we have a large sample of students playing various treatments of a Public Goods game that allowed face-to-face individuals to communicate via written messages, reward and punish others, and receive advice from other groups of students about how to play the game. We found a weak relationship between religion and cooperation in our Baseline treatment, and no effect in the other treatments.

Although we found a few weak effects of religiosity in the study that added organizational context, we believe that our sample as a whole provides evidence for our hypothesis that religious institutions, and the effect these have on individual dimensions of religiosity, are not a strong force to explain generosity, trust, and cooperation among individuals paired within unknown social networks. Although many of these individuals reported to be religious (and in some of our treatments, they were in real religious settings), their proclivity for prosocial behavior was similar to that of secular participants. Based on evolutionary theory, we are not surprised by these results. Although humans may have group-level adaptations that promote prosocial behavior within social groups such as church organizations, individuals may be cautious not to let such behavior spill over to other social transactions where they might be exploited. It can be dangerous to advertise our prosocial or antisocial intentions as these allow people to be exploited for their generosity or punished for their uncooperativeness.

Overall, these results conform to the majority of experimental economic studies, and are consistent with recent cross-cultural results. Cross-cultural studies using economic games show large effects with sensible interpretations (Henrich et al., 2005). In cross-cultural studies using economic games, individual-level variables explain much less total variation than does group-level variation. We think it is likely that, when playing with fellow students and fellow citizens, people from a diverse civil society use nonreligious norms and expectations to guide their play in the games. Our participants play the games much the way student and nonstudent Americans and Western Europeans do.

## NOTES

1. Group selection on *cultural* variation is much more probable than group selection directly on genes (Boyd & Richerson, 1985). Cultural differences between groups are large, evolve rapidly, and often lead to sharp adaptive differences between groups. In the late Pleistocene, sophisticated cultural systems led to the evolution of social institutions mandating a certain amount of cooperation beyond the ancient systems of reciprocal altruism and nepotism. These cultural institutions favored genotypes that were capable of cooperation, and gradually the coevolutionary process built human "social instincts" that were adapted to living in tribal-scale social systems much larger than families (Richerson & Boyd, 2005).

2. Some scholars are not convinced that social institutions are necessary to police free riders and achieve cooperation. They observe that participation in religious rituals and meetings is often costly, and such behavior serves the purpose of defining

religious groups, and to keep the public goods inclusive to only those members who make public sacrifices (Alcorta & Sosis, 2005; Iannaccone, 1992, 1998). In addition to costly signaling, cultural group selection is likely to be an important force because individual-level mechanisms by themselves are unlikely to maintain cooperative behavior (Paciotti & Hadley, 2004).

3. Researchers have explored the links between behavior in experimental games and personality scales developed by psychologists. Kurzban and Houser (2001) used a circular pubic goods game and found that player types are correlated with self-monitoring, self-esteem, neuroticism, and conscientiousness. De Cremer and Van Lange (2001) used the three categories of social value orientation – prosocial, individualistic, and competitive – to predict variation in public goods games. Individuals who were typed as "prosocials" contributed more to the public fund than did the "proselfs." Brandstätter and Konigstein (2001) used a variant of the Ultimatum game and found that some dimensions of the Cattell's personality dimensions predict bargaining behavior. Proposers scoring higher on independence and tough-mindedness demanded more money in the game. Rejection of Ultimatum game offers was associated with persons who were emotionally unstable and extroverted or emotionally stable and introverted. In other research, Boone, De Brabander, and van Witteloostuijn (1999) looked at behavior in five Prisoner's Dilemma games. They found that personality measures of internal locus of control, high self-monitoring, and high sensation seeking were associated with cooperative behavior in repeated games, but not in games with noninteractive settings. Gunnthorsdottir et al. (2002) use a Machiavellian scale to predict behavior in a two-person Trust game. They found that the Mach-IV scale does not predict trusting behavior. Those who score low on the scale, however, are more likely to reciprocate trust.

4. The procedures used by Hoffman et al. (1994) forbid the researcher from even knowing the decisions made by particular individuals. In our procedures, however, we include a questionnaire. Thus, depending on the characteristics of our groups, it might be possible for the researchers to learn the decisions made by individuals by using information related to age, gender, and ethnicity and other identifiable traits.

5. To reduce the problem of colinearity among the remaining variables, we conducted a cluster analysis using *Proc Varclus* in SAS software. Once clusters were formed, we chose a number of final clusters based on analyses of eigenvalues and the cumulative proportion of variance that was explained for each cluster (Pasta & Suhr, 2004). We then selected one variable from each multicluster group. This selection was based on theoretical importance, as well as the variable that had the strongest correlation with its own cluster and weakest correlation with other clusters. We also performed principal components and factor analyses to compare the results. Overall, we found very similar patterns using these conceptually similar methods.

6. Tobit regression models assume that a latent variable extends beyond the censored ranges. Censoring is especially important in the upper limit because a large fraction of participants choose the highest amount to send, and a few participants informed us that they would have liked to send the other player more money than was allowed. All models were fit using STATA software version 9.1.

7. Before completing the questionnaire, participants played an investment game designed to be a measure of risk tolerance. We used this game to help us interpret the

degree to which the Trust game is driven by risk, or by interpersonal trust. In this game, players could choose to invest in an old or new variety of corn. Any money from the 5-dollar amount invested in the old variety would be paid to the participant (with no risk) at the end of the experiment. The payoff for the new variety was decided by the random selection of one number from six. Each number was clearly described in the game script to correspond to a multiplier (0, 0.5, 1, 1.5, 2, and 2.5) that would be multiplied by the amount of money invested. For example, a person who invested \$2.50 in the new corn and drew a "3" would receive $(2.5 \times 1) + 2.5 = \$5.00$.

8. Study 1 involved mainly undergraduates who were recruited for class credit, whereas participants from Study 2 were offered money and recruited based on their organization. In addition, the game methodology differed substantially (double-blind vs. survey), and the social context was substantially different (university lab setting vs. organizational context).

## ACKNOWLEDGMENTS

This research was supported by a generous grant from the Institute for Research on Unlimited Love. We would like to thank Lily Lau for her aid in designing and administering the experiments.

## REFERENCES

Alcorta, C., & Sosis, R. (2005). Ritual, emotion, and sacred symbols: The evolution of religion as an adaptive complex. *Human Nature: An Interdisciplinary Biosocial Perspective*, *16*, 323–359.

Alexander, R. (1987). *The biology of moral systems.* Hawthorne, NY: Aldine de Gruyter.

Allport, G., & Ross, J. (1967). Personal religious orientation and prejudice. *Journal of Personality and Social Psychology*, *5*, 432–443.

Anderson, L., Mellor, J., & Milyo, J. (2010). Did the devil make them do it? The effects of religion in public goods and trust games. *Kyklos*, *63*, 163–175.

Ashley, R., Ball, S., & Eckel, C. (2003). *Analysis of public goods experiments using dynamic panel regression models.* Working Paper No. 03-01. Center for Behavioral and Experimental Economic Science, University of Texas at Dallas.

Atran, S. (2002). *In gods we trust: The evolutionary landscape of religion, evolution and cognition.* Oxford: Oxford University Press.

Baier, C., & Wright, B. (2001). If you love me, keep my commandments: A meta-analysis of the effect of religion on crime. *Journal of Research in Crime and Delinquency*, *38*, 3–21.

Batson, C., & Gray, R. (1981). Religious orientation and helping behavior: Responding to one's own or to the victim's needs. *Journal of Personality and Social Psychology*, *40*, 511–520.

Batson, C., Schoenrade, P., & Ventis, W. (1993). *Religion and the individual: A social-psychological perspective.* New York: Oxford University Press.

Beit-Hallahmi, B., & Argyle, M. (1997). *The psychology of religious behaviour, belief, and experience*. London: Routledge.

Ben-Ner, A., Putterman, L., Kong, F., & Magan, D. (2004). Reciprocity in a two-part dictator game. *Journal of Economic Behavior & Organization, 53*, 333–352.

Boone, C., De Brabander, B., & van Witteloostuijn, A. (1999). The impact of personality on behavior in five prisoner's dilemma games. *Journal of Economic Psychology, 20*, 343–377.

Boyd, R., Gintis, H., Bowles, S., & Richerson, P. (2003). The evolution of altruistic punishment. *Proceedings of the National Academy of Sciences, 100*, 3531–3535.

Boyd, R., & Richerson, P. (1985). *Culture and the evolutionary process*. Chicago, IL: University of Chicago Press.

Boyer, P. (1994). *The naturalness of religious ideas: A cognitive theory of religion*. Berkeley, CA: University of California Press.

Brandstätter, H., & Konigstein, M. (2001). Personality influences on ultimatum bargaining decisions. *European Journal of Personality, 15*, S53–S70.

Burnham, K., & Anderson, D. (2002). *Model selection and multimodel inference: A practical information-theoretic approach* (2nd ed.). New York: Springer.

Camerer, C. (2003). *Behavioral game theory: Experiments in strategic interaction*. Princeton, NJ: Princeton University Press.

Christie, R., & Geis, F. (1970). *Studies in Machiavellianism*. New York: Academic Press.

Darwin, C. (1874). (2nd ed.). *The descent of man and selection in relation to sex* (Vol. 2). New York: American Home Library.

Dawkins, R. (2006). *The God delusion*. Boston, MA: Houghton Mifflin.

De Cremer, D., & Van Lange, P. (2001). Why prosocials exhibit greater cooperation than proselfs: The roles of social responsibility and reciprocity. *European Journal of Personality, 15*, S5–S18.

De Jong, G., Faulkner, J., & Warland, R. (1976). Dimensions of religiosity reconsidered: Evidence from a cross-cultural study. *Social Forces, 54*, 866–889.

Durkheim, E. (1915). *The elementary forms of the religious life*. London: George Allen & Unwin Ltd.

Eckel, C., & Grossman, P. (2000). Volunteers and pseudo-volunteers: The effect of recruitment method in dictator experiments. *Experimental Economics, 2*, 107–120.

Eckel, C., & Grossman, P. (2003). Rebate versus matching: Does how we subsidize charitable contributions matter? *Journal of Public Economics, 87*, 681–701.

Eckel, C., & Grossman, P. (2004). Giving to secular causes by the religious and nonreligious: An experimental test of the responsiveness of giving to subsidies. *Nonprofit and Voluntary Sector Quarterly, 33*, 271–289.

Ellis, L., & Peterson, J. (1996). Crime and religion: An international comparison among thirteen industrial nations. *Personality and Individual Differences, 20*, 761–768.

Fehr, E., Fischbacher, U., von Rosenbladt, B., Schupp, J., & Wagner, G. G. (2002). A nation-wide laboratory examining trust and trustworthiness by integrating behavioral experiments into representative surveys. *Schmollers Jahrbuch, 122*, 519–542.

Frank, R., Gilovich, T., & Regan, D. (1993). Does studying economics inhibit cooperation? *Journal of Economic Perspectives, 7*, 159–171.

Gunnthorsdottir, A., McCabe, K., & Smith, V. (2002). Using the Machiavellianism instrument to predict trustworthiness in a bargaining game. *Journal of Economic Psychology, 23*, 49–66.

Hagen, E., & Hammerstein, P. (2006). Game theory and human evolution: A critique of some recent interpretations of experimental games. *Theoretical Population Biology*, *69*, 339–348.

Henrich, J., Boyd, R., Bowles, S., Gintis, H., Fehr, E., Camerer, C., et al. (2005). 'Economic man' in cross-cultural perspective: Ethnography and experiments from 15 small-scale societies. *Behavioral and Brain Sciences*, *28*, 795–855.

Henrich, J., Ensimger, J., McElreath, R., Barr, A., Barrett, C., Bolyanatz, A., et al. (2010). Markets, religion, community size, and the evolution of fairness and punishment. *Science*, *327*, 1480–1484.

Hoffman, E., McCabe, K., Shachat, K., & Smith, V. (1994). Preferences, property rights, and anonymity in bargaining games. *Games and Economic Behavior*, *7*, 346–380.

Iannaccone, L. (1992). Sacrifice and stigma: Reducing free-riding in cults, communes, and other collectives. *Journal of Political Economy*, *100*, 271–291.

Iannaccone, L. (1998). Introduction to the economics of religion. *Journal of Economic Literature*, *36*, 1465–1496.

Iannaccone, L., & Berman, E. (2006). Religious extremism: The good, the bad, and the deadly. *Public Choice*, *128*, 109–129.

James, W. (1902). *The varieties of religious experience*. New York: Longman.

Johansson-Stenman, O., Mahmud, M., & Martinsson, P. (2009). Trust and religion: Experimental evidence from rural Bangladesh. *Economica*, *76*, 462–485.

Kagel, J., & Roth, A. (1995). *The handbook of experimental economics*. Princeton, NJ: Princeton University Press.

Kurzban, R., & Houser, D. (2001). Individual differences in cooperation in a circular public goods game. *European Journal of Personality*, *15*, S37–S52.

Maltby, J., & Lewis, C. A. (1996). Measuring intrinsic and extrinsic orientation toward religion: Amendments for its use among religious and non-religious samples. *Personality and Individual Differences*, *21*, 937–946.

McElreath, R., Boyd, R., & Richerson, P. J. (2003). Shared norms and the evolution of ethnic markers. *Current Anthropology*, *44*, 122–129.

Momen, M. (1999). *The phenomenon of religion: A thematic approach*. Oxford; Boston: Oneworld.

Norenzayan, A., & Shariff, A. (2008). The origin and evolution of religious prosociality. *Science*, *322*, 58–62.

Orbell, J., Goldman, M., Mulford, M., & Dawes, R. (1992). Religion, context, and constraint towards strangers. *Rationality and Society*, *4*, 291–307.

Paciotti, B., & Hadley, C. (2003). The ultimatum game in southwestern Tanzania: Ethnic variation and institutional scope. *Current Anthropology*, *44*, 427–432.

Paciotti, B., & Hadley, C. (2004). Large-scale cooperation among Sungusungu "vigilantes" of Tanzania: Conceptualizing micro-economic and institutional approaches. *Research in Economic Anthropology*, *23*, 119–147.

Pasta, D., & Suhr, D. (2004). Creating scales from questionnaires: PROC VARCLUS vs. factor analysis. *SAS Users Group international conference proceedings*, Montreal, Canada.

Reynolds, W. (1982). Development of reliable and valid short forms of the Marlowe–Crowne social desirability scale. *Journal of Clinical Psychology*, *38*, 119–125.

Richerson, P., & Boyd, R. (2005). *Not by genes alone: How culture transformed human evolution*. Chicago, IL: University of Chicago Press.

Ruffle, B., & Sosis, R. (2006). Cooperation and the in-group-out-group bias: A field test on Israeli kibbutz members and city residents. *Journal of Economic Behavior and Organization, 60*, 147–163.

Shariff, A., & Norenzayan, A. (2007). God is watching you: Priming God concepts increases prosocial behavior in an anonymous economic game. *Psychological Science, 18*, 803–809.

Sosis, R. (2005). Methods do matter: Variation in experimental methodologies and results. *Behavioral and Brain Sciences, 28*, 834–835.

Sosis, R., & Ruffle, B. (2003). Religious ritual and cooperation: Testing for a relationship on Israeli religious and secular kibbutzim. *Current Anthropology, 44*, 713–722.

Stark, R., & Bainbridge, W. (1997). *Religion, deviance, and social control.* New York: Routledge.

Stark, R., & Finke, R. (2000). *Acts of faith: Explaining the human side of religion.* Berkeley, CA: University of California Press.

Tan, J. (2006). Religion and social preferences: An experimental study. *Economics Letters, 90*, 60–67.

Tan, J., & Vogel, C. (2008). Religion and trust: An experimental study. *Journal of Economic Psychology, 29*, 832–848.

Tylor, E. (1871). *Primitive culture.* New York: G.P. Putnam's Sons.

Wilson, D. (2002). *Darwin's cathedral: Evolution, religion, and the nature of society.* Chicago, IL: University of Chicago Press.

Wilson, D., Near, D., & Miller, R. (1996). Machiavellianism: A synthesis of the evolutionary and psychological literatures. *Psychological Bulletin, 119*, 285–299.

# CHARITABLE CHRISTIANS, PUNITIVE NEIGHBORS: RELIGIOSITY AND ECONOMIC NORMS IN A WATER-SCARCE ENVIRONMENT

Benjamin Jewell and Amber Wutich

## ABSTRACT

*This chapter examines how religion and religiosity shape economic norms in Villa Israel, an urban squatter settlement in Cochabamba, Bolivia. In Villa Israel, residents share water with others to help overcome limited access to drinking water. Using a mixed methods approach, we draw on the results of ethnographic research and economic experiments. The analyses yield three key results. First, there were strong norms of generosity and charitable giving in the community. Second, religiosity was positively associated with generosity. People who adhered to Christian conceptions of charity and frequently attended religious services were more likely to give generously. While wealth was a limiting factor on some families' ability to give water, there was no evidence that the rich and poor endorsed different norms of fair giving. Third, the norms of fair giving varied in the context of the three most common reciprocal relationships in the community (family members, coreligionists, and neighbors).*

**The Economics of Religion: Anthropological Approaches**
**Research in Economic Anthropology, Volume 31, 307–337**

**ISSN: 0190-1281/doi:10.1108/S0190-1281(2011)0000031015**

*Compared with neighbors, exchanges between family members and coreligionists were relatively generous and permissive of self-interest. Based on these results, we conclude that the presence of strong Christian norms of generosity and fair giving is an important institutional mechanism for facilitating water reciprocity in this community.*

In environments with recurrent resource scarcity, such as water scarcity due to drought, attaining the basic resources needed for survival can be a serious challenge. Individuals can either amass goods for their own survival or engage in prosocial behavior with others to facilitate the transfer of goods across the group. The orthodox economic expectation that actors would behave in a rational and self-interested way (Fehr & Gächter, 2000) by hoarding scarce resources has been repeatedly challenged by anthropological work on resource sharing in both ethnographic and experimental settings (Henrich, Boyd, & Fehr, 2004; Wiessner, 2009). Although most of this work in anthropology has focused on food transfers (Gurven, 2004a), some important works have looked at sharing of watering holes and other water resources (e.g., Gluckman, 1964). Trawick (2001), for example, describes the elaborate collaborative irrigation system in an Andean community that was developed in response to persistent water scarcity. These cooperative endeavors rely on shared normative ideas that guide behavior to restrain self-interest in favor of others' needs (Orbell, Goldman, Mulford, & Dawes, 1992; Roes & Raymond, 2003), increasing the likelihood of group survival in a marginal context. While religion has long been identified as an important component in shaping economic behavior (Weber, 2001[1904]), there is little literature exploring how religion shapes exchanges of water. We make two primary contributions to the literatures on religion and economics, as well as resource scarcity: first, we provide a grounded ethnographic context to the role of religion in fostering prosocial behavior in a water scarce environment; second, through economic experiments, we contribute to ongoing debates regarding the role that religiosity plays in shaping economic norms of generosity and fairness.

## BACKGROUND

Debates in anthropology over the role of religion in shaping environmental stewardship or adherence to conservationist ethics (Hames, 2007; Krech,

1999; Smith & Wishnie, 2000) have overshadowed a related branch of research that has focused on environmental factors that may encourage certain religious ethics to flourish over others. Snarey (1996, p. 93), using a standard cross-cultural sample of 186 societies, has shown that cultural groups that live in water scarce environments are significantly more likely to adhere to beliefs in a god "concerned with prosocial moral values." For instance, Persian Muslims incorporated water sharing into their conceptions of morality such that "offering water [was] a pious act. ... According to Shiite doctrine, in particular, pure water is the best gift one can give (without taking payment), for it recalls the thirst of Hussein and his people" (Massé, 1954, p. 225). Roes and Raymond (2003, pp. 134–135) replicate Snarey's finding and argue that belief in a moralizing god with authoritative power over human behavior allows for prosociality to occur through adherence to moral codes enforced by specific sanctioning mechanisms. Because they are passed down from "impartial gods," religious doctrines that promote generosity and fairness, two important components of prosociality, are less likely to be seen as the machinations of greedy individuals (Roes & Raymond, 2003, p. 128).

Prosocial religious moral codes are thought to provide a readily adoptable set of norms for adapting to environmental limitations and other potential threats to survival (e.g., warfare) and might have been critical in the evolution from human societies based primarily on small, kin-based groupings to large groups composed of unrelated individuals (Norenzayan & Shariff, 2008; Roes & Raymond, 2003). Here, we show how religious beliefs, in particular Christian norms of charity, are adopted and utilized in daily interactions with others to facilitate informal exchanges of water in the context of severe water scarcity. Our work examines, in some depth, how these religious beliefs encourage greater economic prosociality and ultimately the ability of groups to cooperatively share a scarce resource. This work grounds past research on the connection between religion and resource scarcity, providing a strong empirical basis to the idea that certain religious beliefs assist human adaptation to adverse environmental conditions.

Religiosity, a measure of commitment to a religious group, appears to facilitate prosociality across a range of resource contexts. The investment of time and money in following religious doctrines indicates to others that an individual is trustworthy (Tan & Vogel, 2008), and appears to facilitate unconditional generosity (e.g., gift-giving, meat sharing, and funeral feasting) across the ethnographic record (Bird & Smith, 2005). Studies from 15 European countries (Scheepers & Grotenhuis, 2005) and the United

States (Regnerus, Smith, & Sikkink, 1998), for example, found that those who attend church regularly are more generous, particularly in terms of their giving to the poor, than those who do not. In addition, there is evidence that individuals with higher levels of religiosity are seen as more trustworthy by nonreligious individuals and are likely to extend trust outside of their church group (Welch, Sikkink, & Loveland, 2007). This increased trust and trustworthiness is essential for cooperative economic interactions, which are further strengthened by the monitoring capabilities afforded to coreligionists who can validate the intentions of others in the context of public participation in ritual activity (Dehejia, DeLeire, Erzo, & Luttmer (2007); Iannaccone, 1992; Ruffle & Sosis, 2007). Our study is the first to examine ethnographically the effects of religion and religiosity on water sharing. We add to our ethnographic detail the economic experiments to confirm the presence of shared norms among residents of a Bolivian squatter settlement.

Experimental research on religiosity and prosociality has produced mixed results. Sosis and Ruffle (2003) found that religiosity, as measured by the frequency of participation in prayer and other rituals, among Israeli kibbutz members increased cooperative behavior in a public goods game. In the communal social and economic system of the kibbutz, prosocial interactions are essential for survival of the community and religious ritual appears to encourage such behavior through confirmation of the commitment of the individual to the needs of the larger group (Ruffle & Sosis, 2007; Sosis & Ruffle, 2003). By contrast, Anderson, Mellor, and Milyo (2010) find no significant difference in contributions in a public goods game or a trust game based on measures of religiosity and religious affiliation among undergraduate students at William and Mary College. However, the authors do find trends in contributions in the two experiments such that participants who reported higher levels of religiosity (i.e., attended church at least four times per month) made higher contributions (p. 172).

Orbell et al. (1992) conducted prisoner's dilemma (PD) experiments in both Logan, Utah (with high levels of religious adherence, particularly Mormon) and Eugene-Springfield, Oregon (listed as having one of the lowest church attendance rates in the country). Like Anderson et al. (2010), they find that religious affiliation has no statistically significant impact on prosocial behavior in the experiments. However, Orbell et al. (1992) do find that frequency of church attendance is significantly positively correlated with prosocial behavior for Mormons in Logan. Interestingly, this result did not hold for non-Mormons in Logan, or for any group in Eugene-Springfield. They conclude that social context matters. In populations where certain religious groups are numerically dominant, a random stranger "will not be, in at least a religious and institutional sense, strangers at all" (p. 303). Ahmed (2008) makes a similar argument when comparing Indian students at a madrasah versus students at a secular university. Students with higher levels of religiosity (i.e. madrasah students training to be imams) contributed significantly more in both dictator and public goods games and were less likely than students at secular universities to contribute zero in both games. Ahmed (pp. 372–373) argues that the "religious environment" is important in experimental contexts, such that "even if religious students did not know the identification of … the recipient in the dictator game (DG), they still might have had some general knowledge that applied specifically to religious students and that could have affected their behavior."

Part of the explanation for this connection between resource scarcity and religious prosociality lies in the way that shared religious affiliation reduces the social distance between unrelated actors. Johansson-Stenman, Mahmud, and Martinsson (2009) look at the impact of social distance on trust within and between Muslims and Hindus in rural Bangladesh. Using a combination of structured surveys and bilateral trust experiments, the authors find differences in reported levels of trust (despite a lack of statistically significant differences in game behavior based on religious affiliation). Both Muslims and Hindus report trusting people within their own religion more than those of other religions, but the two groups differed on their level of trust of other religious individuals versus the general public (Hindus trusted other religious groups more than the general public, whereas Muslims trusted the general public more than other religious groups).

The research on resource scarcity, religiosity, and prosociality indicates that both environmental and social contexts are important for structuring the connection between religion and economic exchanges. While many researchers do not find a relationship between religious affiliation and prosociality in experimental contexts, respondents frequently indicate a belief that members of religious faiths are more trustworthy and generous (Anderson et al., 2010; Orbell et al. 1992). Further, religiosity appears to correlate more with experimentally induced norms of prosociality (Ahmed, 2008). To understand the complex ways in which religiosity, social distance, and norms of prosociality interact, both methods and analyses need to be grounded in the local context.

Our research contributes to this literature by examining how religiosity and social distance influence economic behavior in a water scarce setting, as measured by both dictator and ultimatum games (UGs). We do so by informing how we use experiments with results from ethnographic interviews and using the results of the experiments to aid in our interpretation of the ethnographic findings. Finally, by combining ethnography and experiments in an iterative fashion, we move the study of cooperation in the direction of relying on greater cultural context and creating games that more accurately mirror the real-world social context.

## SETTING

The field research was conducted in the city of Cochabamba, Bolivia (population 608,276). Cochabamba is known for its enormous open-air market, said to be one of the largest in South America. The market is a major draw for migrants from the surrounding Bolivian departments. Migration to Cochabamba tends to occur in waves, following periods of major economic disruption. In the 1980s, the collapse of the tin market and Bolivian mining industry precipitated a flood of migrants from the highland mining regions (McFarren, 1992). Similarly, coca eradication efforts in the 1990s forced farmers in lowland tropical regions to resettle in the city. Economic opportunities in Cochabamba also attract a steady stream of migrants from the rural highlands and the urban centers in the departments of La Paz, Oruro, and Potosi. Thus, newly arrived squatters in Cochabamba bring diverse social and economic norms, including those shaped by rural, mining, urban, and market experiences, to squatter settlements.

This study focuses on Villa Israel, a squatter settlement located in the furthest reaches of southern Cochabamba. Established as a squatter settlement approximately 25 years ago, Villa Israel is now a semi-legal community with electricity, telephone service, transportation lines, schools, a Sunday market, and a health clinic. Initial settlers were recruited to purchase lots in Villa Israel via their connections in highland evangelical churches, mines, and rural communities. Due to the low cost of land plots, the community grew quickly and attracted a wide range of second-wave settlers. The current religious composition in the community consists of a small majority of evangelical Christians (58%), a large minority of Catholics (34%), and a handful of people who report no religious affiliation (8%). The community itself contains 14 small evangelical churches, while one large Catholic church is located just over Villa Israel's border in a neighboring community. Due to the political dominance of first-wave settlers, evangelicals tend to have a more vocal presence in community policies and public life than Catholics. However, there is a great deal of heterogeneity within the evangelical community, with dominations ranging from Baptists to Seventh-Day Adventists, resulting in an array of religious beliefs and practices.

In addition to religious diversity, Villa Israel's urban migrant population is diverse in other ways as well. Residents tend to come from four different Bolivian states: a quarter from Potosi, a fifth from Cochabamba, nearly a fifth from Oruro, and a tenth from La Paz. Three-quarters of adult residents were born in the countryside. Most of the remaining residents were born in highland mining communities or in the cities. Beyond the varied origins of Villa Israel residents, many have complex migration histories that reflect settlers' attempts to thrive in rural farming, highland mines, tropical agriculture, and other cities before settling in urban Cochabamba. The majority of Villa Israel residents speak Spanish and Quechua, with a large minority also speaking Aymara; trilingualism is common in the community. The community is also economically mixed. Villa Israel residents work in a variety of industries, generally in informal employment, including marketing, taxi lines, day labor, construction work, domestic and laundry service, and food vending. Others work in cottage industries such as tailoring, weaving, leatherworking, and animal husbandry. Economic well-being ranges from economically stable to highly insecure. Nearly 65% of households have stable employment and own substantial assets (such as a home or business investments). Just over 35% of households regularly struggle to maintain stable employment and access to basic resources.

Despite the presence of economically stable households in Villa Israel, nearly everyone in the community suffers from at least occasional bouts of water insecurity. This is because the municipal water utility, SEMAPA, is not empowered to provide water services to the 40% of residents living in Cochabamba's south-side squatter settlements (García, García, & Quitón, 2003), including Villa Israel. As a result, all households in the community purchase water from a private vendor. The price of water is four bolivianos (4 Bs) for 200 liters; this represented up to 20% of a standard adult's daily income at the time of research. Because of the link between income and water provision, poorer households do tend to be more water insecure. However, because only a few trucks circulate the community selling a limited water supply each day, even economically stable households may have trouble obtaining water when they need it. Only the wealthiest households – which have large water storage tanks – tend to be buffered from periodic water shortages. Although some alternative water sources exist in Villa Israel (including rainwater collection, a seasonal stream, and a small-scale community water system), these sources do not provide sufficient water to provide community members with safe, adequate, and secure access to water. Indeed, nearly three-quarters of Villa Israel households are unable to obtain 50 liters of water per capita per day, the minimum international water provision standard (Gleick, 1996).

Cochabamba's squatters use a number of coping strategies to survive in the face of severe water shortages. One of the most prevalent coping strategies is sharing of water across households. A survey of people from 23 squatter settlements in south-side Cochabamba, conducted during the dry season of 2008, revealed that 80% of households maintained regular water sharing relationships. Even in the context of high social and cultural diversity in Cochabamba's squatter settlements, shared beliefs about how water should be given and received appear to have emerged to support these frequent exchanges.

## METHODS

We used two methods to examine the role of religiosity in shaping prosocial norms in Villa Israel: (1) ethnography and (2) economic experiments. The purpose of the ethnographic research was to collect high-quality data regarding respondents' experiences of water insecurity, participation in transfers of water across households, and beliefs about economic norms. The purpose of the economic experiments was to measure economic norms in a rigorous, cross-culturally comparable manner (Ensminger, 2002). In this section, we relate how the ethnographic and experimental data were collected in turn.

### *Ethnographic Methods*

The ethnographic research was conducted over 18 months in Villa Israel. The fieldwork began with four months' participant observation conducted during the wet and dry seasons. The participant observation provided the opportunity to conduct grounded observations of day-to-day life in Villa Israel. This included living in the community, participating in community events, fetching water, washing in the river, and becoming proficient in the local dialect of Spanish (which is highly mixed with Quechua). In the fifth month of research, the field team developed an ethnographic survey protocol focused on capturing household-level variation in water insecurity, water sharing, and general economic well-being. The interview protocol was pretested extensively with key informants in Spanish and Quechua.

The ethnographic interviews were conducted with a random sample of 72 households (75% response rate) drawn from a map of 415 homes in the community. The interviews were conducted in a panel format in which each household was interviewed five times over a 10-month period. This allowed the field team to explore seasonal changes in water insecurity, water sharing, and general economic well-being. Interviews were conducted in teams of two, with one interviewer and one note-taker, in Spanish, Quechua, and Aymara. Interviews were conducted with anyone identified as a "household head," defined as a person responsible for resource acquisition and distribution in the household. A total of 101 respondents were interviewed, as up to three respondents were included in each household when they fit the study definition of "household head." Including multiple household heads provides a fuller picture of household economic well-being than focusing exclusively on male or female households.

With regard to data analysis, the focus here is on identifying and describing prosocial norms and the characteristics of sharing relationships in Villa Israel. Simple descriptive statistics are used to summarize the frequency of water sharing events. The qualitative analysis involved iterative coding and analysis of the narrative data collected during participant observation and the ethnographic interviews. In the first iteration, all narratives related to water and prosociality were selected. In the second iteration, narratives were assigned codes related to economic behaviors and strategies (e.g., lending water). In the third iteration, the economic strategies were grouped and coded for reasoning about social norms (e.g., charity). In the final iteration, the narratives were analyzed for overarching themes regarding the moral rationale for engaging in sharing of water.

### *Economic Experiments*

The economic experiments were conducted using two simple and well-known games: the DG and the UG (Ensminger, 2002). The DG, which is one of the oldest economic games, was selected to provide an assessment of generosity norms that is comparable cross-culturally. The DG involves two players; the first player (Proposer) is apportioned a stake and then asked how much she or he would like to provide to a second player (Responder). Both players are anonymous. In the DG, Proposer's offer size is interpreted as a baseline measure of their generosity (Gurven, 2004b). The UG, which is also a very commonly used economic game, was selected to provide an assessment of the norms of fair giving that is comparable cross-culturally. In the UG, a Proposer is again apportioned a stake and asked to divide it with a Responder. However, the Responder can choose to accept the Proposer's offer or reject it; if the Responder rejects, neither player receives their stake. In the UG, the Proposer's offer size is interpreted as a measure of their best guess about Responder's beliefs about the norms of fair giving. The Responder's rejection distribution (that is, their willingness to accept or reject offers at 10% intervals) is interpreted as a measure of their willingness to pay a cost (or not) to punish the Proposer for violating the norms of fair giving (Ensminger, 2002). It is important to note that violations of economic norms can be either stingy (very small) or very large offers that create too great a reciprocal debt, depending on the society and its economic norms (Henrich et al., 2006).

The advantage of using the dictator and UGs is that they have been used extensively in field settings. This allows us to compare our results to a number of established ethnographic cases (Ensminger, 2002; Gurven & Winking, 2008; Henrich et al., 2004). However, one possible critique of this approach is that the games are too simplistic to approximate behavior in the real world (Gurven & Winking, 2008).To address this, at least in part, we created a third experiment: an ultimatum game with a social distance manipulation (UG-SD). In this third game, we told players that they were paired with a family member, coreligionist, or neighbor. Whenever possible, real matches were made; when this was not possible, assignments were made randomly. Players 1 and 2 were kept in separate rooms for the entirety of game play; as a result, participants were unable to guess which community members might be their partners. These relationship categories were chosen because they were the three most frequent sites of water sharing in Villa Israel (barring commercial relationships). Before the DG, UG, and UG-SD, each participant took part in three training exercises: a group lesson, an individual lesson, and a hands-on test. Only respondents who passed the test were allowed to proceed to game play. The exact scripts used for the training sessions and actual game play were those used by Henrich et al. (2004), with a Spanish translation provided by Juan Camilo Cardenas (personal communication). The Bolivian researchers translated the Spanish version into Quechua and Aymara.

The economic experiments were conducted in two rounds (morning and afternoon) of three games each (DG, UG, andUG-SD) during the 14th month of the fieldwork. Conducting the experiments late in the fieldwork ensured that they were carried out in a locally appropriate manner; conducting them in back-to-back sessions on one day ensured that there was little or no strategizing among participants before the experiments began. The experiments were conducted with a random sample of 67 participants (56% response rate) drawn again from the map of 415 homes in the community. Upon entering the local schoolhouse where the games were played, players were separated and assigned to one of two groups. Group 1 players were assigned the following roles: Dictator Game Proposer, Ultimatum Game Proposer, and Ultimatum Game with Social Distance Responder. Group 2 players were assigned the following roles: Dictator Game Responder, Ultimatum Game Responder, and Ultimatum Game with Social Distance Proposer. Because players never repeated their roles, we believe the likelihood of order effects is minimized. The starting stake for each game was 50 Bs (US$6.25), or the daily wage for the highest-paid members of the community. After game play was complete, participants received a payout of real money based on their participation in the day's activities and the outcomes of their game play. Respondents were also provided with a meal, snacks, free daycare, and a 7 Bs (US$0.89) show-up fee for each game.

With regard to data analysis, we explore three distinct questions using descriptive and inferential statistical tests. First, how can Villa Israel residents' game play be characterized with regard to offer size and rejection thresholds? Second, how do religiosity and wealth affect offer size and rejection thresholds? Third, what effect does social distance have on offer size and rejection thresholds? After answering these questions, we discuss how lessons learned from ethnographic research and economic experiments inform our understanding of economic norms in Villa Israel.

## QUALITATIVE RESULTS

### *Norms of Prosociality in Villa Israel*

In Villa Israel, sharing of water across households is a very common strategy for coping with water insecurity and scarcity. Over the course of eight months of survey research, 58% of household heads reported that they had given water to other households within the last week. Over the same period of time, 36% of households reported that they had received water in the previous week. Given the high rate of water sharing in Villa Israel, we asked respondents why they chose to give this scarce and crucial resource to other households. The vast majority of respondents said that they gave water to others because they felt obligated to help the neediest community members.

A number of respondents echoed the perspective of a retired schoolteacher, who said, "When I am able, I prefer to help people who have lots of children and who really need it, regardless of who they are." Summing up the community consensus on water gifts, a prosperous businesswoman explained that help should be given to "those who are in need. ... I would try to choose from among the children or perhaps the elderly, if they asked for help."

To determine the underlying reasons for respondents' professed generosity, we asked them why they felt compelled to help the needy. In response, many Villa Israel residents talked about Christian norms of charity and giving. Such norms are commonly conveyed in the telling of the Good Samaritan parable (Luke 10:25–37) in the New Testament (Roukema, 2004). This is underscored in Luke 14:13–14: "But when thou makest a feast, call the poor, the maimed, the lame, the blind: And thou shalt be blessed; for they cannot recompense thee: for thou shalt be recompensed at the resurrection of the just." This belief is reiterated in John 3:17, when it is argued that no person who has the ability to help and turns away the needy can truly love God (Jacobs, 2007). Voicing a perspective clearly informed by the Bible study, which is common in Villa Israel churches, one of our respondents explained that "God says that you must help those in need ... this compels me to give help to anyone, no matter who they are." Another woman said that she tries to give people a little something because "God sends those people who need help." While these beliefs were held broadly, respondents seemed to find them particularly relevant to water. Explaining why they give away water, a young couple said, "We always help our Christian brothers, we always give ... if we have something to give, we give it ... our neighbors come asking for water and we always try to help them." Acts of generosity appeared to be interpreted by Villa Israel residents as an important form of worship.

While the desire to worship God was an important motivation for generosity among Villa Israel residents, it was not sufficient to motivate water giving among all Christian community members. Rather, the obligation to give to the needy was felt most strongly among those with surplus water and goods. As one particularly generous woman, who often helped impoverished women in her church explained, "If I had more than I needed, I would give a bit away to those who are in need; I would give it away – and not loan it – because I know nobody would give it back." Other household heads, who expressed concern about their own well-being, appeared to feel less obliged to give to the needy. These respondents tended to emphasize the importance of prioritizing their own family's survival over that of other community members. Reflecting a common perspective, a devout but impoverished woman explained, "Right now I have very, very little in my house. I might be able to lend someone a tiny bit, but I also might have to say no because I do not have enough for my own family." The mother of a large, struggling family stated more bluntly, "I wouldn't give anything to anyone because then I would run out and I don't want my children to suffer." Several household heads also expressed concern that unreciprocated water loans could have catastrophic consequences for their own families. As one cautious woman explained, "I would help if I had something to give, but that also might end up making me needy."

In conclusion, then, there seemed to be a consensus that giving water and other goods to the needy was a morally correct and socially desirable behavior. However, only those with surplus water and goods felt a strong obligation to give to the needy; those who were poor, needy, or water insecure felt that their own families' needs should be met before they engaged in charitable giving. While these overarching norms were endorsed by most community members, a close examination of actual water exchange relationships reveals much more nuance in the day-to-day practice of water sharing. In the next section, we focus on the norms of water exchange in the three most common types of sharing relationships: family, coreligionists, and neighbors.

### *Norms of Prosociality among Family, Coreligionists, and Neighbors*

When Villa Israel household heads discussed their desire to help others, they often expressed a preference for giving to family members. In practice, Villa Israel household heads generally allocated surplus goods first to household members, then to nonresidential kin, and finally to other community members. As one young father explained, "The first thing I would do is help my family, then if I have things left over I would give them to anyone who asks until I run out." Another longtime Villa Israel resident was more ambivalent about giving to non-kin: "I would do a little to help anyone who asked, but I would prefer to help one of my family members." Expressing a minority opinion, a hardworking young mother said, "I would not give anything to anyone because they are *otra gente* (strangers); I prefer to save for my little siblings and for my home." This allegiance to family members can play an important role in securing water access for Villa Israel households. For example, one woman explained that, because of water sharing relationships among her extended family, she did not worry about water insecurity. She explained that, "I loan water to my in-laws," but "I also fetch water from my sister-in-law; that's why I don't use the tapstand." Among family members, there was a strong prohibition on charging for water, although people often paid in kind for water provided by family members. Common sharing arrangements included frequent exchanges of water for help with childcare or cottage industries. A few household heads, generally grandmothers, reported that they made regular water donations (without recompense) because "I worry about the little ones." As one Villa Israel grandmother explained, "I lent water to my daughter three times this week because she had to go to work and her kids don't buy water from the truck." As a result, intrafamilial water transfers appeared to have a leveling effect in which impoverished families' water security was enhanced at the cost of wealthier families' water surpluses.

After the preference for giving to family members, Villa Israel household heads generally expressed an inclination to help coreligionists. Again, the desire to give to coreligionists was closely linked to the Christian obligation to help the needy through charitable acts. As one active member of a Christian church explained, he would help any of the "people that I know – not strangers" but "I would give preference to the *hermanos* (evangelical Christians) that I know from church." Another elderly man concurred, but emphasized the importance of neediness in choosing whom to help: "I would give to those who don't have the things they need, to the poor *hermanos*." Several of those who expressed a preference for helping coreligionists explained that they were most familiar with the needs of parishioners in their own churches (e.g., cases of accident, job loss, or family abandonment). Another reason that Villa Israel household heads prefer to give to coreligionists could be social pressure for those with wealth to adhere to Christian charity norms. Charitable acts may provide a visible way for wealthy parishioners to signal their piousness to other church members. From the perspective of the needy, impoverished community members seemed to feel that they could solicit help from church members without fear of stigma or rejection. As a young mother with many children explained, when she was in need, she felt that "maybe I could ask for help from some of the *hermanas* from my church." Indeed, we later learned that an *hermana* from this woman's church facilitated water donations for her when she needed them. Charity among coreligionists was sometimes organized directly by the churches, which mobilized members to donate to worthy cases within the congregation. One woman, who received many gifts after her husband suffered a work-related accident, said "the first and only place I would go to for help would be the Unión Cristiana Evangélica church, because they have done a good job of helping me up till now." Sharing among coreligionists in Villa Israel appeared to be entirely oriented toward gifts (rather than balanced reciprocal exchanges); none of our respondents argued that debts were incurred or should be repaid after the receipt of gifts from coreligionists. At most, recipients of help from coreligionists seemed to feel an obligation to reciprocate broadly by giving to those in need – but only if they were financially able at some point in the future.

Although not considered the most desirable partners, neighbors were the most common source of help and loans in Villa Israel. This is likely the case because neighbors are geographically close and water is too heavy to carry long distances in large quantities. Beyond these practical considerations, some respondents did express a desire to give to neighbors when they are in need. A woman who had migrated to Villa Israel after working for years in Argentina said she tried to assist "a neighbor that I know who really needs help," explaining that the woman's husband beat her so severely that she was not always able to acquire water, food, and other basic necessities. Respondents' familiarity with their neighbors' needs made it more likely they would perceive need and choose to help them. The woman continued, saying "it does no good to help someone who has everything they need and just ran out temporarily; it's important to help those that are really in a bad situation." Based on proximity and familiarity, strong partnerships are sometimes built between neighbors. The owner of a local *chichería* (corn beer bar) carried on a longstanding relationship with the family who lived behind hers; the bar owner said that, several times, she had borrowed money from her neighbor to buy water. Yet, even for those who maintained very active sharing relationships with their neighbors, there appeared to be more emphasis on account keeping, more motivation to secure payback, and more tolerance for explicit self-interest than in family or coreligionist relationships. As a market woman explained, regarding her ability to solicit help from neighbors, "I would go for help to my neighbor and ask them to lend me something, because I know that I would give it back." This consideration of one's ability to pay back water gifts was absent from accounts of exchanges with family and coreligionists. Similarly, when asked if she was willing to help her neighbors, a housewife said, "If my neighbors came to ask for help, I would loan or sell" them what they needed. This is noteworthy because, between family members and coreligionists, there is a strong prohibition against selling water and, to some extent, other basic necessities. Due to the emphasis on self-interest in these exchanges, household heads tended to be less trusting of neighbors than other potential partners.

There was some evidence that social sanctioning was used to punish those who engaged in self-interested behavior – either for those who selfishly refused to give to others or for those who demanded unfair recompense for gifts provided. At one level, nearly all community members engaged in a general criticism of those who behaved selfishly. This is illustrated by a woman's assertion, "Nobody [in Villa Israel] would offer to help an old lady like me." The running social critique of stinginess among Villa Israel residents created social pressure for those who did not wish to conform to the norms of giving. Beyond this, some people engaged in pointed personal criticism of those who did not act generously. In one case, a young woman asked her neighbor to loan her a few buckets of water. When she was refused, the respondent reported, "I bought two bolivianos of water from my neighbor because she is too cheap to give water away." Here, the young woman's retelling serves as a form of social sanction in which the neighbor's miserliness is made public to other community members. Such personal criticisms are considered to be especially harsh when they are targeted at family members. When we asked an elderly shopkeeper who she would go to for help if she ran out of water, she responded, "I would not ask for help from anyone; not even my daughter. I would die. What can I do?" This is a particularly stinging critique in the context of Villa Israel's norms of generosity and giving among family members. In a few cases, there was evidence that some encouraged social shunning as retaliation for self-interested behavior in water exchanges. When a mother of three ran out of water one day, she went to a nearby restaurant and asked the proprietor to sell water. Although willing to sell the water, the proprietor would only agree to do so at an enormous markup over the market value. Incensed, the mother purchased the water in order to prepare the midday meal and feed her children. However, she swore never to patronize the restaurant again and repeated the story to others in the community.

The existence of social sanctions for self-interested behavior demonstrates that there are consequences for those who do not confirm to norms of generosity and giving in the community. Moreover, the norms and sanctions vary depending on whether exchanges are conducted between family members, coreligionists, or neighbors. In the next section, we examine the results of economic experiments to determine the extent to which experimental behavior mirrors the qualitative results.

# EXPERIMENTAL RESULTS

In general, the results from the three experimental games indicate that people seek fair divisions of the stake. The behavior of proposers in the DG and of proposers and responders in the UG indicated that there is a known set of norms that people utilized to guide their game play, but variations based on social distance are present. This point will become clearer as we describe the results of the experiments, in particular the UG-SD.

## *Norms of Prosociality in Experimental Context*

To determine generosity norms in Villa Israel, we first examine the results of the DG. There were 35 pairs of players in the DG. The mean offer in this game was 41.4% (Table 1). This is considerably higher than the average of 20% offered cross-culturally (Henrich et al., 2004). There was a bimodal distribution with a strong mode at 50%, and a weaker secondary mode at 20%. An equal number of proposers offered 100% as did 10%, and there were no offers of 0% (Fig. 1). To determine perceived norms of fair giving, we examine the behavior of proposers in the UG. The mean offer in this game was 43% of the stake with a strong mode at 50% ($n = 33$) (Table 2, Fig. 2). Proposer offers were considerably higher than results from many Western, market-integrated societies as well as most other South American societies (Oosterbeek, Sloof, & Van De Kuilen, 2004). Our results fall in line with findings from Ghana, Zimbabwe and Slovakia (Henrich et al., 2006). If proposers in the UGs were acting purely out of a fear of rejection we would expect to see high offers in the UG and low offers in the DG, when the fear of rejection is removed. Rather, we see that tests of generosity and perceived norms of fairness both indicate a strong preference for an even division of the stake between proposers and responders.

***Table 1.*** Results from a Dictator Game.

| | Dictator Game |
|---|---|
| Number of pairs | 35 |
| Mean | 0.41 |
| Mode | 0.20, 0.50 |
| SD | 0.20 |

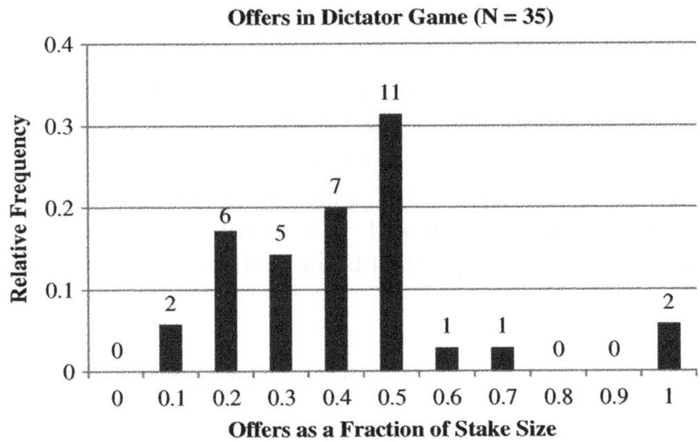


*Fig. 1.* Frequency of offers in a dictator game as a fraction of stake size.

In the UG, we used the "strategy method" in which we elicited responders' entire rejection distribution, rather than simply asking if the responders reject the proposers' offer. The advantage of the strategy method is that we can look at the reported behavior of all players for every possible offer, allowing for a broader picture of conceptions of fair giving (Fig. 3). Responders were somewhat willing to punish low offers, although not to the degree we might expect. There was a rejection rate of 9.1% (3/33) and the mean amount rejected was 53.3% (see Table 2). This rejection rate is in line with findings from the Western United States (9.41%), the Netherlands (9.24%), and Germany (9.52%), but much less than in the United Kingdom (23.38%), France (30.78%), and Spain (29.17%) (Oosterbeek et al., 2004). Although the strategy method reveals a high potential for rejection, the actual rejection rates were low due to the relatively high offers made by proposers who were perhaps well aware of the potential for rejection.

Only about 50% of our responders said they would reject an offer of 0%, and just 20% and 25% would reject an offer of 10% and 20%, respectively. It is noteworthy that responders reduced their likelihood of rejection as the offer size rose, approaching near zero at 50%, but then the likelihood of rejection began to climb again until nearly a quarter of responders reported that they would reject an offer of 100%. This provides strong evidence that responders were seeking to create balanced exchanges, even if it meant sacrificing some monetary gain, rather than conforming to the logic of economic self-interest. Henrich et al. (2006, p. 1767) report that 6 of the 14

***Table 2.*** Results from Two Ultimatum Games.

| | Ultimatum 1 | Ultimatum 2 (Total) | Ultimatum 2 (Religion) | Ultimatum 2 (Family) | Ultimatum 2 (Neighbor) |
|---|---|---|---|---|---|
| Number of pairs | 33 | 31 | 11 | 9 | 11 |
| Mean | 0.43 | 0.41 | 0.42 | 0.40 | 0.38 |
| Mode | 0.50 | 0.50 | 0.50 | 0.20, 0.50 | 0.20, 0.40, 0.50 |
| SD | 0.15 | 0.13 | 0.09 | 0.17 | 0.14 |
| Rejection frequency | 0.09 | 0.10 | 0.09 | 0.11 | 0.09 |
| Rejections | 20% (1), 40% (1), 100% (1) | 20% (1), 40% (2) | 40% (1) | 20% (1) | 40% (1) |
| Average Payout | Player 1: 53% Player 2: 38% | Player 1: 53% Player 2: 37.4% | Player 1: 51% Player 2: 40% | Player 1: 51.1% Player 2: 37.8% | Player 1: 51.8% Player 2: 37.3% |

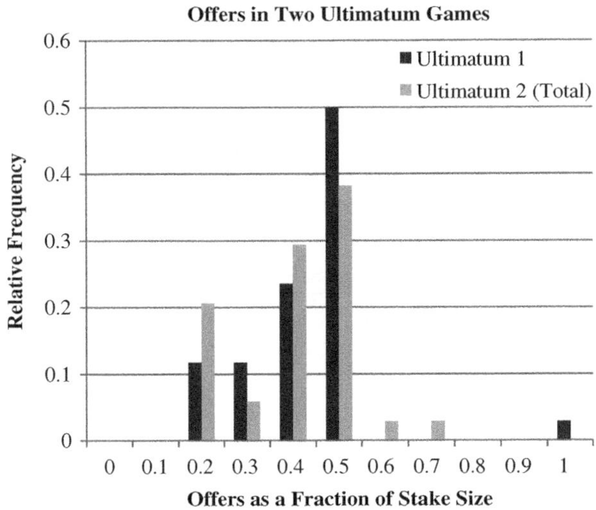


*Fig. 2.* Offers in two ultimatum games based on fraction of stake size.

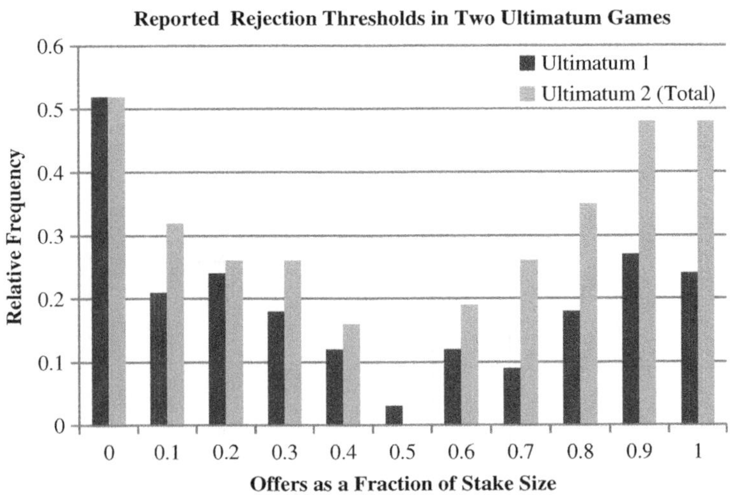


*Fig. 3.* Responder strategy sets in two ultimatum games.

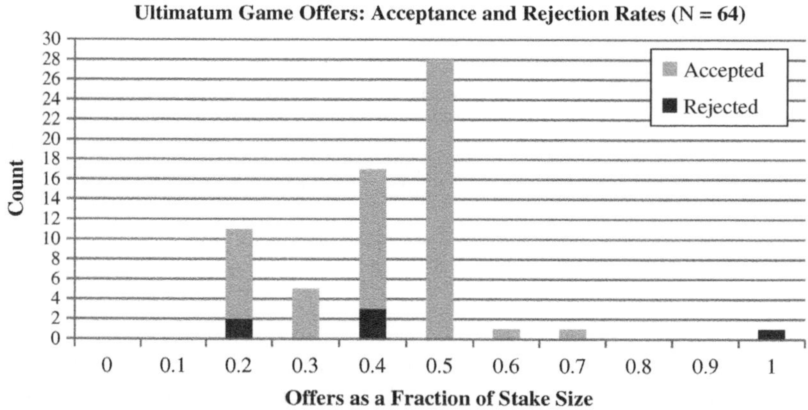


*Fig. 4.* Absolute number of offers, acceptances, and rejecions in two ultimatum games.

nonstudent populations (Samburu, Yasawa, Au, Accra City, Sanquianga, and Sursurunga) they studied had a similar "U-shaped" rejection distribution and that it is increasingly recognized as a widespread finding.

Now, we turn to the special cases of responders who actually rejected the offers of proposers – causing neither player to receive any of the 50 Bs stake (Fig. 4). All three of the responders who rejected their offer had a narrow set of offers they would have accepted. Two of the rejections (one at 40% and one at 100%) deserve further attention because they were unusually large amounts to reject. The player rejecting the 40% offer would only accept offers from 50% to 70%, whereas the player rejecting 100% would only accept 40–80%. Our interpretation of these players' behavior is that the responders were attempting to create a more equitable distribution of the stake. These responders had a relatively narrow conception of "fair giving," which allowed for neither stingy nor debt-creating offers. This indicates that there is, among some respondents, a desire for balanced exchanges that provide the recipient with resources but do not put them in a position of being heavily indebted to others.

## *The Role of Religiosity and Wealth in Shaping Prosocial Norms*

Based on the ethnographic narratives discussed above, we were interested in determining the extent to which two key variables – religiosity and

***Table 3.*** Mann–Whitney U Test for Relationships Between Religiosity and Offer Size.

| | Variable Levels | Dictator Offer | | Ultimatum 1 Offer | | Ultimatum 2 Offer | |
|---|---|---|---|---|---|---|---|
| | | Mean[a] | *P* | Mean | *P* | Mean | *P* |
| Religiosity | ≤4 Services/month | 0.38 | 0.027 | 0.41 | 0.34 | 0.41 | 0.46 |
| | >4 Services/month | 0.53 | | 0.49 | | 0.38 | |

[a]Based on percentage of the total stake size.

wealth – were associated with game play in the DG, UG, and UG-SD. First, we examined the relationship between religiosity and offer size. Ethnographic evidence from Villa Israel indicated that people who were more religiously active would be more generous and adhere to more altruistic norms of fair giving than those who were less religiously active. Religiosity was defined as the frequency of attending church, regardless of denomination. We measured religiosity using a binary variable in which those with high religiosity attended church four times a month or more, and those with low religiosity attended church less than four times a month. We tested the relationship between religiosity and offer size in the DG, UG, and UG-SD using a Mann–Whitney U test. The results indicate a statistically significant relationship between religiosity and offer size in the DG, but not in the UG. Respondents who attended church frequently had significantly higher offer sizes than those who did not attend church frequently (Table 3). Based on these results, we infer that religiosity influenced people to be more generous, but that it had no effect on perceptions of fair giving among participants in the economic experiments in Villa Israel.

Second, we examined the relationship between wealth and offer size. Ethnographic evidence from Villa Israel led us to believe that gifts of water were contingent on the loaner having a sufficient level of wealth. Wealth we defined as the respondent's income level. We measured wealth using a binary variable grouping those with income above and below the sample mean. We tested the relationship between wealth and offer size in the DG, UG, and UG-SD using a Mann–Whitney U test. The results indicate that there was no statistically significant relationship between wealth and offer size in the three economic experiments (Table 4). We believe that, within the context of the games, wealth did not exert a meaningful limit on respondents' ability to make offers to others. All proposers started with a stake of 50 Bs; this experimental setup does not approximate the real-world

***Table 4.*** Mann–Whitney U Test for Relationships Between Wealth and Offer Size.

| | Variable Levels | Dictator Offer | | Ultimatum 1 Offer | | Ultimatum 2 Offer | |
|---|---|---|---|---|---|---|---|
| | | Mean | *P* | Mean | *P* | Mean | *P* |
| Wealth | ≤4200 Bs | 0.40 | 0.27 | 0.43 | 0.17 | 0.39 | 0.49 |
| | >4200 Bs | 0.43 | | 0.44 | | 0.42 | |

situation in which some participants have very limited resources and others have an abundance of resources. That there were no differences in offer size among more and less wealthy respondents seems to indicate that wealthy Villa Israel residents were not inherently more giving than less wealthy residents. Rather, the differences we saw in gifts given by more and less wealthy respondents in the ethnographic data appear to be related to households' limited economic means rather than differences in generosity or adherence to different sets of reciprocal norms. As Gurven and Winking (2008) have argued, further research is needed to utilize experiments that more closely align with the real-world considerations made by individuals in these contexts. Additional statistical tests were conducted on standard control variables that would be expected to impact performance in the experimental games, although none were found to be significant (Table 5).

### *Prosocial Norms among Family, Coreligionists, and Neighbors in Experimental Context*

To determine how norms of fair giving were shaped by specific relationship types in Villa Israel, we examined the results of the UG-SD. There were 31 pairs of players in the UG-SD. While the aggregate results for the UG-SD were very similar to those of the first UG, some differences become apparent when we separate the responders by their relationship pairings. First, we examined the offers made by proposers. Family members offered on average 40%, with a bimodal distribution at 20% and 50%. Coreligionists offered 42% on average, with a single mode at 50%. Neighbors offered 38% with a trimodal distribution (20%, 40%, and 50%). The mean and mode results indicate that there may be a small tendency for coreligionists to be more giving than family members and neighbors; however, a chi-square test did

***Table 5.*** Mann–Whitney U Tests for Relationships Between Offer Size and Demographic and Social Contextual Variables.

| Test Variables | Variable Levels | Dictator Offer | | Ultimatum 1 Offer | | Ultimatum 2 Offer | |
|---|---|---|---|---|---|---|---|
| | | Mean | *P* | Mean | *P* | Mean | *P* |
| Age | 18–35 | 0.40 | 0.15 | 0.43 | 0.618 | 0.42 | 0.71 |
| | >35 | 0.46 | | 0.45 | | 0.40 | |
| Gender | Male | 0.45 | 0.73 | 0.43 | 0.891 | 0.41 | 0.70 |
| | Female | 0.49 | | 0.44 | | 0.40 | |
| Education | ≤6 Years | 0.46 | 0.63 | 0.46 | 0.337 | 0.37 | 0.09 |
| | >6 Years | 0.38 | | 0.41 | | 0.46 | |
| Attend church in | Yes | 0.42 | 0.75 | 0.41 | 0.723 | 0.41 | 0.77 |
| Villa Israel | No | 0.44 | | 0.45 | | 0.40 | |
| Family in Villa | Yes | 0.40 | 0.23 | 0.47 | 0.126 | 0.42 | 0.40 |
| Israel | No | 0.47 | | 0.38 | | 0.37 | |
| Length of residence | <7 Years | 0.48 | 0.22 | 0.45 | 0.845 | 0.40 | 0.82 |
| in Villa Israel | | 0.37 | | 0.43 | | 0.41 | |
| | ≥7 Years | | | | | | |

not indicate that there were significant differences in offer size for those paired with family members, coreligionists, and neighbors.

With regard to the rejection distributions provided by responders, the clearest result is that there is agreement across all three relation types that a 50% stake is a fair offer. Beyond that, there is considerable variation across responders who were paired with family members, neighbors, and coreligionists (Fig. 5). Family members were the most permissive of the three groups, and appeared more likely to accept any offer from someone with whom they were related. Only slightly more than 20% of those paired with a family member indicated they would reject an offer of zero, and 10% said they would reject an offer of 10%, 20%, 40%, 60% and 70%. The curve on the rejection thresholds for family members does trend back up, as with the U-shaped distribution described above for the standard UG format, but not as distinctly. There is a much flatter curve until reaching the US$80 stake size. Coreligionists were more likely than family members to punish less than equitable offers, but less likely than neighbors to punish hyperequitable offers. For coreligionists, the reverse bell curve begins to appear more clearly, with greater than 50% reporting they would reject offers of 0%, trending downward to 0% rejections at 50%, before spiking again at 90% and 100% being rejected by about 35% of responders.

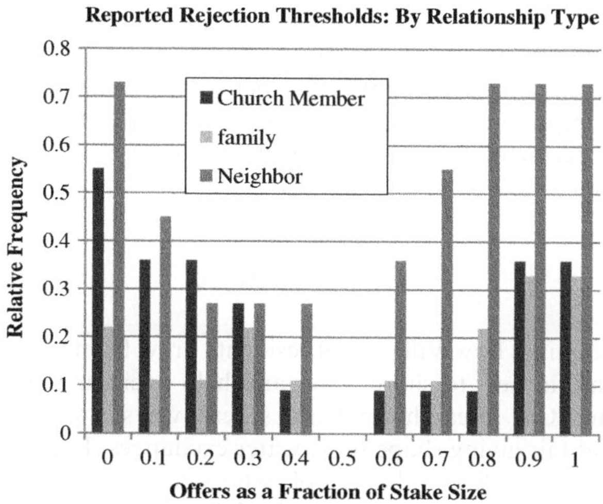


*Fig. 5.* Responder strategy sets based on relationship type in ultimatum game manipulation.

***Table 6.*** Chi-Square Test for Offer Size by Relationship Type in an Ultimatum Game with a Social Distance Manipulation.

| | Relationship Type | *N* | Mean Offer | Chi-Square | Significance |
|---|---|---|---|---|---|
| Offer size | Religion | 13 | 0.44 | 0.49 | 0.78 |
| | Family | 9 | 0.40 | | |
| | Neighbor | 11 | 0.38 | | |
| | Total | 33 | | | |

Neighbors appeared to be acting on the narrowest conception of fair giving, and tended to punish both less and more than equitable offers. More than 70% of responders in this condition indicated that they would reject offers of 0%, 80%, 90%, and 100%. In addition, offers of 10% and 70% would be rejected by 45% and 55% of responders, respectively. As we discussin the next section, these results were consistent with the ethnographic evidence.

We also tested these results using a chi-square test, which did not provide a very sensitive test for differences across the three groups due to the small sample sizes ($9 \leq n \leq 13$) in the UG-SD (Table 6). Thus, there was only one significant difference, at the 80% stake size, in reported rejection rates. In this case, neighbors were significantly more likely to reject an offer of 80% than were coreligionists or family members. This result is consistent with ethnographic reports that neighbors were more rigid in their conceptualization and enforcement of fair giving norms than were family members and coreligionists.

## DISCUSSION

This study examines how Villa Israel residents draw from religious norms of generosity and fairness to share water and help overcome limited access to drinking water. Our research highlights several ways in which the norms of generosity and fair giving shape these water exchanges. First, following Bird and Smith (2005), we found that people who were more religious were more likely to report that giving water was socially appropriate and were more likely to act generously under experimental conditions. In our interviews with people about water sharing, we found that Christian norms of charity were central to understanding water exchanges in Villa Israel. Similar to Scheepers and Grotenhuis' (2005) findings in their European study, Villa Israel residents who were more religious were more likely to stress the importance of giving to the needy. These respondents frequently referred to the Bible and God's exhortations to be charitable to explain why they gave water to needy community members. Our tests for statistical significance confirm that religiosity is correlated with generous behavior. In the DG, which provides experimental conditions that mimic charity, people who attended church at least four times a month had significantly larger offer sizes than those who did not. This finding provides additional support for the findings of Orbell et al. (1992), Sosis and Ruffle (2003), and Ahmed (2008) that religiosity is positively correlated with prosocial behavior in experimental games in environments where people have a reasonable expectation that their game partners will share their faith.

Second, we found that, while the norms of fair giving did not vary between wealthy and poor families, wealth was a limiting factor on some families' ability to give water. A number of Villa Israel residents, even those who endorsed Christian norms of charitable giving in principle, said that they preferred to invest their scarce water resources in safeguarding the well-being of their own family members before contributing to others in the community. Although wealth was identified as an important aspect of the decision-making process in the ethnographic interviews, it did not produce a statistically significant result in the experimental analysis. This could be the result of the experimental environment not acting as a close approximation of the real-world environment in which exchanges occur. That there were no differences in offer size among more and less wealthy respondents seems to indicate that wealthy Villa Israel residents were not normatively more giving than less wealthy residents. Rather, the differences we saw in the ethnographic data appear to be related to households' limited economic means rather than differences in generosity or adherence to different sets of prosocial norms. Our ethnographic finding – that people experiencing resource scarcity hoard resources to safeguard the survival of their kin – is predicted by strict economic rationality (Fehr & Gächter, 2000) and has been verified in a range of resource-poor environments (Booth, 1984; Dirks, 1980; Laughlin & Brady, 1978; Turnbull, 1972). Our contribution is to show, with experimental results supported by ethnographic evidence, that there is no demonstrable difference in the norms of fair giving held by the poor and wealthy in a resource-scarce environment.

Third, we found that the norms of fair giving varied depending upon the social distance between reciprocal exchange partners. Our analysis focused on family members, coreligionists, and neighbors, as these were the reciprocal relationships in which most water exchanges were conducted in Villa Israel. Some Villa Israel residents reported that they gave water away to safeguard the well-being of family members, whereas others described water exchanges as occurring as part of wide ranging and complex exchange relationships that also involved labor, goods, and childcare. As the ethnographic literature would predict (Wiessner, 2009), family members were preferred exchange partners. The findings from the UG-SD supported this, as people paired with family members were the most permissive in terms of the range of offers they would accept. Regarding neighbors, we found that exchange of water occurs most frequently among neighbors, as Sahlins (1972) would predict, due to proximity and opportunity. However, we also found that exchanges between neighbors were the most self-interested and carried a strong expectation of direct payback for loans or gifts of water. Similarly, in the UG-SD, people paired with neighbors were the least permissive in terms of the range of offers they would accept. Regarding coreligionists, several studies show that people are more trusting of coreligionists, although few experiments have found that people are significantly more fair or generous with coreligionists (Anderson et al., 2010; Johansson-Stenman et al., 2009; Orbell et al., 1992). Our ethnographic results clearly show that Villa Israel residents feel a preference for giving to coreligionists, motivated either by church charity drives or the familiarity with church members' needs for charity. Similarly, we found in the experimental results that people were more permissive of coreligionists' large offers (as befits a community in which charity is a well-established and socially acceptable institution), but less permissive of coreligionists' small offers (as we expect to find in a community where stinginess toward the poor is seen as an offense toward God). Our findings contribute to past research showing that religious ties are more likely to yield prosocial behavior; further, by modifying the standard UG to include a social distance component we were able to show how religious affiliation shapes the norms of fair giving in Villa Israel.

## CONCLUSIONS

Here, we examined how religion and religiosity shape economic norms in Villa Israel, a water-scarce squatter settlement in the city of Cochabamba, Bolivia. Our mixed methods analysis, which draws on ethnographic research and economic experiments, yields three key results. First, we find ethnographic and experimental evidence that religiosity makes people more likely to be generous. Second, the experimental results indicate that rich and poor hold the same norms of fair giving, whereas the ethnographic evidence demonstrated that in the real world the poverty limits poor families' ability to act on these norms and give water away. Third, we find ethnographic and experimental evidence that the norms of fair giving vary with social distance, such that people are most permissive with family members, are more punishing of stinginess and more accepting of generosity with coreligionists, and are least permissive with neighbors. Based on these results, we conclude that the presence of strong Christian norms of generosity and fair giving is an important institutional mechanism for facilitating water sharing in this community.

The use of both qualitative and quantitative methods allowed us to iteratively explore the relationship between religion and economic norms. Results from ethnographic interviews were used to inform how economic experiments were structured, ensuring that they matched the local social context. Based on the qualitative analysis, we ran statistical tests on the influence of religiosity and wealth on offers in the three economic games. Our deep ethnographic understanding also allowed for more confident interpretation of the experimental results. While these experimental methods are useful for cross-cultural comparisons, we echo Gurven and Winking's (2008) concern that these experiments may not accurately reflect the complex social reality under which most economic activities occur. In an attempt to address such concerns, we utilized a modified UG based on our ethnographic understanding of the importance of social distance in shaping water sharing behaviors. In future research, this approach to grounding experiments in local context could be used to modify the DG with social distance manipulation to test for effects on generosity.

## ACKNOWLEDGMENTS

This study is supported by the National Science Foundation (Award BCS-0314395), Fulbright-IIE, the Tinker Foundation, Paul and Polly Doughty, and the University of Florida Center for Latin American Studies. We thank our Bolivian colleagues Wilda Valencia, Richard Aguilar, Wilfredo Valencia, and Dominga Choque for their assistance. We are also grateful to Marco Janssen, Juan Camilo Cardenas, attendees of the Lab and Field Experiments on Diverse Social Dilemmas Workshop, and our colleagues at the Center for the Study of Institutional Diversity at Arizona State University for their advice and assistance.

## REFERENCES

Ahmed, A. (2008). Are religious people more prosocial? A quasi-experimental study with madrasah pupils in a rural community in India. Available at http://ideas.repec.org/p/hhs/gunwpe/0330.html. Retrieved on March 15, 2011.

Anderson, L., Mellor, J., & Milyo, J. (2010). Did the devil make them do it? The effects of religion in public goods and trust games. *Kyklos*, *63*(2), 163–175.

Bird, R., & Smith, E. (2005). Signaling theory, strategic interaction, and symbolic capital. *Current Anthropology*, *46*(2), 221–248.

Booth, A. (1984). Responses to scarcity. *Sociological Quarterly*, *25*(1), 113–124.

Dehejia, R., DeLeire, T., & Luttmer, E. F. P. (2007). Insuring consumption and happiness through religious organizations. *Journal of Public Economics*, *91*, 259–279.

Dirks, R. (1980). Social responses during severe food shortages and famine. *Current Anthropology*, *21*(1), 21–44.

Ensminger, J. (2002). Experimental economics: A powerful new method for theory testing in anthropology. In: J. Ensminger (Ed.), *Theory in economic Anthropology* (pp. 59–78). Walnut Creek, CA: Altamira.

Fehr, E., & Gächter, S. (2000). Fairness and retaliation: The economics of reciprocity. *The Journal of Economic Perspectives*, *14*(3), 159–181.

García, A., García, F., & Quitón, L. (2003). *La "Guerra del Agua" Abril de 2000: La crisis de la política en Bolivia.* La Paz, Bolivia: PIEB.

Gleick, P. (1996). Basic water requirements for human activities: Meeting basic needs. *Water International*, *21*, 83–92.

Gluckman, M. (1964). *Custom and conflict in Africa*. New York: Barnes & Noble.

Gurven, M. (2004a). Economic games among the Amazonian Tsimane: Exploring the roles of market access, costs of giving, and cooperation on pro-social game behavior. *Experimental Economics*, *7*(1), 5–24.

Gurven, M. (2004b). Does market exposure affect economic game behavior? The ultimatum game and the public goods game among the Tsimane' of Bolivia. In: J. P. Henrich, R. Boyd & E. Fehr (Eds.), *Foundations of human sociality: Economic experiments and ethnographic evidence from fifteen small-scale societies* (pp. 194–231). Oxford, UK: Oxford University Press.

Gurven, M., & Winking, J. (2008). Collective action in action: Prosocial behavior in and out of the laboratory. *American Anthropologist*, *110*(2), 179–190.

Hames, R. (2007). The ecologically noble savage debate. *Annual Review of Anthropology*, *36*, 177–90.

Henrich, J., McElreath, R., Barr, A., Ensminger, J., Barrett, C., Bolyanatz, A., et al. (2006). Costly punishment across human societies. *Science*, *312*(5781), 1767.

Henrich, J. P., Boyd, R., & Fehr, E. (2004). *Foundations of human sociality: Economic experiments and ethnographic evidence from fifteen small-scale societies*. Oxford, UK: Oxford University Press.

Iannaccone, L. R. (1992). Religious markets and the economics of religion. *Social Compass*, *39*, 123–131.

Jacobs, J. M. (2007). On the difference between social justice and Christian charity. *American Catholic Philosophical Quarterly*, *81*, 419–438.

Johansson-Stenman, O., Mahmud, M., & Martinsson, P. (2009). Trust and religion: Experimental evidence from rural Bangladesh. *Economica*, *76*(303), 462–485.

Krech, III, S. (1999). *The ecological Indian: Myth and history*. New York: Norton.

Laughlin, C. D., & Brady, I. A. (1978). *Extinction and survival in human populations*. New York: Columbia University Press.

Massé, H. (1954). Persian beliefs and customs. New Haven: Human Relations Area Files. Available at http://www.yale.edu/hraf/collections.htm. Retrieved on September 1, 2010.

McFarren, W. (1992). The politics of Bolivia's economic crisis: Survival strategies of displaced tin-mining households. In: L. Benereia & S. Feldman (Eds.), *Unequal burden: Economic crises, persistent poverty, and women's work* (pp. 131–158). Boulder: Westview Press.

Norenzayan, A., & Shariff, A. F. (2008). The origin and evolution of religious prosociality. *Science*, *322*(5898), 58.

Oosterbeek, H., Sloof, R., & Van De Kuilen, G. (2004). Cultural differences in ultimatum game experiments: Evidence from a meta-analysis. *Experimental Economics*, *7*, 171–188.

Orbell, J., Goldman, M., Mulford, M., & Dawes, R. (1992). Religion, context, and constraint toward strangers. *Rationality and Society*, *4*(3), 291.

Regnerus, M., Smith, C., & Sikkink, D. (1998). Who gives to the poor? The influence of religious tradition and political location on the personal generosity of Americans toward the poor. *Journal for the Scientific Study of Religion*, *37*(3), 481–493.

Roes, F. L., & Raymond, M. (2003). Belief in moralizing gods. *Evolution and Human Behavior*, *24*(2), 126–135.

Roukema, R. (2004). The Good Samaritan in ancient Christianity. *Vigiliae Christianae*, *58*, 56–74.

Ruffle, B. J., & Sosis, R. (2007). Does it pay to pray? Costly ritual and cooperation. *The BE Journal of Economic Analysis and Policy*, *7*(1), 1–37.

Sahlins, M. (1972). *Stone age economics*. New York: Aldine de Gruyter.

Scheepers, P., & Grotenhuis, M. (2005). Who cares for the poor in Europe? Micro and macro determinants for alleviating poverty in 15 European countries. *European Sociological Review*, *21*(5), 265–268.

Smith, E. A., & Wishnie, M. (2000). Conservation and subsistence in small-scale societies. *Annual Review of Anthropology*, *29*(1), 493–524.

Snarey, J. (1996). The natural environment's impact upon religious ethics: A cross-cultural study. *Journal for the Scientific Study of Religion*, *35*(2), 85–96.

Sosis, R., & Ruffle, B. J. (2003). Religious ritual and cooperation: Testing for a relationship on Israeli religious and secular Kibbutzim. *Current Anthropology*, *44*(5), 713–722.

Tan, J. H. W., & Vogel, C. (2008). Religion and trust: An experimental study. *Journal of Economic Psychology*, *29*, 832–848.

Trawick, P. (2001). The moral economy of water: Equity and antiquity in the Andean commons. *American Anthropologist*, *103*(2), 361–379.

Turnbull, C. M. (1972). *The mountain people*. New York: Touchstone.

Weber, M. (2001/1904). *The protestant ethic and the spirit of capitalism* (T. Parsons, Trans.). New York: Charles Scribner's Sons.

Welch, M. R., Sikkink, D., & Loveland, M. T. (2007). Radius of trust: Religion, social embeddedness and trust in strangers. *Social Forces*, *86*(1), 23–46.

Wiessner, P. (2009). Experimental games and games of life among the Ju/'hoan bushmen. *Current Anthropology*, *50*(1), 133–138.

Printed and bound by CPI Group (UK) Ltd, Croydon, CR0 4YY

15/09/2026

14962364-0004